"Mr. Danish's clever use of the history of one of the greatest voices ever to sing, Maria Callas, and a little known part of that history, her early life during turbulent times in the world, gives this a truly romantic and involving idea.... I loved it and any opera lover would too. Easy, readable and knowledgeable about life, music and all the stuff that happens in between....!"
   - Aprile Millo, Metropolitan Opera Star

"Mr. Danish's exceeding knowledge of and passion for the medium of opera suffuses every line of this cinderella narrative, one that provides a thrill ride for both the novice and the seasoned opera fan. The Tenor is impossible to put down...."
   - Samuel Juliano, *Wonders in the Dark*

"As an operatic diva that has sung over 100 performances with the Metropolitan Opera, I can say without hesitation, that "The Tenor" is a riveting and accurate tale of life imitating art! Peter Danish's story telling ability is lyrical and powerful as he explores the life of an opera singer through passion, longing, romance and war! The accuracy of his descriptions about a singer's journey, his musical and operatic references and his colorful characters, including the incomparable Maria Callas, make this a must read!"
   - Victoria Livengood, Metropolitan Opera Mezzo Soprano

"Whether Peter Danish is writing about music, history or travel in his vastly entertaining novel, "The Tenor," his words fly off the page. The whirlwind of images invites the reader into a world that will be familiar to some, foreign to others—but captivating to all. Read it!"
   - Richard Sasanow, Editor-in-Chief BWW Opera

"The easy flowing prose of Mr. Danish's historically engaging novel is expertly paced and eloquently depicted. As an opera singer who has sung hundreds of performances around the world I think this book will be a compelling read for music lovers and an exhilarating story for all readers. Bravo, Mr. Danish!"
    - Korliss Uecker, Metropolitan Opera Soprano

"Each page of Tenor is as rich as a box of Italian chocolates. By page 8 I already found 7 lines I wanted to steal. Dive in and trust author Peter Danish to sweep you up and lead you through a remarkable adventure! I couldn't put it down."
    - Tom Dudzick, playwright, *Over the Tavern*

"Facts and fiction playfully intertwine in this opera lover's delight!"
    - Alberto Ferreras, award-winning author, B as in Beautiful

"The Tenor was not what I was expecting. Yes, it's about opera. Yes, it's an homage to art and artists. Yes, it's about dreaming fulfilling one's destiny. But-it's about all those things without being fussy or precious. It's decidedly unfussy--because it's about people who work really hard....Peter Danish creates characters you root for. He has woven a tale that keeps you wanting to find out what happens next! I think they call those page-turners!"
    - John Cariani, Tony Award Nominee, playwright, *Almost Maine*

"With his far-reaching opera expertise and keen insight into the Italian soul, Peter Danish draws us into his captivating story of the joys and heartaches of the performer's life. The result is a satisfying read for book lovers and opera lovers alike. Bravo, Il Tenore!"
    - Erica Miner, Award-winning Author, *Murder in the Pit*

The Tenor

Peter Danish

PEGASUS BOOKS

Pegasus Books
3338 San Marino Ave
San Jose, CA 95127
www.pegasusbooks.net

First Edition: January 2014

Published in North America by Pegasus Books. For information, please contact Pegasus Books c/o Caprice De Luca, 3338 San Marino Ave, San Jose, CA 95127.

Although the novel is very loosely based on a true story, *The Tenor* is a work of fiction and not intended to be a historically accurate depiction of the lives or the careers of any of the characters contained within. Though none of the characters are real, some are composites of many people whom the author met and interviewed in the preparation and research for the book. Any similarities are not intended and purely coincidental.

Library of Congress Cataloguing-In-Publication Data
Peter Danish
The Tenor/Peter Danish – 1st ed
p. cm.
Library of Congress Control Number: 2014900099
ISBN – 978-0-9910993-4-4

1. FICTION / Romance / Historical / 20th Century *. 2. MUSIC / Genres & Styles / Opera. 3. HISTORY / Modern / 20th Century. 4. HISTORY / Military / World War II. 5. BIOGRAPHY & AUTOBIOGRAPHY / Composers & Musicians.

10 9 8 7 6 5 4 3 2 1

Comments about *The Tenor* and requests for additional copies, book club rates and author speaking appearances may be addressed to Peter Danish or Pegasus Books c/o Caprice De Luca, 3338 San Marino Ave, San Jose, CA, 95127, or you can send your comments and requests via e-mail to cdeluca@pegasusbooks.net.

Also available as an eBook from Internet retailers and from Pegasus Books

Printed in the United States of America

To Sanela,

my wife, my life and my muse.

You make it all worthwhile!

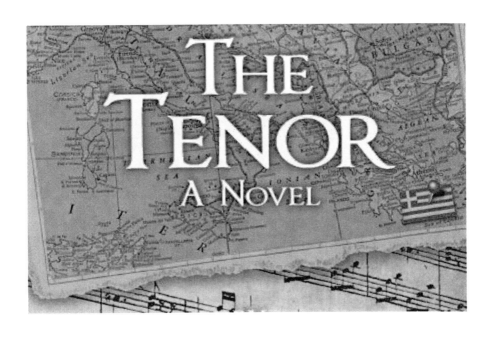

THE TENOR

A NOVEL

PREFACE

A few years ago, I was reading a biography of Maria Callas, written by Ariana Stassinopoulou – who would later become known to the world as Arianna Huffington. In her book, there was a very brief but incredible story about an Italian soldier. History has no record of him and his name is unknown, but he inspired me more than I can possibly explain. I decided that he deserved a life and a story of his own.

It would be impossible for me to thank everyone who assisted in the creating of this book. If I tried to name them all I would surely leave out far too many. The dozens and dozens of people whom I met in my trips to Italy and Greece, who generously shared their stories and answered my endless questions, please know that your contributions are greatly appreciated and they provide all the color and the texture of the story, and your personal anecdotes about life "back in the day" are the very breath and lifeblood of the book.

Thanks go out to Marcus McGee, Caprice De Luca and Chris Moebs at Pegasus Books for having faith in the book. Thanks to Alla Generalova for her tireless, unfailing editorial eye. Special thanks to Heather Wood for her invaluable advice throughout the process and particularly for her encouragement, when prospects for success looked bleakest. And to all the poor souls I asked to read the early drafts over the last few years!

And a very special thanks to my friend, Georgia Prosalenty Vasilakopoulos, and the late great Jimmy Ziotis (of the Skylark International Cafe in Nyack), for their tireless help, guidance and insights on all things Greek! *Efharisto para poli!*

– Peter Danish

THE TENOR

New York, March 1965
Chestnuts

AT FORTY FIVE YEARS OF AGE, Pino Vaggi considered himself a reasonably lucky guy. He was in good health, had a successful business, good credit, some money in the bank and the nice reputation of a respected artist around his little neighborhood. Yet he was plagued by feelings of restlessness, of a destiny unfulfilled. What he'd considered his true calling and sole reason for existence had been dangled before him and snatched away ages ago. Like so many others, he once had grand plans to dedicate his life to the creation of art, but over time, the business of surviving cooled his passion for such noble pursuits. Necessity wielded a cruel whip and he had plenty of marks to prove it.

The aroma of roasting chestnuts emanating from a street vendor's cart caught him in a visceral way as he stood waiting for the light to change; they'd always been his favorite. In the spring, the trees in the little Alpine town of his childhood had brimmed with them and in the fall they covered the ground in a velvety, light-brown blanket.

There was hardly a meal in his household that hadn't contained them in some shape or form. Breakfast might have been ground chestnut cereal, lunch might have been served on bread baked with chestnut flour, and dinner always featured chestnut pasta for a first course. As an adult, he could hardly pass a street vendor without the aroma stirring some warm memory from his youth. It was a burden he bore virtually every day since moving to New York decades ago. The Italy of his salad days was a distant memory, and yet he continually found himself fighting off the phantoms of the past.

He took another deep nostalgic breath and a strong sense memory broke through the surface. Suddenly, he was five years old, back in his mother's kitchen and the aroma was everywhere. It brought along other memories too, equally familiar but not as pleasant. He thought of the village chimneys bellowing black smoke and the smell of fresh bread wafting from them and the terra cotta roofs on which they sat. Those images and that world were no longer his.

He had no idea who now occupied his childhood home or his room. Some new arrivals had long since called it home and had removed any sign of the previous occupants who once breathed life into those stones and mortar. He didn't bother shooing away ghosts of the past; he'd lived with them for so many years that he hardly noticed them any longer.

A taxi's horn interrupted his daydream and he returned to the present. The hot, dirty exhaust of the traffic filled his nostrils as his eyes watched the warm air dancing on the blacktop, distorting everything passing through it. It always amazed him how clearly he could remember every inch of his mother's kitchen, down to the minutest detail, but he could never remember where he'd left his car keys.

History never appealed to him as a young man, but as he grew older, it became an obsession. It was one of life's great ironies, he thought, that his passion for history grew in *indirect* proportion to his ability to remember anything. Luckily, his sense of humor got him through many such "ironies."

As he crossed Canal Street, the sun was just beginning to dip behind the Westside skyline. The unique golden glow of early spring in New York reflected warmly off the windows of the buildings, its shadows creeping eastward like a gauzy spectral army on the march. As a child, he'd been told that in the USA they had streets paved with gold. When he first arrived in New York and saw that light turning everything in its path to gold, he thought, *that must have been what they meant.*

This was his favorite time of year. It reminded him of "the old country," but the rapid pulse of traffic passing before his eyes reminded him that tonight would be the most monumental night of his life and he needed to stay focused. At the next corner, waiting for the light to change, the aroma of roasting chestnuts caught him again. Despite his best intentions, he simply couldn't help but surrender to its call.

His passion for chestnuts wasn't a trait he'd inherited from either of his parents. His father loved to roast them for the children at Christmas, but it was more the ritual, the ceremony that he enjoyed than the taste (not to mention the smiles that they invariably produced). Pino's mother possessed a singular distaste for chestnuts having less to do with their flavor than with their ever-expanding culinary dominance in the region. She would often declare, "What I wouldn't give for some *real* flour to bake with!"

He and his parents possessed strikingly dissimilar tastes in food and sadly, as he grew older, he came to realize that there would be very few things that he and his family would have in common. Time blurred the memories, but chestnuts remained one thing that always reminded him of happy times spent with his family in the old stone house in that little mountain-top village.

The scream of a police siren brought him back to the present. A little boy holding his mother's hand stared at him in curiosity. Pino laughed to himself, thinking how silly he must look to passers-by. How long had he been standing there, staring into space? His watch said: 5:15pm. Still plenty of time, but he couldn't afford to dawdle any longer.

While daydreaming, he'd missed his turn. Where the heck was he anyway? He glanced around at a hazy sea of closed faces as the smell of taxi exhaust burned his throat. He looked back at the little boy next to him who, judging by his smart clothes and his mom's two-hundred dollar handbag, was a child of privilege. But all their money couldn't protect him from breathing the taxi exhaust every day.

Would that boy ever know the peace and tranquility of Collagna, the solitude and the quiet majesty of the mountains and the cold crisp air that folks breathed there, that Pino had known growing up? Pino smiled a deep melancholy smile at the child and paused to ponder the wonderful gift of poverty, in all its shabby glory, that his own parents had bestowed upon him.

Pino had tried hard to explain to his own daughter what the mountains, so high and so majestic, meant to him. He described the sky of the mountains, so clear and so bright that it had to be the blue of heaven itself. He told her of the house he was born in, made of stone, no heat or air-conditioning, and only a large wood burning stove. But he could only describe them accurately and vividly in Italian and sadly, she had never shown any desire to learn her father's native tongue. They'd had exchanges like these hundreds of times, invariably with the same result. She tolerated his musings about the glorious past, but in her eyes he could see that she still viewed him as some coarse peasant who had crawled out of a storybook called "Italy."

The mountains, the great plateau, the giant evergreen trees and the royal blue sky were miraculous to Pino, but they were miracles of the past, a past that he could hardly even remember any longer. In his youth, the vast open spaces of the Apennines had made him feel small and insignificant. Now, the crowds and the noise of New York gave him the same sensation. It was ironic given how self-assured and cocky he'd been in his youth.

A taxi bearing a bumper sticker that read *"Honk if you love peace and quiet!"* pulled up in front of him and he laughed out loud. *"New York in a nutshell,"* he thought. Glancing up at the "Pedestrian Crossing" sign, Pino remembered his mother's comment upon seeing the sign when they first moved to New York: "Okay, but where do *Catholics* cross?"

The light changed and the world jumpstarted. The sign on the corner read *Mulberry Street.*

"Okay, focus! Pick up tux. Shower. Shave. Buy flowers. Get a cab."

He was cutting it closer than he wanted. This waxing philosophical was becoming a habit of late and he had to keep it under control. Episodes like this, and there had been several of them, helped him get through some difficult times. But tonight he needed a cool, clear head. He strolled across Mulberry Street, heading east.

Stepping out of the sunlight into the growing shade, he noticed it was getting colder, so he turned up his collar against the brisk wind blowing north from the Battery. The weather report predicted thunderstorms and he could see the threatening clouds gathering to the west. It wouldn't have mattered if there were a blizzard blowing. Tonight he had enough energy to light up all of Manhattan.

In spite of his relative comfort and security, he viewed his life as a long series of failures and missed opportunities. The losses were always easier to count than the gains, as they left marks. His father once told him that he was made of soft wood, like pine.

"The good thing about pine," his father had said, "was that it was strong and it could bend a lot without breaking." The bad thing was that it showed a dent from every blow it received, and Lord knows he'd seen his share of dents.

The long years doing a job he was never really cut out for, while at the same time turning a deaf ear to his life's true calling, had exacted a toll. The stores of Pino's spiritual capital had been taxed to their very limit when finally, it happened.

Hope. He thought back to the day only a few months earlier when *hope* literally walked back into his life and in an instant, the loneliness, desolation and depression parted like clouds after a sun shower. Armed with a renewed sense of purpose, he made phone calls, sent out invitations, bought clothes, etc. He was a young man again, reckless and silly. His middle-aged heart bounced like that of a child.

The evening and his future were a blank canvas and for once he was certain that *he* would be the one holding the brush. It was his chance to put it all right. He'd been waiting over twenty years and he wasn't going to be late. Tonight, if all went right, he might actually achieve, crazy as it sounded, a measure of immortality.

PART ONE: ITALY 1930

CHAPTER ONE

A NIGHT AT THE OPERA

"HURRY, PINO! The train leaves in twenty minutes, with or without you!" Rosemaria Vaggi wasn't exactly a doting mother but she did like to keep up appearances, and after weeks of telling the entire town that her husband was taking her and the children to the opera, nothing short of an earthquake was going to spoil her evening.

"Did you hear me? Let's go!" she called out from the bottom of the stairs as she straightened her hat in the hall mirror. She was a fair-skinned beauty in a plump, old-fashioned kind of way with long auburn hair that was always pulled back in a tight bun, except for church on Sundays and on such rare occasions as a night at the opera. High-strung and temperamental, she never dealt well with the rest of her family's consistent lack of punctuality. *Clearly it was a trait the children had gotten from their father.*

In the kitchen, Antonio Vaggi was tying a bonnet on his daughter's head, careful not to catch her hair in the knot, as he usually did. Little Maria, only five years old, didn't understand why she was wearing her Sunday clothes on a Saturday afternoon but she was thrilled to receive a brand new silk bonnet for the occasion. In her current state she would not have been out of place in one of Raphael's Angel frescoes.

At that moment, upstairs in the bathroom, Pino Vaggi, age ten, wished he had a bonnet to cover his stringy mop of hair that, despite two applications of lard, simply would not stay put. He didn't dare appear before his mother in that state, but time and his mother's patience were running out. He wet the comb again and dragged it across his scalp one last time, but it got hopelessly snagged. He panicked and yanked and yanked as hard as he could, but it would not give.

"You've got one minute!" called out the sentinel at the base of the stairs.

His father used to joke, *the real length of a minute depended upon which side of the bathroom door you happened to be on,* but Pino knew his mother wasn't in a joking mood. He knew what he had to do. He opened the medicine cabinet and took out a pair of scissors. He raised them up, bit his lip and prayed for the best. He snipped his hair gently just beneath the knot, then quickly matted his hair down as best he could with his hands.

After flushing the evidence down the drain, he glanced back in the mirror. Hope stirred in his heart that he just might get away with it. In spite of his tragic hair, he thought he cut a fine figure in his grey wool suit, but just to play it safe, he knelt down and said a quick *Ave Maria*.

"Oh no! Tony, it's starting to rain," Mrs. Vaggi cried out, as Pino trotted down the stairs and straight out the door.

"It's just a drizzle, Mama," said the boy, hoping the rain might mat down his hair further.

"It'll take more than a little rain to spoil the evening," Mr. Vaggi said, kissing his wife, "Now let's go and have a wonderful night."

Papa was hardly a poet, thought Pino, but he knew just what to say in such circumstances. When Pino saw the look in his mother's eyes, he knew he was safe. She was back on cloud nine and nothing would change that.

The skies opened and rain poured down as the taxi reached the station. Pino could see and smell the smoke from the engine as they rushed inside. They boarded the long black train and walked the length of one car, then another, then another. Pino figured by the time they reached their compartment they would already be in Milan.

Finally, Papa stopped and opened the door to an empty compartment and they all filed in. The compartment had two light brown leather benches facing one another and could easily sit six people. The leather had an odd pungent smell to it and Pino knelt down to sniff it.

"Stop that!" said his father, grabbing Pino by the collar and dropping him on the seat next to his sister, who couldn't help but giggle. The compartment seemed enormous to Pino, and he hoped that the other seats would remain unoccupied for the duration of the trip. His father sat back, yawned deeply and soon nodded off to sleep. *"Papa could sleep through an earthquake,"* thought Pino.

His father was a butcher by trade, and some would say the work suited him. A short, stout man with thinning, jet-black hair and a small thin moustache, his only striking physical features were his enormously muscular arms.

He was a third generation butcher and tenth generation *Collagnian*. Life in Collagna, the slow pace, the neighborly familiarity of the people, the general daily "sameness," the peaceful stunning vistas and the crisp cool mountain air were all to his liking. It was a life that few would call exciting, but one that fit his demeanor well.

This trip to the opera was actually his wife's idea, but the thought wasn't altogether unpleasant to him. He was never a great fan of the fine arts, but he realized that he really didn't do many things with his family other than eat dinner with them, and thus he hoped that the experience might be memorable for them. His knowledge of opera was virtually non-existent, but he did recognize most of the popular arias, owing to his parent's collection of 78 rpm recordings by singers whose names meant nothing to him. It all seemed so stuffy.

Mrs. Vaggi playfully described her husband's taste as "completely unencumbered by culture." His preferences in music ran closer to the Neapolitan style that so many northern Italians found vulgar.

"Neapolitan music was fun. What's wrong with having fun?" Papa Vaggi thought.

He fondly remembered the first radio the family owned; it was the envy of the entire town. It was bigger than the kitchen stove and the sound was deplorable, but it gave them a connection to the outside world that few others in their little village possessed. Unfortunately, it seemed all of the musical programs on the radio were opera! The State seemed to view opera as the only art form worthy of such distinction. Over the years, he had come to a kind of *simpatico* with it and he was actually looking forward to the performance with great anticipation. Secretly, he also hoped it would lend him an air of distinction in the community. At the very least, it would give him something different to talk about at the bar, other than the usual soccer scores or Mussolini and his crazy fascists.

Mrs. Vaggi chose the evening and the performance. Initially, Mr. Vaggi was pleased with the selection of *Romeo and Juliet* because it was a story he knew and could easily follow. Yet his disappointment knew no boundaries when he learned that the opera would be performed in French. Nonetheless, he was determined to "rise above it."

Pino and Maria were singing and mimicking operatic poses when the door to the compartment opened and two young men in black shirts entered and sat down. Apparently Papa had not reserved the entire compartment after all.

"Papa, why do we have to go to the opera? I don't like the opera," said Pino. His sister giggled, sensing that the question would land him in hot water.

"That will be enough, thank you," declared his waking father in a tone that should have been message enough.

"But Papa, I don't like the opera," he repeated.

Pino's father rubbed his eyes and leaned forward with a stern look on his face. "I'm not going to say it again!" As he sat back, his glance fell upon one of the black-shirted newcomers. Their eyes met for an instant and Mr. Vaggi's look turned to one of disdain. The newcomer returned the hard glance, sitting up, head erect. Pino's father snorted and was about to open his mouth to say something when he felt his wife's hand touch his arm. When he turned toward her, the look in her eyes stopped him in his tracks.

"Not tonight," she whispered gently. His anger faded as he smiled and kissed her. She was right; this was not the time or place for politics.

Pino sat in silence for the remainder of the journey, but the little scene between his father and the black-shirted man didn't escape his attention. He made himself a quick mental note to ask Papa about it later. Volumes could be filled with the mental notes Pino planned to ask his father about, but most were forgotten shortly thereafter.

Upon reaching Milan, the Vaggi family streamed out of the compartment. As Mr. Vaggi passed through the door, one of the black-shirts said in a pointedly sardonic voice, *"Buona sera."* Pino watched as his father paused, swallowed hard, then with flared nostrils continued after his family through the corridor of the car, muttering: "Damn fascists."

They disembarked the train and walked the length of the platform into the massive granite lobby of the station. It was by far the largest and most beautiful building Pino had ever seen. As they proceeded to the front of the station to catch a taxi, Pino looked back at the spectacular facade, with its magnificent archways and mammoth columns. He thought it was far too beautiful a structure to be a train station. *It must have been a great Roman temple once, a place where the senate sat and passed laws and killed Christians and things like that.*

That was only the beginning. Milan was incredible. It sprawled out in every direction as far as the eye could see. So many lights, so many buildings, so much noise and so many people! As the taxi raced along through the busy streets, passing storefront after storefront, and restaurant after restaurant, Pino thought, *a million people must live here!* The drizzling rain and accompanying fog added a soft misty glow to the busy tableau outside the taxi window.

Pino's bliss was interrupted when the taxi screeched to a halt, causing the entire family to topple about the compartment. A group of pedestrians appearing in the middle of the road caused the driver to slam on the brakes to avoid hitting them.

"Everyone ok?" Mr. Vaggi asked. Shaken but not injured was the verdict as everyone's attention turned to the pedestrians in the taxi's headlights.

They were crossing the street carrying signs, which Pino couldn't get a good enough look at to read. What was unmistakable was the fact that they were all wearing the same black shirts as the two men on the train.

The driver apologized to Papa Vaggi and began muttering under his breath. There was something aggressive about the demeanor of the crowd and Pino was nervous. The driver, impatient with their pace, tapped his horn. Several members of the group stopped and looked in the windshield at the driver. One came right up to the bumper of the car. His face was pugnacious and his stance confrontational. For a second he just stared at the driver, and then he slammed his fist on the hood of the car, scaring the wits out of Pino. Mama Vaggi screamed and Papa grabbed her hand. Little Maria was the only one in their group who seemed to be enjoying the show.

"Easy now," Mr. Vaggi said. "It's alright. Everything's fine." The black-shirts continued on their way and the taxi driver resumed driving to the opera house as if nothing had happened at all.

"These *fascisti* are so touchy! They can't read or write but they sure talk loud!" the driver joked, completely unbothered.

Mr. Vaggi laughed and winked at Pino who was more shaken than he let on. *Who were these fascists anyway?* he thought, and resolved once again to bring up the matter with his father when the time seemed appropriate. But tonight was Mama's night. He had heard his father say it repeatedly, and Pino didn't want to do or say anything that might spoil it.

The taxi dropped them off in the piazza in front of Teatro alla Scala. As they pushed their way through the crowd in front of the theater, Pino observed the dingy color of the theater and wondered why anyone would paint an opera house yellow. *The train station was much more impressive*, he thought.

Passing through the entrance and making their way through the foyer of the opera house, Pino's opinion changed drastically. It was suddenly something out of a storybook: marble floors and towering columns, with gold everywhere. As he gazed around in wonder, Pino felt that despite the fact that he was wearing his best Sunday clothes, he was still somehow underdressed.

His father told them to stay put while he checked their coats. Pino was more than content to stay right there and examine the designs in the marble blocks that made up the floor. It was so polished that he could see his own reflection in it and he thought for a second that it might be glass. It made him happy just to look at it.

His mother was not quite so thrilled. Her husband had returned from checking the coats and was motioning for them to go back outside. It was clear that Pino's mother had absolutely no intention of doing so. She grabbed an usher and thrust their tickets in his face. He squinted at them, and then he too pointed to the door leading outside. He made a circular motion with his hand that caused Mrs. Vaggi to grab the tickets from him and storm away toward the door. Mr. Vaggi grabbed Pino and Maria's hands and followed after her.

Pino's mind was racing. *I'll bet we're here on the wrong night! Wouldn't that be funny?* But, when he saw the look on his mother's face, standing outside waiting for them, he knew it was no laughing matter.

"What difference does it make which entrance we use?" said Mr. Vaggi, taking the whole matter in stride, but Pino's mother wasn't having it. They walked around the corner of the building along with a fairly large group of people headed in the same direction. Their destination was a side stairway above which hung a sign saying: *GALLERIA.* Pino didn't quite understand, but it appeared to him that their tickets did not permit them to enter through the beautiful main entrance.

They were "relegated" to something known as the *GALLERIA,* and his mother was very disappointed, if not embarrassed about it. They went along a broad corridor, with a long marble floor, through another door, and then up a flight of stairs, then another, and another.

Often his mother's anger would flare up like a sand storm in the desert, seemingly out of nowhere and then it would be gone just as fast as it arrived. But it was not to be the case this time.

"Mama, I'm really excited. Aren't you?" Pino offered, hoping to return some of the glitter to the occasion, but his mother didn't want to be cheered up. As they ascended what seemed like ten flights of stairs, Pino thought for certain she would cry. She stopped on the landing before the final flight of stairs and composed herself. She had little need to, however, because when they reached the top of the stairs, something happened - something magical.

In the hallway, a gentle-looking old usher with long sideburns and a bushy moustache smiled at them and took their tickets. He led them down the hall to a doorway with a dark, red velvet curtain hanging in it. He stopped, knelt down and took little Maria by the hand.

"Is this your first time at the opera, sweetheart?" he inquired in a sweet, grand-fatherly tone.

Maria nodded bashfully.

"We don't usually get visitors your age, dear. It was very thoughtful of your mama and papa to take you with them to the opera. Not many little girls get the chance. I think you are going to have the time of your life."

The usher smiled and winked at Mrs. Vaggi, who was beginning to get caught up in the proceedings. He led Maria right up to a curtain and stopped.

"Now, close your eyes and don't open them till I say so."

He took the velvet rope that held the curtain back off its hook.

"Ready? Now!"

With that, he yanked back the curtain and a collective gasp burst through the entire Vaggi family. There were no words to describe it. Maria and her mother ran inside and right up to the railing. Pino and his father followed close behind.

Pino was sure he had entered paradise. In front of him, he beheld the most breathtaking theater that anyone could have ever imagined. Everywhere he looked there was plush red velvet and gold. The entire auditorium was aglow in gaslight, creating a warm, dreamy, mystical aura. Pino felt Goosebumps up his back and arms, and for that one moment, he completely lost himself in a sense of awe. If the evening had ended right there, it would already have been memorable. It had been one wonder after another.

He stepped up to join his mother and sister at the railing and looked down at the stage and the orchestra pit. Everywhere, there were people milling about - aristocratic-looking people, in tuxedos and furs, bejeweled, holding opera glasses. Pino glanced at his mother. There were tears in her eyes, but they were different than the ones she'd nearly spilled only a moment earlier. Papa surveyed the theater with a cursory eye and he seemed suitably impressed.

"Pino, look at the beautiful chandelier!" exclaimed his sister.

It has to be ten meters across, he thought.

"Papa, they should build a theater like this back home," Maria continued.

Mr. and Mrs. Vaggi laughed out loud at the thought. Mr. Vaggi slipped his arm around his wife's waist and gently hugged her. It seemed that complete family harmony had finally been achieved.

As the lights went down, they settled back in their seats and Pino hugged his mother. She in turn took his little hand and squeezed it hard. He then looked at his father, who was trying his best to stifle a yawn. It was apparent that the magic that Pino felt was lost on his father. He didn't appear unhappy, but merely content; wearing the sort of expression that Pino had seen on him after a good meal.

The audience applauded when the conductor appeared and he acknowledged the applause with a polite bow. Then silence.

Pino was biting his nails and sitting on the edge of his seat. The opening chord of the score struck him like thunder. His jaw dropped, and his eyes widened, feeling warm and wonderful. He forgot that he was in the Gallery; for the entire theater had become his private parlor and the musicians were performing just for him.

Pino was familiar with the story. What child in Italy wasn't familiar with *Romeo and Juliet*? But something was different. The lady singing was beautiful! She had long dark hair draping down over her gown and sang like an angel, her voice liquid gold. The man singing, while somewhat short and stout, sang like a god! And he had the loudest voice Pino had ever heard.

When he sang to Juliet up upon her balcony, it was the most beautiful song he'd ever heard. Even though he understood not a word of French, the meaning was apparent. And the *music*! *Oh*, the music! This didn't sound anything like the scratchy, hollow-sounding records his parents played on the victrola at home. This sound was nothing short of magic!

As the curtain fell at the end of the first act, Pino leaned forward and rested his chin on his hands. Touching his face, he discovered he was crying. He'd never been moved to tears by anything before and wasn't sure what to make of it.

By the time the final curtain fell, Pino was an emotional wreck. His heart raced and his hands shook. He was perspiring and crying. He was completely unaware his family was even still there. This was the most wonderful, glorious thing he'd ever seen. His place in the universe was changing. *It's almost as if God is here right now in the theater* he thought. *Showing me this divine sound and vision of how beautiful and joyful life should be. This is how I want to spend the rest of my life.*

CHAPTER TWO

THE MAESTRO

EARLIEST RECORDS SHOW that the village of Collagna was a popular rest stop for pilgrims making the trek from the northern provinces to Rome. Located just before the Cerreto Pass, marking the midway point in the range, it was a logical spot for weary pilgrims to seek repose from their travels.

In more modern times, Collagna was a modest town with one church, one school, and one train station. There were, however, a half dozen taverns. One of the taverns was actually an inn with rooms available for modern "pilgrims" weary from travel who stumbled upon the fair hamlet, and fresh cheese and warm focaccia were always in abundance. The town was probably as indebted to France and Switzerland for its culture and cuisine as it was to Italy, but those thoughts were rarely considered and never spoken aloud.

The word "provincial," in its loveliest and most charming sense applied. A traveling salesman once remarked, with accuracy, that Collagna had "more sheep than people!" However, for all its bucolic charm and natural beauty, Collagna was hardly the ideal place to begin a career in the arts. Such was the fate of Pino Vaggi.

By the time he was twelve years old, Pino was already known around town as "Little Caruso." Whether in school, in church, or doing chores, he was invariably singing, humming, or whistling an opera aria. Everyone loved to listen to him and he knew it. It made him quite cocky. Father Michele, the parish priest, remarked on it often to his parents, stressing the importance of humility in the Christian faith. But it was actually Father Michele who gave Pino most of the sheet music the boy had been learning from. The priest was quietly hoping to mold Pino into a fine cantor for Sunday services.

There was precious little Pino's parents could do to deter townsfolk from contributing to the boy's already growing ego. Hearing a Verdi aria from the lips of one so young was simply too much for them. How could they be expected *not* to coddle the boy? Thus, his cherubic cheeks got more than their share of affectionate pinches.

In truth, Pino's parents were quite proud of their son. They were pleased that he was polite and well-mannered and that he was generally loved throughout the village. He displayed remarkable poise, intelligence, and maturity for his age.

Mrs. Vaggi was a bit concerned that the boy was neglecting his school work for his singing. She loved his singing and believed he had real talent, but did not want him pursuing it at the expense of his other studies.

Mr. Vaggi's only concern about Pino was that the boy showed virtually no interest at all in sports. After almost sacrilegiously informing his father that he "detested" soccer, Pino's parents gave him a pair of ice skates for Christmas, hoping to tap into some primitive alpine sporting urge. Unfortunately, he could not have been less interested in the skates. Still, in a show of maturity, and determined not to be a complete ingrate, he made a great spectacle of his procession through the snowy streets of the town toward the frozen lake carrying his shiny new silver skates.

His pilgrimage did not go unobserved, attracting the attention of several of his more curious classmates, who followed at a respectful distance. By the time he reached the lake, a veritable parade followed him. He really hadn't wanted an audience for his maiden voyage, but it was too late to turn back.

His first tentative step onto the ice was met with a deep, low-pitched cracking noise, almost a howl. The Gods of Sport were trying to send him a message, but with such an audience in attendance, he dared not retreat from his mission. He took a deep breath and strode out onto the frozen lake. He hadn't gone ten feet before the ice beneath him gave way and he found himself knee-deep in freezing water.

So the boy is no good in school and no good at sports—what else was there, really, Mr. Vaggi thought. At first the concern vexed him but it eventually passed. One fact that did not escape him, however, was that Pino had relatively few friends. It wasn't that his classmates didn't like him, but being so focused and so driven at such a young age made close friendship with him more work than most young children were willing to do. For his part, Pino rarely played with other children his age because, as he told his parents, "a career in the arts requires total commitment," although the words sounded almost laughable coming from the mouth of a pre-pubescent child. His father wondered who in the village was filling the boy's head with such ideas.

Still, it was impossible to imagine a childhood in Italy that was completely devoid of soccer. Thus, when pressed upon by his friends he would reluctantly answer the call. At twelve years old, Pino was blessed with an opera singer's voice and a pudgy body to match. Accordingly, he had to face a harsh reality early on, a fact both universal and inescapable. Simply put: the fat kid was always the goalie. His physical gifts lent themselves better to his primary passion, singing.

Pino's first real music teacher was Maestro Franco Ivaldi, a giant of a man with a spectacular mane of silver hair and a booming baritone voice. He lived alone in a tiny stone house on the very edge of the town, where civilization met nature, beyond which lay the twisting trails to the mountain's summit which were known only to skiers and climbers.

Like most of the houses in Collagna, the maestro's was made of stone and had a pitched sandstone roof. Like the people in Collagna, the homes were hardy. They would often outlive many generations of families. The stone also provided the additional benefit of a wonderful natural acoustical quality for the maestro's pupils. At one time the maestro had kept a studio next to the church in town, from which he conducted his lessons. However, in the years since his wife passed away, his home gradually became his primary studio.

The road to the maestro's house could accurately be called the road less traveled. It was a mere thread of a road, a path of gravel and stones choked with tufts of grass and moss. The trees on either side had thrust out branches to make progress even more eventful. Their roots protruded from the ground and looked like the skeletal remains of some prehistoric creature. A large fallen tree had been left to rot and countless shrubs grew wild and ugly around it.

This building would become Pino's home-away-from-home, his school and his sanctuary.

As for the maestro himself, no one in town was sure exactly how old he really was. His appearance and vitality were those of a young man, but the years spent cloistered in the darkness of his studio and in the choir loft of the church had shielded his skin from any prolonged exposure to the sun. Consequently, he had glorious, creamy-white skin.

As far back as anyone could recollect, he had always had gray hair, which with time had become pure white, with the occasional streak of silver in it. He was once a tall, slender, graceful man, but time, gravity and a lifetime spent over a piano had reduced him to near-hunchback stature, so much so that at times, the top of his head seemed lower than his shoulders, giving him the appearance of a vulture. Yet when he stood erect, he was a giant and commanding presence.

The community as a whole found the maestro a cold and distant creature, devoted to his art and not especially skilled in the social graces, but Pino disagreed completely. He understood the maestro immediately and found him to be the warmest, wisest, and most trustworthy soul in the entire world.

At their first terrifying meeting, Pino thought the maestro looked out of place in this century, thinking he belonged to a distant, mystical, medieval age—an age when men wore puffy shirts of lace and capes and rode in horse-drawn carriages that rattled down cobblestone roads, a time of impeccable manners and language and learning and books. Providence seemed to have plucked him out of history and dropped him in Collagna just in time to cross paths with "Little Caruso."

Pino imagined that the maestro had tried to cultivate and maintain a visage like one of the great composers of the past and in this he was most successful. He spoke in a resonant baritone, the voice clear and crisp, with just a hint of arrogance. A born teacher, the maestro was possessed of the singular quality of total confidence. It radiated throughout his body, shooting from his fingertips as he caressed the keyboard and booming from his throat as he spoke. It was both intimidating and awe-inspiring, and Pino felt equal measures of both.

The maestro had begun his not-so-illustrious career as a gifted concert pianist. A native of Fornova, a village on the river Taro in northern Emilia-Romagna, by the age of thirteen he was considered a prodigy and received a generous "gift" from a wealthy patron to continue his studies in Bologna. The great city was a far cry from Fornova, but its institutions of higher learning were noted predominantly for the studies of law and medicine, not the arts. It wasn't Milan. Yet, it was in Bologna that Franco Ivaldi developed and polished his skills and soon earned the enviable reputation as a "sight reader extraordinaire!" He could glance at a sheet of music only once and be able to play it from memory. Moreover, his gift of perfect pitch made him an adept accompanist for singers, as well. But, as is often the case, the gift came with a corresponding burden.

A little over a year after he moved to Bologna, and against his better judgment he agreed to play at the wedding of a wealthy friend. He was promised a tidy sum for the performance and he certainly needed the money, but he desperately hoped no one from his conservatory would ever learn of it. At the reception, he became the subject of a particularly ill-advised wager of the bridegroom.

The wedding was a black-tie affair at a fancy hall and it was clear that no expense had been spared. Unfortunately, the groom's ribald sense of humor got the better of him. He bragged to his bride's inebriated brother that the piano player was a savant, blessed with such an amazing ear that the brother could literally sit on the piano keyboard and Franco, the pianist, could name all the keys that he sat on! The bet was made and the brother proceeded to leap up on the bandstand and drop his hind quarters on the keyboard in full view of the entire wedding party.

The guests were shocked and the father of the bride was not amused. As the wine-soaked brother dandled on the keyboard, heedless of the affront he was causing, his father climbed onto the rostrum and dragged him out of the hall by the hair. A near-riot ensued, and although he played no active role, Franco's name was forever associated with the prank. Sadly, the incident achieved near-legendary status in certain affluent circles in Bologna, circles that might have been helpful to the career of a young musician, had circumstances been different.

As if fortune hadn't frowned upon him enough, Franco began to notice a dull nagging pain in his left hand while playing. At first he ignored it, but soon it became intolerable and he was forced to consult a doctor. "Strained ligaments" was the diagnosis and "rest" was the prescribed remedy. After a few days, he felt better, but when he resumed playing, the discomfort soon returned. It seemed no amount of rest could completely eliminate the pain. Distraught, Franco sought the advice of his teacher at the conservatory. His instructor was a practical man and his sober advice was to concentrate on teaching and accompanying singers. There would always be work for a good accompanist.

A good accompanist! Was that what he was to be reduced to? A good accompanist? He was thunderstruck. At first he rejected the thought and determined to find another doctor and another treatment. In the end, it was not to be. The strained ligaments diagnosis was followed by one of nerve damage, and with those two words a grand career ended before it even began.

Riches and fame held no value to him whatsoever; they were distractions, the kind that always seemed to fill his path, the kind that separated the very good from the great. Franco Ivaldi dreamed only of perfection, not of personal aggrandizement or financial gain. Now it appeared that perfection would be denied him.

Franco Ivaldi, concert pianist, would become Franco Ivaldi, master accompanist. Eventually, after having accompanied hundreds of Italy's finest singers and studying their strengths and weaknesses, watching their preparation and learning their techniques, he became Franco Ivaldi, master vocal instructor. It was a career that suited him better than he expected, and as a result he spent many happy years in service of the arts as a much sought-after vocal instructor. His return to the Apennines was in reality his wife's decision, but he never regretted it. The hectic pace and the dog-eat-dog lifestyle of the city never appealed to him anyway.

Over the years, he had taught hundreds of students of varying levels of talent and commitment, but the child standing before him in his studio now was causing him fits. Pino Vaggi was by far the most gifted and technically advanced pupil that Franco had ever heard. Aside from the fact that he had a gorgeous natural tenor of extraordinary brilliance with a richly balanced tonal quality, his breath control and phrasing were far superior to half the professional singers the maestro knew, and yet Pino was only twelve years old! It was unthinkable!

Looking at the boy's face for the first time, the maestro saw a young man upon whose plump pink cheeks there lay like morning dew a layer of cockiness that would either become his greatest asset or his worst liability. Although he would not and could not admit it, for the first time in his life, the maestro was secretly terrified! Terrified that he might say or do something that would have even the slightest negative impact on the boy's progress.

Another vocal teacher might rush the boy on an accelerated career path, which undoubtedly could bring financial rewards, but might be devastating to the voice, and the thought that the world might never hear a mature Pino was intolerable to the maestro. It unnerved him, but he knew that there was only one true path, and his job, his duty, would be to see that Pino stayed on it.

Pino's studies consisted of piano, violin, voice, and music theory, but none of the lessons held any interest for him other than voice. Consequently, he neglected the disciplines that bored him, to the extent allowable by the maestro, of course.

"No! No! Like this!" roared the old man. "You must always keep the fingers gently curled. You see? Like this! Capische?"

"*Si, Maestro.*"

"Good, good. You start to understand. *Va bene, basta,*" he said, closing the cover to the piano. "Pino, do you understand why I insist that you practice the scales so much? Why we do the same exercises over and over? Hmm?" The only answer the boy could think of was one that he dared not say. So instead he simply nodded.

"Why?" inquired the maestro, calling his bluff. Pino paused as if to compose his thoughts, and scratched his head, hoping for divine intervention and then gave up, shrugging his shoulders.

"Pino, Pino, Pino…," said the old man, his voice the very picture of disappointment. "These scales must become more than just notes; they must become language for you. You have to have them so committed to memory that ninety years from now, God willing, as you lay on your deathbed, you still won't be able to get them out of your head."

Pino rolled his eyes and sighed.

"Don't make faces! It's the same with singing. You must possess a thorough understanding of the theory behind the music before you can sing. You must be a complete musician, Pino, not like the ones out there today that don't even know when they are singing off-key."

The maestro turned back to the piano and lifted the cover.

"Now this note is C," he said as though he was talking to an infant, and he struck an octave above middle C. "Now sing it!" he commanded in a terrible voice. Pino sang the note, but he was flat. "No. Like this: Seeeeee."

Pino attempted the note again, but once again he was flat.

"Make the pitch higher."

Again he tried and again he was flat.

"Flat, flat, flat. Higher!"

Pino tried desperately to hit the note and the maestro continued to pound the note on the keyboard. It built up to a fury as the maestro began to hit C's all over the keyboard and then started to sing it himself! Finally Pino hit the right pitch and the maestro cried out.

"Aha! Stupendo! Now hold it!" Pino struggled to hold the note. "Hold it, hold it!" the maestro cried, placing his hand on Pino's diaphragm. "Breathe from here! Four more beats and I'll let you go hoooooome."

As they both ended the note together, Pino felt faint and the maestro started to laugh a demonic laugh.

"You didn't think you had it in you! *Eh? Eh?*" cried the old man. Pino could only shake his head in exasperation. The maestro grabbed Pino and hugged him warmly.

"Tell your papa that Maestro is very proud of you. Eh! You are making wonderful progress."

Just as Pino smiled proudly, the maestro broke the hug and smacked the boy violently in the head. Pino just stood there in shock. "But you are still lazy! And a lazy musician is no musician, so I have got to keep you working hard. It is for your own good! One day you will thank me! Mark my words, Pino!"

"*Si, Maestro. Grazie. Ciao,*" spoke the confused *tenore*-in-training.

"*Ciao, Caruso!*" answered the maestro as warmly as he knew how. This *commedia dell'arte* went on for days and weeks, and ultimately years. Pino and the maestro gently sparred with one another, each seeking the other's soft spots to exploit. On the surface, it appeared that there was no love lost between the two, but in reality, a deep-rooted respect and fondness characterized their relationship, and upon occasion, some genuine affection even snuck in.

As in every Italian family, the dinner table was where most of the real living, dying, discussion and decision-making took place, and *Casa Vaggi* was no exception. The events that shaped the family's world had their roots at that table, between courses of salad, pasta, meat and fish. Missing dinner was not only unacceptable; it was unthinkable. The dining room was the site of some of the family's greatest joys as well as its most heated battles.

One such evening was on the occasion of Pino's thirteenth birthday. On a cool, cloudy October night, having just completed his lesson at the maestro's studio, Pino dashed home for what was certain to be a special dinner. For the children's birthdays, Mama Vaggi always prepared their current favorite dish. On that particular night, Pino had expressed an interest in fish. That seemingly harmless request brought about one of the turning points in young Pino's life.

Living on a mountaintop afforded the residents of Collagna an abundance of truly wonderful foods, none of them aquatic. The region produced delightful lamb, venison, veal, rabbit and wild boar, as well as some of the finest cheeses in Italy, and the very best truffles and chestnuts, but fish were somewhat problematic. In the summertime, when the rivers were high, fresh fish were in abundance, but in the autumn, the mountains got very cold very early and fish were few and far between. If fish were available at all, they were brought in frozen, by truck from the city, and at considerable cost.

But a birthday was special and if it was fish that Pino wanted, it was fish that Pino was going to get; at least that was Mrs. Vaggi's point of view. Mr. Vaggi wasn't quite as convinced, but in such matters, it was Mrs. Vaggi who prevailed.

Thus, given the uniqueness of his request and the trouble that it caused, it was probably the worst imaginable day for Pino to break unwritten rule number one: he was late for dinner.

It really wasn't his fault; the Maestro had started one of his rambling reminiscences about the "old days," and about how he heard "Ponselle sing *Lucia* one night and *Aida* on the very next," and although the clock on the wall told Pino that he was running late, he couldn't seem to find an appropriate time to interrupt. By the time the old man ran out of steam, the damage was done.

The days were getting shorter and it was already dark out as Pino dashed through the streets all the way home. As he burst through the door, the looks on his parents' faces told him that no explanation would suffice. So he knew better than to offer one, and simply said, "Sorry," as quietly as possible and took his place at the table.

"Go wash your hands, Pino," his father said, walking into the living room where the radio was playing a news broadcast. Pino nodded and ran upstairs to wash as though washing would be the first step toward atonement. From downstairs, he heard nothing but the sound of the radio. Like most children his age, he feared his father's silence more than his rage, and it seemed that silence was in order that evening. Like a gladiator headed into battle, he took a deep breath and entered the lion's den.

As usual, the dinner table was set for a king, with no fewer than five fresh vegetables, and fresh chestnut spaghetti in a light pesto sauce. The soup was a hot bean creation with a sprinkle of *pecorino* cheese. The main course was a gorgeous sea bass, stuffed with fine herbs. It seemed a shame to Pino that this wonderful meal would be tarnished by the silent tension that hung over the room. After Pino's father mumbled grace, the table became a mad dash for food.

"So, Pino, what did you learn today?" asked Pino's mother, trying to save the evening from disaster. Unfortunately, Pino didn't follow her lead.

"At school or at conservatory?"

"At school, of course."

"Ah! I learned nothing at school. They have nothing to teach me."

"Oh, really?" his father asked, not amused.

"Let me put it this way: what they have to teach, I have no need to learn. I can't fill my head with math, and science and things. I need to focus my energy on my music if I am to have a successful career."

His father's eyes burned and Pino noticed that they were red, as if he had been crying. Pino had never seen his father cry, so he dismissed the notion. The only other possibility he could think of was…

"Pino, no one would be more proud of you than me if you became a successful singer," added his mother, gingerly, "but that doesn't mean you should neglect your other studies. They help you prepare for life in ways that music can't."

"Look at the Maestro," Pino lumbered on, "he never even went to high school, much less university."

"The Maestro?" barked his father, "OK, let's *look* at the Maestro."

Little Maria covered her ears.

"Papa, no yelling!" Mama interjected.

"He lives in a rat hole, in a small town on top of a mountain, and has to play the organ in church on Sunday and at funerals and weddings in order to scratch out a living. Is that what you want?"

"Papa, it's his birthday! Please!" Mama implored.

"But Papa, you yourself said he was the greatest musician you'd ever heard, didn't you?" countered Pino.

In fact, Papa Vaggi greatly admired the maestro. He often thought about how the old man had chosen to spend his golden years living alone in peace and quiet, confident of his life's work expertly done and able to turn a snobbish nose to those "posers" in Milan and Rome who had not a fraction of his talent or class. Still, it was not a life Papa Vaggi relished for his own son and he knew he had to hold his ground.

"That's exactly my point, Pino! It takes a lot more than talent to have a career in the arts, it takes drive, ambition and…"

"Oh, and who has more drive and ambition than me?" Pino interrupted.

"And, it takes more than that!" his father went on, "It takes luck, lots of it! It's a very fickle profession."

"*La donna è mobile, qual piuma il vento!*" sang Pino, causing his father to boil over.

"Don't you dare make jokes when I'm speaking! You listen when I'm speaking!" he raged and pounded his fist on the table, causing all the glasses to rattle.

The silence returned. The only sound was the radio, still playing softly in the living room. The announcer's voice, which Pino tried to ignore, but couldn't, said something that jarred the boy.

Wait! Did he just say we are at war?

Pino's attention was suddenly drawn to the news broadcast where an announcer was saying something about Italy marching into Ethiopia. He was afraid to change the subject, but he realized something else was afoot, something much more serious than his being late for dinner.

"Remember this," his father continued, "one day, God willing, you will be married. You will have a wife. You will have children. Now this may come as a shock to you, but children need to eat. Some eat more than others. Some even expect *fish* in the off season! And food must be paid for, *capische?*"

"*Si, Signore,*" Pino said in the most respectful tone he could manage.

Ever the peacemaker, his mother sensed it would be a good time to change subjects.

"All right, that's enough! Let's talk about something else," she interjected, trying her best to infuse the conversation with some much needed levity, but the silence returned, only for a few seconds, before it was broken by little Maria.

"Pino, could you do me a small favor?" she asked sweetly.

"How small?" he inquired.

"You know my friend, Gia?"

"Of course."

"Well, our spring dance is coming up and…"

"Oh, no! Not a chance!" declared Pino, finally drawing a smile from his father. Maria, however, wasn't giving up.

"Come on, Pino, she's very pretty!"

"She smells like a shepherd," he retorted.

"Hey, that's not very nice! Come on now," his father said, trying hard not to laugh.

"Go on, Pino, what would it hurt? I think she's lovely," added Mrs. Vaggi, sensing she had successfully changed the subject.

"I guess, but she's just, well, I don't know. She's just not my type," said a perspiring Pino.

The reply touched a nerve, and he feared he might have angered his final ally, his sister.

"What does that mean? What's wrong with her? Why isn't she your type?" she asked as Pino dabbed his forehead with his napkin.

"She's so…too, I don't know, too provincial."

"Provincial?" cried out his mother as his father burst out laughing. "Where did you learn that word?"

"Obviously at conservatory, because at school they teach him *nothing!*" blurted out his father in the midst of a belly laugh. "Excuse us, Signore Vaggi, but in case you haven't noticed, this isn't Paris! You live in a town of two hundred and eighty people in the Apennines!"

The harder they laughed, the angrier Pino became. Eventually, calmness returned to him.

They just don't get it, he thought. He'd show them.

"Pino, don't get angry," his father said. "If you don't want to go to the dance with Gia, no one is going to force you, even if we do think it's a good idea. All I'm trying to say is that you seem to think you have it all figured out at fifteen."

"Thirteen."

"Fourteen, thirteen whatever."

When Pappa Vaggi got an idea in his head, it stayed there, and time and truth could not dislodge it. He could be presented with irrefutable evidence, but it made not a dent in his absolute certainty that he was correct.

"I just want you to consider something that you may not have thought of: what you want out of life at thirteen won't necessarily be what you want at twenty. What you want at twenty won't be the same at thirty. You see where I'm going with this?"

"Yes, Papa, thanks" said Pino warmly, thinking he was out of the woods.

"That's all right, son. Maria, tell Gia that Pino would *love* to take her to the dance."

"What?" Pino exclaimed, and a good-natured pandemonium ensued.

Things seemed, at least for the moment, back to normal, and after a dessert of *torta nera*, a regional specialty made from walnuts and eggs, Mama and Maria cleared the table. Papa disappeared and returned with a long, odd-shaped bottle in his hand, which Pino instantly recognized as *grappa*. It dawned on Pino at that moment that his father had been drinking earlier, probably after hearing the news about Ethiopia.

Papa Vaggi got two glasses from the cupboard, slammed them down on the table with a proud smile and poured his son his first-ever glass of *grappa*. Pino had watched his father drink the nasty stuff for his entire lifetime and this moment was obviously some sort of rite of passage. It meant much more to Papa than Pino, because the boy had no desire whatsoever to taste the bitter liquor. On that night, however, there would be no avoiding it. He raised the glass to his lips and sipped the grappa under his father's watchful eye.

"I may be dead wrong, but I'll bet you're going to love this!"

As usual, he was dead wrong. The *grappa* didn't disappoint: it was awful, by far the foulest thing that had ever passed Pino's lips, which were now on fire. He tried desperately not to spit it out, but he was losing the fight.

"Heh, heh, how do you like it, son?" asked the beaming papa.

"Great," Pino barked back, the fire now spreading to his throat.

"There's an old saying, 'it was your first, but it won't be your last!'" Papa said as he poured himself another glass and hammered it down.

Pino would have been perfectly content for that to have been the last *grappa* he ever drank, but he realized it probably wouldn't even be his last one of the night. After one more drink, the two men sat in silence as the radio continued to play in the next room.

"Papa," he asked gently, "A few minutes ago, I thought I heard the announcer say that we went to war with Ethiopia today. Did you hear anything about it?"

"Hmm," his father grunted, "let's talk about it tomorrow."

Pino let it drop, guessing for that subject tomorrow would never come.

After a few minutes of silence, he excused himself and ascended the stairs to his room. His room was small and cozy, with wide plank flooring and exposed beams in the ceiling. A small writing desk in the corner with a lamp was the only furniture in the room, save his bed. He crashed onto the comfortable feather bed and mulled over the events of the day.

He knew then that his father was never going to be satisfied with his career choice, but he hoped that eventually the old man would come around a little. His mother didn't seem to have a problem with it, or at least, she never let it show.

It was unpleasant to think that in addition to all the hard work he would have to put in on an artistic level, he would have an equally hard time winning over his parents. *Didn't they understand how hard it was? Couldn't they be even a little supportive?* No matter, he thought, even if they had no faith in him, he had enough faith for all of them.

With that thought bringing him an uneasy peace, he rolled over and pulled out a large book from under the bed. It was a scrapbook of newspaper clippings about different singers. It was not a comprehensive collection, since his town was hardly a regular stop on the touring schedule of any legitimate singer.

He read the larger daily papers from Milan in the town's little library and often took to "borrowing" pages from them to contribute to his growing scrapbook. His latest clipping was from the *Corriere della Sera*. It was a review of the great tenor, Beniamino Gigli. He had recently done a recital in Milan for which he received a twenty minute standing ovation. The crowd even followed him back to his hotel and cheered until he came to his window to acknowledge them.

Gigli was Pino's favorite tenor in the world. It was partly because people often compared his own voice to Gigli's, and partly because Gigli sang with a delicacy and eloquence that, to Pino's ear, Caruso and Martinelli lacked. Another reason, which couldn't be overlooked, was the fact that Gigli was born in a tiny village near the town of Ancona, and he was the son of a humble shoemaker. His modest beginnings gave Pino great hope for his own career.

Pino rolled over and held the scrapbook against his chest. He wished he lived in Milan. There was something to see and hear every night in Milan. He could hear all the world's great singers and learn lessons he could only dream about in Collagna.

The more he thought about it, the angrier he got. He never allowed himself to consider the possibility that he was fooling himself, and that a simple peasant boy from "cheese country" really couldn't have a career in opera.

Obviously, his musical education couldn't compare to the kind afforded young singers in Milan, but he resolved to make up for that with complete dedication.

And of course, his father's persistent positive attitude and support was always a great confidence builder. *Thanks Papa!* His mind raced. He hated Collagna. It was a prison, a prison on a mountaintop in a faraway land. At some point, Milan must become his new home!

His troubled thoughts were interrupted by a knock at the door. Pino closed the scrapbook and replaced it under his bed.

"Come in," he mumbled and his sister Maria burst through the door and leapt onto the bed next to him.

"Sorry I got you into that," she said with a smile.

"Don't worry about it."

"If you don't want to go to the dance with Gia, it's fine. I just thought that you liked her. Or maybe she liked you. I don't remember. Anyway, I'm sorry."

"Apology accepted," he said, putting a loving arm over her shoulder. He loved his sister dearly. She was his rock and only real friend in the world. She was too young to be a real confidante, but she was an exceptional listener and his "one-person" fan club and tireless cheering section. No one dared utter a negative word about her brother in her presence. Irrespective of their ages, she was his protector and at times it bothered him, but more often he felt lucky.

"Hey Pino, could you do me a serious favor? Not about the dance."

"Like what?"

"Please don't talk to Papa that way. One of these days, you're going to give him a stroke."

Not her too! He thought, but he was in no mood to debate. *A Stroke? Where did she learn that word?*

"He just doesn't understand."

"Exactly! So you shouldn't drive him crazy. You'll both just get more and more frustrated with each other."

"Maybe, but he's got to give a little, too!" Pino retorted defiantly, hoping to appear less martyr-like, but it was lost on Maria. She just loved him, regardless. She hugged him and kissed him on the cheek.

"Besides, I know you're going to be a *huge* opera star one day. You're the best singer in the world!" she said, earning yet another big hug from her brother. "And I'm still your biggest fan, but we can't kill Papa in the process, *va bene?*"

"Yeah," he laughed as he hugged her. *God, she's smart for a kid*, he thought. As she got up to leave, she stopped just short of the door and smiled mischievously.

"So, does this mean you'll change your mind about the dance?"

Pino's reply was a pillow flung at her as she ran out the door giggling. He got up to close the door, but he stopped.

His parents were talking softly downstairs. He got down on the floor and crept to the top of the stairs as stealthily as he could, despite creaky floorboards, and tried to eavesdrop on their conversation. The radio was still playing in the living room, but not loudly enough for him to make out the announcer's words. In between brief patches of silence, he heard his mother and father speaking.

"How did it happen?"

"How do these things *always* happen?"

"Will it be bad?"

"Probably."

"How long do you think it will last?

"Who knows? Turn it up. Here it comes."

The radio got louder but all Pino could hear was the scratchy sound of some distant disembodied voice, whose words were more shouted than spoken.

A solemn hour is about to strike the history of the Fatherland...

"The Fatherland? Who does he think he is? Hitler?" snorted Papa.

"Quiet, Tony!"

Not only is an army marching towards its objective, but forty million Italians are marching in unison with the army, all united because there is an attempt to commit against them the blackest of all injustices, to rob them of a place in the sun... With Ethiopia we have been patient for forty years. Now enough!

"Tony, I don't understand. What does he mean? 'For forty years we've been patient,' what did Ethiopia do to us?" Mama inquired.

To sanctions of an economic character we will reply with discipline with our sobriety and with our spirit of sacrifice.

"Sanctions? What kind of sanctions?" Mama asked, "Discipline and sacrifice? Tony?"

"It means other nations may halt trade with us because of this war and we will be in deep shit."

"What's that supposed to mean?"

"It means rationing. Gasoline rationing. Food rationing. Who knows what else? Jesus, hasn't this country dumped enough hardship on us already? Goddamn Fascists!"

To sanctions of a military character we will reply with acts of war!

The last remark needed no interpretation and an icy silence followed. The broadcast continued but Pino didn't hear another word. He crawled back to his room and closed the door. Climbing back into bed, he pulled the covers up over his head in confusion.

His problems of only minutes ago that seemed to carry the weight of the world suddenly seemed trivial. Italy was at war with a country he'd never even heard of. Rolling over, he got on his knees and with the covers still hanging over him; he folded his hands and said his prayers.

The next morning at school, the entire class was abuzz with discussion of the war. Pino's teacher, Mrs. Toniolo, read what appeared to be a prepared statement explaining to the students that Italy had been forced into action against its will and that the war was not an act of aggression but rather the last resort of a peaceful nation protecting its own interests.

The explanation only further confused Pino. He glanced around at his classmates and wondered if they felt the same. His closest friend at school was Allesandro Biaggi, another student of the Maestro, whose father was the Chief Magistrate of the police. Allesandro always seemed to have his finger on the pulse of everything going on in town and Pino often received tidbits of information that Alle had learned covertly from his father. During lunch break the two boys chatted, but it was hardly what Pino expected.

"The truth is," Allesandro stated in an authoritative manner, "Ethiopia is not the real problem. It's the solution to the problem."

Pino shook his head in bewilderment.

"Italy's population is growing rapidly; too rapidly for its own good, economically speaking."

Pino remained confused but by then he was too embarrassed to say anything.

"Italy needs many materials that are not found within our borders, so we need to import them from elsewhere. Now do you get it?"

The answer was "no" but Pino's reply was, "I *think* so."

"So where and how do we get the materials we need?"

"We invade Ethiopia?" Pino stammered.

"Right!"

"What do they have that we need?" Pino asked, and oddly enough, the question caught Allesandro off-guard. He knit his brows for a second before replying.

"All kinds of things."

Pino realized Allesandro wasn't as knowledgeable on the subject as he pretended to be, and it was Pino's guess that Allesandro's speech was probably a regurgitation of something he'd heard his father say. No matter, he was interesting and he knew far more information on the topic than Pino ever would.

"Furthermore, "Allesandro continued, "this solves both problems. Ethiopia provides land for Italy's over-population, and raw materials for the folks back home. And the best part is, it's one more country that accepts our lire, get it? We buy stuff with our own currency. So, Ethiopia is the 'solution' to the problem," Allesandro concluded with great satisfaction, looking as though he were expecting applause.

"Oh, of course!" said Pino, "I get it now."

That night over dinner, Pino shared Allesandro's theory concerning the war with his father, to which he received the following reply.

"Stay the hell away from that kid! He sounds crazy!"

"But, Papa, his father told him--"

"Who is this kid anyway?" Papa inquired with an incredulous grin.

"He's my school friend, Allesandro. He studies with the Maestro too. You know his father, Captain Biaggi, the Chief Magistrate."

At the mention of the Chief Magistrate, Pino couldn't help noticing his mother and father exchange glances. His father's demeanor changed to one of unmitigated disgust.

"Son, I think you're old enough to know what I'm about to tell you," his father stated in a matter-of-fact way that caused Mama to stop drying the dishes. He moved his chair till he was face to face with his son. "The only reason we went to war in Ethiopia is because our Premier Mussolini is a crazy lunatic with a death-wish!"

"Tony, stop it!" Pino's Mama cried.

"He is an ugly violent man, who only understands one thing: brute force. That's all any of them understand, these Fascists, violence and more violence. And your friend's father only has his job today because he's a goddamn Fascist too!

"Tony, that's enough!" screamed Pino's mother in a tone he'd never heard before.

They sat in silence again, with her voice still ringing in their ears. More and more often they found themselves this way. Papa got up and poured himself a glass of wine.

"Mussolini is from this region you know. He was born in Dovia, I think," he said, taking a long swallow of the wine and smiling. "They say he never touches alcohol." He looked at the wine in his glass, "Well, I'll tell you this much…I don't trust an Italian who doesn't drink wine!"

He winked at his son to try to relieve some of the tension in the room, and felt bad for having raised his voice, but he had no intention of stopping until he'd said his piece.

"Pino, these men came into power after the great war because the country was a mess and they brought order to it. But how did they bring it? Hmm? I'll tell you: brute force. That's how. They're not exactly what you'd call educated or learned men."

He paused to take another sip of wine and Pino took the opportunity to interject.

"But, Papa, I've heard the Duce talk on the radio. He sounds very smart."

"Oh, he *is!* Make no mistake, he certainly is. No one can come so far, achieve so much, in such a short time, without being smart! And I don't mean book smart, he had no education or political experience at all! What he had, Pino, was complete and utter ruthlessness."

The look in his father's eyes frightened Pino but he dared not say anything.

"These are bad men, Pino. They have no morals, no character. I'm embarrassed to say that they got their start right here in Emilia-Romagna, but it's true. They would betray their brother to steal his house. They will lie, steal, cheat and deceive to get their way."

Pino's knees were rattling under the table. His father spoke of these Fascists the way Father Michele spoke about Satan in church. If these men were so heinous, how was it they were allowed to roam about freely? And how did one become the head of state? And why hadn't any one even mentioned them to him before?

Pino's head was reeling. He needed to know more but he didn't know what to say. He looked at his mother who was biting the edge of a dishtowel, and staring out the window. The kitchen was colder now than when he entered for dinner and Pino wanted to ask his mother to build a fire in the wood-burning stove, but he sat speechless.

"They came to power by eliminating their enemies in any way necessary--first in a small time way, and then eventually on a grand scale."

Pino was confused and he looked it. His father saw it in his eyes.

"Let me give you an example. Suppose you are a Fascist and you happen to be the Mayor or the...um...oh, let's say the Chief Magistrate of a town."

"Tony don't!" warned Pino's mother, but Papa continued.

"And because you are a Fascist, you have lots of enemies. Whenever a crime is committed in your town, you have one of your enemies arrested for the crime. You then have a quick tribunal convict him, and guess what? One less enemy! This way you look like you have solved the crime, and you have eliminated one more of your 'problems'. You continue in this manner until all of your problems have been eliminated. *Capische?"*

Pino didn't like what he was hearing, but he understood only too well his father's meaning, still, he had trouble accepting it as true. He was shaken and he needed to do some thinking. His cherubic little face, always so rosy and cheerful, was so contorted from these strange, awful, new, discoveries that his father simply had to stop.

"I'm sorry, son," Papa said with a huge sigh, "I know it's a lot. I didn't mean to dump all of this on you, but I thought I owed it to you to tell you the way things are." He got up, stretched and messed up Pino's hair, again trying to diffuse the situation, but it was useless.

"Papa," Pino asked very slowly, "Is Allesandro's father a bad man too?"

Mrs. Vaggi stared at Papa with a steely glance and flared nostrils. Papa hesitated and rubbed his eyes. He scanned the floorboards, as if he might find the answer in one of the dark crevices.

"I think…I think, I've had a little too much to drink tonight," was all he said on the matter before leaving the room.

That night, Antonio Vaggi didn't sleep a wink. He didn't toss and turn either. He just lay in bed wondering how things had gotten so crazy. Until that point, he'd always thought he'd been an exemplary father to his children, but he recognized that lately he'd been drinking a bit too much and losing his cool a bit too often, particularly with Pino.

Maria on the other hand was a total angel, *thank God*, and never any trouble. Of course, she hadn't reached puberty yet. He knew he didn't possess the head or the patience for domestic issues, and thought it wise to leave such matters to his wife.

Rosemaria Vaggi was a doting mother, whether she liked to believe it or not, and she hoped to instill in her children the virtues of honesty, patience, generosity and above all else kindness. Antonio Vaggi, on the other hand, wished for more practical qualities, like common sense, thrift and a good work ethic. Not that he possessed any of these qualities himself, but he thought it well for his children to have them. But now, with the possibility of war approaching, things were going to get tougher before they got easier. With the greatest and worst war of all time still fresh in his memory, not even the biggest pessimist could ever have imagined another war on the horizon so soon.

With that last troubling thought in mind, he rolled over to try to sleep. He thought for a moment about saying a prayer, but dismissed the thought. He wasn't the praying type. Although he regularly attended church, he really wasn't religious at all. His father had told him years before: 'lead a decent and honorable life, and you'll never be beholden to anyone.'

He smiled at the thought.

"Oh, Papa, if only it were that simple!"

CHAPTER THREE

A TENOR IN CRISIS

THE NEXT MORNING THE SUN ROSE; Pino looked out his window just to be sure of it. A wild deer was in their yard eating the last of his mother's roses, completely unconcerned about the war in Ethiopia. It made him smile. He heard the door slam and saw his father outside chasing the deer away from Mama's roses. He had a cup of espresso in his hand and he stood there facing the autumn sun as if he was trying to inhale the very sunlight itself. Pino leapt out of bed, put on his robe and ran quietly down the stairs and out the back door to the yard.

"*Bongiorno*, Papa!" he said with a smile.

Papa Vaggi turned around to see his son and smiled.

"What gets you up so early today?"

"I saw you chasing the deer from Mama's roses, that's all," said Pino.

"Lucky for that deer that I saw him before your mother did," said Papa, "or we'd be having venison for dinner tonight!"

Despite the brilliant sunshine, it was still quite cold and Pino began to shiver. His father put an arm around him and rubbed his arm.

"Papa," started Pino, unsure of exactly what he wanted to say, "I'm sorry I was late for dinner last night, and for the way I behaved." His father chuckled and gave him a good squeeze.

"That's alright. I suppose I owe you a bit of an apology myself."

"No, Papa. You don't!" Pino protested.

"Yes, I do. To your mother, too." He spoke in a tender voice that was unfamiliar to Pino. "You had better get ready for school."

"Yes, Papa." said Pino as he headed back to the warmth of the kitchen.

"Oh, by the way," his father began.

"Yes?"

"Don't mention to anyone what I said last night. Given the news, it's probably best."

"Sure, Papa," said Pino with a smile, thinking that for the first time in his life his father was talking to him like a man.

The hike up the hill to the maestro's house initially deterred some of his students, but he found that he could schedule lessons well into the evening in this more remote location without knocks at the door from irritated neighbors.

The maestro's house had become Pino's second home. The library serving as the primary studio was filled from floor to ceiling with opera and symphony scores. Pino could spend days on end rummaging through them. He believed that the maestro had the score to every opera ever written. There were hundreds and hundreds of them. Their exact filing system eluded Pino. In some cases it appeared that they were ordered alphabetically, yet others appeared to be grouped by language, still others by voice type. Pino guessed that he could spend dawn till dusk, every day for a year in here and still not read half of them. It was a humbling thought and a constant reminder of the work before him.

Had Caruso really studied *Boris Godunov* or *Eugene Onegin* or *Götterdämmerung?* He must have, thought Pino. To be the greatest of all time, he must have studied *all* the great masters and their works. The thought of learning German and Russian terrified Pino. He had a difficult enough time mastering a few words of French. During one lesson, after a successful rendering of the "Flower Song" from *Carmen*, which Pino had memorized phonetically, the maestro praised the boy on his fluid phrasing. His triumph, however, was short-lived when the maestro asked him to explain Don Jose's motivation and the symbolism of the flower. The perspiration on Pino's brow announced more clearly than any words could that he had been caught unprepared. The maestro was constantly yelling at his students for one reason or another, but it was his silence that they feared most of all. His look of disappointment was piercing, and had been known to wobble the knees of even the bravest students. Yet the maestro could never be accused of being cruel to his pupils. The day after a silent scolding, warm hugs and tender words of encouragement were always in order and he administered them with the grace of an artist and the affection of a parent. Having no children of his own, his students were his legacy.

The trip home down the hill from a lesson with the maestro was always a relief. Pino usually ran, seeing just how fast he could go without losing control. Usually, his schoolbooks were the only casualty.

One afternoon, Pino headed down the hill faster than usual, running furiously through the streets like a man possessed. Without stopping, he burst through the front door, ran straight through the kitchen, past his mother washing the floor, and up the stairs. He didn't stop until he crashed, with a tremendous thud, onto his bed. His terrified mother ran screaming up the stairs after him and found him curled up on his bed, crying into his pillow.

"Pino! Pino, what's wrong? Pino, what happened?"

"Nothing," he said.

"Nothing? You come through here like a crazed dog, and then say it's nothing?"

"It's…I'm embarrassed to tell you."

"Embarrassed? Pino! I'm your mother! There's nothing you can't tell me, whatever it is."

"It was my lesson. It was the worst lesson I've ever had. Maestro was so angry with me, he sent me home."

"Is that all?" She sighed. "Oh, Pino. You had me terrified."

"What do mean, *is that all?*" He expected indifference from his father, but not her!

"Pino, you had a bad day. Everybody has bad days. Caruso had bad days. Gigli has bad days, and even Pino Vaggi has them. Now stop your crying before your father sees you."

Although her words gave him no comfort, he did begin to feel a little foolish for carrying on so.

"I'm sorry, Mama. I just…"

"I know, I know."

"No, Mama, you don't know." He paused to take a deep swallow. "I can't sing anymore. I'm awful!" He started to cry once more.

"Pino, don't be ridiculous! Of course, you can. You have the prettiest voice I've ever heard."

"Not anymore! My voice sounds worse and worse every day."

"Relax. This is silly. I'm sure that it's just a phase you are going through. It will pass."

"I hope you're right," he uttered with a deep sigh of resignation.

"Of course, I'm right. I'm your mother," she blurted out. Then, trying hard to be conciliatory, she added, "Now, tell me what you want for dinner because you've had a bad day and tonight you get whatever you want. How's that?"

Pino smiled and wiped away his tears, knowing that it was the best she could do. Dinner was always her chief negotiating tool and one could never overstate its importance, but that effect was primarily on her husband, not Pino. Nonetheless he played along.

"Why don't you make veal, Mama, Papa likes that best."

"This meal is for Pino, not Papa!"

"I know, but make veal anyway."

"That's very sweet of you, Pino, but here's what we'll do," she smiled proudly, "We'll make veal, but, we tell him it's what Pino wants, eh?"

She gave him a great big hug, and everything was right in the world. That is, until the very next afternoon at 4:30 pm when Pino did an encore performance of his mad dash through the door, across the kitchen, up the stairs and onto his bed.

"Again?" she muttered to herself as she turned back to the sink to turn off the water. She grabbed a towel to dry her hands and started toward the stairs when the door again burst open. This time it was the old maestro, panting desperately.

"Maestro, my God! Are you all right?"

"*Si, si*, I'm fine," he managed to get out between gasps. She led him to a chair, then grabbed a wet towel and wiped his forehead.

"Ooooh, I'm too old for this," he moaned.

"What are you doing?"

"Trying to keep up with that *testa dura* son of yours," he said, wrapping his fist against his head. "He bolted out of my studio like a rabbit."

"Why? What did you do to him?"

"What did *I* do to him? Nothing!"

"Nothing? Two days in a row he comes home crying his eyes out for nothing? He's just a little boy, Maestro, and you work him too hard! What are you doing to him in that studio? Can't he sing anymore? If not, that's fine, his lessons cost us a fortune. But don't--"

"*Basta!* Rosemaria! Let me speak already!" the old man cried.

Exasperated, she sat opposite him at the table.

"Can I have some water first?" he requested pleasantly.

She got up and brought him a pitcher of water and a glass, but before he could start, Pino appeared in the doorway, looking like a general, defeated in battle, about to issue the terms of his surrender.

"Mama. Maestro. I've come to a decision," he declared in a shaky voice. "I've given it a lot of thought, and I've decided I am going to give up singing." His mother and the maestro looked at each other in shock. "I know you both are disappointed, but my voice sounds worse and worse every day and I realize now that no matter how much I try, no matter how hard I work, I will never be able to have a career in the opera with this voice."

"But, Pino!" his mother cried in astonishment.

"No, Mama, I've made up my mind."

"Pino, come here a moment, will you?" the maestro asked in a conciliatory manner.

The boy approached and stopped about three feet in front of him.

"Come closer. Don't be afraid."

Pino stepped directly in front of him and the old man thrust his arms around him and hugged him violently. Pino began to cry like a baby. Pino's mother dabbed a tear away and felt conspicuously absent from the moment. The maestro stroked Pino's hair and gently kissed his temple. Pino just kept on bawling. It was a cathartic cry, one that had been building up for some time and had finally been given its release. Eventually, Pino ran out of tears and began to sniffle.

Sensing a break in the action, the maestro started to chuckle to himself. The chuckle soon became a laugh. Suddenly, Pino angrily thrust himself away from the maestro.

"You laugh? You think it's funny?" he cried out.

"Really, Maestro," added Pino's mother.

"Such drama! Pino, I swear, you really have the personality of a diva. You know that?" He continued to laugh as Pino glared at him in shock. "You aren't going to quit singing, because there's nothing wrong with your voice!"

"No! You're just saying that. I'm not deaf. My voice is cracking everywhere!"

"Of course it is! You still don't get it? Your voice is changing!"

"Is *that* what it is?" Mama Vaggi exclaimed with newfound clarity.

"Yes! Little Pinuch here is becoming a man!" the maestro stated with pride.

Pino just stood there mystified, unable to utter a word.

"Your voice is changing. It happens to everyone, but for singers, well now, you're going to have to work a little harder to reach those high notes!"

"But I sound awful! I can't hit any of the notes!"

"No, Pino, you don't sound awful. You're just stuck between voices, your old one and your new one."

"My baby's voice is changing," gushed Mrs. Vaggi.

"Mama, please! But what...what if it's no good? I've worked so hard!"

"Pino, relax. You're going to be a wonderful tenor. That's why I've drilled you so hard on your technique. Even if your brain forgets the lessons, your throat muscles never will. Got it?"

Pino didn't look convinced and his mother came around the table and hugged him. "My little Pinuch. Soon, I won't be able to call you Pinuch anymore."

"In just a few weeks, your voice will be good as new, probably better, more colorful, more mature." said the maestro in an authoritative voice.

"So this is a good thing?" the boy asked incredulously.

"Unless you want to sing *castrato* roles for the rest of your life, it's a *very* good thing," added the maestro, bringing positive closure to the situation.

Pino rushed back into the maestro's arms and hugged him once more. The general frustration growing inside him the last few months had manifested itself in resentment: resentment of his peers, his parents, and to some extent himself. He held onto the maestro like a life raft. He figured that he probably spent more time holding another human being in the last ten minutes than he had in the last year. Whether he wanted to admit it or not, it felt good. Life was good again.

It was impossible to fully describe Maestro Ivaldi's influence on Pino. He was mentor, role model, confessor, colleague, conspirator, and in many ways a brother. Undoubtedly, Pino was the maestro's favorite student. Most people assumed it was because of Pino's undeniable talent, which they believed the maestro craved the credit for nurturing. If Pino struck it big, the maestro would be recognized as his Svengali and bask in the reflected glory. In reality, the maestro possessed no such agenda. Rather, he saw in Pino a miniature portrait of himself at that age. He knew the pitfalls and the difficult choices that lay ahead of the boy, and he was painfully aware of the mistakes that he had made in his own career. He would make absolutely certain that Pino would not repeat them. He would do this for all of his students, but in Pino he saw his toughest task as well as his greatest opportunity; the opportunity for that elusive *perfection*.

As usual, the maestro was right. Pino's voice recovered, but it took longer than the maestro thought and caused Pino more than a few anxious moments. As Pino's voice began to even out, he became aware of some very noticeable changes in the color of its low end. More specifically, it now *had* a low end, a rich chest register. Remarkably, the mid-range had also changed, developing a burnished, velvety quality that, at first, sounded foreign in his own head. The new sound soon grew on him, and he found himself holding his notes longer and longer just to hear that sound.

The ease with which the air passed over his vocal cords and the glorious tones it produced had seduced Pino, but the maestro quickly put an end to any frivolous self-indulgence. He recognized all the traditional tenor pitfalls, even the ones that were very popular to the masses, and would tolerate none of them.

Pino must travel the road of the artist. For the time being, like Tannhäuser, *"while others walk the soft grass, he must walk barefoot on stones and thorns. While others drink from the stream, he must drink in the hot sun. While others sleep in a soft bed, he must sleep in the snow and ice."* He must toil and labor for his art, and not fall victim to the dangers of early success. It was clear to the maestro that Pino would soon be a legitimate tenor capable of finding work on his own. Thus, it was more important than ever for Pino to concentrate on his technique, that it might be permanently branded into his brain and his throat muscles. It was the maestro's last, greatest mission, his final goal and milestone. It was the very least that he could do for this boy who had brought him so much joy, and so much vitality, so late in life.

These were the thoughts that accompanied the maestro to bed at night and that greeted him each morning, giving him a renewed sense of purpose. Years ago, when his wife had died, he had begun a slow, unconscious descent into reclusiveness. At first it was a natural period of bereavement, but eventually he realized that he enjoyed people's company less and less. Finally, he began to notice that he hardly spoke at all anymore. He didn't really miss conversation, not being much of a conversationalist even when he was young and relatively gregarious.

The maestro married fairly late in life, at age forty-four, but that had not prevented him from enjoying nearly two decades of nuptial bliss. His wife was a music teacher from Castel Nuovo, a town just a few kilometers away. Some said that their meeting was predestined by the stars, because no one could imagine a more perfectly suited couple. They had met on a train bound for Milan. Their mutual destination was a performance of *Lucia di Lammermoor* at Teatro alla Scala. The maestro would later pronounce the evening a "cosmic concurrence." The term spoke volumes about their relationship and ultimately their marriage.

They first noticed one another on the station platform, glances meeting by chance followed by pleasant smiles. Then, by the greatest possible coincidence, their seats happened to be facing one another. As they sat in silence, the maestro would occasionally glance up from his newspaper to sneak a peek at her. During one such glance he noticed a gold pin on the lapel of her coat in the shape of a violin. *A musician?*

Just then she looked up and their eyes met for an instant, but the Maestro quickly looked away. Yet, out of the corner of his eye, he detected a hint of a smile on her radiant face.

At the next stop, the people sitting next to each of them got up to depart, leaving them alone. For the first time in his life, the Maestro could sense sexual tension. He didn't say a word, yet he was keenly aware of every slight movement she made. This was totally unlike him. He felt detached, as if he was a voyeur, watching all of this happen to someone else, but his racing heart told him otherwise. It was all too real. What should he do? If he spoke, what would he say? He was totally inexperienced in this sort of thing and was suddenly disappointed at his own inadequacy. Surely, he hadn't felt this way in years, but the romantic in him knew that he must seize the moment before it slipped away.

But he did nothing. He sat in nervous silence like a teenager. The trip seemed endless, but soon it would be over and she would be gone. As he sat there waiting for some divine intervention to show him the way, *it happened!*

She folded her newspaper and placed it back in her bag. She then shuffled through the bag looking for something. This went on for a moment until she found what she was searching for. She removed a book from the bag, opened it and began reading. But it was not just *any* book! It was the libretto to *Lucia di Lammermoor!*

"Grazie, Signore!" he said speaking to the Creator himself. These were the first words the maestro's future wife heard him utter that evening, in that compartment, on that train. It was indeed a cosmic concurrence.

CHAPTER FOUR

SOLA, PERDUTA, ABANDONATA

FATHER MICHELE HAD BEEN THE PARISH PRIEST for over ten years and suspected that his tenure in Collagna might soon be up. It was a mixed blessing. Being the pastor of a community in the remote Apennines initially held no special ardor for the priest who previously had held posts in Milan and Ravenna. When he arrived, ostensibly to "fill-in" for the indisposed pastor, who was in declining health and advancing years, and who simply couldn't handle the bitter mountain winters any longer, Father Michele fully expected it to be for the short term.

Something happened, however, the day he arrived in Collagna. That something was called San Giovanni Battista. The old relic of a church had first been mentioned in the histories of the region in 1153, but it was probably much older. At first sight, it took his breath away and he knew it would be his destiny.

It wasn't long before the church became a part of him and he of it. He set about learning the long history of the church and its critical role in the history of the region. The community fell in love with the energetic priest who showed so much interest in their past. It was a match made in heaven or at least very close to it, because, as Father Michele was so fond of saying, "at 3,800 feet, no church in Italy was closer to heaven!"

His arrival in the community came at an auspicious time, just as the ruling Fascist party was becoming notoriously indifferent to the Catholic Church. In this remote region, Father Michele was able to avoid much of the unpleasant intrigue that plagued so many of his fellow pastors in other parishes. Father Michele expected Pino to be an altar boy just like most of the boys in Collagna, but the thought never appealed to him. Pino was too willful for his own good and hardly what one would call pious. So when Pino's natural gift made itself known, Father Michele took great pleasure in recommending the choir loft rather than the altar for Pino.

For his part, Pino was just as happy to be in the choir loft. The choir members rarely paid any attention to the goings on downstairs, except when cued by the maestro to sing. Maestro Ivaldi was at the helm of the organ at Vespers as well as at Sunday Mass. Pino liked to think of his time in the choir loft as free lessons, because at the conclusion of the Mass, the maestro would invariably have some comments about his singing.

Father Michele and the maestro had a cool relationship, which the choir members loved to gossip about, imagining all kinds of nefarious reasons for their mutual indifference. Pino hated the gossip, and had no time or patience for it. His aloofness gave the impression to many of the other choristers that he was a conceited little shit. He wasn't concerned with them, and believing they were all just jealous, he probably did act like just the little shit that they thought he was.

On cold winter mornings, the maestro was in the habit of bringing a liter of hot brandy to the choir loft in his music bag. As a general rule he would partake of it in a regimented manner: one capful after the opening prayer, another after the Apostle's Creed, and two during the sermon — as the sermon would invariably go on for a bit. It kept him comfortable and warm in that drafty icebox of a choir loft.

One Sunday, in the dead of winter, the snow kept most of the choristers home from Mass, and most of the parishioners too, so Pino played the role of one-man choir. He thought it would be fun, since there was virtually no one there, to do some different songs, to get a rise out of Father Michele. The maestro just grunted disapprovingly; he was not himself that day, either.

Halfway through the Mass Pino found himself trying hard not to fall asleep. He rested his head on the railing of the choir loft and closed his eyes. *Just for a minute* he told himself. He awoke to find the few members of the congregation seated beneath him looking up at him, their faces contorted.

What's going on? Why are they staring at me? He immediately noticed a sound, a horrible noise. *What was it?* He turned around and to his horror the maestro was slumped over the console of the organ. Pino gasped!

"Maestro! No!" he cried, and he raced to the old man's side. He tried to lift the maestro off the keyboard but the old man was too heavy. The organ continued to howl dissonantly beneath him. Just then Father Michele appeared followed by two altar boys. The priest pushed Pino aside and sat the maestro back in the chair. His face was pure white. Pino felt an icy pain shoot through his heart.

"Giovanni, quickly, go get Doctor DeMauro. Hurry!" Father Michele barked and the boy dashed down the stairs. The priest then took the old man's wrist looking for a pulse, and started gently slapping him on the cheek.

"Franco! Franco! Wake up! Come on! Wake up!" he implored. To Pino's eyes there was no sign of life. Pino ran to the maestro's side and took his hand;

it was cold as ice. This couldn't be happening! Pino started to cry as he rubbed the maestro's hand to warm some life back into it. Suddenly, Mrs. Alfiero, the baker's wife, appeared with a glass of water and a handkerchief and started wiping the maestro's forehead.

"Franco!" cried the priest, "Come on! Wake up!"

After a few minutes of no response, Father Michele took out his rosary beads and started to pray.

"No!" Pino cried and started violently shaking the old man.

Just then Dr. DeMauro arrived and told everyone to stand back. The choir loft was already too crowded and Father Michele motioned for the boys to go downstairs. Pino didn't move.

"*Pino!* Wait downstairs," the priest ordered and Pino reluctantly obeyed. He stood at the base of the stairs and listened as the doctor went to work. It was only a matter of seconds before he heard the magic words.

"He's only fainted. He's alright." Upon hearing those words, Pino collapsed. He was shaken, but at least the maestro was alright. A moment later he heard a more familiar sound.

"Argh! Get that away from me!" It was the maestro's gruff voice and it never sounded so sweet to him.

"It's just ammonia salts, Franco, relax," said the doctor.

"I don't care, get it away!" said the feisty old man.

"You fainted. Now sit still for a moment and relax," ordered the doctor. "Probably the heat in here combined with the cold out there. Take a drink of water and then we'll get you home."

Pino let out a huge sigh of relief upon hearing the news. Knowing how proud the maestro was, he was certain the old man wouldn't want anyone to see him this way. Pino also didn't want the maestro to see him crying, so, with the situation in hand, he decided to head home.

Walking through the vestibule of the church past the confessionals, Pino decided it was high time to go to confession; not today, but sometime soon.

That evening at home, Pino related the story to his parents, trying not to get too emotional. The event gave them all pause, but for reasons obvious, it shook Pino much deeper. It forced him, once again, to consider life without the maestro. It was a bleak thought. He gazed around the table at his parents and wondered with a troubled and guilty mind if losing either of the two of them would affect him as much. It was an honest enough question, but he decided not to give the matter further thought as there was nothing to be gained by knowing the answer, either way.

The final cadenza at the end of *"La Donna e Mobile"* had always given Pino trouble. His tendency to scream the final high C also gave the maestro fits. He taught Pino at least three ways to avoid losing the difficult final note, but Pino usually panicked and forgot what he was supposed to do and instead just belted out the note, letting the chips fall where they may. Luckily, his high notes were so thrilling that he got away with it, *but not in the maestro's presence.* Nothing escaped his glance or his ear.

One evening, at a small concert in the church basement, with the maestro not in attendance, Pino finally sang the aria feeling no trepidation at all as he approached the end. He navigated the cadenza without even the slightest difficulty and the audience went wild. Pino bowed, acknowledging their applause, tipped his head to his accompanist and strode proudly off the stage. *Damn, the first time I nail that cadenza and the maestro isn't here to see it!*

Maestro Ivaldi's arthritis and emphysema had been acting up again for the past few months. He managed to work his way around the arthritis for years but the emphysema was something altogether different, making even the simplest of tasks difficult, particularly in the unforgiving Collagna winter. A lifetime of smoking had ravaged his lungs and the doctor gave him direct orders to cut back on cigarettes, and work, and to slow down in general. Unfortunately, the maestro was famously bad at taking orders and wound up hospitalized more than once.

This particular event, a showcase of several of the maestro's better students, was arranged by Alfredo Gianasi, the cantor in church. Alfredo was a part-time cantor, part-time organist, full-time philistine and a devoted, card-carrying Fascist party member. With the maestro indisposed, Alfredo had become the full-time musical coach, director, and impresario in Collagna.

It was not that Alfredo lacked passion or dedication for the art, or that he hadn't studied under reputable teachers, or even that he lacked artistic temperament; rather it was simply a profound lack of talent that had held him back. But joyously oblivious to this fact, he went about his day and duties like a modern day Giuseppe Verdi. A "statesman for the arts," he called himself. Alfredo was an elderly music teacher residing in his native village and was totally unknown beyond it, though his pretensions to high-art were faithfully supported by his fellow Fascist-party villagers, whose complete and total confidence in his genius was just as real as the outside world's complete and total neglect of it.

At the side of the stage, Alfredo stood waiting with a towel. Pino grabbed it and dried his face and hair.

"Bravo, Pino! Bravo!" he exclaimed, patting Pino on the back. "Your *legato* was simply beautiful. You sounded just like Gigli. You know that? But maybe tomorrow we work on your agility a little bit? Eh?"

Pino thought for a minute, then spoke softly.

"Maestro?"

Somehow the title never seemed to come easy when speaking to Alfredo. That word had always been reserved for Maestro Ivaldi, who wore it so well.

"I can't come for a lesson tomorrow. I have something personal which I must attend to, but I'll see you again on Saturday."

Alfredo's nostrils flared and his back arched. He wasn't used to disrespect from his students. Pino may have been the old maestro's prize pupil, but to Alfredo, he was just a pampered lazy brat, incapable of accepting direction. Unfortunately for Alfredo, Pino was still undeniably the most talented young singer he'd ever heard. But that was immaterial to Alfredo when it came to matters of respect.

"Pino, don't get lazy now. You're at a critical stage in your development. I must insist."

"This one time, I'm afraid, I must insist," interrupted the boy.

Then Alfredo dropped a well-timed bomb for which Pino was unprepared.

"I plan to send you on auditions next month. You can't afford to skip lessons now."

It was a cheap shot, but it always worked. The word "auditions" hit Pino like a bucket of cold water. His eyes popped open and his jaw gaped. He didn't even try to mask his emotions. This was what he had always been waiting to hear. Sometimes, it seemed as if Maestro Ivaldi might never utter these words, but Alfredo just did.

"Auditions? Really?" He paused for a moment to drink in the satisfaction, but it was short-lived, as a sudden wave of guilt overtook him and he arrived wearily at a moment of clarity. "Wait a minute. I can't come tomorrow. I just can't. And that's that. I'm sorry, but my agility will have to wait until Saturday." With that, Pino turned and left the stage. As he walked away, he felt Alfredo's eyes on his back, but he dared not turn back. He was on a one-way street, a street that had been paved long ago, and he would not let himself be seduced by any shortcuts, no matter how attractive they might seem.

Still wearing his borrowed, ill-fitting tux, Pino walked to the lower village. His only guide was a blinking red cross. As he got closer, he could see the north entrance to the medical center that passed for a hospital. He entered the door and stopped at the desk for a second to catch his breath. Pino walked gingerly down the hall, searching for his appointed destination. At the door, he paused, wiped the perspiration from his brow, and ran a hand through his messy hair.

He entered the room, and to his surprise, there was a nurse seated just inside the door. Before he could utter a word, she put a finger to her lips to tell him to be quiet. He nodded and shut the door slowly. He turned and approached the bed. A small lamp on a table next to the bed was the only light in the room and its amber glow hardly reached beyond the edges of the table. The bed and its occupant lay in total darkness. He wished that he had stopped to buy flowers or a small gift of some sort, but it was too late for that now.

After a minute or two of standing in silence, his eyes adjusted to the darkness. Before him, on the bed, lay his mentor, his veneer of invincibility gone. For the first time in his life Pino thought the maestro looked old. In his sleep, he labored for each breath, and it seemed as if each exhale might very well be his last. His brilliant white mane appeared dull and matted and his skin looked like leather stretched for tanning. It was an image Pino wasn't prepared for and his thoughts drifted back to his first meeting with the old man.

Pino's mother had dressed him in his Sunday clothes and spent at least a half-hour trying in vain to get the boy's hair to look presentable. Once Pino had passed inspection, they were off to the maestro's studio. Along the way, Pino's mother warned him not to get any dirt on his shoes, a nearly impossible task, and she stopped no fewer than three times to straighten Pino's tie and to brush dust or lint off of his shoulders. It was quite an ordeal, one that Pino didn't understand at all. What did all this primping have to do with music? Finally they reached the studio and Mama Vaggi inspected her son one final time. Not perfect, but close enough.

The maestro's studio was a veritable wonderland for Pino, full of violins, music stands, metronomes, all kinds of woodwinds, a big shiny brass tuba and a mammoth concert grand piano. Pino was in heaven. He couldn't hide his glee, nor could his mother manage to contain it. The only thing missing was the maestro himself. Pino imagined the maestro to be a brooding genius, a consummate artist, cloistered away in this magical studio, making music for no one but himself. Pino loved him before he ever set eyes on the man.

As his eyes scanned the studio, stopping on one joyful vision after another, the sound of a door creaking brought him back to reality. He whirled round toward the sound and suddenly his heart sank. There before him in the doorway stood "the monster." Maestro Ivaldi was the tallest man Pino had ever seen. His hair was gleaming silver and his eyebrows jet black. His fingers were long and thin and they gently stroked his chin as he examined the new specimen before him. He appeared to be one part mad scientist, one part vampire. He didn't look angry, but he was anything but happy.

Suddenly, to everyone's surprise, Pino took a step forward and extended a hand.

"Piacere, Maestro," he said firmly. The maestro said nothing. They stood in awkward silence for what seemed like an eternity. Finally, the maestro smiled a half-smile and shook the boy's hand, and Mrs. Vaggi let out a tremendous sigh of relief.

"Confidence is important in any career," offered the old man, "but in the performing arts it is essential. Vital." Pino had no idea whatsoever what the maestro meant but he smiled and nodded his head. "We begin on Monday. *Buona sera, Rosemaria.*" With those words, he was gone. Without even singing a note, Pino had unwittingly, passed the first test. In fact, one might say he already graduated to the next level at the first meeting. The maestro left the room already in love with the boy's cockiness.

In his memory, this moment was a microcosm of their future relationship.

Pino approached the maestro and sat next to him on the bed. For an instant he thought about waking him, but thought better of it. He then started to hum very quietly, just enough for the maestro to know that there was company. The maestro stirred under the covers and smiled. Pino then began to sing the words to him, in German. The maestro knit his brows and without opening his eyes quietly spoke.

"What *is* that?"

"I learned it at conservatory this week."

"That's not what I asked you."

Pino fidgeted nervously before answering. "It's Wagner."

An arrow through the heart might have had a less devastating effect. At hearing the name Wagner, the maestro began coughing violently. Pino expected a reaction, but not the onslaught he was about to endure.

"Assasino! Wagner? *Why,* Pino, *why* do you want to kill me?"

"Maestro, no! I just thought, well, it's called 'Dream' and when I saw you sleeping so quietly, I thought..."

"You thought you'd come and sing some Wagner to disturb my dreams! I see. What *stronzo* has you singing Wagner?" Pino thought carefully about his answer, not wanting to upset the maestro any more than he already had, but the direction they were headed seemed already determined.

"Since you've been sick, Alfredo has taken over my lessons at the conservatory."

"Alfredo!" cried the Maestro, "Alfredo is *cafonne*, a buffoon. And worse he's a Fascist! *You* should be teaching *him*."

"Yes, Maestro, but there are no other teachers in Collagna and I need to keep working."

"Fine. Work then, but do not let that imbecile tell you how to sing. Do not change one single element of the technique that I taught you. *Capische?*"

"Yes, Maestro, I understand perfectly."

"Singing Wagner? Are you insane?"

"But, Maestro, he's my teacher. What choice do I have?"

"What can I do, Maestro?" cried the old man in mocking tones, "Help me! Help poor, poor Pino! Boo-hoo! Don't be a baby Pino, it doesn't suit you."

Pino decided to pursue a different attack.

"Alfredo says next month he will start sending me on auditions!" announced the boy proudly, fully expecting the maestro to be impressed.

"Singing Wagner, no doubt! An excellent idea, truly."

The salvo missed its mark but, undeterred, Pino continued, leading with his chin.

"We haven't decided what I'll be singing just yet, but he's had me working on *"Trovatore"* and *"Aida"* as possible audition pieces." The maestro put his hand on his head in disbelief as Pino continued. "You see, Alfredo says there are no Verdi tenors right now so I should concentrate on..."

The maestro had heard enough. "No, no, no!" he interrupted. "There are plenty of Verdi tenors, *all bad ones!* And you will soon join their ranks if this is the kind of repertoire you choose!"

"But, Maestro, it makes sense! Think about it. Alfredo says it's a simple case of supply and demand."

"Supply and demand? Pino, are you a singer or an accountant?"

"Alfredo says I need to expand my repertoire to include more difficult pieces and to stop singing the same simple arias over and over."

"Simple? No aria is *simple*! Only a complete fool would suggest so, and Alfredo is just such a fool! Are you really so conceited to believe you have *mastered* Bellini? *Mastered* Puccini?"

Pino turned away from the maestro and nearly started to cry. He desperately wanted to start auditioning, and he knew deep down that he was ready. Why couldn't the maestro see it? He paced around the room for a moment in silence. He knew that the maestro had never steered him wrong, but he also had not heard him sing in months! Pino resolved to convince him that the time was right. He turned toward the maestro to speak, but before he could utter a word, the old man beat him to the punch.

"Pino?"

"Yes?"

"Sit down. You're making me nervous."

Pino sat down on a chair at the other end of the room and stared at the floor. For a long moment they sat in silence. Although he knew he should feel compassion for the bedridden maestro, right at that instant all Pino felt was frustration and impatience. Sooner or later the maestro would be gone, and without him, who would show Pino the way? There was only Alfredo. For better or for worse, Pino knew he dared not alienate him. It was true that Alfredo was a hack, and a shameless self-promoter, but it was equally true that he would soon be all that Pino would have. The thought worried and sickened him, but he had to prepare for that eventual reality.

"*Cilea,*" trumpeted the maestro, smashing the silence.

"What?" inquired the boy, looking up from the floor.

"*Lamento di Federico.* You know it? No?"

"Of course. Why?"

"Sing it."

"Now?"

"No, at my funeral, *stronzo!*" the old man bellowed.

Pino nodded, paused for a moment to clear his throat and began to sing, but he was immediately interrupted by the maestro.

"Do you plan to sing from a chair at your audition?"

Pino heaved a heavy sigh and stood up slowly. Not halfway through the aria, the maestro interrupted him again.

"*Basta!* I have heard enough. This will be your audition piece. Now go home, I need to sleep."

Pino was running out of patience.

"Excuse me, Maestro, but Alfredo really doesn't think..."

"Pino! Don't be a fool!" screamed the maestro. "This is your life, not some game. You've worked too hard. Alfredo doesn't know *merde!* And, you can tell him I said so! Tell him that this is what you are going to sing and that's that! Show some backbone, Pino! Start acting like a man!"

Sadly, the best Pino could manage was a nod of his head and a sad half-smile.

"*Si, Maestro. Buona notte.*" he said. Just when the evening looked blackest, the maestro began to laugh, to himself at first, then out loud.

"Pino, wait," said the old man, in the tenderest voice Pino had ever heard from him. "Come here. Sit with me."

Pino reluctantly sat on the bed with the maestro, his feelings in chaos. The old man struggled to sit up and Pino helped, moving the pillows behind him. They resumed their awkward silence, but this time the maestro wasn't angry. He was smiling. His smiles came few and far between, and they usually made Pino feel uneasy, but this smile was different than any he'd ever seen on the maestro's face. This was one that would be indelibly ingrained in Pino's memory for the rest of his life. This smile radiated pure love.

"Pino, you can sing whatever you want at your auditions. I just want you to understand that in my heart, I truly believe that there is no singer in the world today who sings that aria as well as you. No one."

The old man's words were poetry to the boy.

"You understand that aria, because you live it. It is your world. The story of the poor shepherd boy living in the mountains is near to your heart and life, *capische?*" The boy nodded. "That's why it sounds so genuine and honest when you sing it."

No words ever spoken to him meant so much.

"*Grazie*, Maestro."

"No, Pino, thank *you*. You can tell Alfredo that I recommended it if you like or you can tell him to drop dead, okay? But from now on, you make the decisions."

He hugged the maestro the way he always wanted to hug his father but never could. The maestro kissed him on the forehead and gently pushed him away, as if to say: 'go forth.' But, in typical fashion, a moment later, the old man drained all the sentimentality from the moment.

"But you tell Alfredo that if he has you singing any more Wagner, I'll get out of this bed and strangle him with whatever strength I have left!"

This time it was Pino's turn to smile, equally radiant, but also somewhat melancholy.

"*Ciao*, Maestro. *Grazie*," he said as he got up to leave. Strolling toward the door he stopped, flashed a wicked smile and turned around. "Maestro? Does this mean I can tell Alfredo we can't sing any more Strauss *either?*"

"Pino, when did you become a Nazi?" the old man shook his head, "You want to put me in the grave? Your voice is a *bel canto* voice. You know what that means? It is not meant for contemporary music. It's not of this century. It is of the last. And that is a rare gift. Remember: *Bel canto, bel canto!*"

"I will."

"Pino," said the old man, his voice suddenly more severe, "sit for just another second, won't you."

The boy dutifully did.

"I don't know exactly how to say this, but, I'm not going to be here forever, you know. Soon you will be on your own. You need to start using your head. Times are changing so fast lately and there are a lot of bad people out there, really bad people."

Pino thought back to his father's lecture on the Fascists and wondered to what the maestro was alluding.

"Never forget that, and never forget this: the world only heaps riches and acclaim on the strong, the ambitious and the ruthless."

Pino though for a second. To his knowledge, he possessed only one of those virtues.

"Soon you are going to have a lot of very hard decisions to make, and I won't be there to guide you. You will be tempted in your career and in life by shortcuts and quick fixes. Don't take them. Remember, to sacrifice for art is a rare privilege. It is something to be grateful for, not something to regret." Then he griped Pino's hand very tightly. "Always, always, always stay true to yourself." He paused to let the words sink in, then resumed in lighter tones, "Now get the hell out of here and let me sleep."

"*Grazie* Maestro," said Pino, thinking he might have just graduated. As the boy left, the maestro fixed his glance on him.

"Pino," he said with a smile, "don't look so serious. You know what they say, "you don't stop laughing because you get old. You get old because you stop laughing."

"*Buona notte, Maestro,*" he said with a smile, as the old man rolled over to sleep.

"*Strauss! Agh, che bruto!*" the Maestro murmured to himself.

The blessing of the maestro was more important than all the other accolades or applause he had ever received. In the deepest regions of his mind, Pino suspected that this was what he had worked for all along, a deep-rooted desire to please the maestro, much in a way that a child seeks to please his or her father, and armed with it, Pino walked home proudly, confident and more convinced than ever that he was destined for greatness.

CHAPTER FIVE

WINNING BATTLES, LOSING WARS
MAY 1936

THE WALK HOME FROM THE MAESTRO'S STUDIO was always a
pleasant one. It was downhill all the way! Alfredo, on the other hand,
conducted his lessons near the town square in a small spartan studio that
he referred to as *Il Conservatorio Ufficiale di Collagna*. It could be correctly said that
the contents of the studio provided an accurate depiction of its occupant. All
around the perimeter of the studio lay the evidence of a lifetime spent in self-
aggrandizement; trophies, framed certificates, letters of recommendation, most
of which were from Fascist Party Officials and not artistic associations.

Conversely, Maestro Ivaldi's studio held none. The old maestro felt all the
frames in Alfredo's studio created the clinical antiseptic feeling of a doctor's
office. His own preference ran towards that of an ill-kept library. He liked to say
that the general untidiness was by design to make his students feel more at ease,
but it wasn't true. He simply lacked the patience to return things to their rightful
place, or even to assign them a rightful place for that matter. The only benefit
afforded by Alfredo's location was that Pino could pass his father's shop near
the center of town and drop in to say hello on his way home.

One day, Pino dropped by his father's shop to poke his head in and say
hello, but to his surprise he found the shop closed. Papa Vaggi rarely closed the
shop before five pm on a weeknight and never on a Saturday, but today he was
nowhere to be found and it was only four o'clock. Pino's first thought was that
his father wasn't feeling well and went home early. But if that was the case, his
father would almost certainly have left a note in the window saying so.

Suddenly, he heard a loud crash followed by the distinct cackling sound of
distant laughter. Pino followed the sound down the block and around the corner
in curiosity. He soon found himself in front of DeLuca's bar, one of the smaller,
louder and by all accounts, most opinionated watering holes in the town.

The establishment had been in the DeLuca family for several generations
and had a well-worn, friendly look to it that radiated old-time hospitality. Truly,
the bar possessed those qualities, provided a guest was willing to listen to
interminable war stories, soccer debates, and the legend of how General
Garibaldi had slept there during his exile. There were paintings of Garibaldi

everywhere and a large photograph of King Victor Emmanuel III hung just above the bar. The establishment screamed out nationalism, but the pride it spoke of was for a different Italy.

Noticeably absent were any photos of *Il Duce*. There were no banners declaring: *Tutto nello Stato, niente al di fuori dello Stato, nulla contro lo Stato,* "Everything in the State, nothing outside the State, nothing against the State" or "*Me ne frego,*" "I don't care," or any other Fascist sayings. Such ideologies found no welcome at DeLuca's for it was well-known in these parts that the DeLuca family had been fiercely anti-Mussolini since *Il Duce* dissolved the Italian Parliament, where Marcelo DeLuca, the family patriarch, had held a seat. In the process, Mussolini also named himself *de facto* dictator.

Being strongly anti-fascist was a dangerous business. Being publicly anti-fascist was suicide, especially in a small town, but it earned the DeLucas a level of respect that was unimpeachable and their business flourished as a result.

The cheering, Pino soon learned, was in response to the news that Italy had finally conquered Ethiopia. The war was over and the boys were coming home! Pino couldn't wait to rush home to tell his father the news. As fate would have it, he didn't have to wait, because from the crowded bar, a figure was flailing at him. It took Pino a second to realize the figure was actually that of his hopelessly inebriated father, barely able to stand upright. Pino smirked to himself, thinking, 'This should be good!'

"Pino! Come in, boy!" he called out, and Pino joined him at the bar. The pandemonium was infectious and Pino was soon caught up in it. Everyone was laughing, singing and kissing each other, the wine and beer flowing freely. "Have a drink, son! The war is over!" said Papa, spraying his son with his words. Pino smiled and found himself hugging his father like he was "one of the boys". It gave him a distinctly "mature" feeling. "Gino! Give my son here a shot of *grappa!*" Papa called out.

No! Not grappa! Anything but grappa! Pino thought, but it was no use. The two men downed one *grappa* after another and literally laughed until they fell over onto the floor.

Pino thought, *Hey, maybe I was wrong. Grappa's really not all that bad after all! It just took a little getting used to, that's all.* Right at that moment, he felt exactly the same way about his father. As they laughed and tried their best to get up off the floor, a number of the patrons started singing.

"Thank God, this nightmare is over." Pino's father blurted out. "I'm not sure exactly what we won," he paused to consider his words, "but at least we won!" Pino and Papa clinked glasses at that. "Let's pray we never have to go to war again!"

"Amen!" said Pino, absently, listening to the crowd sing, as his father stared at him through drunken eyes and smiled a broad fatherly smile.

"Go on, Pino! Show these bums what real singing is!" he shouted.

Pino thought for a moment and shook his head.

"I really don't sing this kind of music, Papa," he said.

"Sure. Sure. Of course," Papa Vaggi said, with obvious disappointment.

Pino desperately wanted to save the moment and wracked his brains, *what could I possibly sing here?* He couldn't think clearly. His mind was blank; he couldn't remember any songs at all. *Damn, that grappa makes everything foggy!* He looked up at the picture of his king hoping for some inspiration and a second later it came to him. It wasn't very "showy" but it was appropriate. He swallowed, coughed, cleared his throat and slowly began to sing. At first, amid the cacophony of noise, his voice couldn't be heard at all, but slowly, one by one, the voices silenced and listened.

"Va' pensiero, sull'ali dorate; va ti posa sui clivi, sui colli,"

Fly, thought, on wings of gold; go settle on the slopes, on the hills.

"Ove olezzano tepide e molli, L'aure dolci del suolo natal!"

Where, soft and mild, the sweet airs of our native land smell fragrant!

It was the chorus from Verdi's *Nabucco*, the song of the Hebrew slaves, yearning to breathe free. The piece had become something of an anthem in Italy during the reformation years after the Great War. With its deeply spiritual message of hope, tinged with a sentimental longing for a bygone era, it was the ideal choice for that crowd, on that day. To Pino's great surprise, the entire bar knew every word and a warm electricity ran up his spine as the tearful crowd began to sing along.

"Del Giordano le rive saluta, Di Sion le torri atterrate…

Greet the banks of the river Jordan and Zion's toppled towers.

"Oh, mio patria, sì bella e perduta! Oh, membranza sì cara e fatal!

Oh, my country, so lovely and lost! Oh, remembrance so dear and despairing!

"Arpa d'or dei fatidici vati, perché muta dal salice pendi?

Golden Harp of the prophets, why dost thou hang mute upon the willows?

"Le memorie nel petto raccendi, ci favella del tempo che fu!"

Rekindle our bosom's memories, and speak of times gone by!

"O simile di Sòlima ai fati traggi un suono di crudo lamento, o l'ispiri il Signore un concento che ne infonda al patire virtu!"

Mindful of the fate of Jerusalem, either give forth an air of sad lamentation, or let the Lord imbue us with the fortitude to bear our sufferings!

The song ended with the entire bar singing the final chorus in harmony. Even Pino's father sang along. The final note sparked a thunderous ovation and Pino was mobbed by the crowd. It was a moment he'd treasure for a lifetime, but it was nothing compared to what happened as he turned toward his father. Antonio Vaggi was sitting on a barstool not three feet away from Pino, weeping uncontrollably. In his entire life, Pino had never seen his father cry. It was a shocking sight. He desperately wanted to hug him, but he just couldn't.

His father pulled him close and whispered to him: "Pino," he said, choking back tears, "there are really only two kinds of people in the world." As he paused to take another breath, Pino was certain the next line would be: "Good people and bad people," because he'd heard his father repeat this expression countless times over the years. Yet what followed was not what he expected at all. "Son, there are sheep…and there are shepherds. Don't be a sheep."

No one would ever have accused Antonio Vaggi of being a poet or even of having a way with words, but the few syllables he'd just uttered were the most eloquent ones Pino had ever heard. He'd finally reached communion with his father.

CHAPTER SIX

LABORING FOR ART

UNFORTUNATELY, 1937 WAS NOT THE PEACEFUL YEAR that all of Italy had hoped for. Achieving an overseas empire in Ethiopia was not enough to satisfy the *Duce*'s ambitions. Some said his next venture was merely an attempt to divert public attention away from the growing economic crisis at home, others believed it was the obligatory gesture of coming to the assistance of a fellow fascist. Whatever the reasons, by mid-1937, Mussolini had committed some seventy thousand troops to aid Franco's fascists in the Spanish civil war. The *Duce*'s hopes that the war would be a brief one were soon dashed by Russia's offer of assistance to the opposing Republicans, and unfortunately, as the conflict dragged on so did Italy's involvement on a grander and grander scale.

At the time, most Italians couldn't understand what was to be gained by choosing sides in a civil war. Of course, they couldn't have guessed the breadth of the *Duce*'s lofty future ambitions. What most Italians did understand quite clearly was that times were hard. The economy was stretched to the breaking point by the *Duce*'s adventures in Africa and any further actions would be a heavy burden to bear and require a great deal of sacrifice domestically. After having just emerged from a period of economic strife, the *Duce* was asking his people once again to tighten their collective belts for "the greater good."

Like many small European towns, Collagna didn't offer a great deal of choice in terms of career opportunities. Tradition was unchanged for generations: the baker's son became a baker, the tailor's son became a tailor; and the butcher's son became an opera singer. *Opera singer?* The renewed sense of pride that Antonio Vaggi had in Pino's career choice was rapidly waning, and the barbs and quips from the various tradesmen in town were hitting closer and closer to the heart. It wasn't that he wanted Pino to follow in his footsteps and become a butcher, but he wanted him to become *something, anything.* Anything that brought home a decent wage, that is. These thoughts began to consume him as he watched his son pass by his shop each day en route to his lesson, then again, as he strolled home from his lesson. *Was an unemployed opera singer really an opera singer at all? How long would the boy continue to take lessons upon lessons upon lessons, with no real future in sight?*

He held in his hand a note Pino had written and left on the kitchen table saying he'd be home late for dinner as he had rehearsal at church for a funeral he'd be singing that weekend. The thought of Pino becoming a cloistered hermit, playing the organ in church on Sunday was unbearable. As a boy, he was always so full of life and passionate about everything he did, from soccer to his schoolwork, but once music had entered his life there was little room for anything else. Mr. Vaggi liked music as much as most, but he'd always considered it merely a pleasant diversion, hardly a career path suitable for a man. Yet this was the life that his son had chosen and there was seemingly no stopping him. Well, he thought, perhaps it's time his son got an education in some of life's more practical realities, unpleasant realities, not necessarily to dissuade him in his career choice, but rather to put into perspective all the sacrifices his family had made for him along the way. Maybe, just maybe, he might decide to give a little something back to the family, a contribution toward the household.

He gazed upon the note, regarded his son's penmanship and marveled. It flowed like a mountain stream, with graceful loops all uniform in length and style. How hard did the boy work to get it so perfect? Or, like his singing, did it just come naturally? Papa Vaggi knew his own penmanship looked positively barbaric by comparison. And while he couldn't care less about his own poor handwriting, it did bring him just a slight sense of grief that the boy was now certainly old enough and sufficiently intelligent to sense his father's deficiencies in…many things.

But for God's sake, he was sixteen years old! *It's time he started to pull his own weight. By the time I was sixteen I was already supporting my entire family!* Between work and his family responsibilities, Antonio Vaggi had never really had the time or the opportunity to cultivate his mind in any real or meaningful way. *But what harm had it done?* He was no worse off for it. He owned a house and a successful business. Well, relatively successful.

With that thought in mind, he washed his hands and closed up the shop, determined to have a conversation with his son over dinner that evening. From that point on, he told himself, things would be different. He locked the front door to the shop and proceeded directly to DeLuca's bar.

The maestro didn't like listening to the phonograph because he thought it sounded positively dreadful. For that same reason, he didn't like listening to the radio, either. But, with relatively few guests visiting his hospital room and colder weather coming on, he decided to accept the gift of a radio from one of his more well-to-do students, Allesandro Biaggi. It would help keep him company on the loneliest nights.

He accepted the gift with mixed emotions, because he knew and disliked the boy's father, Chief Magistrate Biaggi. A radio set was expensive and the maestro didn't like to think about where the magistrate may have gotten the money. Like everyone else in town, the maestro suspected that Magistrate Biaggi secured his position by virtue of his affiliation with the Fascist party in the region, and he was probably correct. In truth, however, the maestro actually had no problem with that part of the equation. Connections or relations, people got jobs that way all the time. It was nothing new. And, frankly, to him the Fascists were not the worst thing Italy had ever seen, either. Maybe they went a little too far once in a while, but that, he felt, was the cost of order in a disorderly country, and post-Great War Italy was certainly that. The maestro's problem with Biaggi was a purely personal one: the magistrate treated people with unusual cruelty, and it was beginning to rub off on his son, Allesandro. The maestro always liked the boy, but in recent months he detected a note of hostility in him that was disturbing. When the maestro prohibited the singing of German in the studio, the boy demanded to know why. The maestro's decision was based ostensibly on his personal disgust with Hitler, but knowing the boy's family and its political affiliation, the maestro wisely chose not to share his rationale with Allesandro.

A lifetime spent working in the arts had introduced the maestro to a great deal of odd and zany characters, and more than a few different lifestyles, but the one overriding lesson that he learned from all his experiences was a simple one: respect. The only way to get an orchestra composed of musicians from different countries, speaking different languages to work together smoothly was through respect. It was so simple it was ludicrous. Yet in the magistrate, he noticed a profound lack of respect, and that, thought the maestro, was completely intolerable in a person holding such a position. Consequently, he felt considerable trepidation accepting the gift of the radio.

As it turned out, the radio proved an ideal companion for the bedridden maestro. Because it spoke *at you* and required no dialogue, he could listen for hours on end without getting tired, as he often did of conversation. The only difficulty was the persistent clatter of annoying political broadcasts for which he had no patience whatsoever. He kept the radio on a little cart that could be rolled right up to his bedside for listening, and discreetly stowed away when visitors arrived. The voices of the newscasters and the musical programs eventually became his friends and he would often get annoyed at having to turn off the radio when visitors arrived. So his frustration was compounded on the evening that he received a surprise visit from Chief Magistrate Biaggi.

The visit seemed at first perfunctory but cordial, nonetheless the Maestro couldn't help having a little fun at the magistrate's expense.

As Biaggi entered and approached, without opening an eye the maestro spoke.

"Visiting hours are over."

The magistrate laughed. "How are you my old friend?" he asked offhandedly.

"At death's door. And it's drafty. So if you don't mind -"

"In that case, I won't keep you." He smiled to himself at the little clever double entendre.

"Not at all! It's always a pleasure saying goodnight to you, Captain. Goodnight!"

"But first, I need to ask a small favor."

"Of course you do," said the maestro with a yawn.

Biaggi stepped closer and tripped over the maestro's slippers beside the bed. Annoyed, he kicked them under the bed.

"My son, Alle, is having some difficulties with that new teacher, Alfredo. Out of respect for you, I have come to you first rather than speak to the teacher myself. Alle misses you terribly and this new teacher is treating him poorly, perhaps even disrespectfully. Do you think you could speak to him?"

"Of course, I'll speak to Alle, but he is a very stubborn boy, you know."

"Not Alle, you fool!" he thundered. "Alfredo! Talk to him!"

"You talk to him! You're both *Fascisti*. I'm sure you have much in common."

Biaggi turned away in frustration. He hated coming to the old man cap in hand. It was demeaning, but he had no choice.

For his part, something about the conversation didn't sit well with the maestro, either. It was almost as though he was being probed and cajoled into providing some sort of information about Alfredo that the magistrate was unable to discover for himself. The maestro never cared for Alfredo, that much was certain, but he also resented being used. He was no informer and he didn't like being treated as such. Just as he was about to give the magistrate a well-earned piece of his mind, the officer spun around with new energy. Something had caught his eye and he smiled.

"So, tell me, how do you like the radio?" he asked sweetly, rolling the cart away from the bed and against the wall; placing himself between the maestro and the radio, as if he were saying, *You'll have to get past me to get it back.*

The maestro's nostrils flared. *The bastard!* he thought. *So that's how it's going to be, is it?* But, as he opened his mouth to speak, he felt a twinge in his chest. It was just a pinch, a little tightness. He'd had them before and the doctor always yelled at him for getting so worked up. He took a deep cleansing breath and decided not to argue. He'd live to fight another day.

"Magistrate, you must forgive me, but I grow fatigued. Could we possibly continue this chat another time?" the maestro inquired softly.

"Oh, certainly, certainly." the magistrate replied, assured of his victory. "If you think of anything you wish to tell me, to help the situation, please let me know. I'd prefer not to have to deal with this teacher myself, if possible. You understand, I'm trying to teach my son to fight his own battles and all. In my official capacity, it would be awkward. I'm sure you understand."

"Of course," the maestro nodded. They said polite goodbyes and the magistrate departed.

The maestro adjusted his pillows, completely puzzled. None of this added up. *Why wouldn't the magistrate handle Alfredo in the thuggish manner that he treated everyone else, particularly if he offended the officer's son?* It made no sense; something was wrong with the picture. The twinge returned, this time in his back. He ignored it again. It generally went away in a few minutes, and besides, he was trying to concentrate. What would make this bellicose man treat a lowly music teacher with such patience, the very patience that he was famously lacking? Whatever it was, one thing was for certain: Biaggi could count on no help whatsoever from the maestro.

In the midst of all his bravado, an unpleasant thought crossed the maestro's mind: he didn't want to do anything to cross the magistrate *too* much. Although he hated to admit it, he had come to rely upon the radio and didn't want to lose it. He knew the magistrate was just the sort of petty, vindictive person to take it back. No, he couldn't allow that to happen. With a troubled mind, he tried to figure out a solution.

Could it be believed the Magistrate was turning over a new leaf? Of course not. *Could Alfredo actually have some damaging information about Biaggi?* Ridiculous – Alfredo was a fool! Besides, even if he did try to besmirch the magistrate in some way, who would believe the word of a cretin like Alfredo versus the word of … At just that moment, a match was struck deep in his mind, illuminating an absurd possibility! He sat up in bed.

"That's it. They're both *Fascisti!*" he said aloud. "The last thing the Magistrate wants is to cause any trouble for another Fascist. First, it wouldn't look good. Second, heaven only knows what might happen if that *idiota* Alfredo decided to make trouble for the magistrate with the Party. They would probably still side with the magistrate, but he would have a black spot on his record and there would always be doubts. Ha! And Alfredo was just the kind of crazy *patso* to do it! I'm sure the Magistrate knows it too. He wants it all to go away. Ho, ho, ho! Oh, this is rich!"

He rubbed his hands together with a sinister laugh, then reached over to turn the radio back on, but it wasn't there. It was still against the far wall where the magistrate had rolled it.

"Damn *Fascist!* Making me get out of bed!" he muttered as he threw back the blankets and stepped onto the ice cold floor.

"Ooooh! That's cold!" he cried, as a chill shot up his spine and all the way to his fingertips. He looked for his slippers but they were too far under the bed for him to reach without getting down on his hands and knees.

"*Va fan*....never mind!" he muttered to himself as he tiptoed as quickly as he could over to the radio. When he reached down to grab the cart, the twinge struck again; this time strong enough to get his attention. He reached inside his robe and rubbed his chest. His hands felt icy cold against his skin and he pulled them out to blow on them and rub them together. He couldn't get the chill out, so he rubbed harder.

Damn, was it winter already? He couldn't stand on his tiptoes any longer and allowed the soles of his feet to touch the cold tiles. The feeling was like a cold iron spike thrust up through his heels all the way to the base of his brain. The twinge was now a sharp, shooting pain in the middle of his back and coming around his ribcage. The pain was blinding, nearly causing him to double over, but all he could think about was warming his hands, his freezing cold hands. At that instant, he vaguely remembered hearing once that persons having a heart attack reach a moment in which they must make a decision either to fight or to surrender. He looked down at his hands, at the long thin white fingers that once moved so fluidly and gracefully, that had brought so much joy to so many, and he smiled. He slowly rolled the cart over to the bed and sat down on the edge. He turned on the radio and lay back in bed, pulling the covers back over his legs.

The newscaster was saying something about Spain and the Republican defeat. It didn't matter. He turned the dial until he came upon his favorite music station and he began to laugh. In fact, he laughed so hard he nearly cried.

Wagner! They were playing Wagner! How sublimely ironic life is, he thought as he folded his hands.

As the chorus of pilgrims sang, *"Saving grace is dealt to the penitent, one day he will go into the blessed peace, Hell and death cannot harm him!"* the maestro smiled and softly said to himself, "Hmm. We shall soon see." And with that, he closed his eyes for the last time.

Sadly, the maestro's death came and went without much fanfare. Pino sang the *Ingemisco* from Verdi's Requiem at the funeral and Alfredo conducted the choir. It was a very dignified service, and everyone present agreed that the maestro would have wanted it that way. Pino had prepared himself emotionally for the loss of his teacher for several months and was determined not to shed a tear at the service. He was only partially successful.

The autumn chill had come early to Collagna that year and by October, the trees were nearly bare. The ground was covered in a colorful blanket of red, brown and gold leaves which made the climb up the hill to the graveyard slippery. The grave, too, was awash with fall colors, the ground already covered with leaves, giving the scene a cheerier look than it deserved.

As the casket was lowered into the earth, Pino broke down and sobbed uncontrollably. The cemetery was located at the base of the mountain and not many mourners made the journey. Pino thought it just as well, since so few townsfolk had taken the time to visit the maestro while he was still among them. He was tired of the phony, philosophical musing, always in abundance in Collagna whenever someone died, and even more tired of the would-be philosophers themselves. Among the mourners were most of the maestro's pupils, Pino's "brothers and sisters." Allesandro and Marco were there along with the pretty blond girl, whose name he still didn't know.

Life without the maestro wouldn't be easy. In all of his dreams and delusions of grandeur, he'd always imagined the old man standing in the wings cheering him on. Now, it was clear, the road would be a lonely one. If only his parents understood him like the maestro did, that would make it all worthwhile, but he wasn't wasting any more time on that romantic notion.

He sat alone by the maestro's grave until nightfall. His parents would be worried, but he didn't care. In the distance, he could see the lights of the town. The flames from the fireplaces and hearths reflected through the windowpanes, the flickering lights looked like fireflies buzzing about.

Focus. That's what the maestro had always told him. Expend energy only toward your goal. He knew there would be stumbling blocks but he'd simply have to navigate them. The first stumbling block was Alfredo.

"Think liquid," Alfredo advised. "The voice must flow evenly throughout the range from top to bottom like liquid." The advice was technically sound, but somehow Pino kept wondering where his teacher had learned the expression. In fact, Pino would put all future commands from Alfredo through equal scrutiny. Alfredo loved his catchy expressions and often beat them to death before disposing of them completely.

"Let the air do the work." "Pretend you have no upper lip." "The mouth must open top to bottom, never side to side." All of these expressions, and so many more had found their way into the Gianassi "voice-lesson graveyard." Pino considered each piece of advice and weighed it on its own merits, but he couldn't help thinking *how committed to these ideas could Alfredo possibly be if he only used them for a few weeks, then tossed them aside, never to be heard from again?* Pino didn't need this additional concern but there seemed no way around it. He would use Alfredo for what he could provide and disregard all the trivial nonsense and petty mental games.

"Count, Pino! One, two, three..."

Pino clapped his hands as he sang, although he felt ridiculous doing it.

"No, no, no!" yelled Alfredo at the top of his lungs.

Pino stopped singing and slammed shut his music book. The two men stood in tense silence. Pino told himself not to get angry, not to play Alfredo's game, and above all, not to insult him. He slowly packed his music into his bag as Alfredo watched.

"I'm sorry," he said faintly as he left the studio. He walked home, seriously considering never returning. But he knew that doing so would mean that Alfredo had won. He'd never let that happen, he had promised the maestro.

Pino wasn't a fatalist but he couldn't help noticing a certain recurring phenomena. He could always count on his family to provide the least possible support just when he needed it most. He would bet his allowance that his father would say something nasty just when he needed a kind word. Tonight would be no different, he was certain.

The smell of liquor on his father's breath when they sat down to dinner alarmed Pino. His father would often stop at Flavio's or DeLuca's on the way home for a drink, but in his entire life Pino could not remember his father ever showing up for dinner in this condition. The effect was dramatic and the silence at the dinner table was palpable: four sets of eyes were staring down at four sets of dishes.

Pino's mother glanced from face to face trying to read something in the expressions. Unfortunately there was nothing to read.

"Is it my imagination or are we unusually talkative tonight?" she asked.

The kids shrugged their shoulders but said nothing. Mr. Vaggi didn't even acknowledge the question.

"How about you, Pino? What's new at school?" Pino simply grunted. "Didn't you say you have some auditions coming up or something?" his mother continued.

"I wish," he said, a little bit too smugly. The remark had the magic effect of bringing his father out of his private world.

"What do you mean, *you wish*?" he inquired angrily.

"I mean, Alfredo says I'm not ready yet," replied Pino. It wasn't what Mr. Vaggi wanted to hear. In truth, whatever Pino had said wouldn't have mattered. His father was looking for a reason to explode.

"What the hell does that mean? When *will* you be ready? You've been taking lessons for seven goddamn years!"

"Papa, that's enough," said Mrs. Vaggi.

"Don't tell me how to raise my son! It's about time he starts looking for a job and starts to contribute to this family!"

"I don't care what you think. The dinner table is no place for that sort of language!" she replied.

Pino's father could never bear hurting his wife's feelings. Full of anger and guilt, he wiped his mouth and stormed out of the room.

"Is Papa alright?" asked little Maria, in a voice that would have made angels cry.

"He's fine, honey, he just had a hard day at work. He'll be fine."

The answer satisfied Maria but Pino wasn't buying it and his mother knew it. She hoped he'd let the matter drop without further discussion and luckily he managed to read her mind and do just that. He ate his meal in silence, then retreated to the safety of his room.

Later that night he found himself back in his little perch on the floor at the top of the stairs struggling to hear his parents' conversation, but they weren't saying much. The radio was playing a news broadcast which made absolutely no sense to him. *Germany had invaded Austria?* Somehow, German troops were now on the northern Italian border! *What was going on?* He wished his mother would turn off the water in the damn sink so he could hear.

Just as he dared to crawl a bit further down the stairs, a plank squeaked so loudly that he was sure his parents had heard it. Amazingly they hadn't. In a minute, his heart rate returned to normal and he sat on the top step. The sound of the radio and the sink echoed up the stairs to the second floor which was otherwise ghostly silent.

A board creaked behind him and he swung around. He noticed Maria's door was ajar. The night wasn't as frightening now. Its particular language of creaks and cracks no longer held any terror. The only terror was approaching him slowly, smiling quietly in her pink nightgown. She opened her mouth to speak but Pino covered it.

"Shhh! If you promise not to say a word," Pino whispered, "you can stay here with me."

She had no idea what he was talking about but the offer implied something mischievous so she immediately agreed. They crawled next to each other at the top of the stairs and he whispered in her ear.

"I'm trying to hear the radio, so you have to be completely silent."
She nodded.

The water was finally turned off and the radio could be heard loud and clear. Papa Vaggi was muttering to himself again and Pino thought he might actually be talking in his sleep. A moment later, the radio dashed that theory.

"Jesus Christ, Rosa, they're practically in the Alps already! That didn't take long." Mr. Vaggi roared.

"Tony, we have an agreement. They signed it last year. You heard the Duce. We are an Axis from Rome to Berlin. They're not the enemy!"

"Tell that to those poor bastards in Vienna! They were allies too! They even speak the same goddamn language! They are a cold and cruel people, Rosa. Never forget that."

The announcer went on to say: "a nation that needs the help of foreign troops to keep its independence no longer deserves that title…"

It was all Greek to Pino, but one thing was certain: the Germans had invaded Austria and that put them right in Italy's backyard and from what he could deduce from the radio, it appeared they had done so with the blessing of Mussolini. Axis or no Axis, it didn't exactly foster a feeling of security.

"Pino," Maria whispered, "I don't understand. What's going on?"
He toyed with the idea of lying to her, but decided against it.
"It sounds like the Germans have marched on Austria."

"When you say 'marched,' do you mean they're at war?" she asked. He honestly didn't know the answer and had chosen that word specifically not to upset her, but she was too smart.

"I'm not sure. We'll probably find out tomorrow." Seeing his sister's eyes aglow with fear, he decided it was best to get her back in bed.

"Let's go now, before they hear us."

Before he could move, he heard something that made his blood run cold.

"Tony, what are they going to do to Mr. DeLuca?" his mother asked.

Mr. DeLuca? thought Pino, nervously.

"Who knows? Lucky for him he's got money and some connections. If he didn't, he'd be dead already."

Pino's heart froze.

What? Dead already?

"That bastard Biaggi has always had it in for him."

Pino hastily got up off the floor and dragged his sister with him. He'd heard more than he wanted to and felt sick. He put Maria in bed and told her they'd talk first thing in the morning, then he collapsed onto his own bed, shaking. This certainly explained his father's drinking. *What was happening to the world? Mr. DeLuca arrested? He'd be dead already if it weren't for his connections! And it was all because of Alle's father?* The cold night got colder and no amount of blankets could remove the chill from Pino's bones. Once again, his own problems seemed more and more trivial. He desperately needed to talk to his father and sort things out, but who knew when that opportunity might present itself.

Oh, Maestro! Where are you when I need you? Pino thought for the first time since the maestro's passing. He pulled the covers over his head and tried to sleep, feeling more frightened and lonely than he'd ever felt before.

The next day, dinner began on precisely the same note on which it had ended the previous night.

"Well, what do you have to say Pino?" his father asked.

Clearly no answer would suffice, so Pino tried to turn the question around.

"What do you want me to say?"

"I want you to say 'you're right, Papa.' I'll get a job and start to help out around here."

This was not the conversation Pino had hoped for. Never realizing that his own spells of brooding silence might actually be baffling or hurtful to his parents, he sat like a statue. Eventually, his father's stare proved too much. Pino measured his words carefully, or at least so he thought.

"Papa, I can't. At least not right now. It's not a good time."

"That's all I ever hear. 'It's not a good time.' It's never a good time! When will it be a good time?"

Pino's mother tried to deflect the question with one of her own.

"Pino, do you think you're ready to audition?" she asked.

"I don't know. Maybe," he answered.

"Maybe? Don't you even *want* to work?" his father yelled. "I mean, aren't you *embarrassed*? Can't you sing somewhere that pays or do something that resembles a job?"

"I really think that if I went to the National Conservatory in Milan I'd have a better chance," he added, ignoring his father.

"The National Conservatory in Milan?" Mr. Vaggi exploded.

"I'd have better teachers, work with better singers and have more exposure to people who could really help my career. If I stay here...well I just don't think I'm getting anywhere by staying here. I don't think Alfredo will ever feel that I'm ready."

"So you'll just keep taking lessons upon lessons and continue to line his pockets. Well, I've had just about enough of it. I'm going to have a talk with that thief tomorrow. Goddamn Fascist! Why don't you ask him to get you into the National Conservatory? That's how everyone does things nowadays! They control everything, the jobs, the banks, the school admissions. Get it? It's about time you wake up and smell the goddamn coffee!"

"Shut up, Papa!" Mrs. Vaggi reprimanded her husband in a voice Pino had never heard. With tears in her eyes, she turned her attention to her son. "You really think you know better than your teacher, Pino?"

The thought of his mother crying was unbearable to Pino, so he toned down the rhetoric.

"Mama, I know my voice," he said, "and I think I've learned all that I can from these small-time, local voice teachers."

But Mr. Vaggi had had just about as much of this conversation as he could take.

"I think what you need is a little lesson in reality," he said. "Times are hard. Your mother and I can hardly afford your lessons here. It's time you grew up and started acting like a man!"

Try as he may, Pino never seemed to say the right thing at the right time, nor did he remain silent when silence was the best option.

"Papa, if I get a job now, I'll never have a career in the opera. Do you want that?"

"Oh, no you don't! Don't try to make me feel guilty. For nearly ten years now..."

"Pino," his mother interrupted. "We've paid for your lessons up till now, and we have no problem continuing to pay."

His father looked at her in disbelief.

"However," she continued, "if you want to move to Milan, to the National Conservatory, then you've got to find some other means of paying for it. We just can't afford it. And that's the end of the discussion."

The hollow silence that had overtaken so many dinners round that table returned again. Pino had never felt so selfish before. Although he hated to admit it, he actually began to understand his father's point of view. He looked at his father's face and he saw sadness behind the anger. He suspected that his father felt guilty as well, for not understanding his son and guilty for not be able to provide everything that the boy required emotionally and financially. While Pino thought he understood his father's frustration, he couldn't fathom why his father consistently felt it necessary to take out his own frustrations on his son.

That night, alone in his room, Pino lit a candle and sat at his little desk. After listening to make sure no one would disturb him, he pulled a letter out from under his desk blotter and quietly filled out the application to the National Conservatory, sealed its envelope, and blew out the candle.

CHAPTER SEVEN

Giving something back

COLLAGNA HAD THREE LEGITIMATE TAVERNS, two hotel bars and one bar masquerading as a restaurant. The latter was known as Café Fritz. It was not a bar in the traditional sense but it was even less a restaurant. Café Fritz had seating for about thirty people and another dozen or so could fit at the bar, but more often than not, the bar crowd spilled over into the restaurant area, commandeering tables, chairs, waitresses. It was, generally speaking, a jolly place, and travelers heading up the mountain on a ski trip would usually find it more inviting than most of the other local watering holes, which were more exclusive to the "neighborhood crowd". Consequently, Café Fritz was not held in high regard by many of the locals.

In fact, many viewed it as a cancer eating at the heart of their charming little community. Pino's parents were strong proponents of this view. They didn't like the transient type of people that such an establishment drew. They noted with disgust that Café Fritz was the only bar in town which the police had ever been called to (in a professional capacity, that is).

Herman Fritz, or "Herr Fritz," as many of the children liked to call him, was of Austrian-Jewish extraction and had moved to Collagna some ten years prior, to marry the love of his life, a local beauty named Loretta DiFranco. The two had met in Parma, where she had been attending university. His family was in the hotel business and was interested in acquiring some properties outside of Austria, where the growing anti-Semitic undercurrent had become unsettling. Herman was visiting Parma for several months to locate and negotiate interest in a local hotel. It was in that hotel that he first met the striking Alpine beauty. He, too, was very handsome and possessed great confidence, which she found extremely attractive as well. It was clear that he came from money and that certainly didn't hurt. Loretta was a bright and ambitious girl who didn't want to spend the rest of her life in Collagna and the two quickly became friends, then lovers, then fiancés.

She knew her family would be an obstacle at first, but once they met Herman, and he had the chance to charm them, she was certain they'd come around. When her papa learned that Herman owned hotels, she thought, he would undoubtedly be impressed and his approval of the match would be assured. Herman even decided to sweeten the deal a bit, telling Loretta that he was interested in buying a hotel or lodge in an area quite like Collagna, hence the birth of Café Fritz.

Herman bought the establishment virtually sight unseen. The price was extremely reasonable and, as he was anxious to impress his future in-laws, it seemed the perfect proof of his good intentions. The family's initial reaction was one of shock, but Loretta stood firmly beside her fiancé despite the expected objections. The fact that he was Jewish was problematic to both of her parents, who wanted and fully expected a Roman-Catholic son-in-law, but they were not willing to sacrifice their daughter's happiness for it. Reluctantly, they accepted her decision, and Loretta was overjoyed.

For the first few months, their happiness knew no bounds. Unfortunately, in their hasty courtship, the subject of children was given but a cursory conversation: they both wanted children. Neither of them had the foresight of discussing the issue of the religion of the children. For some inexplicable reason, both thought the other completely unreasonable about it. To Loretta, it was a foregone conclusion that the children would be Catholic; there was really no room nor reason for debate or negotiation. Herman was aghast at his fiancé's stubbornness on the issue, remarking that he fully believed it was her parents and not her speaking. The debate became an argument, the argument a fight, until finally the couple was hardly on speaking terms at all.

Sadly, Loretta's family couldn't stay on the sidelines and used the matter to poison the union, not merely with their daughter but with the extended family and the townsfolk as well. After all, in Collagna, everyone knew there were really only two religious denominations: us and them. Herman found himself on the wrong side of that line and never had a chance. Their engagement had no formal breakup of any kind. The two simply drifted further and further apart and, in the accompanying silence, their relationship faded away.

Herman buried himself in his work, breaking his back to turn Café Fritz into a first class establishment, which he did most successfully. He chose not to leave Collagna specifically to be a thorn in the side of the DiFrancos, whom he detested with all of hell's fury. It was easier for him to hate them than to hate Loretta, whom he chose to view as a victim of the family's poison. Over time, he became less and less interested in keeping up the standards of Café Fritz and eventually its fine reputation faded and a seedier clientele seeped its way in.

It was really no surprise, given the way Pino's luck was running, that his first foray into the work force would be in just such a place. He had no prior knowledge of the reputation of the place, because such nonsense had always bored him, or about how his family might react to the knowledge of his employment there. All he knew was he had a job. Signore Fritz would pay him 100 lire per week to sing four twenty-minute sets of Neapolitan songs for his customers nightly, plus all the tips that he earned.

Pino was elated! He thought he was stealing the money. Although he never really cared for Neapolitan songs, he knew that he could sing them in his sleep, and more importantly, he could tell his father that he was finally going to make a contribution to the family. The thought filled him with pride as he considered his father, working like an animal every day to provide for the family. For the first time in his life, Pino would be a breadwinner.

He decided to share the good news with his family over dinner, because that was where such matters were discussed. Pino waited until the meal was over before, bursting his buttons with pride, he dropped his bombshell. He scanned the table to absorb their expressions, but before he could manage one pass, his father dropped his own bombshell.

"No son of mine is going to work for Jews." And he said nothing more.

After dinner, Pino went outside and walked for miles. He had no destination in mind, just away from his father. *What difference did it make who he worked for? It was a job, wasn't it? And since when did his father hate Jews?* His mind was spinning out of control and he wandered aimlessly. After several hours of walking, it had grown very dark and Pino wasn't sure exactly where he was so he sat down to rest. *How could his father be so awful?* It was clear to Pino now that his father couldn't appreciate his art because his father couldn't appreciate anything! How could Pino expect him to appreciate Verdi when he wasn't capable of appreciating even the slightest gesture of human kindness? It was just another in a seemingly endless string of disappointments his father would lay upon him. Never again would he go out of his way to please the old man. If Papa didn't like his job, that would be his tough luck. If he threw Pino out of the house, fine, Pino would just move in with Alfredo.

A cloud crept over the moon and Pino felt the cold of night coming on. All the wonders of the Apennine autumn had vanished. The breathtaking colors of the plateau, the mist of the valley after a rain, the smell of the crisp morning air had all gone. He had a premonition of impending doom and for a moment thought that the devil himself resided in their tranquil little village.

A tremendous wave of fatigue overcame him and he began to shiver. All he could think of was sleep. He looked around to get some idea of where he was but it might as well have been the moon. He'd never get home in this darkness.

Suddenly, he noticed something glittering on the ground in front of him and reached to pick it up. As he did, he noticed a number of such luminescent objects. He recognized them immediately. They were black quartz reflecting back the hint of moonlight like a great black sequined blanket stretching out around him. The glitter only added to the desolation of the landscape. He realized now that he'd wandered all the way to the river bed of the Rio Biola and was halfway to the neighboring town of Busana. The walk back would be a long and sobering one. He looked up at the sky and the stars were starting to peek out from behind the clouds. He smiled a sad smile and the stars smiled back at him. He picked up another piece of quartz to give to his sister and placed it in his pocket as he began the long trek home.

He resolved at that moment that all the timidity, propriety and shyness that had bound and handicapped him until now would be done with. The storybook of his youth, in which he was but a character, must close. A new book, which he himself would author, would be written.

Signore Fritz liked to tell new customers that he was directly related to the famous Fritz family of the popular Mascagni opera *L'Amico Fritz*, but he had no documentation of any kind to support this claim. Of course, everyone in town knew it to be false, but nonetheless, he thought the connection provided him with an air of sophistication to newcomers. If it did, it was the only hint of sophistication about him that remained. In recent years he had grown bitter and bellicose and his café reflected it. Much like him, the café was loud, dark and dangerous-looking. Yet he had found a niche and business was brisk.

The success of Café Fritz was an enigma to the people of Collagna. They didn't care for him or his café and certainly no self-respecting local would be caught dead inside it. Still, it flourished. Perhaps it was the townsfolk themselves, their intolerance and generally suspicious nature that enabled a place like Café Fritz to thrive. Strangers arriving in town undoubtedly got a warmer welcome there than at any of the other local taverns, and the music certainly was louder and livelier than any other place in town. Thus, it was entirely reasonable that vacationers passing through would be drawn to such a place for a night out.

It took Pino all of five minutes to determine that he hated the place. He hated the noise, the seedy clientele, the smoke, the odor, but above all, he hated Herr Fritz. To Pino, Fritz was a nasty little man who never seemed to have a nice word for any of his employees. No one was spared; not the bartender, nor the waitresses, the bus boys, not even the entertainment. What amazed Pino most was that patrons could have such a wonderfully festive evening, completely oblivious to the misery of the staff serving them.

Because Pino worked intermittently throughout the evening, he had plenty of time to watch his boss in action. Once, he heard Herr Fritz bragging about how little he paid his entire staff, particularly the entertainment! It gradually became clear to Pino that his new boss had only hired him because he believed the boy would work cheaply. Pino wasn't even aware of what a bargain he was. He hoped to get the opinion of someone else, one of the other employees, but didn't feel close enough to any of them. The only person he really even spoke to with any regularity was Paolo, the bartender, and, of course, to a lesser extent, his accompanist, Simone. Calling Simone an accompanist was actually a bit of a stretch. He was a tired, old-time saloon piano player, who knew hundreds of songs by heart and could pick up almost any tune in just one listen, but he couldn't read a note of music! His most interesting feature, in Pino's view, was the extraordinary fact that Simone was nearly stone deaf! At fifty years of age, but looking some twenty years older, he'd spent the better part of his life inside of a bar either playing piano or drinking, or both. Paolo told Pino to be careful of what he said around Simone, suggesting that the piano player could hear a lot more than he let on, and that Signore Fritz would frequently send him into a crowd to do reconnaissance, since people would generally speak freely in front of him. Then, like a good soldier, he'd report his findings back to the boss. Apparently, Paolo spoke from experience, having been burned by the piano player once before.

Paolo was a tall, thin, handsome Tyrolean creature, who looked like he should be mountain-climbing in *lederhosen* and a hat with a feather in it, rather than tending bar. His family were mountain folks as far back as anyone could remember and he possessed a congenial, laid-back, mountain pleasantness that pervaded everything he did. This amiable personality combined with his gift of gab made him a natural bartender.

Paolo had an unspoken policy of buying back the fifth drink for customers at the bar (the third drink for regulars and better tippers). One day, early in the afternoon when the place was empty, Signore Fritz sat at the bar and ordered a *Negroni*, made from Campari and gin. He threw the drink back in one swallow and ordered another. This went on for some time and Fritz and Paolo were chit-chatting about the bar and soccer, generally having a very pleasant time.

Maybe the boss wasn't such a hard ass after all, Paolo thought. Running a place like this required an iron hand and Fritz was just a little bit over-zealous in his management style. Paolo thought things would be different now that he and the boss were finally "simpatico."

In an instant, everything changed and Paolo never even saw it coming. When Signore Fritz finished his fifth *Negroni*, he announced it was time to get back to work. He took out his wallet to pay for his drinks, as was his custom, and asked Paolo how many drinks he'd had. Paolo rang him up for his five drinks, but Fritz made no attempt to pay. Instead, he just looked at Paolo and scratched his chin and knit his brows.

"All the dirt and scum that come in here, you buy them back their fifth drink, but you charge me?" asked Fritz, springing his trap. "I just want to know how come?"

Paolo was frozen, not with fear but with anger, anger for his contemptible boss who pretended to be his friend, and anger for the son-of-a-bitch that had squealed on him. Ready to be fired, Paolo took a deep breath and held it. But nothing happened. Fritz got up, took a few bills out of his wallet and left them on the bar, and walked away. From that moment on, Paolo had to be extremely careful about giving away free drinks. He knew that it would directly affect his take home pay, since a good portion of it was from the tips he made. Although he had no proof, he guessed immediately that Simone was the rat, a belief that was shared by several other employees. Despite his vow of vengeance, Paolo was too good-natured to harm anyone. Instead, he decided to humiliate Simone by letting him know that everyone in the place knew he was a rat; that would be enough punishment in itself.

In the end, he did nothing. He thought about it and concluded that he was above publicly embarrassing anyone no matter how lowly the wretch may be. *What would I have gained? A few minutes of cheap satisfaction? Not worth it.* In any event, he was mindful of Simone from that day forward.

One evening, as a full house of diners and revelers were eating, drinking and being merry, Pino was having trouble with Simone. Halfway through "*O Sole Mio,*" Simone seemed to be falling asleep. The tempo was all wrong, first too fast, then too slow. Pino struggled in vain to follow the nodding accompanist, but it just wasn't working. At the conclusion of the song, Simone let out an audible sigh of relief which the audience found hilarious. Pino bowed and left the stage to the sound of polite applause, but he was furious. He rushed through the crowd to the back of the restaurant like a man on a mission and was out of breath and perspiring when he reached the manager's office. Signore Fritz was inside smoking an enormous cigar and counting money. Pino paused to catch his breath and fix his tie before entering.

"Signore Fritz, I've finished my last number of the evening."

"That's nice," he answered not looking up from the roll of bills he was counting.

"I'd like to get paid now, so I can go home." Signore Fritz just kept counting, ignoring Pino. Then he wrote something on a little yellow notepad.

"Signore, I'd really appreciate my money now, please. I've got lessons in the morning and I really need to get some sleep." Without looking at him, Signore Fritz chuckled.

"Oh, yeah. That's right. Opera singer. Well, let me give you some free advice. Save your money kid, you're not that great. *Capische?*"

There was a long pause, a moment of fury. Pino felt his cheeks grow scarlet, but he managed not to lose control.

"I understand very clearly. I also understand that you owe me for two night's work. I'd like it now before the smoke does any more damage to my voice." Fritz turned and smiled at the cocky tenor. He squinted one eye at him for a second, then blew two lungs-full of smoke into Pino's face.

"I'm *really sorry* about the smoke," he said, as he counted off some bills and stuffed them into Pino's shirt pocket. "Call me when you get to La Scala. I hear they don't allow smoking there," he added, laughing to himself as he walked away. Pino's anger was boiling over as he strode over to the bar and ordered a drink. It was only a glass of red wine, but to Pino it might as well have been *grappa*. He swallowed it like a shot and coughed like a teenager taking his first drag from a cigarette. He wanted to go home but he was in no mood to deal with his family. He sat there and surveyed the crowd, his thoughts on Signore Fritz and how he would get even with him.

Out on the floor, a pretty waitress whose name Pino could never remember, was being harassed by a drunken customer who grabbed her around the waist and forced her to sit on his lap. She'd been teasing him and acting very coy and he clearly got the wrong impression. She was trying politely to break free of his grasp but it just wasn't happening. He was slobbering all over her shoulder and neck. Suddenly, to his surprise, she stopped struggling and turned around to face him. She gingerly kissed her fingertip and planted it on his nose. As he reached for her hand, his eyes closed in bliss, and she nimbly slipped away. His entire table burst into laughter, and the man grabbed his heart in a ridiculously melodramatic gesture.

"*Ciao, Bella,*" the drunk cried in a tortured voice. Without missing a beat, he then turned back to his table, picked up his drink and toasted the waitress. He began to sing *La Donna é Mobile*, in a sloppy drunken yell. Soon his table joined in; then the whole restaurant started to sing.

Pino picked his head up from the bar and smiled. Soon, he too started to sing along. Suddenly, his face lit up and he rushed to the piano, where Simone was nodding off.

"Simone, play it!" he cried.

Simone took a second to comprehend what Pino was saying; then another to recognize the tune. By the time he got started, the crowd was beginning the second verse. Pino took the lead, singing in full voice, but the crowd was too loud for him to be heard. Frustrated, he jumped up on top of the piano. This got their attention and they all began to quiet down. Soon it was just Pino and Verdi in all their glory. The crowd was enthralled. Pino finished the aria with a tremendous cadenza and a spectacular high C and the crowd went wild! It was like Italy had won the World Cup! Pino politely bowed to the audience, then smiled a triumphantly defiant smile at his boss. Jumping down from the piano, he waved to the crowd and headed straight out the door.

As he walked home, the winter air bit into his face. He thought about what Paolo had told him and decided to abandon any further plans for retribution. He didn't need any more trivial distractions and that was how he perceived Fritz; an insignificant distraction. "Focus" he reminded himself, like a mantra.

His family was a different matter. He had more difficulty staying focused around them. Reaching home, he entered quietly so as not to wake anyone, but his mother was up and waiting for him at the kitchen table with the radio playing softly in the living room. He entered and sat down quietly near the stove to warm his hands. The winters in Collagna were fierce enough to turn a man's bones as brittle as match sticks and Pino thought his bones might snap. His mother kindled a fire in the big old wood burning stove and they sat before it. The open door cast a warm orange light throughout the kitchen as she went to the cupboard and drew out a loaf of bread and a wheel of *pecorino* cheese, which she in turn laid on the table without saying a word. Pino hated the silence that was creeping into their lives but felt powerless to stop it.

"What are you doing up so late, Mama? Can't you sleep?"

"I got a little restless thinking about you down there at that restaurant, so I turned on the radio to listen to the news."

"Calling Café Fritz a restaurant is a bit of a stretch."

"Yes, but I'd rather think of you singing at a restaurant than some dirty, filthy bar." She poured a cup of tea for herself and Pino, who pulled his chair closer to the fire.

"Is this what you really want? Singing in bars? Is this how you expect to start a career?"

"Mama, don't even start! You and Papa insisted I get a job, so I got a job."

His mother sighed yet another heavy sigh and nodded her head.

"And they let me use the piano anytime I want to practice. It's not like we can afford a piano."

The remark hurt and seeing his mother's reaction, Pino tried to lighten the conversation. "Besides, I was a big hit there tonight."

"Really?" his mother added incredulously.

"Really! Everybody in the place stood and cheered when I sang *La Donna é Mobile!* You should have heard them. It was incredible." His mother smiled sadly and took a sip of tea. "Mama, why don't you and Papa come and hear me sing some night? It would really mean a lot to me. I mean, you never come to hear me sing anymore. You never come to lessons. You never come to hear me perform anywhere."

"Where do you perform? In bars? No thank you. Once you get some work, some legitimate work, then your Papa and I will come hear you sing. Why don't you do a recital?"

"A recital? Really, Mama, do you have any idea how much it costs to put on a recital? You know all my money is spent on lessons. I can't afford to rent a hall and an accompanist to do a recital. Are you going to pay for it?"

The comment hit another nerve but he continued anyway.

"Look. You asked me to help out around here, and I have. Yet all you do is criticize."

"Pino, I'm trying to help. You're too stubborn to listen."

"Listen to what? All I do is listen, and all I hear is criticism! Mama, come and hear me sing, then, you can tell me if you think I should really reconsider a singing career. Otherwise, please stop lecturing me!"

They'd reached an impasse.

"My little Caruso, my little Pinuch. What am I going to do with you? I wish I knew how to help you, but I don't. You think I enjoy seeing my baby so unhappy, so frustrated? I have plenty of faith in you, but you've got to have a little faith in me, and in your father. It's not so easy being a grown-up. You'll soon see."

As they sat in silence, from the living room Pino heard the announcer on the radio say something about Germany and someplace called the Sudetenland. Lately, it seemed like Germany was the headline news every night.

"What's going on with Germany, Mama?" he asked as politely as he could, knowing that he'd never find the courage to breach the subject with his father.

"Apparently, Germany invaded Czechoslovakia today."

Pino pondered the information. *First Austria, now Czechoslovakia* he thought.

"Mama, do you think Germany will invade us too?" he asked, sheepishly like a small child. She smiled and stroked his cheek.

"No. They're our allies. We signed an agreement with them. Don't worry about it."

"Papa's worried, isn't he?"

"You have to remember, Pino, your Papa fought in the last war. He hates anything to do with war. And like most men his age, he's not looking forward to another one."

"Why? Papa's too old to be a soldier." She smiled and took his hand.

"But his son isn't."

It was a thought that in his wildest dreams Pino had never considered.

"Pino, we're still fighting in Spain and who knows when that will end," she said sadly. "You'll be eighteen soon and you'll have to join the army like everybody else. We just pray it's over before you have to enlist."

He sat there with a stupid look on his face trying to appear mature. Of course, in the back of his mind he always knew he'd have to serve but he managed to keep the thought well buried. Eighteen always seemed so far off in the future.

"You look exhausted," she said. "Get some sleep. We'll talk some more tomorrow."

He got up and kissed his mother.

"*Buona notte*, Mama."

"*Buona notte*, Pino," she said faintly as he climbed the stairs.

He fell onto his bed and started to take off his clothes. The stench of cigarettes was overwhelming and he thought he'd be sick, but he lacked the energy to be sick. He sank back onto the bed and started to drift away toward unsettling dreams.

Slowly, his door opened and unseen and unheard, his sister Maria tiptoed inside the room. Blissfully unaware of the kind of day Pino had had, she shut the door, took two strides and leapt onto the bed. Startled, Pino screamed out and Maria fell down laughing.

"Are you crazy?" Pino bellowed.

"Gotcha!" she laughed.

"What's wrong with you? If we wake up Papa..."

"I never see you anymore! Between school and lessons and working at the bar."

"I'm sorry. It seems like all I do all day is apologize to people."

Maria gave him a big hug and climbed on top of him.

"Why don't you come to hear me sing?" he said.

"Yeah, right, I'll just tell Papa, "Papa I'm going down to Fritz' bar tonight to hear Pino. Don't bother to wait up."

"You could come to one of my lessons."

"The maestro wouldn't mind?"

"When was the last time you heard me sing?"

Maria scratched her head. "Hmm, I don't know. A year or so?

"No! It can't be that long," Pino exclaimed.

"Maybe more."

"Really?" Pino felt embarrassed. "Wow. I didn't realize. I'm much better, now."

"But I already think you're the best singer in the world."

"I wish Papa felt that way," he said.

"Give him time."

"I'm trying."

"Try harder."

"Sometimes I think he'd be happier if I just became a butcher."

"Probably," she blurted out, as she got off the bed and headed for the door, "By the way, Gia said to say hello!"

CHAPTER EIGHT

DISTRACTIONS

MAESTRO IVALDI ONCE TOLD PINO that the reason why romance languages sounded so pleasant to the ear was the preponderance of vowels. The French language, he noted, had over forty phonetic vowel sounds in it, whereas English, for example, had only twelve. Consequently, the likelihood of a rhyme occurring naturally was infinitely greater in the romance languages than in the Germanic or Slavic languages. In addition, there was just no way around the fact that you couldn't hold a note if it was a consonant.

To Pino it seemed like German, Russian and English had nothing *but* consonants in them! He was certain that despite the existence of some undeniable masterpieces in these languages, (*Eugene Onegin* in Russian, *Fidelio* and the Wagner operas in German) most of them were clearly "second-string" works, simply because they had the tremendous liability of ugly language.

All of these thoughts were pulsing through Pino's mind as he sat in the waiting room of Alfredo's studio. His sudden concern for Anglo-Saxon and Slavic languages was precipitated by the lesson going on in the room next door, where a singularly beautiful female voice was singing a ravishing soprano aria. Pino had sat through countless lessons of his colleagues noting their strengths and weaknesses and picking up pointers on repertoire. In this case, however, both the aria and the language were foreign to him. Judging by the number of consonants and breathy "ch" sounds, Pino guessed it to be Russian, but he couldn't be sure. He sat back in his seat and allowed the music to wash over him. This was by far the most beautiful aria he'd ever heard in a language other than Italian or French, and yet he'd never heard it before. He thought he knew, or was at least aware of all the major concert arias, but clearly he was mistaken. How did this one sneak past him? He would have to discuss this with Alfredo, but that could wait. Right now, he was the audience, not the singer, and he allowed the music to rush into his private little world and fill him with a warm, joyful sensation.

Pino's bliss was interrupted when another colleague of his plopped down beside him on the couch in the waiting room.

"Bongiorno, Pino. *"*

"Ciao, Alle.*"*

Pino wanted to avoid a conversation with Allesandro and he turned away
and opened a score on his lap, pretending to study. Since the day Signore
DeLuca was arrested, Pino made a conscious effort to avoid Alle and hoped his
friend hadn't noticed. He knew eventually their lessons would overlap and he'd
be forced to see him, but Pino resolved not to discuss with him anything but
singing. The degree of anger in his father's voice whenever he mentioned Alle's
father, the Chief Magistrate, frightened Pino. Everyone in town was talking
about Magistrate Biaggi and not in the kindest of terms, and Pino was certain
Alle had to know of it. Yet, if he did, he had a good poker face, because he
carried on as if absolutely nothing was amiss. The situation was something Pino
didn't understand and didn't want to understand. He had a tough enough time
staying focused. As naïve as it sounded, he just wanted everyone to get along.

All of his attention was currently directed at the soprano in the other room.
He looked up from the score and tried to see around the corner into the studio,
hoping to get a look at the girl, but she was just out of sight. Once again he
turned his attention to his score, but it was no use; he couldn't concentrate.
Determined to get a look at her, he gently slid his chair forward, hoping no one
noticed. Then, leaning forward again, he craned his neck like a giraffe to peek
through the doorway, but all he could see was a part of her back and a flowing
mane of golden blonde hair. For a second he closed his eyes and thought he
detected a faint trace of perfume, or perhaps it was the smell of her hair. He
began to drift; the faint smell, the exotic music and the beauty of her voice
combined to intoxicate him, and he felt goose bumps on his skin and a chill up
his spine. Sitting there in his chair, swaying to the music, his dream was rudely
interrupted.

BAM! The sound was so loud that Pino leaped up out of his chair. The
music stopped in the other room. There on the floor before him lay his
mammoth *Ricordi Complete Tenor Arias Volume One.* In his trance-like state, the
book had fallen from his lap and onto the floor. He sheepishly leaned over to
pick it up.

"Nice work," Allesandro teased.

"I just wanted to find out the name of the aria."

"Uh huh. Whatever you say." In the other room Alfredo cleared his throat
loudly, a sound Pino knew well. It reeked of annoyance and disapproval. Pino
ignored him completely.

"What language is that?" he asked Allesandro.

"Polish."

"No, seriously!"

"I am serious. Wait, no, it's Czechoslovakian."

"*Now* you're putting me on," said Pino, incredulously.

"You've really never heard this before?"

"Never."

"It's very popular."

"Maybe in Poland it is," he said with a laugh.

They sat back in silence and Pino remembered the radio broadcast from the previous evening. Somewhere northeast of them, German troops were marching into Czechoslovakia. It seemed a bit ironic that on this particular day he would hear his first Czechoslovakian aria. Perhaps it was some kind of stupid joke that Alfredo found amusing.

"It's Dvorak!" barked Allessandro.

"Huh? Oh."

"Whew! Czech, now there's an ugly language!"

"No uglier than German," mused Pino.

"Hmm...maybe, but nothing's as ugly as Russian."

"Agreed," they both chimed out in perfect harmony. He didn't want to get into any kind of international discussion with Alle, fearing the conversation might drift to politics, so he sat back and again began to analyze the voice singing in the other room. He wondered if he'd seen or heard her before. No. He couldn't have. He'd certainly have remembered that voice.

"Well, I'll say this: she sure makes the most of an ugly language." He paused and looked at his music. "Hey, Alle, you think we have an advantage singing in Italian?"

"Of course we do. You can't compare the Slavic and Germanic languages with the romance languages. They have almost no vowels. You ever try to hold a high note while saying *Ich!*"

Pino pondered for a moment and smiled. He never really considered himself lucky in any way, yet he couldn't argue with the logic.

"I guess." Pino laughed, "I just wish I could make my German sound as beautiful as she makes Czechoslovakian sound."

"I thought you had sworn off German?" Alle asked in a wisecracking voice. Pino didn't want to engage him on this subject but couldn't think of a convenient way out.

"I have," he replied, "and remember, maestro said no German would be sung in his studio while Hitler is in power."

"*That* maestro is dead. I doubt very much that Alfredo shares his sentiments," Alle said in a sardonic tone of voice that made Pino nervous.

"Well," Pino retorted, "art is art regardless of politics. Right?"

"Whatever," answered Alle with a yawn.

Pino knew his remark was stupid and he was embarrassed for saying it, but just then the aria came to a close and the two boys sat up straight and discreetly tried to fix their appearances.

"Very good, my dear. That will be all for today," said Alfredo in the studio.

"*Grazie,* Maestro. *Ciao.*" Her speaking voice was nothing to write home about, certainly nothing compared to her singing voice, but none of that mattered, the most important words were about to be uttered, not by the girl, but by Alfredo.

"*Ciao,* Gia," he said clearly and distinctly, and Pino nearly fainted.

"Gia?" He said out loud. "No!" Then, to his great dismay, she walked out of the studio and right past him as he sat there with his mouth open wide like some primordial creature. She put on her coat and her eyes met Pino's. It was the girl whose name he couldn't remember from the funeral. She was the single most gorgeous thing he'd ever laid eyes on. She had big dark, wide-set eyes with enormous eyelashes and the alabaster skin of a Madonna with a sheen like December snow. Two big dimples dotted her chubby cheeks and she bit her lower lip.

She had just a hint of a twinkle in her eyes as she smiled a shy smile at him.

"*Ciao,* Pino," she said as she quickly turned up the collar of her coat and left the studio, music books in hand. Pino sat there dumbfounded, his jaw still hanging open in disbelief.

"Gia?" he muttered stupidly.

"Why do you keep saying that?" asked Alle. "She's here three times a week. You must have noticed?"

It was no use. Pino was in another world.

"I have, I mean...I know. She's actually my sister's friend."

"Uh huh, whatever you say," said Alle.

Alfredo's nasal voice brought the comedy to a close and Pino grabbed his book and entered the studio. He placed his book on the music stand and clothes-pinned back the pages.

"Anytime you're ready, Maestro Vaggi," snorted Alfredo. Pino nodded politely and cleared his throat.

"And what will we be working on today?" the maestro pleasantly inquired. Pino's devilish side suddenly took hold of him and he slammed his fist on the piano.

"Tannhäuser!" he shrieked.

Alfredo grabbed his heart in shock and Pino nearly fell over laughing. Alfredo failed to see the humor and so began another in a seemingly endless string of lessons working on material that Pino now knew as well as his daily prayers.

As he ran through his scales and then through Act One of Puccini's *Tosca*, Pino's mind was in Eastern Europe. He realized that somewhere a war was going on but he was listening to Dvorak and thinking about Gia.

Gia. How about that? Gia.

The lesson concluded and Pino packed his books. He passed Allesandro on his way out of the studio and nodded politely. He couldn't be bothered thinking about petty politics right now. Grabbing his coat off the rack he noticed something that gave him pause. A small pinkish-white scarf was hanging on the last hook. He drew closer to investigate. In the studio, Alle began to vocalize. Pino took the scarf down off the hook and examined it.

Could it be hers? he thought. *She did leave in quite a hurry.* It was a simple light wool scarf, not particularly special in any way, save the fact that Gia might be the owner. Who else could it belong to? Pino had seen Alle enter and he didn't remember him wearing a scarf. The color surely wasn't "manly" enough to belong to Alfredo. Then he pressed the wool to his face and he was overwhelmed by the delicate fragrance. Alfredo and Alle certainly didn't smell this good. It had to be hers, he concluded, and he relished the thought of returning it to her. He gently rolled the scarf up and tucked it away in his coat pocket. With a giddy heart, he skipped out the door and strolled home, all the way discreetly caressing the scarf in his pocket like it was a holy relic – which indeed it was.

CHAPTER NINE

EVERY GOOD BOY DESERVES FAVOR

ALFREDO GIANASSI STARED AT THE PICTURE of Maestro Ivaldi that hung in the waiting room of his studio. He wanted to take it down for a long time, but was afraid some of his students would get angry. Alfredo thought of himself as everything that the old maestro wasn't: intelligent, articulate, and above all, ambitious. Had the old bird had one ounce of ambition in his body he might have been one of the greats. Alfredo remembered watching him conduct an entire concert performance of *Norma* from memory. Another time, he could recall the maestro filling in for an ailing pianist on a recital tour of Chopin and Liszt. Without rehearsal, the maestro sat at the piano in the town hall theater and performed some of the most difficult music ever written for solo piano. He was blessed by God with a particular gift. Alfredo had never seen anything like it before. He himself possessed no such talent. Although an accomplished and somewhat celebrated musician himself, he had to toil for his art. Ninety percent perspiration, ten percent inspiration, he remembered someone once had said, and in his case it certainly applied.

He had overcome many obstacles in his life but none so challenging as the young man that stood before him in the waiting room. Pino had become Alfredo's obsession. He knew that this boy was no ordinary talent, but he was unsure how to harness it. The boy had too many of the old maestro's silly habits. Furthermore, he saw in Pino the embodiment of the maestro's philosophy that only after complete mastery of the art could one hope to achieve any kind of success.

Alfredo had no patience for such nonsense. Even at seventy percent of his capacity, Pino could have an enormously successful career. There was no need to beat dead horses; the boy was smart. He wouldn't develop bad habits. Those habits were the result of laziness, and that was one thing that Pino could never be accused of. But he was too damn cocky for his own good. Alfredo wanted Pino to begin his career soon, because he believed that at such a young age, the boy would need the counsel of a veteran of the industry. Alfredo was poised to play mentor, agent, whatever was necessary. Today would be the test and he had planned for every possibility.

The final note in the aria, *"Di quella pira"* from Verdi's *Il Trovatore* is not actually written in the score. Nonetheless, it had long been a tradition for Italian tenors to interpolate a high C at the end of the aria. In fact, it had become the standard, and anytime a tenor failed to attempt the note, he was almost certainly greeted by a collective groan of disapproval from the audience. As the final high C approached, Pino felt no trepidation. He had nailed all four earlier ones without incident and now he was rolling. As he hit the note and held it far longer than the half note called for in the score, Alfredo stopped playing and just listened. He stared at Pino without saying a word. A palpable tension was growing when suddenly, quite unexpectedly, he began to clap his hands. Confused, Pino just smiled and nodded.

"*Bravo. Bravo*, Pino, now you are ready. Go and sing," Alfredo muttered with a slight feeling of resignation.

"What?" Pino stammered.

"Go out and sing. There's nothing more I can teach you." Pino's jaw dropped in shock. These words, which he thought he might never hear, meant so much that he couldn't think straight. "You're a man now and you've got to behave like one as you embark on your career." Pino remembered his father using virtually the same words, but ironically, the circumstances could not have been more dissimilar. Suddenly, a voice could be heard in the distance calling Pino's name. Alfredo wheeled around as Pino's sister Maria burst into the studio like a wild animal. She dashed across the room and leapt into Pino's arms, knocking them both to the floor.

"What the hell are you doing?" Pino screamed.

"Pino! You've been accepted!" she cried and hugged her brother.

"What?" She pulled a letter out of her coat pocket.

"The conservatory, Pino! You've been accepted!"

"Would someone care to explain to me what's going on here?" asked Alfredo impatiently.

"The National Conservatory, Maestro! In Milan! Pino's been accepted." Maria cried. "When I saw the letter, I knew what it was and just had to open it. Please don't be mad."

Pino read the letter in complete shock.

"This is unbelievable! Unbelievable!"

Alfredo wasn't exactly thrilled at this new development. It really didn't fit into his master plan for Pino, but he couldn't burst the boy's balloon now, so he decided to play along.

"This is wonderful news!" exclaimed Alfredo.

Suddenly Pino stopped dead in his tracks and dropped the letter on the floor.

"Pino, what's wrong?" he asked. "First you can't contain yourself, now you look like your dog just died."

Dejected, Pino sat on the bench next to Alfredo.

"I only applied to prove to myself I was good enough," he said.

"So? Apparently someone else agrees!" cheered Alfredo.

"It doesn't matter who else agrees, we can't afford it."

"Can't afford what?"

"The National Conservatory, my family could never afford it." Alfredo saw his opportunity and seized it.

"But, Pino, the National Conservatory is public, not private. It's not very expensive at all."

Pino didn't look convinced.

"But when did you go to Milan to audition?" asked Alfredo.

"I didn't," said Pino. "Maestro Ivaldi wrote a note to the Director of the Conservatory on my behalf. They were friends from way way back. The Director said that Maestro Ivaldi's endorsement was worth more than any audition."

Alfredo was burning up.

"Well," he said. "I'm sure once they hear you sing, they will certainly give you a scholarship."

"How can you be so sure?" Pino asked.

It was then that Alfredo set his plan in motion.

"Pino, I'm very disappointed with you," he said shaking his head. "Maestro Ivaldi was not the only one with connections. I'm not without my own influence you know."

He winked and Pino's eyes lit up once again. Suddenly, Pino remembered what his father had said about Alfredo's political connections. Was it possible that Pino could use the Fascists to his own benefit? Releasing a scream of joy, Pino picked up his sister and whirled her around the room, nearly knocking Alfredo over.

"Whoa! Easy Pino, I'm an old man."

"Finally, I'll have my chance!" Pino cried out, "And Papa can't complain!"

"He'll find something to complain about anyway, but who cares!" cheered Maria.

"Wait a second," he said turning to Alfredo. "Maestro, why didn't you tell me before that you had connections at the National Conservatory?"

Alfredo anticipated and fielded the question like a master.

"Because you weren't ready yet. Now you are. You used to have to concentrate on hitting the notes. Now they come easily and you can concentrate on interpretation," he said placing a hand on the boy's shoulder, "But Pino, make no mistake, this is only a beginning. Now the real work starts!"

"I know, and I'm ready for it!" he said confidently. Then grabbing his sister by the hand, he ran out the door to begin his new life.

The first person Pino wanted to share his news with was Signore Fritz. It was a tad spiteful but he couldn't help himself.

As he approached the Café, he saw Paolo standing in the alleyway outside the kitchen entrance crouching down behind some crates of fruit and vegetables. Something about the scene made Pino uneasy, so he sent his sister home, saying he'd join her shortly. As he got closer, Paolo noticed him and motioned for him to keep silent. He drew up alongside the restaurant quietly and joined Paolo behind the crates.

"Something big is going on," whispered Paolo and he pointed in through the open kitchen door. Looking through the kitchen, Pino could see Signore Fritz having a heated discussion with someone, but he couldn't make out who it was.

"You can't do this to me! This is the first I've heard about this!" Fritz screamed and Pino's blood curdled. The other voice spoke so quietly and calmly that Pino had to struggle to hear his words.

"Signore, I'm afraid there is absolutely nothing I can do," the voice said.

Pino recognized the voice but couldn't seem to place it.

"A letter was sent to you on September 1st stating that by decree of *Il Duce*, as a Jew who had immigrated to Italy after January 1, 1919, you had exactly six months to leave the country, and you are hereby relieved of your Italian citizenship."

"I don't have Italian citizenship, you Fascist asshole!" Fritz erupted.

"Nonetheless," continued the other man, "you have until March 1st of 1939 to sell your belongings and leave the country."

"And what if I don't?" Fritz challenged. A silence fell over the restaurant. Pino could hear footsteps and he crouched down low.

"I trust I've made myself perfectly clear. Good day, Signore Fritz."

"Get the hell out of my restaurant, you bastard!" yelled Fritz. His scream was followed by a crash, which Pino guessed was the sound of a bottle being thrown. He glanced over at a flabbergasted Paolo. Slowly, they raised their heads to look over the crates and saw the front door to the restaurant fly open. Chief Magistrate Biaggi, accompanied by two officers, marched out.

Of course! Pino thought. That was the voice he'd recognized. Pino marveled at Signore Fritz' courage. Nobody dared speak to Chief Magistrate Biaggi that way. Unfortunately, all the bravado seemed pointless.

"Holy shit, Pino! Fritz is screwed!" Paolo ejaculated.

"Yeah, it sure sounds that way." Pino agreed.

"Since when did we start expelling Jews from Italy?" Paolo asked with a half-laugh.

"Beats me." Pino relied dryly, not seeing the humor.

Yet, it was true enough. In a devastating series of decrees in the summer and early fall of 1938, Mussolini in effect wiped out the citizenship of virtually all Italian Jews, and in doing so, ostensibly, took away all their rights. They could no longer attend school, or belong to a scientific or artistic organization. They could no longer marry an Italian or own land or even serve in the Italian military. It was particularly crushing news to the many German Jews that had found refuge in Italy from Nazi persecution.

Pino didn't know exactly what to make of this news. He had no love for Signore Fritz, although, he was fast developing a newfound respect for him after listening to the way he'd held his ground with Magistrate Biaggi. But there was something inherently wrong with what was happening. Much as he regretted it, this was something he simply couldn't avoid discussing with his father.

He considered the ironic timing; it seemed every time Pino got some shred of personal good news, he was greeted by an equal share of bad news from the world around him. It wasn't fair, he knew, but in light of what he'd just seen happen to Signore Fritz, he felt like he was getting off easy. A light-hearted thought came to him and he chuckled to himself. He realized it also meant that he'd just lost the only job he'd ever had! His life was about to change and although it was everything he had hoped for, he was more than a little nervous. Not merely because it was a big step and because of the turmoil going on around him but because he no longer had any excuses. If he didn't succeed now, he had no one to blame but himself.

CHAPTER TEN

QUESTIONS AND MORE QUESTIONS

THE NEWS OF PINO'S ACCEPTANCE to the National Conservatory swept through the town like the autumn wind through the valley. In no time at all, everyone was wishing him success and he was bursting with pride. On the home front, a cooler reaction was anticipated and received.

Pino's father was very proud but he couldn't seem to bring himself to show it. He was torn. He wanted to show his son he was proud of him but he also didn't want to send Pino what he considered the wrong signal. They'd discussed the matter and he had said no. He didn't want to reward his son for so blatantly disobeying him. So he decided, to the extent possible, to remain indifferent to the news.

Over dinner that first night, Pino didn't push his luck, keeping remarkably calm about everything that had transpired. He did, however, feel a burning desire to speak to his father about Signore Fritz. He chose to wait until dessert and even then opened the subject with the utmost care.

"Papa, something strange happened on my way home from my lesson. I stopped off at work on the way and Signore Fritz was arguing with Chief Magistrate Biaggi."

His father began laughing to himself. "A match made in heaven, an atheist and a Jew."

"Papa, did you know that Italy is deporting all the Jews?"

"Good riddance."

Pino was aghast. He was done. He'd spent what he considered a lifetime making excuses for his father's behavior but this was something he couldn't rationalize. He looked at his mother who simply sighed and shook her head. She was tired and there was just no use in arguing. Despite the best of intentions, their arguments invariably ended in screaming and slammed doors followed by long bouts of silence. It appeared she was done fighting, and for the time being, so was Pino.

The following Saturday was gorgeous. Brilliant sunshine lit up the mountainside and flooded the valley. The streets of the town were brimming with pedestrians for the first time in weeks. The winter had been a particularly nasty one and even a hint of a thaw was gratefully welcomed. Even though it was still quite brisk out, the golden sunlight created the illusion of warmth and the majority of Collagnians were eager absorb their share of it.

That afternoon, Pino went to confession for the first time in as long as he could remember. He was bursting with questions about Signore Fritz which he now couldn't see the point in discussing with his father. In the past, Maestro Ivaldi would have been his natural sounding board for such questions; another reminder of the great void his death left in Pino's life. So, with nowhere else to turn, Pino decided to talk to Father Michele.

After the usual formalities of the confessional, Pino got down to the real reason for his coming, explaining what had happened to Signore Fritz, his father's subsequent reaction, and Pino's own anger and disgust with his father.

It didn't take long for the priest to realize who he was listening to behind the curtain. The theme of their conversation spoiled Father Michele's mood and soured his stomach. Suddenly that third glass of wine with lunch and the second espresso after it seemed particularly ill-advised and he'd wished he'd taken his own often-given advice on moderation.

"My, my, my! My son, you've got a lot of issues here, difficult ones; issues that don't have simple answers. First, let me say that the church has always frowned upon the persecution of anyone regardless of their religion. I don't know the exact details of what happened to Signore Fritz but if it is unjust, the people doing this to him will have to stand before God one day and bear the brunt of His anger for it."

The thought pleased Pino, but then the priest made a left turn into territory which the boy didn't expect.

"Most religions speak in the same way on this subject, my son. There is even an old Jewish proverb that says: there is no justice unless mercy is part of it. And the Muslims say: whoever is kind to his creatures, God is kind to him. What I'm trying to say is that it is really not a religious issue at all, although some may use religion as a pretext."

Pino had never met a Muslim and Signore Fritz was the only Jew he'd ever known but he thought he understood what the priest was getting at.

"Remember, our Lord Jesus Christ said: 'I give you a new commandment, that you love one another even as I have loved you.' He didn't say love just the Catholics! Everyone is your neighbor, my son."

The words struck a resonant chord with Pino.

"Let me add one thing only about your Papa. He is not a bad man, and you should always respect him. Remember the fifth commandment: 'Honor thy father and thy mother.' It's perfectly natural for young people to go through a period of resentment of their parents. It's important not to fan the flames and make the fires greater than they need to be. I can't condone what your Papa said, but I suspect he may have some unresolved issues that may color his judgment in certain cases. Everyone does once in a while. That doesn't mean he doesn't love you. Not everyone shows their love in the same way. Everyone is gifted in different ways. Not everyone can be a great opera singer, you know."

Pino smiled. Listening to the priest speak made him feel better. *Maybe he should come to confession more often,* he thought. Although, he didn't really answer any of Pino's questions, Father Michele did provide some good sound advice in a broad sense. Feeling more comfortable, Pino continued his questions.

"Father, why are we at war in Spain?"

"Ah! God only knows!"

That was the best answer yet, but, still feeling a little unsatisfied with the interview overall, Pino decided it was time to do his penance. Father Michele was infinitely more diplomatic than his father but ultimately his answers provided little to ease Pino's troubled conscience. Pino always felt better leaving the church than entering but this time he felt particularly fresh as he stepped into the sunlight and breathed in the cool mountain air.

Old Signore DeLuca wouldn't be breathing the same air today, he thought. And Signore Fritz had less than a month to breathe his last breath of crisp clean Apennine mountain air.

Italy had been a fair model of tolerance in the early part of the twentieth century, so to many Italians, Mussolini's inconsistent behavior on the issue of anti-Semitism was confusing and troubling. The *Duce* went to great lengths to detail the differences between the Fascist and the Nazi purviews on the subject, stating "Fascism is a regime which has its roots in the great cultural traditions of the Italian people. National Socialism (Nazism) on the other hand is savage barbarity." Yet despite his eloquence on the subject it became increasingly difficult to see the differences in the two philosophies in terms of their application.

This was particularly troubling to the King, who simply couldn't stomach what he perceived as Mussolini's consistent kowtowing to the whims of Hitler. The Pope went a step further, publicly condemning the anti-Semitic policy of the government, stressing the folly of following the lead of such a regime as Germany. In spite of the opposition of the public, the Church and the King, Mussolini continued his anti-Semitic agenda and further distanced himself from the goodwill of the people he governed.

The day that Herman Fritz left Collagna was a sad one. He'd made few friends during his tenure in the town, but still a small crowd had gathered to see him off. To Pino, he looked like Canio in *I Pagliacci*, carting all his earthly belongings to the train station. The crowd was polite but Pino wondered just how many present were well-wishers and how many came simply out of morbid curiosity. Unwilling to satisfy them, Fritz defiantly wouldn't reveal his destination.

Pino approached and shook his former boss's hand without a word.

"Keep practicing, kid. You'll get there," Signore Fritz said with a wink before grabbing his bags and climbing the stairs to the platform. The remark made Pino smile. As he glanced around at his neighbors, Pino noted with some sadness that none of his family was in attendance.

CHAPTER ELEVEN

GIA

L IKE MOST ALPINE TOWNS, Collagna was incredibly cold in the winter, and stunningly beautiful, fair and picturesque in the summer. When Fabio and Angelina Mastrangelo first visited the town, it was late spring, and the flowers were simply breathtaking. They had heard of the area from a friend who was an avid skier. Although they weren't really the outdoor type, they thought that a week hiking in the mountains might be romantic. They were not disappointed. In fact, they made a pact to return each year at that same time.

After three years of spring vacations in Collagna, they decided to make the town their permanent home. They bought a small house at the edge of town not far from the ski trails. Fabio was a tailor by trade, but Collagna already had a tailor and demand was not sufficient to warrant another. Nonetheless he opened his tailor shop and quickly lost his shirt. It was Angelina that had the idea to make and sell clothes from their shop rather than provide the standard alterations and repairs like the other town tailor. They quickly developed a moderately successful business. A year later, Gia was born.

At birth, Gia had exceptionally big, wide-set eyes that gave many the impression that she suffered some kind of birth defect. In her early teens, her eyes looked far too big for her head and she was subjected to the ridicule of her classmates. Her one true and constant friend through it all was Maria Vaggi. Maria had always thought Gia quite beautiful in an exotic way. Her support helped Gia through virtually every pubescent crisis. Their friendship for life was sealed early on and for years they were inseparable, despite the extreme differences in their respective personalities. Maria was always alive, aware and bubbling with life. Gia was just the opposite: shy, retiring and extremely self-conscious, especially about her eyes.

However, as she grew, her big dark eyes became her most striking physical aspect. In fact, the ugly duckling had become a swan in virtually every way. So much so, that by the time she was sixteen, she was regularly compared to Greta Garbo in *Camille*. Consequently, and not so surprisingly, it became her favorite movie.

It was *Camille* that inadvertently started Gia on a musical career; more accurately, it changed her musical direction. She had been taking piano and violin lessons since childhood and was considering a career in music when she first saw the movie. Her parents were not thrilled with Gia's obsession with the film, its subject matter being a Parisian courtesan's affair with the son of a well-to-do society member, and her subsequent death from consumption. But the legendary Greta Garbo and the dashing Robert Taylor made the film so much more than that to Gia; it represented the triumph of love over all obstacles, despite the film's tear-jerking ending. Collagna had only one cinema and films generally stayed for several weeks; this fact afforded Gia the opportunity to see the film nearly ten times, sneaking in with Maria, over and over.

One afternoon while waiting for Pino to finish a lesson, Maria overheard Maestro Ivaldi joking about Gia's obsession with the film. During that lesson, the maestro informed Pino that Verdi's *La Traviata* was actually based on the same novel as *Camille*. This meant nothing to Maria but she shared this tidbit of information with Gia, who that same day, set off to the library to find a copy of the score to *Traviata*. She was awestruck; here was *Camille*, but set to music! Not by just anyone, by Verdi! She read the score voraciously and couldn't believe her eyes. Although he'd changed Camille's name to Violetta, otherwise the story was virtually the same. Yet, despite the similarities, the operatic setting made the story seem more epic in scope, grander in vision and more touching than she could ever have imagined. Here was a glorious masterpiece unlike anything she had ever known before. It was at that moment that Gia Mastrangelo gave up the violin and the piano forever, and began her career as an opera singer. She simply had to perform this music and this role. It was made for her, and she for it. She was already an exceptional musician and she sang in the church choir. How difficult could it be?

Pino and Gia's inevitable courtship was anything but traditional. He was travelling back and forth on the train to the Conservatory in Milan every week and Gia remained in Collagna, continuing her lessons. Week after week, Pino would return to Collagna and ask Maria about Gia: "Will you be seeing her? Is she coming over? Did she ask about me?" Meanwhile, on the home front, Gia would ask Maria virtually the same questions! Maria had to maintain a careful balance. At first, she found it amusing, and strangely empowering. She loved to tease her brother and watch him sigh, so desperately in love with Gia. It wasn't like Maria to be cruel, but this opportunity was, she figured, once in a lifetime. One day, they would all laugh about the comedy that played out before her, but for the time being she had to be careful to steer the two young lovers toward their eventual marital bliss. Without her, she was certain, they would mess things up. It was the least she could do for the two people she loved most and whom she desperately wanted to see together.

Pino's schedule prevented them from having a normal courtship. Bad timing coupled with Gia's shyness and Pino's relative inexperience provided the relationship with a comical series of misadventures masquerading as "dates."

Despite the runaway success Pino was enjoying in Milan, more often than not, his thoughts were in Collagna with Gia. He dutifully took the train home each Friday morning and spent the weekends with his family and pursuing his new "girlfriend." He would rush home just to be with her and then when they actually saw each other, he was terrified and acted awkwardly aloof.

Why she had any interest in him, he thought, was difficult to fathom. But this was one gift horse he wouldn't be looking in the mouth. For weeks on end, Pino would hang around Alfredo's studio hoping just to see her pass by and to casually say hello. He knew that she liked him, Maria assured him of this, but he still couldn't seem to get his courage up to actually speak to her. His dreams each night consisted exclusively of her; her singing, her hair, her eyes, her lips. In his mind they'd already become lovers but they still remained virtual strangers in reality.

Although the facts seemed to speak for themselves, it wasn't until Pino's senior recital (for which he asked her to be his date) that Gia actually acknowledged that they were even "seeing" each other.

However, in spite of what Maria called "their own best efforts to screw things up," it was blatantly obvious to even the casual observer that they were very much in love, and it was just a matter of time before they would be together.

CHAPTER TWELVE

School Days

P INO'S DAYS AT THE NATIONAL CONSERVATORY were marked with success after success. The faculty and his classmates alike began to recognize that a particularly exceptional talent was in their midst. Serious discussions were taking place about how long they would wait before setting up major auditions for him. Pino wasn't at the conservatory more than a few months before the Directors had privately decided that he was already sufficiently advanced to work. His knowledge of the repertory rivaled their own and his near perfect vocal production was something to marvel at. In their collective minds, it was just a question of how much more professional polish he required.

For Pino, the classes he took were considerably easier than he'd expected them to be. His training was far more advanced than that of his colleagues. In fact, he often felt that he could probably teach most of the classes himself! Thus, each evening during his daily prayers, he said a special one specifically for his patron saint Maestro Ivaldi, whom he had to thank for any and all of his current or future success.

Pino's voice was developing a beautiful honey-hued tone and a balance throughout the register that would have been the envy of any tenor short of Gigli. In addition, his technical mastery was rapidly becoming the stuff of legend throughout the school. There was more than a little talk of "the mountain boy with the natural gift," or "the God-given gift" or "the born tenor," and frankly Pino did little to dispel them.

He was always a bit perturbed by the fact that it was impossible for them to accept or believe that anyone from so remote a location without "proper" musical instruction could possibly have "developed" the skills that he possessed. It was easier for them to believe in divine intervention; that he was some sort of freak of nature. It irked him, but he let it go. He was confident that he'd have the last laugh when he was singing at La Scala.

His trips home to Collagna were long and tiring, but they provided balance for him.

Mama Vaggi began to notice a pattern in her son's behavior. Every Friday, upon his arrival, he'd practically knock the door down. Then gradually, as the weekend progressed, he'd get more and more melancholy and sit around the house like a love-sick puppy. She found it hilarious, but knew better than to say anything that might hurt him, *sensitive artist that he was.*

It became apparent that music was no longer the only thing in Pino's life and his mother found ample evidence to support this among his school books while cleaning one evening. She consistently tried to get Pino not to dump his books on the kitchen table when he came home, but he was hopeless. Gathering the books together to bring them up to his room, she noticed a letter with a fancy seal on it. It was already open so she felt little guilt in examining its contents. She read the letter in astonishment. It was from the opera house in Bergamo. Pino had been extended an offer to sing there in the upcoming season!

She put the letter down and sank into a chair. Pino was offered a job as an opera singer – a paying job! But there was more! In the same envelope, she found another letter from an opera company in Pesaro. It too contained an offer! She felt dizzy. It was too much for her to process and she began to cry. The tears were partly for her baby, now a man, of whom she was immeasurably proud, and partly for her husband, whom, she reasoned, could now give himself leave to be proud of his son.

How could Pino possibly not say anything about this? She puzzled over the question for a second then decided not to push the matter further. He'd make the information public in his own way, in his own good time. Containing herself, however, would be another matter altogether!

To his mother's great consternation, Pino chose to keep mum on the subject throughout the entire weekend. When time came for him to head for the train station Sunday night, he gave his mother a perfunctory kiss on the cheek and departed without saying a word about the job offers. He simply sighed and smiled sadly at his sister, who tried her best not to laugh at her love-sick brother. Their mother watched the interplay between her children and thought with a laugh, *is it possible that he's that far gone?* She would be having a conversation with Maria the moment Pino left, to get to the bottom of this. As the door closed behind her son, Mrs. Vaggi wanted to scream. This was what he'd been waiting for his entire life and now he acted as if it meant nothing at all.

Pino had always acted as if girls meant nothing to him whatsoever. Initially, his mother found it amusing but as he got older, she had to admit, it did trouble her a bit. It wasn't natural for one so young to be so career-oriented. He never really showed any evidence that he was going through puberty at all. More than once the thought had crossed her mind that perhaps, he *just didn't like girls.* She couldn't bring herself to think anything further on the subject; it was too troubling to her. She liked to think of herself as open-minded but when it came to matters of her *own* family things were different.

It prompted her own visit to Father Michele to seek out his counsel. The meeting was meaningless because she became nervous and never got around to discussing Pino at all. The fact that her son had already chosen a harsh and unforgiving career path was difficult enough. That road would be made all the more difficult if he were… if he…if he *didn't like girls*.

The revelation of this mystery girl in Pino's life provided his mother with more than a modest measure of relief. The fact that anyone could divert his attention from his singing so completely had been unthinkable only a few weeks earlier. One thing was certain: whoever this mystery girl was, she had clearly woven a spell over her little tenor.

CHAPTER THIRTEEN

TIMING IS EVERYTHING

FOR THE FIRST TIME IN HIS LIFE, Pino could say he was truly happy. He was in love with life and the future finally seemed promising. All of his hard work was beginning to pay off. As Pino's joyful world view focused exclusively on his singing and his first girlfriend, the world around him was undergoing a great tectonic shift.

On February 12, 1939, Pope Pius XI was planning to address the world in a radio broadcast to call for a world-wide disarmament conference. It would have been an exceedingly daring gambit on the part of the pontiff to thrust the church right in to the wheels of the oncoming Axis machine. But on February 10th, just two days shy of the historic occasion, something altogether unexpected happened: he died. And his historic encyclical died with him.

There were celebrations nationwide in March as Maria Giuseppe Giovanni Eugenio Pacelli was coronated the new Pope Pius XII. More good news arrived only days later as word reached home that the Spanish Civil War had ended and the troops would be returning. The nation, weary from wars in Africa and Spain, and in the throes of economic despair, was in desperate need of some good news, and this provided a glimmer of hope.

Mussolini was riding a wave of popularity for having been the catalyst in brokering the "peace" between Germany, France and England. His principle goal of resurrecting Italy's respect abroad and thereby ensuring a key role in all international negotiations was achieved. He was publicly critical of Hitler's aggression and was repeatedly quoted as having no desire or predilection toward supporting him in any further hostile activity. This resonated well with his tired and intrinsically pacifist nation but unfortunately, his overwhelming lust for power mixed poorly with his multitude of weaknesses; vanity, egoism and above all else petty jealousy - and a jealous heart neither hears nor heeds the voice of reason.

Not content to stand on the sidelines while Hitler won victory after victory, Mussolini was determined to grab his own share of military glory. He detested the role of peacemaker, despite the fact that it had brought him a measure of international regard, and sought to redress that image with a more warlike one. While his efforts in Africa earned him some modest acclaim, his half-assed support of Franco mired his military reputation in a deep morass.

Mussolini soon showed the world how he planned to redeem his military standing. In a case of inconceivably poor planning, and bad timing of *biblical* proportions, the *Duce* chose the holiest day on the Christian calendar, Good Friday, April 7th, for Italy's invasion of Albania. Once again he found himself at loggerheads with the Pope, the King and the vast majority of Italian citizens. Timing was everything. The Pope was on the job less than a month when all this transpired. The King and the monarchy overall had lost a bit of its moral-high ground through its support of the Fascist campaign in Ethiopia. And the public was weary from back to back wars that they neither wanted nor understood. The anticipated outrage never really materialized.

Unfortunately, the Albanian invasion did little more than underscore the ineptitude of the Italian military. Poorly trained troops, indecisive command, general confusion in the ranks and sadly antiquated equipment combined to make a battle out of what should have been a simple exercise. Hitler was discouraged by what he saw and advised Mussolini against any further unilateral actions. Although they eventually achieved their goal, the action was an embarrassment, and the spirits of the nation sank once more.

It often took weeks for news to reach the Apennines, so the arrival of spring was unencumbered by stories of failed Albanian invasions. Still anxiety was running high in Collagna. Signore De Luca's arrest and imprisonment was not discussed in public but was clearly on the minds of all. His transfer from the local precinct jail to the regional prison did not bode well and nothing could buoy the spirits of his family.

Pino was having a political crisis of his own. One morning, Papa Vaggi was running late for work and in his haste, forgot his newspaper. While finishing his own breakfast, Pino glanced at his father's newspaper and came across an article about his favorite tenor, Beniamino Gigli. Instinctively, he reached for a pair of scissors to clip out the article to add to his scrapbook, but as he began cutting the article out, he noticed the accompanying photo. It showed the great maestro at a pro-Fascist rally in Milan. Pino put the scissors down and began to read the article. At first he could not believe his eyes, but soon it became clear: Gigli was a Fascist.

How could this be? For some strange reason, based on no empirical data whatsoever, Pino imagined that only policemen, politicians and bankers were Fascists, not artists! The article became more troubling the more he read. It seemed that Gigli was not merely an outspoken fan of Mussolini, he was a full-fledged proponent of Fascist doctrine and fanatical supporter of the regime.

It was a crushing blow to Pino, who had come to idolize the great tenor. He didn't know what to make of this discovery. Here is a man, thought Pino, in an unassailable position, given his stature in the music world, and yet…

Could a great artist such as Gigli share the hateful ideology of the Duce? Seeking some sort of solace or at least a stable area of philosophical "middle ground" Pino tried to think who else he knew to be Fascist. The only people he could think of were Chief Magistrate Biaggi and Alfredo. While he, personally, didn't care for either of the two, he had a hard time believing they were really evil men, although he knew his Papa might not share that opinion. With a troubled heart, he headed for Alfredo's studio to see if the maestro could fit him in for an impromptu coaching session. He really had no interest in a coaching but he did want to ease his curiosity, and thought a heart to heart with Alfredo might in some way prove helpful.

"Ritorna Vincitor!" rang from Alfredo's lips, seeing Pino in his vestibule. "The Great Maestro Vaggi has chosen to grace us with his presence. To what do I owe this great honor?"

Pino laughed and hugged Alfredo. It was not the way that he usually greeted his teacher but for some reason at that moment he was feeling a bit nostalgic for the old studio, and even for Alfredo.

"I was hoping you could fit me in for a coaching sometime this weekend." Pino said hopefully.

"Hmmm, let me see," said Alfredo shaking his head and scratching his chin. "Don't be silly, of course I can fit you in. Drop by any time after three tomorrow and we'll see what those big city teachers have done to your voice. And hopefully, just hopefully, we can straighten it out."

Pino suddenly regretted the idea, but it was too late now. He saw that Alfredo was looking very tired and drawn and he wondered if the maestro was sick.

"So, Pino. Tell me, how do you like Milano?"

Pino saw his opening.

"It's so, so big. It's a little overwhelming. And the people there are very different. They pay a great deal more attention to fashion and politics than we do here." Knowing that Alfredo was both a fastidious dresser and a Fascist, Pino hoped the remark would hit him in a soft spot, while still appearing to open the subject in a casual way. It did.

"Ah, Pino," said Alfredo happily, "finally you are having your little eyes opened to the ways of the world! You are beginning to understand that your little town is not the center of the universe and the way people here walk, talk, and think are not the only ways. This is good! I've never felt truly at home up here in the mountains, with folks that spend their days arguing over the price of a pound of pork." Alfredo totally failed to grasp that the remark might be offensive to the son of a butcher and carried on musing. "Trivial, Pino, it's all so trivial. Nothing here ever changes, for generations it's been the same. This is no place for artists like you and I. An artist needs to be constantly challenged. To do that, he must be around other artists. To do that, he needs to be in the city." Alfredo closed his eyes dreamily. Pino thought this a good time to gently nudge the conversation.

"I saw in the paper that Gigli did a concert in Milano last night," said Pino.

"He did indeed!" trumpeted Alfredo, "for the *Duce*. He is the *Duce*'s favorite tenor, you know. I believe Toti Del Monti and Tito Schipa were there as well."

Del Monte and Schipa were Fascists too! Jesus, who else? thought Pino. Alfredo, as if reading his mind, continued.

"And if I am not mistaken, the great Pietro Mascagni also."

No! thought Pino. *How could the composer of "Cavalleria Rusticana" be Fascist?*

"Ah, what I wouldn't have given to be there at their side. One day soon, the Party will make this a great country again. You'll see."

Pino decided the time had come to roll the dice.

"Alfredo, tell me something. I thought the Fascists were all about violence and force. How can an artist support that kind of thinking?"

Alfredo came out of his dreamlike state and looked squarely into Pino's eyes.

"Who told you that nonsense, Maestro Ivaldi?"

Pino froze, sorry he had brought up the subject.

"Well, yes. He did say it. But I've heard it from other people too," he said, not mentioning that the "other people" of whom he spoke were his parents.

"I'll bet you haven't heard that kind of talk in Milano, have you?" Pino honestly couldn't say he had, or at least he hadn't noticed. "I thought not. No, Pino, that kind of small-minded thinking is reserved for the small-minded people that populate our small towns. It's beyond them to understand greatness, great art, great ideas, great civilizations. It's not their fault, mind you; it's simply not within their grasp."

Pino suddenly remembered precisely why he so disliked Alfredo.

"But Pino, luckily for you, you've managed to rise above it. Collagna won't be your home much longer. You'll see the way things really are and you'll move on."

Pino walked home slowly, past the church, De Luca's bar and his father's shop. He didn't stop in to say hello; he had too much on his mind. *Alfredo really is an ugly, angry, hateful man,* he thought. Yet, so many truly great artists were Fascists just like him. *Was it possible that people capable of creating such beauty were equally capable of being despicable human beings?* It made no sense, but it was a possibility he'd have to consider. Then he remembered how he felt when he heard Alfredo's political connections might be able to help him in his own career aspirations. He didn't think of himself as a bad person, he just figured he'd use Alfredo's connections to further his own interests, then toss them aside. No harm done. Or was there? Perhaps these artists were simply doing the same thing but on a greater scale. Maybe they *had* to support the government for one reason or another. Maybe they were being coerced into doing it! He wasn't doing a very good job convincing himself, but on a certain level he needed to believe it. He'd hang on to that slim hope for the time being, but just the same, tomorrow he'd start shopping for a new hero.

CHAPTER FOURTEEN

THE STAIRCASE

WHY WAS IT CALLED 'THE STAIRCASE?' Pino had wondered about the name since he first visited the theater as a child. He remembered, with irony, the seemingly endless stairs his family had to climb to reach the gallery. Yet the name hardly seemed appropriate for such a venerated hall. He learned the reason for the odd title was that the opera house was built upon the ruins of a medieval church: Santa Maria della Scala.

Each time Pino visited La Scala, he made a point of stopping to look at the mammoth statue of Leonardo da Vinci that stood at the center of Piazza Scala, and wondered why there wasn't a statue of Giuseppe Verdi in the *piazza*. Da Vinci wasn't a composer. What did he have to do with opera? Pino thought the statue of da Vinci would be better suited for the *piazza* a few blocks away in front of the church that housed his celebrated "Last Supper." But then again, no one asked him.

Since his arrival at the conservatory, Pino tried repeatedly to see the famous *al fresco* painting but had no luck. Each time he visited the church of Santa Maria Della Croce, upon whose wall "The Last Supper" was painted, it was closed for restoration. This went on for weeks and months and eventually Pino began to believe the painting wasn't really there at all! He imagined that it was probably moved into storage for safe-keeping in case of war or perhaps someone had accidentally damaged the priceless treasure and the church was trying to cover it up. He was full of conspiracy theories.

The day of Pino's La Scala audition came much more quickly than he had expected. He still had virtually no performance resume. Aside from several small productions at the conservatory, Pino's performance history was limited only to recitals. When his professor recommended him, based on his successful regional auditions, he was shocked; shocked and ecstatic. He realized that this was only a first audition and that most singers had to audition many times before they ever got a contract, but he wasn't worried. He had complete faith in his ability and firmly believed that none of the singers he'd heard on stage in the past year were any better than him.

Although the auditions were closed to the public, frequently singers' friends and family managed to sneak into the audition hall. Pino wanted no such audience. He knew he would be nervous enough without that added pressure. He didn't tell his parents or even Gia. The only person he told was Maria, and that was only because he thought he would bust if he didn't tell someone.

The fateful day arrived without any fanfare. Pino got up, washed and dressed, like he always did. Considering that this was the single biggest audition of his life thus far, he felt surprisingly little apprehension. This made him especially confident as he wandered down the street toward the conservatory. His day would be very much like every other day. Since his audition wasn't until four thirty in the afternoon, he'd have to sit through a class on music theory (today's subject being counterpoint) a vocal interpretation class (which would serve as a good warm up) and finally a keyboard class (which offered him the opportunity to clear his mind and concentrate on something other than the impending audition). As he ambled down the street, he thought that, all in all, he couldn't have asked for a more well-laid-out day. Things were all falling into place.

The day went without incident. Music theory was dead boring, interpretation proved an excellent warm-up, and keyboard was a pleasant diversion. Exercises in the Dorian mode, one of Pino's favorites, relaxed him and made him slightly contemplative. When class let out Pino headed for the recital hall. He pronounced himself in perfect body and mind for the upcoming date with destiny.

He arrived at the recital hall at four sharp and to his profound surprise, he found himself totally alone. He looked around the room, perplexed. He checked his watch and pulled out his letter of confirmation with the time and date on it. Everything seemed to be in order except for the fact that no one was there! He began to get nervous. *Could there be a mistake? Could he be the only one scheduled today and the judges were late?* It wouldn't have been the first time that happened. *But what about the accompanist? Where was he?* And it was awfully dark and cold. No. No. No. Something was definitely wrong, but what could he do except wait?

He heard a noise on stage and ran down the aisle to the apron of the stage to see who it was. The noise continued: a rattling, clanking sound. He climbed onto the stage to look around.

"Hello! Is anybody here?" he called out. A curtain on the left side of the stage pulled back and a janitor with a bucket and a mop appeared. "Sir, what happened to the auditions scheduled here for this afternoon?"

The janitor coughed and cleared his throat before speaking.

"A pipe busted. Water everywhere," he said. "Auditions have been moved to the opera house for today."

"What? Oh, no!" Pino exclaimed. He was frozen. Was there time? He'd have to run for it. With that, he dashed out the door like a gazelle. His heart and head pounded as he ran. The opera house was only a block away but he couldn't afford to walk.

When he arrived at the stage entrance, there was a large handmade sign saying, "Auditions this way". He burst through the stage door and looked for the sign-in table which he found with no trouble, but there were only two singers to go before him, ten minutes at best to catch his breath, compose himself and warm up. He headed backstage and tried to relax, but the backstage area was a madhouse! There must have been a dozen singers, all warming up, vocalizing at the same time. Pino was suddenly terrified. He couldn't stop perspiring and couldn't catch his breath. Everything was going wrong! He gratefully accepted a cup of hot tea but it did nothing to calm him.

He sat on the floor in the bathroom and tried to compose himself. How could this have happened? After all his careful planning, everything that could go wrong, did go wrong. He tried to focus. He was here to sing, and sing he would. Everything else was immaterial. He got up and washed his face with cold water and took a deep breath.

I'm as good as any of these singers, he told himself in the mirror. *No, I'm not. I'm better than them. I'm going to go out there and make you cry. I'm going to sing like a god. I am going to move you like you've never been moved. When I'm done, you will never forget me.*

He wasn't sure where the words were coming from, or if he believed them, but he spoke them like a mantra. He felt goose bumps all over his body, not a chill but a feeling of warmth that enveloped him like a blanket. The maestro was with him. He could feel it.

"Today I will make you proud, Maestro." With that thought, he went backstage and joined the others waiting for their chance at greatness. The singers were being called to audition in alphabetical order. Thus, Pino Vaggi was assured of being one of the very last singers to be heard. He knew that meant the judges would be tired, restless and probably hungry. *Why shouldn't they be? He was!* They had probably sat through dozens of big, heavy, dramatic arias, each designed to wring the last imaginable drop of emotion out of them. How could the judges not be numb after hearing one after another of those apocalyptic odes? And wasn't he about to perform yet another of them? The thought stopped him cold. Suddenly, he wasn't so confident about his selection. His hands got cold. He planned to sing *"Lamento di Frederico,"* by Cilea. It was what the Maestro had suggested and Pino was especially comfortable with it, but it was another dirge-like, heart-wrenching number. Could he possibly hope to make an impression on the judges with such a piece?

There were just two singers left backstage and Pino was the more nervous of the two. A singer was on-stage doing a dreadful rendition of "*E lucevan le stelle*" from *Tosca*. The sound coming from his mouth was tight, dry and forced. It made Pino much more confident. At least, he knew, he would sound better than this poor soul. Pino smiled to himself at the thought, but then he caught himself.

What am I thinking? At least I won't be the worst? *That's not why I'm here.*

He got up from his chair and walked over to the table where he'd left his music bag. The singer inside finished and Pino stopped to listen to the polite applause.

"Marco Tomasini," called a voice from within the theater, and the last singer backstage with Pino stood up, cleared his throat and headed for the stage.

"*In bocca lupo*," Pino said, wishing him luck.

"*Crepi lupo,*" the singer acknowledged.

Pino was gathering his sheet music together when he heard the words that changed his entire career.

"And what will you be singing, Mister Tomasini?"

"*Lamento di Federico*, by Cilea."

Pino's heart stopped. "What!" he cried. He dashed to the side of the stage to see his worst nightmare coming true. As he did, the entire contents of his bag poured out onto the floor.

This can't be happening! he thought. *He couldn't possibly sing the same aria!* He fell to the floor in dismay. Gathering his wits, he madly searched for something that might provide his salvation.

"Maestro, what do I do?" Pino cried out, completely oblivious to the crowd forming around him. He listened to the singer performing *his* piece and gnashed his teeth. Although this singer was far more polished than the last, this audition piece was sure to put the judges to sleep. Just then Pino stopped, and a candle of thought was lit. A plan was rapidly forming in his head and this singer had put the final piece in the puzzle for him. Pino was about to make the riskiest move of his entire career. He had been preparing for this audition for weeks and had worked extensively honing and polishing his interpretation of "*Lamento di Federico*," but he would not be singing it! Something in his brain told him he had to throw caution to the wind and take a chance. He would perform a different aria, one that he hadn't sung in months! One so radically different from anything the judges had heard all day that they would have to sit up and take notice! He was sure it would work.

The singer was nearing the end of the aria when Pino found the sheet music he was looking for: *"Ah, mes amis,"* from Donizetti's *La Fille du Regiment*. The aria was a killer. A career-ender, with a staggering nine high Cs! Yet it was bright and upbeat and Pino just knew he could deliver it with more style than anything he had heard yet.

"Pino Vaggi," a voice called out from the auditorium. He hadn't even noticed the other singer had finished. Pino took a deep breath and strode out on-stage. He was remarkably calm, he thought, and even smiled as he handed the music to the accompanist and nodded politely to the judges. He was pure electricity.

"And what will we be hearing this afternoon?"

"'Ah, mes amis' from *La Fille du Regiment* by Donizetti," Pino proudly declared.

The judges nodded to him to proceed. He cleared his throat and nodded to his accompanist.

The aria, justly famous or infamous, for making or breaking careers, was a welcome change of pace for the judges, and Pino could sense it immediately.

"Ah, mes amis, quel jour de fete!" But it was more than simply a change of tempo; it was a change of mood. It was joyful.

"Je vais marcher sous vos drapeaux." The aria tells the story of a poor country bumpkin going off to join the army to impress the girl he loves. As he sang, Pino sensed the same affinity for the material that he felt for the Cilea piece. It was just as the Maestro said.

"L'amour qui m'a tourne la tete," And the high Cs poured out of Pino like melted butter, liquid and creamy. He was practically dancing as he sang. He was rapturous.

"Desormais, desormais, me rend un heros!"

He had done it! He was sure. And as he nailed the final high C, he held it until the entire audience began to cheer! Up until that moment he was unaware there even was an audience! The judges, mildly annoyed by the audience reaction, couldn't help but applaud themselves, realizing they'd witnessed something truly special.

Pino was shaking with excitement and tears began flowing freely down his cheeks. He bowed as deeply and gracefully as his nerves permitted. As he stood up and turned to leave the stage, he noticed someone jumping up and down in the rear of the hall. He laughed to himself, before realizing it was none other than his sister Maria! To his astonishment, standing next to her was Gia! If that was too much to believe, then the sight of his mother and father applauding sent him over the edge. It was a sight he'd come to believe would never happen. He regained his composure, bowed again and quickly headed for the wings. Before he could reach them, his eyes met Gia's and she blew him a kiss. He froze for a moment, then got hold of himself and blew a kiss back. Maria playfully punched Gia in the arm as she gushed.

As he reached the wings and heard the congratulations of his colleagues, all he could think of was his sister; she must have set this whole thing up. He picked up his music, which by now was everywhere on the floor, and laughed out loud. It was completely inconceivable to him that his father was a party to so covert an action. Not that his father couldn't keep a secret, but rather that he simply did not possess a single spontaneous bone in his body.

Later that evening, Pino's father insisted on taking them all out to a fine dinner. For the second time in his life, Pino felt like a man in the company of his father. Sitting at the head of the table and controlling the conversation was as thrilling for him as the audition. He was feeling almost giddy when his father asked for quiet.

"A toast," he said, dramatically, "to my son, Giuseppe Vaggi. Tenor with Teatro alla Scala!"

"*Salute!*" they all cried, clinked glasses and cheered.

"Let's not get ahead of ourselves here," Pino said, reeling them back to reality. "This was only the first audition."

"Don't be modest now. I heard you out there tonight. Of course they'll offer you a contract," his father boomed.

"I know, but still, I'd rather not jinx it."

"Anyway, even if you don't get La Scala, now you can sing in just about any opera company in Italy, no?" Mrs. Vaggi added, slyly alluding to the other offers that Pino incomprehensibly insisted on keeping to himself.

"Well..." he said.

"Nonsense!" his father interrupted, "there is no other opera company! La Scala will be Pino's new home."

Pino looked at the man that had been the source of most of the pain, confusion and disappointment in his life and put his arm over his father's shoulder.

"You know," Pino laughed, "listening to him tonight, it's really hard to believe that only a year ago he wanted me to be a butcher!" Papa blushed and they all laughed.

Pino had been shyly ignoring Gia. He darted a furtive glance at her and their eyes met for an instant, but then they both looked away. He looked back for just a second, and then glanced down at her hands on the table. He wanted to touch them but he didn't dare. The right time would come.

The dinner was wonderful but interminable and when it finally wound down everyone was exhausted, except Pino. He could have danced all night. But the hour was getting late and the yawns more frequent, so he called for the check. His father grabbed the check and paid for the meal, leaving an exorbitant tip for the waiter.

At the coat check, Pino handed his father and mother their coats. As he placed Maria's coat on her shoulders, he kissed her on the cheek, and she responded with a wink. He then helped Gia put on her coat and as he did, he allowed her hair to brush against him. He deeply inhaled and she turned around to face him. They stood in awkward silence for a second, her big dark eyes hypnotizing him.

"I've never heard you sound better than tonight," she said in a voice so soft he could hardly hear.

"Oh, um, thank you, thanks," he clucked awkwardly. They were again in silence.

"Are you two coming?" his father asked with a yawn.

"One second, Papa." His father left, shaking his head.

"So, um, are you still singing?" he asked, hoping to sound thoughtful and sincere.

"Uh huh."

"With Alfredo?"

"Yeah, the good old Conservatorio Ufficiale di Collagna."

"Maybe I could stop by sometime and hear one of your lessons. I mean, if you don't mind."

"I'd love you…I mean, I'd love *for* you to hear me sing," she said with a flirtatious smile.

"Great! Maybe, um, we could get a cup of coffee sometime and talk?"

"Look, Pino, I don't know how to say this. I really like you. But if you don't ask me out on a real date soon, I'm going to kill you!"

He didn't answer but stammered a few indecipherable words. Gia looked over her shoulder to see if anyone was looking. Then quickly, she wheeled around and kissed Pino on the lips and ran out the door. Pino touched his lips with his hand and smiled. Things simply couldn't get any better than this.

CHAPTER FIFTEEN

JUST WHEN YOU LEAST EXPECT IT

"INDIGNATION WITHOUT ACTION," was the world's consistent response to all of the Axis acts of aggression. Mussolini must have seen it. As Hitler rearmed, then rolled into the Rhineland, then Austria, then Czechoslovakia, the world was outraged but impotent. The *Duce* watched as the world grew more and more desensitized to the systematic steamrolling of helpless nations. This made the invasion Albania possible. Although the actual Albanian campaign was carried out with the precision of the Keystone Cops, it did represent another Italian victory and propelled the Duce into his next ill-advised enterprise.

In a move that shocked the nation, Mussolini signed the notorious "Pact of Steel" with Hitler, binding together Italy's military future with Germany; and some would say, signing their fate.

Despite the anti-German demonstrations erupting in Milan and Rome, Mussolini felt he was in many ways ensuring peace for his beleaguered nation. However, as in its recent past and in a foreshadowing of things to come, Germany could not be counted on to keep its word. On the very day after signing the Pact of Steel, Hitler met with his chancellery and began outlining his plans for invading Poland.

The news of Italy's entry into the Pact of Steel with Germany rang through the villages of the Apennines like a death knell. The Albanian campaign separated another class of anxious eighteen-year-olds from their homes and families. After three years of war, the absence of young men in the valley was impossible to ignore. The labor force was becoming increasingly comprised of young boys and older men and the already bleak economic situation got a little bleaker.

Antonio Vaggi was never afraid of an honest day's work; priding himself on his ability to put in a sixty-hour work week and still never miss a meal with his family. Yet, he couldn't deny that it was getting more and more difficult to keep this up in the current climate. There were simply fewer mouths to feed in the town and business was bad. He had had a plan, but with each passing day it was looking less and less likely that he'd be able to fulfill it.

Pino and Gia were by then a full-fledged "item" about town. When Pino's mother finally realized that the "mystery girl" who had enchanted him was in fact little Gia Mastrangelo, Maria's best friend, she thought it absolutely hilarious! The girl whom he had once proclaimed a "shepherdess" had now completely won Pino's ardor. Of course Mrs. Vaggi adored Gia, who wouldn't? The girl was positively adorable, utterly charming and above all, the most well-behaved child she'd ever encountered. She just hoped that her *testa dura* son wouldn't do anything stupid and let this one get away!

Pino and Gia loved the movies. More accurately, Gia loved the movies and Pino loved Gia, so accordingly, Pino loved the movies, too. The cinema was their private little world. They would always sit in the very back row in the corner. The view wasn't very good, but the privacy couldn't be beat. It was there that they learned all the events that would shape their world. Pino had traded in listening to the radio in favor of watching the weekly newsreels at the cinema with Gia. No matter how bleak the news appeared to be, it seemed worlds away from them in the warm darkness of the cinema in their little mountaintop village. It was in that warmth that Pino heard the news of Germany signing a "Pact of Non-Aggression" with the Soviet Union in August of 1939. It made him sit up and take note.

"Does this mean we're allies with the Russians now?" Gia inquired.

"I guess," Pino said, unsure of anything anymore, "If they can't do anything without our approval, then I guess we agreed to it. And that, I guess, make us allies." He wasn't very convinced with his own logic and decided to go back to the old faithful radio for the details.

That evening when he returned home, he found his parents listening intently to the radio broadcast. Apparently, news still got to the radio a lot faster than the newsreels. The agreement was signed days before and anti-Russian demonstrations were breaking out nationwide. Politicians and commentators were calling for the Duce to denounce the Pact of Steel in light of this egregious violation of its tenets, both in letter and spirit.

Pino was dumbfounded, but pulled up a chair and sat alongside his parents. In his little rose-colored, gossamer-filled existence of the past month, he'd completely shut out the rest of the world, which evidently was continuing to spin out of control.

"This man, I truly don't understand," said his father. "He says over and over and over that the Bolsheviks are the greatest evil on earth and yet now…" he trailed off, laughing. "What a fool! How could he possibly be so stupid as to trust a man like Hitler? Jesus Christ Almighty! Any idiot could see that the man is a menace and can't be trusted. My daughter Maria would be a better *Duce*!"

Pino laughed at the idea but realized that his father's laughter wasn't out of amusement but from disbelief.

"How many times can we be led down the garden path by this man? Rosemaria, tomorrow we must go to church and say a *novena* for him. Truly a greater fool has never lived!"

"But, Tony," Mama Vaggi interjected, "he reconciled with the Pope and he had his children baptized. He must be more spiritual than you think."

"Oh, Rosemaria, please! That's all politics. He's been an atheist his entire life! But at least that was one thing I agreed with him about. Between the Church in Rome and the Bolsheviks in Moscow, Rome is the lesser of two evils!"

Pino couldn't help laughing again. His papa, the most bellicose man he'd known, was actually quite funny when he was despondent.

"Ah, Pino, my son, laugh now, for tomorrow we shall all be crying." His father stood up from his chair and began to sing – an opera aria nonetheless! *"Ridi, Pagliaccio!"*

Canio's famous lament over his unfaithful wife from *"I Pagliacci,"* seemed strangely appropriate at that moment, but Pino couldn't bring himself to join his father. He moved his chair closer to his mother's and took her little hand in his own. She stroked his arm and forced a sad little smile.

"How's Gia?" she asked, trying to change the subject.

"She's wonderful. We went to the cinema tonight."

"You take her to the cinema every night! You need to do something different for a change."

"What can I say, Mama, she loves the movies!"

"And you love her, don't you?" she asked. Pino just blushed and shrugged his shoulders. "That's alright, Pino, I really like her, too. You could do far worse. Don't let her get away."

Italy had allied itself with Germany on the evening of Gia and Pino's first kiss, so it only seemed appropriate that two months later, as Pino and Gia were on the verge of entering the next level of intimacy, another crisis should disturb their plans.

For several weeks, Pino's father had taken to working late at the shop. With Pino no longer working at Fritz's and the overall economic malaise of the region deepening daily, Mr. Vaggi needed to put in the extra time just to try and make ends meet. Mrs. Vaggi and Maria contributed by joining an afternoon knitting circle in town. They made clothes for the less fortunate of the village as well as sweaters and gloves to send to the regional army post in Reggio.

Pino's schedule left him little time for such altruism, but he desperately wanted to make a contribution. He consistently reminded himself that once he secured a regular contract he'd have plenty of money and he'd be able to help out his parents in ways he couldn't presently imagine, and the fastest way to make that happen would be to stay more focused than ever. He still had heard nothing from La Scala.

One Friday afternoon in late August, Pino was walking home from the train station through the center of town. He'd caught an early train and thought he'd surprise Gia by showing up at her singing lesson. His timing was off by just a few minutes, for as he approached Alfredo's studio, Gia was already skipping down the lane like a school girl. His heart leapt and he ran after her and caught her just as she was about to enter the library.

"Hey! You're home early!" she cried out.

"Don't go to the library," he said, "it's so nice out, let's go for a walk in the mountains."

She jumped into his arms. They strolled, arm and arm, back to Pino's house to pack a small picnic basket to take with them. The mountains were spectacular in the summer and they were only a short walk away, Pino thought, remembering his mother's admonishment about doing "something different."

As they reached his house, Gia took a small basket from the kitchen counter and immediately began filling it with fruit, cheese, bread and a small bottle of soda pop. Seeing things in good hands, Pino ran upstairs to change his clothes. He tossed his books on the desk and kicked off his shoes. He wanted to get comfortable but also wanted to look nice. He really didn't have that much to choose from. He took off his school pants and put them in his dresser. He took out his cotton summer pants and noticed to his dismay that they were soiled at the knees. He didn't want to wear dirty pants, even if they were going into the mountains. His other options were his heavy wool dress pants, his heavy wool casual pants or his Sunday pants, which really weren't an option at all. *Damn*, he thought with a sigh. It was either going to be comfortably dirty or uncomfortably presentable. *Not much of a choice*, he thought as he mulled it over in his head.

"I'm ready, Pino," said Gia, entering his room and finding him in his underwear. He quickly grabbed his dirty cotton pants and held them up in front of him in embarrassment. He thought she'd depart immediately, but she didn't.

He thought she'd at least cover her eyes, but she didn't. They stood in silence for a long minute. Pino couldn't breathe. He felt feverish and thought he'd melt. He became aware of his own breathing, he could hear it. But she didn't leave. She came closer. Only inches apart, their eyes locked in a longing embrace, Pino could smell her hair and he dropped the pants to the floor. He threw his arms around her and kissed her like a wild animal.

In a series of moans and grunts, they fell onto the bed, their bodies writhing against one another. He ravaged her neck and shoulders and she moaned in ecstasy. She grabbed his hair and pulled his mouth back onto hers. He felt his hands wandering all over her body to places he'd never gone before. Suddenly, he felt a stirring sensation in his loins that overwhelmed him. He pinned her arms back on the bed and thrust himself upon her, again and again. He stopped, only for a second, to look in her eyes, to find some sign that he was right, that she felt as he felt, that she wanted what he wanted.

"Hello! Who's home?" Mrs. Vaggi's voice said from downstairs. Pino's heart stopped. They froze on the bed in terror. "Pino? Is that you?" she continued.

Gia jumped up and started fixing herself in the mirror.

"Answer her!" she whispered urgently.

"Um, yeah, Mama. I got home a little early. I'm just changing," he said pulling on his pants and grabbing his shoes. He looked in the mirror and his face was bright red. He'd never pass inspection this way. He took a couple of deep breaths and fanned himself. He was sweating like a beast of burden. Gia on the other hand, now looked fresh as a daisy.

"I'll go talk to her. You cool off for a minute," she said, heading out the door.

"Ciao, Signora!" she said pleasantly as she descended the stairs.

"Ah! Gia! I had no idea you were here. Give me a kiss!" Mrs. Vaggi said.

Pino put his shoes on and laced them up. Gia was clearly a better actress than he was, so he'd let her go on for a minute and he'd follow her lead.

"We're going for a picnic," she said. Then, lowering her voice so that Pino couldn't hear, she continued, "Signora, please don't be angry with me. I made him go back and change. He was dressed like we were going to the Ritz for New Year's Eve! I laughed at him and hurt his feelings. He got all red and embarrassed. Please don't say anything!"

Mrs. Vaggi covered her mouth, stifling a laugh. She almost cried. She couldn't have loved this girl more if she was her own.

"I know, he's a disaster!" his mother whispered, "He goes so overboard all the time! So serious! His father is just the opposite; he would go to the opera in his butcher's apron if you let him!" Taking Gia by the hand, Mrs. Vaggi led her over to the living room. "You need to get him to relax more," she said in serious tone. "He needs something else in his life other than the music, it's not healthy. Take more walks, go swimming, go horseback riding, something outdoors, you know."

Pino appeared and Gia gave Mrs. Vaggi a covert wink.

"Ready to go?" he asked.

"Ay! Pino! You're pants are filthy!" said his mother. "You expect a lady to be seen with you when you look like a ditch digger?"

"Nice to see you too, Mama." He said. "Let's go, Gia." As they wandered through the foothills they didn't say much. They just let the warm summer breeze wash over them and fill their senses with the thousand fragrances of the valley. After a while, they stopped and sat down on a large flat rock resembling a big tree stump.

"You're a pretty good actress, you know that?" Pino said, taking a bit of an apple.

"Yeah, I know," she agreed with a big smile and putting her arms around his neck she kissed him. "I guess you're pretty lucky to have met me."

"You have no idea."

Given the way things were going, it should have come as no surprise when Adolf Hitler blatantly defied the pact he's signed only months earlier and invaded Poland. It seemed like the world had seen this movie before. Hitler would claim a nation was a potential threat. He'd then amass troops on its borders, and eventually say the nation's constant provocations had become intolerable and he would invade them. At least he was consistent. But in the past, he had not had a binding agreement stating he'd do no such thing without the prior consent of his Axis partner Italy. In reality, the agreement did little to prevent Hitler from doing as he well pleased. In Italy, nervous citizens wondered if their *Duce* would honor the terms of the agreement and go into battle with his partner. As before, anti-German demonstrations again erupted all across the nation. A mutual assistance agreement signed by Great Britain and Poland did little to help matters. The entire Italian nation held its collective breath waiting to see what would happen.

Two days later, Britain, France, Australia and New Zealand declared war on Germany and World War II was well on its way. Just when it seemed there would be no avoiding conflict, Mussolini did something no one expected. He declared Italian neutrality. He actually stood up to Hitler and said that his nation was not prepared to wage such a war at this time and refused to be dragged into it.

With a sigh of relief that could be heard from the Alps to Sicily, the Italian people went back to work rebuilding their wounded economy. What no one realized was that Mussolini was deeply vexed by the public's response to his declaration of neutrality. He viewed himself a revolutionist and a revolutionist's sacred duty was to wage war not proctor the peace.

The stock market going up did little to appease him. With international business beginning to flow again, he was indifferent. As the Italian shipping industry regained its sea-legs, he yawned. None of this mattered or appealed to him. Glorious victory on the battlefield was his manifest destiny, he was certain of it. Yet, even a cursory glance at his country's military and economic situation left him convinced he was not prepared to go to war...yet.

Sitting in the last row of the cinema, Pino and Gia watched as Hitler overran Poland right before their eyes. They saw President Franklin Delano Roosevelt of the United States declare the U.S. neutral in the conflict. They saw Canada declare war on Germany, thus ushering in the battle of the Atlantic. The entire war seemed to be just another movie that they were watching. And even though the movie was being acted out on not-so-distant shores, they would snuggle in the warm darkness of the theater and nothing in the world could touch them.

For several months, Pino saw progressively less of his family. An unhappy pattern was forming. Dinner was no longer an unbreakable engagement as Papa was always working late and Mama was always working with one or another of her social groups. Maria was the only member of the family Pino was seeing on a consistent basis. With his nineteenth birthday rapidly approaching, Pino began to consider how lucky he had been. Most of the other guys his age in Collagna were called up for military service on their eighteenth birthday. Luckily his status as a full time student had exempted him from the first round of call ups. He knew it wouldn't last forever, especially if Italy went to war again.

He thought about finding a job in town. He had now amassed a half-dozen offers to sing in respected regional opera houses, but accepting them would end his trans-Lombard commute and make his dates with Gia much less frequent. The last thing he wanted to do was take a position that would take him away from her for six months or longer.

He also wondered what effect it would have on his parents. Now that his father had come into the fold somewhat, Pino didn't really want to take a chance on spoiling it.

His mother spoke to him about having a party for his birthday, but he rejected the idea. He claimed not to be in the mood for a big bash, but in reality, he didn't want them spending a lot of money on a party when times were tight. Instead, he would prefer a nice dinner with the immediate family and, of course, Gia. The only luxury he would allow himself was the choice of the main course, and for that he chose a local delicacy, *cinghiale*, wild boar, and if possible, some polenta with porcini mushrooms from the forest nearby. It was not a small request, but not completely outrageous either and he knew that it would be a favorite for everyone present.

Maria met Pino at the train station on his birthday and told him that she wanted to treat him to an ice cream for his birthday. Pino, having already made the special request of *cinghiale* for dinner, didn't want to do anything that might spoil his appetite, but he couldn't refuse his sister. Maria's offer kept him away from the house while his parents and Gia prepared a feast fit for a king. Mama prepared the roast *cinghiale* while Gia stirred the polenta, adding just the right amount of ground chestnuts. For the occasion, there would be fresh polenta and crispy fried polenta, a special request from Papa Vaggi. Three bottles of *Rosso di Montalcino* were decanting, and knowing his son's fondness for *grappa*, Papa had ordered a special caraway seed *grappa* for the occasion. The table looked like Christmas dinner by the time Pino and Maria arrived.

There are certain times in a person's life when everything just fits. These times are few and far between and even fewer and farther between if you don't take the trouble to notice them when they happen. Pino's birthday dinner was one such occasion. An embarrassed Gia was prodded into singing, *"Buon Compleano a Ti"* and Papa said a more moving Grace than Pino had ever heard. He sat at the head of the table and basked in the glow of his loved ones busily chatting and devouring the monumental feast before them. Looking out at this miracle of serenity, he wished he was a painter instead of an opera singer so that he could capture this moment in oil on a canvas to preserve forever.

Melancholy with wine, he started thinking that perhaps he hadn't been the easiest person in the world to get along with the past few years, with all of his special needs and idiosyncrasies. Apparently, his family was still capable of capturing that old magic, now and again. Over the course of the meal, he felt a great bundle of adolescent resentment finally burning itself out, and he promised himself that he'd try harder not to allow the embers of that resentment to flame up any more.

He felt someone touch his hand. Gia was smiling broadly at him, the smile that he now cherished like a secret possession that no one else knew about or could share. He was crazy about her and wanted nothing more than to be seen standing beside her. She was so beautiful, he thought taking her hand into his own.

"Excuse me for just a minute," Papa said, wiping his mouth and getting up from the table. Mama Vaggi followed him into the living room.

"I think Papa's drunk!" Maria laughed, sliding down closer to Pino and Gia.

"Yeah, and for once he's not screaming and yelling!" Pino said.

"I'm going to go check on him," said Maria, getting up and dashing after her parents.

Pino took advantage of the unexpected moment of privacy to sneak in a quick kiss.

"I think we got set up," said Gia.

"I'm not complaining." Pino said leaning forward to kiss her again.

"Could you come in here for a second, Pino?" his father called out from the living room.

Pino snapped his fingers and said, "Drats! Just as it was getting good!"

He got up and Gia took his hand. They turned the corner to enter the living room and saw Mama and Papa Vaggi standing against the far wall holding up a large tablecloth. They both had "cat that ate the canary" grins on their faces and looked like they were about to burst with excitement. Pino was confused. The wine blurred his thoughts and he failed to grasp the significance of the tablecloth. He stared at it with searching eyes but came up blank. He looked at Maria who was biting her nails on the verge of tears. He was missing something. *It was a plain white tablecloth, what could it mean?*

At that moment, like a toreador, his father yanked away the table cloth and revealed Pino's birthday present.

"Happy Birthday Pino!" they all cried out in unison.

Pino's jaw dropped. He was frozen. Against the wall stood a beautiful, walnut colored, upright piano. He was stupefied. A piano? He slowly moved towards it and placed his hands upon the keys. How in God's name could they afford it? The answer was simple: they couldn't! But there it was just the same. In an instant, Pino's brain registered a thousand thoughts; his father working overtime, his mother and Maria taking jobs. This was what it was all about. He turned around to face them and found himself awash in a sea of proud faces. His mother hugged Maria and his father stood with his arms folded proudly beaming.

"I…I'm speechless," he stammered, "This is the greatest gift anyone ever received. Mama, Papa, Maria, I don't know what to say."

"Play something!" Gia said. He approached the piano and gently stroked the yellowing keys. It wasn't a new instrument to be sure, but to Pino, it might as well have been a brand new Steinway concert grand. This was the kindest, most generous gesture his family had ever made and it came in a time of their greatest need. Looking at the instrument, he thought about the tremendous sacrifice it must have meant for his entire family to provide this for him. He realized then that he'd completely misjudged them. Father Michele was right; everyone shows their love in their own way, according to their capacity to do so.

Pino whipped around and ran into his father's arms. He squeezed him like he never had before. They weren't the types for grand shows of emotion, but in this case exceptions were in order. The entire family joined in a great big bear hug which Pino wished would last forever. It was the perfect closure to a perfect day; a day he'd later call the greatest of his life. It was an affirmation of faith that he neither expected nor believed possible. *Maybe, just maybe*, he thought. *I won't have to do this all alone after all.*

CHAPTER SIXTEEN

ALLIANCES

NOVEMBER 30TH, 1939, in an act of unprovoked aggression, the Soviet Union attacked Finland. In Italy, anti-Soviet demonstrations emerged alongside the anti-German ones already going on. The *Duce* shared their sentiments but the German pact with the Soviets placed him in an awkward position. He couldn't outwardly renounce the Soviets without angering his ally, Hitler, who despite obvious evidence to the contrary, repeatedly assured him that the Soviets had no aggressive designs on Eastern Europe.

However, mounting pressure from the King, the Pope and the Italian people was forcing him to take some kind of stand on the situation. The King believed that the Soviet issue provided the ideal opportunity for Mussolini to denounce the Pact of Steel and repudiate Italy's obligation to Germany therein. But the *Duce* could not muster the strength of character to do the right thing. With tremendous booty seemingly there for the taking, Mussolini cringed at the idea of prolonged neutrality.

With lightning speed and frightful precision, the Nazis struck. On April 9th, Germany invaded Denmark and Norway. On May 10th, the siege extended to France, Belgium, Luxembourg and the Netherlands. On May 15th, Holland surrendered. On May 28th, Belgium surrendered. Watching Hitler's forces march unchecked across the continent was too much for the *Duce*, and on May 30th, he wrote to Hitler stating Italy's "impatience to be at the side of the German people in the struggle against the common foe." Declaring his nation was ready, willing and able, he fixed a June 10th date for entry into the conflict.

On that fateful evening, every radio in Italy heard the *Duce's* message. It was a night few Italians would ever forget.

"An hour marked by destiny is striking in the sky of our country, the hour of irrevocable decisions. We are entering the lists against the plutocratic and reactionary democracies of the West, who have always hindered the advance and often plotted against the very existence of the Italian people…At a memorable meeting in Berlin, I said that, according to the laws of Fascist morality, when one has a friend, one goes with him to the very end. We have done this and will do this with Germany, with her people and with her victorious armed forces."

The image of Mussolini standing on his balcony declaring war on France and England was brought to Collagna via newsreel, the way virtually all national and international news made its way to the mountains. It was by no means the fastest way, but it could generally be counted on for accuracy. Some locals would see the same feature film over and over just to get the current news.

After months of seeing the same images over and over, each time with a different country in the starring role, it became apparent to Pino that things would get a lot worse before they would get better. He and Gia never spoke about it, ever. There was an unspoken understanding that the subject was taboo, because it seemed to be the only real threat to their happiness. Finally, one evening after the feature ended, it was too much for Gia to bear.

"Do you think you'll get called up?" she asked timidly.

"I'm nineteen. I'm already on borrowed time."

"But we're at war and they haven't called you up yet?"

"Just lucky so far, I guess."

"But what about your singing?"

"What about it?"

"You're not just going to give up on it - are you?"

"Of course not, but I've got to be realistic. Sooner or later I'm bound to be called up. And then I've got to concentrate on staying alive, not singing."

She squeezed him tightly, shivering at the thought.

"Don't talk that way. Don't even think that way."

"I'm trying not to, but I want to be prepared when the time comes."

"*If* the time comes! You're scaring me, Pino. Please stop."

Pino turned to her and looked deeply into her eyes. He wanted to tell her something, but couldn't. He kissed her passionately, trying his best to make everything all right. They kissed and kissed again, then embraced each other as if it were for the last time. They sat in the dark of the empty theater until an usher told them it was closing time.

Silently, they walked hand in hand through the empty streets toward Gia's house.

"So, I guess it's pretty late." Pino said.

"Uh huh."

"I guess I'll see you tomorrow then?" he said in an off-hand and careless manner, hoping to lighten the moment, but his ploy would hardly have deceived a toddler. She only nodded and dashed into the house.

When Pino got home, the lights were on and his mother and sister were in the kitchen listening to the radio. He knew they were waiting for him. He shut the door and hung up his coat. He really didn't want to talk to them right then but he knew it couldn't be avoided.

"Can I have some coffee, Mama?" Pino asked.

"Isn't it a little late for -" she started to say, but stopped. "Sure," she said getting up to fetch a cup from the cupboard. Pino sat down at the table and waited for the questions to begin. He didn't wait long.

"Well?" Maria asked, watching him over the rim of her glass. "Did you tell her?"

He shook his head. His mother placed the cup in front of him and reached out her hand to rub his shoulders.

"I tried," he said. "But when she saw the newsreel, she started crying, and I just couldn't."

"But, Pino," Maria interjected, "you'll be leaving in three days."

"Don't remind me." He took a long sip of coffee and sighed.

"Maybe it's best I don't tell her, and just leave."

"Don't be ridiculous. She'd never forgive you if you did that," said his mother.

"You want me to tell her?" Maria offered.

He thought for a moment then stood up.

"No, I'll tell her tomorrow after church. We'll go for a walk and I'll tell her."

"Pino, your father and I want to throw a little party for you before you go," his mother said, looking at him with a lump in her throat.

"I'd prefer you didn't. You've don't too much already."

"But, Pino..."

"No, Mama! I don't want to make a big deal of this. Every boy my age in the country is going and so am I and that's that."

"But the whole family will want to wish you well."

"The family? What family? Those people who never come to visit? Who never come to hear me sing, now suddenly they all want to wish me well? I'm sorry, Mama, but I can do without their well wishes! Goodnight!"

As he stormed upstairs, Maria put her head on her mother's shoulder and held her hand sadly. There was nothing that either of them could do or say that could possibly make the situation any better or easier.

The one public place that Pino had yet to be seen with Gia was church. When they were a little bit younger, both had sung in the church choir under Maestro Ivaldi, but since his death the choir held little appeal for either of them.

She was understandably curious when he asked if she would accompany him on Sunday since being seen together in church meant that their relationship had reached another level. Of course, she agreed.

Pino fidgeted like a child throughout the Mass and Gia thought it was adorable. She was under the impression that he was still embarrassed to be seen in church with a girlfriend. She smiled to herself but wouldn't do anything to further embarrass him. She didn't dare hold his hand. She hardly looked at him, but soon the temptation to touch him proved more than she could bear. She gently slid her hand off her lap and onto the wood of the pew. Then, slowly, almost imperceptibly, she slid her hand next to his, then gently on top of it. At that moment, she immediately knew something was wrong. His hands were ice-cold and clammy, emotionless.

A bell was ringing as they left the church. To Gia it sounded like a death knell. She felt little relief when Pino took her hand as they silently walked down the street. They looked like just another couple in love as they sat under a tree in a park. Upon closer inspection, they looked much like a young couple who were breaking up: one was crying and the other speaking, but emotionless. Gia suddenly got up and ran away. Pino chased after and caught her. She wanted him to catch her. She wanted him to hold her forever. For the first time it was clear to her just how deeply in love with Pino she really was and just how large a void he would leave if he never returned.

The train station was buzzing on the day Pino left. It seemed there were more able-bodied young men in Collagna than he had realized and apparently they all got the letter at the same time. As he looked around the platform, he noticed men aged fourteen to forty, all headed off to the same uncertain future. Bags in hand, Pino found himself saying his goodbyes to his family much like all the rest of them. He wanted to tell everyone something profound and deeply moving, a thought they could keep in their hearts to remember him by in the event that he not return. There was only one problem; when he gazed upon them, his heart sank, and he decided that the best thing to do was to do nothing, to downplay his leaving as best he could and try to keep a lid on his emotions.

"OK, I'm all loaded up. Time now for the tearful good-byes, right?" he said sarcastically.

"Oh, Pino," his mother cried and hugged him. He realized that this might be the very last time he would feel her embrace and his emotions were torn. He was angry with himself for letting his emotions get the better of him, and he fought desperately to hold back the tears.

"I'll write the first chance I get, Mama," he promised.

He let go of her and moved down the line to his sister.

"What, no tears?" he asked.

She was tougher than he was.

"I promised I wouldn't," she quipped confidently, and with a smile, she took a gold chain from around her neck and put it on her brother. The chain had a small medallion on it.

"What's this?" he asked.

"It's my Saint Christopher medal. Take it. It'll protect you." She said. He hugged her fiercely. He'd come to lean on her more and more and knew she'd be sorely missed.

"You're in charge now," he said with a wink, "take care of them till I get back," he whispered in her ear. She kissed him on the cheek and he knew she would take care of them. He didn't want to let go of her, partly because he might never have the chance to hold her again, and partly because next he'd have to face his father. Yet, when he reached his father, his fears proved unfounded. Papa Vaggi looked at him, beaming with pride, maybe even love.

"*Buona Fortuna*, my son," his father said as he shook Pino's hand firmly and grabbed and tugged his cheek. It was a very strange moment for Pino. He wasn't quite sure why, but his father's gesture made him feel more calm and secure. The only wars Pino had ever known were with him and he'd been a fierce adversary. But the state of peaceful coexistence at which they'd recently arrived gave Pino a great feeling of relief. If he'd had to leave with the relationship unresolved, it would have gnawed at him. Instead, he left with his father's blessing. It gave him the confidence he needed for his next goodbye.

Gia was trembling, her dark eyes red and puffy from sobbing. He thought of all of the movie heroines they'd watched together that looked so beautiful when they cried. What a contrast real pain and fear made. Real pain and fear could not be hidden. Pino took her hands into his own and kissed them. He shot a look at his family and silently shooed them away and they obliged. After they reached a secure distance, Pino began the hardest conversation of his life.

"Look, hey, it's not the end of the world," he said with a sad smile.

"I know."

"I didn't want you to go home sad..." He paused and took a deep breath.

"How can you say that?" Gia interrupted.

"I'll write every day, and there won't be a moment when you won't be in my thoughts."

"Don't be ridiculous," she said. "You said yourself, your only priority was to stay alive. You can't afford to be distracted by anything else."

"I won't be distracted by anything if I know that you'll be here waiting when I come back."

"You know I will," she promised. He looked into her tear-filled eyes and saw his own reflection. He was nearly crying himself. Closing his eyes, Pino took a hard swallow and kneeled before her. Holding her hands against his chest, he uttered the words that would change his life forever.

"In that case...Gia Mastrangelo, will you do me the honor of being my wife?" he said in a voice that surprised even him. Gia nearly fainted.

"What?" she said so quietly that he couldn't actually hear it. He repeated the message in words that left no room for confusion.

"Will you marry me?" She burst into tears.

"Yes! Oh, my God, *yes*!" she cried out. Pino's family was about twenty feet away trying to be polite, but Gia's cry caused Maria to sneak a peek at them.

"Oh, my God!" Maria shrieked.

"What is it?" her mother cried, and turned to see Pino on his knee in front of Gia, and Maria wildly running toward them.

"Ah! Was that what I think it was?" Maria screamed.

Gia leapt into Maria's arms.

"Maria! Pino asked me to marry him!"

"Oh! I'm so happy for you!"

Mrs. Vaggi kissed Gia and Mr. Vaggi shook his son's hand forcefully.

"Your cup runneth over, Pino," he said in a quiet voice. Pino couldn't help but agree. The world stood still for just a moment. He saw the joyous faces spinning around him and wondered why all this good fortune would be showered upon him at just such a time, but he knew it was useless to ask. He just floated about his body smiling and glowing, wishing it wouldn't end.

Unhappily, the train whistle broke the euphoria and reality returned with a crash. Everyone stopped. Pino looked at Gia. She rushed into his arms.

"I love you," he whispered in her ear.

"I love you, too," she beamed.

The two young lovers separated, unsure if it would be the last time they'd ever see one another. Pino saluted his family like a good soldier, picked up his bags and stepped up onto the train. He dropped the bags on the top step and ran back into Gia's arms. Their last kiss was neither deep nor passionate, but rather soft and tender as if they had crossed over to a new plateau. They separated once more and he kissed her hands. He ascended the stairs once more and blew them all a kiss. The train began to move slowly and its jerking motion nearly knocked him off. Gathering himself up, he saluted his family one last time as the train rolled off into the distance.

PART TWO:
WAR

CHAPTER ONE

BASIC

W
ITH FRANCE'S IMMINENT SURRENDER staring him in the face, Mussolini leaped into the fire hoping to grab some of the spoils of war for himself. It was no secret that he coveted the French Riviera that bordered his own *Cinque Terre* as well as the Mediterranean island of Corsica which lay just north of Italy's Sardinia. His strategic interests in Africa ran from Tunisia on the Mediterranean to French Somaliland on the east coast of the Indian seaboard.

With two dozen divisions on the French border poised and ready, the first wave of attack was set. Surprisingly, the first blows of the war were not to be upon France. On June 12, the Italian Submarine Bagnolini sank the British Light Cruiser Calypso in the Mediterranean and the Italians were finally on the scoreboard. The next day, the Italian destroyer Strale sank the British submarine HMS Odin off the Gulf of Taranto, and on June 16th, the British submarine HMS Grampus was sunk by Italian destroyers. The battle for the Mediterranean was underway and proceeding better than *Il Duce* could have imagined.

Italy should have stuck to the water, because the ground war would be an altogether different story. On June 17th, with a severely ill-equipped and under-prepared army, (ironically, the very same day the France requested an armistice with Germany) Italy launched its initial ground attack through the Saint Bernard Pass in the Alps.

As if God himself resisted the advance, a massive snowstorm halted their march almost immediately. In the south, the Crown Prince of Italy led the assault on the second front along the Riviera toward Nice, with similar results. Despite their numerical advantage, the Italians could only gain five miles of the French coast, occupying territory up to Modane. Overall, the invasion of France was a disaster of epic proportions.

On June 24th, the French surrendered to Germany and the campaign was for all intents and purposes, over. Fearing a great loss of face, Mussolini demanded that France surrender to Italy as well or the fighting would recommence. The French capitulated and Italy had won a victory (of sorts).

In his barracks on the outskirts of Turin, Pino greeted the news of Italy's victory with a cry of joy. The good news spread throughout camp like wildfire, and along with it the dim hope that the British might also be ready to surrender. The base heard countless sagas of bravery and heroics of both the Italian Navy and the Regia Aeronautica as well. It made the drudgery of basic training slightly more bearable. For a tenderfoot like Pino, basic training was pure hell and nothing he'd faced in life thus far had prepared him for either the physical or mental demands it presented. Marching, calisthenics, marching, rifle training, marching, obstacle courses, marching, wading through water, marching, target practice, and more marching; nothing came easy to the displaced mountain boy.

Initially, fortune appeared to be shining upon him. He glowed with pride at being selected for the elite Alpine Division, but his glow diminished when he learned that he was actually chosen for the division simply because of his mountain upbringing. The Italian Army boasted both Mountain Infantry and Alpine Infantry, and as the titles would suggest, they were designated as such because of their particular affinities to conduct operations in mountainous regions. The basic difference between the two groups was simple: Mountain divisions operated at altitudes up to two thousand meters and Alpine divisions were specifically chosen to operate at insanely high altitudes above three thousand meters.

Generally, the Mountain units were composed of an infantry division with "animal transport," meaning the artillery regiment's weaponry was transported in horse-drawn carts or on pack animals. The infantry received no special training in mountain warfare, but rather, were chosen largely because of their mountainous mailing addresses.

The Alpine division, by contrast, was an elite unit also composed of mountain men, but who received meticulous special mountain warfare training. They were in superior physical condition and expert marksmen. In addition, each regiment had its own artillery, engineers, and auxiliary services permanently attached. The prevailing thought process at the time was that any invasion of Italy would come by way of the Alps, surrounding the country's northern borders, thus such divisions were not merely logical but critical to the nation's defenses.

The war began for Pino virtually the moment he arrived in Turin. As he assembled for his very first inspection, his commander, Captain Salerno, commented on the size of his suitcase and the size of his belly.

"I thought all you mountain boys were long and lean?" he asked.

"Obviously not all of us," Pino said with a smile. The smart remark earned him the first in a series of lectures on protocols which he chewed, swallowed and digested like an overcooked piece of beef. Pino quickly learned that any attempts to correct his commander's misconceptions about the mountains and the people who resided in them were better left unsaid.

Captain Salerno was a large, portly man with dull facial features that appeared to have been sanded down. He possessed the flat nose of a boxer and a huge dimpled chin that suggested stubbornness and the ability to take a punch. Pino guessed his Commanding Officer was Sicilian from his accent but he couldn't be sure. In addition to the physical trials of basic, Pino also found himself the unwitting recipient of a daily Italian lesson. His understanding of, and patience for, southern Italian dialect was limited. His father had told him for years that there really was no such thing as a dialect. These were merely provincial people who were too dumb or just too lazy to learn their own language. Pino shared his father's opinion, but wisely decided not to share it with anyone.

Pino's regiment, the 3rd Alpine of the 1st Taurinese Division, was a rag-tag group from all over the country. For some reason, he had expected everyone in camp to be from the north, like him, but that was not the case. Apparently, some years earlier, the army, fearing mutinies, had adopted a policy of grouping together recruits from different regions specifically to prevent any conspiracies from forming. More often, it resulted in tension and lack of trust between soldiers due to gaping differences in dialects, values, and customs. To Pino, it seemed to run counterintuitive to the entire "elite Alpine unit" idea. Soon, many other illogical concepts would present themselves that he'd have to contend with. For example, his CO simply could not fathom the fact that a young man from the Apennine Mountains had never held a gun in his hands.

How do you hunt? What? You've never hunted? And you live in the mountains?

Pino was tempted to tell him that they no longer had to "catch" their dinner and actually had running water and electricity, too, but he thought better of it. The irony was immense. Pino considered his Captain a buffoon and his Captain considered him a bumpkin. Clearly, the two men were on a collision course and it was just a matter of time before they collided. Sadly for Pino, he didn't yet realize that in this situation it didn't matter who was right. The ranking officer was right, always.

The crash occurred exactly one month from the day he arrived in camp.

"What do you mean you've never been on a horse before?" Captain Salerno howled.

"Just what I said. I've never been on a horse before! And *yes, I'm from the mountains!*"

The instant the words left his mouth, he regretted them. He thought about apologizing but he was sure that would only make matters worse. To his profound surprise Captain Salerno didn't utter a single word. He merely smiled.

Two days later, Pino was packing his things and headed for an uncertain future aboard a train headed for Piedmonte, carrying with him a letter detailing his failure to live up to the standards of the Alpine unit. His dismissal and re-assignment was swift and came with the admonishment that he had one strike against him and military prison was in his future if he slipped up again. He was rattled by the news but rallied himself at the chance to start fresh with the lessons he'd learned in Alpine securely tucked away in there back of his mind. The army, he began to realize, was an unforgiving business and he had already failed the first test.

The 3rd infantry regiment of the 29th Piedmonte Division was waiting with open arms for its new recruits and Pino prayed he could slip in unnoticed with the rest of the newcomers. Aside from a sideways glance and a sneer from the Corporal reading the roll, Pino did just that. He quickly found his place in the barracks and set off determined to turn over a new leaf. The Piedmonte Division was regular army and its training regiment, while exhausting, posed no real problems for Pino. He felt like he'd gone to bed in one world and awakened in another; a world where he might actually succeed.

Each day, after seemingly endless hours of exercise and training, Pino and his comrades would head back to their barracks and one by one the exhausted men would fall into their bunks and pass out, except Pino. He would sit on the edge of his bunk until he caught his breath. Then, he'd look around to see if anyone was watching, and if the coast was clear, he'd pull a book out from under his bed, the big Ricordi book of Tenor arias. He'd lie on his side to conceal it from onlookers and start to read through it. It was the one connection he allowed himself to keep with his previous existence. This ritual went on unnoticed for days and he felt secure that while he couldn't vocalize in the barracks, he could to some extent keep up with his studies.

His body ached like it never had before, but he began to notice a marked improvement in his stamina. He also noticed how flat his belly was becoming, and so quickly! He actually liked his new lean body and thought that if he got through the war in one piece he would never allow himself to return to his portly past.

One of the primary reasons for his weight loss, in addition to the introduction of exercise to his world, was the fact that the food in the mess hall was completely inedible. Pino never considered his mother the greatest cook in the world, but he soon developed a newfound appreciation for her culinary skills. He expected bland food in the army but not repulsive food, and the gruel that he ingested morning, noon and night was, in his opinion, not fit for a dog. Consequently, he suffered the additional pleasure of a digestive system that regularly went on strike. Eventually, his brain told him, he'd get used to it, but his body staunchly refused to get with the plan.

Daily in the mess hall, Pino would sit down with his company and pray for the best, earnestly hoping that he wasn't the only one suffering, but his closest acquaintances showed no outward signs of any gastrointestinal discomfort, which once again caused Pino to rethink the quality of his mother's cooking.

The same country wide selection process that puzzled him so in the Alpine Division existed in regular infantry as well, thus the mess hall was a veritable cacophony of dialects. There were three soldiers in his company with whom he became especially close. In truth, there was only one, but that one was close to two others and Pino found himself becoming a member of their extended gang.

Antonio Amonte was without question Pino's closest friend and confidant in the company. He was from Todi and the son of a butcher. Pino laughed: two butcher's sons in the same company. It had to be karma that they would be friends. Amonte was tall and thin with dark skin and jet–black hair that combined to give him movie-star good looks. Soft-spoken but possessing a sardonic sense of humor, he was the only person in the company to whom Pino had spoken about his opera singing. It was a decision he would come to regret.

Wrapped up in acclimating to his new world, it was weeks before Pino realized that the information flow in the company wasn't nearly as good as in the Alpine Division. In Alpine, virtually every day announcements were made broadcasting news of Italian victories in the war. For some reason, regular army didn't feel compelled to share current events with the rank and file. Secretly, Pino feared the dearth of news meant that there was no good news to tell.

One morning, as he sat down to breakfast with Amonte, they were joined by two of Amonte's buddies from basic. They looked to Pino like the Italian equivalent of Laurel and Hardy. Marco Bernardi was a huge, hulking beast of a man from Naples with large dirty hands and short-cropped, thinning hair. His unpleasant face was bulbous, had the greasy complexion of one that hadn't washed for days, and wore an almost perpetual scowl. He had jowls like a man twice his age and a weak chin that almost disappeared into his throat when he lowered his head. As if written in the stars, it wasn't long before Bernardi became Pino's chief antagonist. One of the things that Pino couldn't stand about Bernardi was the fact that he found it virtually impossible to speak without the use of a nearly continuous flow of profanity. It was the first thing that Pino noticed about him and the thing that stuck out most. Pino didn't consider himself a prude but in his worldview, Bernardi was a repugnantly vulgar man.

Raimo Carlucci was a skinny little squirt with the voice and smirk of a rodent. He was a big city boy from the heart of Rome, but possessed none of the refinement, intelligence, or culture which Pino expected to find in one with an urban upbringing. Carlucci was sharp as a tack but in a sneaky cunning sort of way that Pino distrusted. For some reason which Pino couldn't put a finger on, Carlucci's demeanor always reminded him of Alfredo or the "snitch" in a Hollywood movie; the guy you could count on to squeal to the police or sell you out to your enemy.

Pino didn't really care for either of them but they were Amonte's friends, so before long they became his friends as well. Eventually, Pino came to realize that Carlucci really wasn't a bad guy at all, he simply went along with anything and everything Bernardi said, and Bernardi was, in Pino's opinion, a textbook case of *cafonne*.

When they joined Pino and Antonio at breakfast, the peace was irreparably disturbed. Much to Pino's disgust but hardly to his surprise, Bernardi slopped up his cold cereal like a barnyard animal.

"Just like mama used to make," he said, and no one could tell if he was being facetious.

"Yeah, I hear it's extremely nutritious," said Pino. "Hey, how often do we get mail around here?" he continued, changing the subject.

"Supposedly, every two weeks," answered Carlucci.

"Why? Mama sending you chicken soup?" Bernardi chuckled.

"Or the latest *Opera Digest?*" quipped Amonte. Unfortunately, the remark didn't go unnoticed by Pino or, more unfortunately, by Bernardi.

"*Opera Digest?*" he asked with a look of disgust.

"Yeah. Vaggi here is an opera singer." Amonte added.

"I didn't know that," said Bernardi with a smirk.

"Yeah, really, practically made it big just before getting called up."

"Tough break," laughed Carlucci.

"I'll live," said Pino with a yawn, hoping to put the conversation to rest, but Bernardi had no intention of letting it go just yet.

"Why don't you sing something for us, Vaggi?" he asked.

"I never sing this early in the morning," Pino retorted smartly.

"Go on. Give it a shot."

"Forget it. You're wasting your breath."

"Come on, Vaggi, just a few bars of something."

"Drop it, guys, I'm not singing."

Bernardi stood up and cupped his hands like a megaphone to make an announcement.

"Regazzi! We have an esteemed guest with us today, directly from the Royal Opera House." Pino got up and shoved Bernardi but he didn't so much as budge.

"Cut it out!" he yelled and grabbed Bernardi's arm, but like a cat, Bernardi spun around and bent his hand back in a hammerlock, as Pino cried out in pain.

"Now, that's more like it! Sing, Vaggi! Sing!" Pino writhed in agony, thinking his wrist would break, when suddenly the MPs rushed in and broke up the altercation. Pino didn't want any trouble, knowing he already had one strike against him from Alpine, but trouble had found him. Despite his best efforts, it would not be the last such skirmish with Bernardi. The next day, found Pino and Bernardi scrubbing toilets in the latrine. It was humiliating labor to be sure but to truly infuriate his colleague, Pino loudly sang Neapolitan songs as he worked.

"You know, you just can't beat the acoustics in a bathroom," he said, triumphantly smiling as Bernardi scowled at him with his usual menacing stare.

"O sole mio, sta'n fronte ate!"

Night time in the barracks was quiet time, with soldiers passing the time playing cards or writing letters home to loved ones. Typically, Pino would study his music until he grew bored or until his eyes hurt. Then he'd consider writing a letter to Gia or his family, but the feeling would soon pass. He was never much of a letter writer and he hadn't written to either Gia or his family yet. He knew that eventually his procrastination would make him feel terribly guilty. Alone in the dark, night after night, after everyone else had turned in, he sat on the floor next to his bunk to try to write. Much to his surprise, he found gathering his thoughts together more difficult than he had expected. Pino started to compose his first wartime letter to Gia numerous times before finally completing it.

My love,

I hope that somehow this will reach you. Sorry it took so long to write but it has been crazy. I started in Turin but things didn't go so well there, so they transferred me to Piedmonte – apparently my lack of hunting and horseback riding skills made me a poor choice for Alpine combat – heck, I could have told them that! Have you ever been on a horse? They seem to think mountain folk spend all day hunting, fishing and marrying their cousins. Most of the guys here are pretty nice and I've made a close friend, Antonio (his Papa is a butcher too – what are the odds of that?) They do tease me a lot about my singing though, but I don't let them get to me. I have managed to fit in a little studying here and there; it keeps me sane and reminds me of you.

They say training is supposed to last sixteen weeks but the rumor is we'll be shipping out of here by the beginning of next month. We still don't know where we'll be headed, but as soon as I find out, I'll write and let you know. As far as news goes, I used to think we were in the dark in Collagna, but here it's a total blackout. They don't tell us anything. If you write, please let me know the latest news – and not just about Collagna! That's all for now.

Te adoro,

Pino

P.S. - I've lost quite a bit of weight. You'd hardly recognize me now!

Reading it back, he was disappointed. It was impersonal, disjointed and didn't say very much, but he wasn't really in the mood to write. He'd write again, soon, and more often, he promised himself. Writing made him sleepy, so he climbed back into his bunk and joined his brothers in arms in search of Elysium.

The art of soldiering wasn't coming easy for Pino. For weeks he went through all the motions with the rest of his comrades in arms, but he sensed something was missing. For one thing, his uniform was a joke; the jacket was laughingly too big and the pants itched terribly. With ill-fitting boots added to the mix, he was one miserably uncomfortable fighting machine. Discomfort aside, there was something important missing in his disposition, as well. The first time he pulled the trigger on his rifle in target practice, it terrified him. The noise was deafening and the kick nearly took off his shoulder. Looking across the field at the target, the outline of a human form on paper, served only to magnify his concern. At some point the target wouldn't be paper. It would be a real live person, a person that would be fixing its aim on him. In such a pinch, he knew he'd be able to react correctly, but it never came naturally. At least not the way it came to Bernardi, who never looked happier than when he was shooting something. Even Amonte had the forbearing of a tiger when he put the rifle to his shoulder. Maybe *he* was that mountain boy who spent his youth hunting and fishing and riding horses! Pino's natural abhorrence of violence put him at a disadvantage as a soldier. He knew that, but to what extent, he'd have to live and learn.

Slowly but surely, Pino's resentment of his commanding officers was fading away. Even Captain Salerno of the Alpine division was no longer as evil in Pino's mind. Sure, the captain had ridden him hard and, Pino still believed, somewhat unfairly. But all things considered, that battle of wills now seemed foolishly unnecessary and probably at least partly Pino's own fault. In retrospect, the captain was doing him, and by extension his comrades in arms, a favor.

In addition to the physical workouts and combat training, the division was lectured repeatedly on military strategy and tactics. To Pino, it might as well have been in Chinese. Day after day he learned about the principles of employment, the *Guerra di rapido courso*, or war of rapid decision doctrine that all such principles were based upon. As far as he could gather, the entire concept was based on three different divisions working in concert. First, Celeri divisions, which were composed of infantry and mounted cavalry, which would provide reconnaissance. Second, tank brigades, which were designed for penetration, encirclement, and exploitation. Third, motorized divisions, designed for rapid maneuver over a wide range and for the reinforcement of mechanized or fast moving units

Infantry was at the heart of the system and absolutely critical, but infantry-artillery integration was close behind. Armor was to function in the role of infantry support and tanks would operate in concert with cavalry units.

The battery of officers delivering the lectures stressed that the concept was ground breaking and audacious, bold and nearly perfect. Success was virtually guaranteed, if executed with the proper degree of surprise, speed, intensity, sustained action, and flexibility. Pino couldn't help but be impressed by their confidence and mastery of the subject matter. He wasn't exactly sure what it all meant, but he liked the fact that victory was all but assured. Glancing around at his comrades, noting the puzzled expressions on their faces, he took solace in the fact that he wasn't the only one in complete oblivion. If this stuff was so critical to learn, why didn't they provide notebooks and pencils? Surely nobody would remember a word of it the moment they left. Bernardi managed to sleep through virtually every lecture and never once got caught, a fact that irked Pino terribly. Amonte would be able to recite this stuff, chapter, book and verse, while Bernardi would yawn and say "whatever." Yet, they'd be expected to stand side by side on the field of battle and function, as the officer said: "hand in glove". *Viva Italia!*

CHAPTER TWO

WORD FROM THE FRONT

PINO'S LETTER ARRIVED IN COLLAGNA after just a few days and Gia was understandably elated. None of the other boys who departed along with Pino had written home yet, or at least none of their letters had yet been received. She wasn't sure why, but she was proud of this fact. She'd begun keeping careful tabs of such things. The radio was her sole source of information now.

Since Pino's departure, the cinema held little appeal to her and was a constant reminder of his absence. She might have dismissed the fact that a war was going on at all except for the radio, and the fact that there were no longer any young men seen on the streets and in the taverns of Collagna. The only place she saw any boys her own age was at the conservatory and the only boy there was Allesandro. For some reason, he had yet to be called up for service. Gia didn't know Alle very well but from what she could deduce for herself, he seemed like a nice, polite, if somewhat loud, young man. Her opinion was not shared by the rank and file of the town. A great many of the townsfolk believed he had been spared service by virtue of his father's political connections. This resulted in resentment bordering on hostility toward the boy, who unfortunately was becoming increasingly belligerent. All of this was completely unfair to Alle. In Gia's opinion, true or untrue, what could he possibly have done about it? Magistrate Biaggi seemed every bit the pernicious man that everyone called him, but Alle certainly played no part in his father's political circles. It was cruel to punish him for it, she thought, recalling what Father Michele had said in mass about: "visiting the sins of the father upon the son." She was certain that eventually Alle would do his service like every Italian and all this would blow over, but in the meantime she would try her best not to act like the rest of her neighbors, who treated the boy like a pariah.

The day Gia brought Pino's letter to the conservatory to show Alfredo, Alle was there. She proudly displayed the letter for both of them and they read with gusto.

"My dear," said Alfredo, blushing," I'm not so certain Pino would appreciate you sharing this letter with everyone. Its contents are a bit personal, no?" Of course the thought occurred to her, but it wasn't all that personal and it was more important for her to let everyone know that even in the face of a war, her fiancé (she loved the way that sounded) was thinking of her. Alle did not share her sentiment.

"He's got more important things to do than write letters," he quipped. And with those few words, he forever lost Gia as a supporter.

"It took him months to write one letter, Alle," she said tartly "I'm sure he waited for an appropriate moment."

"Don't misunderstand me, Gia," he said sweetly, "All I'm saying is that Pino is hardly what you would call a 'warrior' if you know what I mean. He's my friend, too, remember and I want him coming home in one piece. The best way to do that is to learn what it means to be a soldier." Despite his apologetic tone, she was furious with him.

"He's right, you know," Alfredo agreed.

"And what exactly do you know about being a soldier, Alle?" she asked. The barb hit the mark as a look of dark indignation crossed his face.

"The function of a citizen and the function of a soldier are inseparable, that's what the Duce says. We all have to serve in our own way."

"And how pray tell do you plan to serve?" she demanded, "Singing the National Anthem at Fascist rallies?"

"That's enough!" boomed Alfredo, stepping between them like a boxing referee. Alle grabbed his coat and stormed out of the room, but Gia was sure that would not be the last such discussion they would have on the subject. Alfredo sat down on his piano bench and looking at her, shook his head in disappointment.

"I really thought you were smarter than that, my dear." She didn't care what he thought. She wasn't going to tolerate anyone saying a negative word about Pino – no one! "We are at war, my dear. And war does funny things to people. It adds so much stress to our already stressful lives that it's a miracle we all don't crack up."

"We're only at war because of your *Duce*, Maestro," she boldly stated.

"Yes, I suppose that is true, but sometimes war is inevitable, Gia. Nobody wants to go to war but often not going to war is worse. Inaction can sometimes cause as much damage as action. I don't expect you to completely understand this but, sometimes great men have to do..." he paused for a long time to choose exactly the right wording. "How can I put this gently? Sometimes, great men must do things that *appear*, and I do mean appear, for want of a better word, things that appear *bad* in order to serve the greater good. Do you understand?" She hadn't a clue. "For example, a great man must be in a position of power to effect change. To achieve this greater good, he must gain this power and maintain this power, and sometimes he must make some very difficult decisions and do some unpleasant things. But the end more than justifies the means. Don't you see?" She didn't see and she didn't want to see. She wasn't even sure she wanted to continue as Alfredo's student. Something broke within her that day, something that could never be fixed. As Alfredo smiled and touched her under the chin, she wanted to slap away his hand. She'd never felt such revulsion before and it sickened her. She needed to get out of the studio and fast.

"Excuse me, Maestro, I'm afraid I'm not feeling well," she said as she grabbed her coat and Pino's letter.

"And, your lesson?" said Alfredo.

"I have to go," she said and rushed out the door. It was the last time she ever set foot in the *Conservatorio Ufficiale di Collagna.*

CHAPTER THREE

BACK TO BASICS

SIX WEEKS PASSED FASTER THAN PINO could have imagined. As suspected, the sixteen weeks of training never materialized, and one gloriously sunny morning he found himself in formation on a parade ground listening to his commander deliver the information they'd all been waiting to hear. The commander spoke from a small platform in front of them that wasn't there the day before, so Pino concluded the announcement would be an important one.

"At 0800 tomorrow, companies A, C and D will ship out. Have your gear ready and checked. You will have one final inspection at 0600. Company B will remain on the base until further orders. That is all. Dismissed."

That's it? he thought. *No details of any kind?* As the men broke off and headed in different directions, Pino and Amonte wandered back toward their barracks, perplexed.

"He didn't even say where we were shipping out to," Pino noted.

"No, he didn't," said Amonte.

"You think that's good or bad news?"

"I wouldn't care to guess. I'm still trying to figure out how we got allied with Germany."

Pino laughed. Amonte always knew just how to put a situation in perspective, he thought. He was glad to have met him and hoped they'd remain together after the various deployments were executed.

"God, I hope it's not Russia," Pino muttered aloud.

"I doubt Hitler trusts our fighting skills enough to send us to Russia," Amonte reassured. The next morning came quickly. A bugle sounded the call and the soldiers scrambled, gathering all their belongings for inspection. Pino started to pile up all his belongings and shoved as much as he could into his kit bag, but it didn't all fit. He tried and tried, taking things out and rearranging them, but it was no use. Looking down at the pile, two items stuck out like sore thumbs: Gia's scarf, which he'd never part with, and the *Ricordi Tenor Aria* book. With great trepidation, he picked it out and flipped through its pages. He knew most of it by heart. It was his last vestige of civilization. The bugle blew again as Pino agonized. He glanced at the table of contents which he could recite from memory and his eye stopped on a title he'd forgotten about. *"In Fernam Land"* from Richard Wagner's *Lohengrin* was the only German title in the book and the only aria in the entire collection that Pino had not worked through until it was written on the inside of his eyelids. He turned the pages until he came upon the aria. It was familiar, but not overly so. *"In a far off land…"* the words began, but the third blast of the bugle left him little time to think. He tore the page out of the book and folded it neatly and placed it in his bag. It would give him something to chew on during the trip, wherever they were heading. The book, which had been his most prized possession, his Bible for all of his formative years, was tossed into the trash with the remnants of the morning's breakfast. It felt strangely liberating to him to turn his back on the trash can and walk away. With a smile, he looked at his watch.

"Va bene! Ten more minutes and I've officially survived basic," he thought with a sigh of relief.

Bernardi had a similar problem fitting his things into his kit bag, but he arrived at a different solution. Surveying the mess that used to be his footlocker, he deviously looked around to see if anyone was watching, then shoved all the stuff under his bed.

"Anybody hear where we're shipping out to?" he asked.

"One of the MPs said North Africa," Amonte answered. "I heard two of 'em talking last night. If they're to be believed, we invaded Egypt last month."

"Egypt? Why, Egypt? And how come nobody tells us a damn thing anymore?"

"Egypt, wow! Hey Vaggi, that's too bad." Bernardi said sarcastically.

"And why is that?" Pino politely inquired.

"Well, all that dry desert air is liable to make mince-meat out of your vocal cords. Better ask your mama to send you lots of hot tea and cough drops."

"Lay off him, will ya?" said Carlucci, showing heretofore unseen backbone.

"Would you mind refreshing my memory here for a minute, Bernardi?" Pino asked. "What's your problem? Did I say something about your *mother* or something?"

"Maybe, I just don't like your face. Or your "my-shit-doesn't stink" attitude. And let me tell you something else: I don't like the fact that somewhere out there I may need someone to cover me, and that someone might be you. It scares me. *Capische,* choirboy?" Bernardi shoved him as he walked past him and out onto the grounds. Pino shook his head, then sat down on his bunk and finished collecting his gear. He thought about the next letter to Gia and what it would say:

"Dear Gia,

I know you'll probably find this hard to believe, Gia, but somehow I've managed to get a reputation as a mama's boy. I guess it's my singing. I probably never should have told anyone that I was an opera singer. But, somehow, I thought that would impress them and they would treat me with respect. Clearly, this was one of the biggest miscalculations of all time. Anyway, I've got to go now, because today we ship out. I still don't know where we're being stationed but as soon as I find out, I'll write. I miss you more than words can express.

Per Sempre, Pino."

The thought made him smile, but he realized that Bernardi's comments were serious. Did anyone else doubt his soldiering skills? He looked around the barracks and saw stern faces gathering their gear. They were all young like him and green like him, just like him. If anyone didn't trust him, none of them had let it show. Pino grabbed his pack and walked out onto the grounds with a serious face but a troubled heart.

The entire company repeated the previous day's exercise and assembled in front of the reviewing stand again. The commander walked back and forth inspecting them, again. Only this time, he didn't look as happy. The men glanced nervously at one another as the commander began to speak. "Congratulations, men, you've all passed basic training. In celebration of this momentous occasion, at 1200, transports will arrive at the main gate to carry all of you to your first stop in Bologna." Surprise filled the faces of the men. "Bologna?" thought Pino, in confusion as the commander continued. "Once in Bologna, you will bunk down for the night before boarding trains in the morning which will carry you south to Taranto."

"Taranto?" said Amonte.

"That's eight hours by train," said Carlucci.

"It beats the hell out of Russia," quipped Bernardi.

"Oh, baby. I love southern cooking!" Carlucci added.

Sounds too good to be true, Pino thought, and it was.

"I see a lot of smiles out there, well, you can lose them right now. In Taranto, you will be briefed on your mission and receive your specific marching orders. You will be drilled for several days before boarding armored amphibious personnel carriers which will carry you to your ultimate destination..." The commander paused for what seemed like an eternity. The men held their breath and crossed their fingers. "Greece," he thundered.

Pino opened up his eyes and knit his brows.

"Greece?" said a disappointed Bernardi.

"Are they on our side?" Amonte asked.

"Beats me," answered Pino, clearly confused. The confusion was short-lived, as the commander continued.

"For those of you who aren't up on current events, I'll briefly fill you in. As most of you know...well, some of you might know, in the past six weeks, Italy has made several advances in northern Africa; specifically Egypt and British Somaliland. With our troops advancing into Egypt, the British Navy will undoubtedly flee Alexandria. The logical port of call for the English fleet will be in Greece. Thus, to prevent the enemy from finding safe harbor, Greece must be eliminated as a place of refuge.

"Great, I'm invading Greece," Pino thought.

"The invasion has already begun. Earlier this week, eight armored divisions struck across the Albanian border and are pushing towards Athens as we speak. We will join them in the second wave in ten days' time. Transports leave at 1200. Have your gear ready and checked. Now, go forth. Be proud of your country and your mission. Believe, Obey, Fight! That is all. Dismissed."

CHAPTER FOUR

THE ROAD TO HELL

THE ROMANCE THAT PINO HAD ALWAYS associated with trains was nowhere to be found as the army transport train rolled through the early morning mist *en route* to Taranto. The stop in Bologna was brief, and the 5:00 am departure made it seem even briefer. The four newly christened soldiers sat facing one another, trying to sleep, with the exception of Bernardi, who slept like a stone.

"I'm not so sure about this," Pino whispered, so as not to wake Bernardi.

"No one asked you," replied Amonte. "For what it's worth, Greece sounds a hell of a lot better to me than Africa."

The argument seemed sound, but the thought of approaching combat anywhere worried Pino. He looked at Bernardi sleeping next to him and nudged him gently.

"Hey, you awake?" he asked and got no answer. Then more boldly, Pino shook him. "Come on, quit pretending to sleep. We're having a serious discussion here. Why are you so quiet?" Bernardi opened his eyes slowly and turned to face Pino.

"I wasn't sleeping. I was thinking."

"Yeah, thinking about sleeping," Pino quipped.

"Or food,' Amonte added smugly.

"Yeah, ouzo, souvlaki!" Carlucci stated, like an authority on Greek cuisine.

Bernardi brought the conversation back home.

"I can't wait to shoot somebody," he said looking Pino straight in the eyes, with a frankness that unnerved him. While Bernardi yawned and closed his eyes again, the rest of them sat in silence. His words brought into focus an unpleasant reality none of them had quite grasped yet. The thought pierced Pino's tired brain and sent a cold chill through his body.

Pino sat back in his seat and looked out the window. The moon was sinking on a misty blue night overlooking the sea, giving way to a dull blue-grey morning. As the yellow moon faded into the breaking day, in his head, Pino could hear Gia singing the "Hymn to the Moon," from *Rusalka*, the aria he first heard her sing that day in the Maestro's studio; the cry of the Little Mermaid yearning to be with her Prince, and imploring the Moon to hear and help her.

"Oh, Moon in the velvet heavens, your light shines far, you roam throughout the world gazing into human dwellings. Oh, Moon, stay a while! Tell me where my beloved is! Oh, tell him, silver moon, that my arms enfold him, in the hope that for at least a moment he will dream of me. Shine on him, wherever he may be and tell him of the one who waits for him here!"

The words seemed appropriately fitting. He missed the warmth and security of that studio, and he missed Gia, but he especially missed the maestro. He sighed and turned over to try and catch some sleep.

As the train headed south toward Taranto, another division was headed north toward Taranto. Only this division was composed of English fighter bombers. In all, two aircraft-carriers, five battleships, ten cruisers, thirty destroyers, four armed trawlers and a large number of merchant marines were bearing down on the Italian fleet as it slept. The Italian Navy was large and formidable, comprised primarily of battleships, heavy cruisers and swift destroyers and the Gulf of Taranto was its principle base of operations. It seemed completely incomprehensible that a handful of antiquated English bi-plane torpedo bombers could possibly inflict any serious damage to the largest and most painstakingly guarded port in all of Italy. Yet when the dust cleared, the Italian fleet lay in ruins.

On the evening of November 11th, twenty-one British Swordfish fighter-bombers launched from the air-craft carrier H.M.S. Illustrious in the Mediterranean near the Greek Island of Cephalonia. For some odd reason, the air-raid sirens in Taranto went off twice that night in false alarms prior to the arrival of the English and perhaps this fact contributed to the complete state of surprise that the bombers found upon their arrival. The Italian Navy possessed no radar but they had a fairly sophisticated acoustical early warning system designed to detect the sound of airplane engines from far off. It proved sadly lacking.

In two waves, the British struck. The low-flying Swordfish were World War I fighter bombers that flew very slowly and made easy targets. Despite the relative ease spotting the incoming targets, the Italian anti-aircraft batteries couldn't seem to find the mark and the English lost only one plane in the attack. In all, two pilots were lost and two taken prisoner. It was a remarkable success for the British. The second wave was even more successful than the first, striking land based targets as well as anchored ships.

Taranto, the largest and most well-armed anchorage in the Mediterranean was effectively liquidated in just under two hours. Four of the Italian navy's six battleships were in smoking ruin along with two of its heavy cruisers. The two remaining battleships, the Giulio Cesare and the Vittorio Veneto were given immediate orders to steam north to Naples to escape the onslaught. The physical damage to the Italian fleet paled in comparison to the psychological damage that the attack left in its wake, effectively dashing forever *Il Duce's* dream of ruling the Mediterranean.

The famous *sole* of southern Italy was nowhere to be found when the train carrying Pino and his pals reached Bari, the last stop before their final destination of Taranto. Bari was simply gorgeous, a coastline of immense natural beauty with the vast Adriatic sea visible from the window of the train. Pino had never seen it before and the rocky coast spreading out before him was positively striking. He'd only been to the seaside once in his lifetime on a family vacation to the *Cinque Terra* on the Italian Riviera. At the time, the sea didn't impress him much. He must have been too young to appreciate it, he thought, because as he looked out at the crystal blue water before him, his breath was taken away. It looked both stunningly beautiful and profoundly peaceful. Yet somewhere out there across this deep blue pond lay Greece, where he'd soon be traveling to kill the enemy and conquer the country for his own. It still seemed completely unreal to him, but he was sure something would happen sooner or later that would snap him into shape and help him tap into his inner warrior.

Taranto was located in what could be called the upper arch of the boot of Italy, where the heel met the sole. As the train approached the last stop on its long journey, Pino could see large mountains in the distance that dominated the west side of the Gulf of Taranto. The Appenino Calabrese range ran for hundreds of kilometers and could be seen from all around. Two harbors comprised the port of Taranto; an inner harbor known as the Mare Piccolo and the greater outer harbor known, not surprisingly, as the Mare Grande. The two were connected by a canal making the port a virtually closed harbor except for one entrance to the southwest. The outer harbor, at four kilometers across, was one of the greatest deep water harbors in the entire Mediterranean and the pride of the Ionian Sea.

All Pino knew about Taranto was that the famous folk dance the Tarantella was said to have originated there. Originally, the dance was supposedly done to ward off the effects of spider bites. He'd learned the latter fact from Bernardi, so he regarded it with the appropriate degree of incredulity.

Pulling into the train station, it appeared that the morning fog hadn't yet lifted, despite the fact that it was nearly midday. From the moment the soldiers disembarked the train, it was clear that something was terribly amiss. There were no transport vehicles to pick them up and carry them to camp. There was no one to greet them at all at the station. As the enormous mass of soldiers piled out onto the platforms, confusion began to spread. Captain Adamo, always appearing in control of any situation, told his men to sit tight while he sent messengers to reconnoiter.

The unmistakable smell of burning oil hung in the air and what had appeared to be fog was clearly the residue of smoke from some not-too-distant fire.

"This does not look good," Pino said to Amonte.

"No shit," said Amonte pointing to the black clouds of smoke on the horizon. "What do you make of that?"

"God knows," said Pino, looking at Bernardi, who was nodding his head as if to say, "Finally!" As the heat of battle appeared to be closer than ever, Bernardi's demeanor became increasingly manic. Pino was more frightened of him than of any unseen enemy, because Bernardi gave the appearance of someone who simply wanted to inflict pain; whom he inflicted it upon was immaterial. From the looks of things, he would get his wish sooner rather than later.

Before long, the situation became apparent. A massive attack had rendered the Italian fleet dead in the water. No transports had come for them at the station because all available personnel were at the harbor dealing with the aftermath of the attack. A vast cloud of English fighter bombers drifted into Taranto harbor completely undetected during the night and decimated most of the fleet. They also learned that while the Navy had been dealt a devastating and crippling blow, almost miraculously, the loss of life had been mercifully small; a total of forty casualties. Given the gravity of the attack, the small number of casualties was shocking, and as Pino surveyed the smoking ruins of the harbor, he was convinced it was a complete miracle. In the utter chaos that reigned, one thing was certain: they would not be boarding any ships anytime soon.

The housing that was earmarked for the new arrivals had been converted into make-shift triage and field medical units. Pino's entire company was immediately pressed into service; some carrying the wounded, some fire-brigade, some construction and demolition. It was nothing that they were trained for but circumstances dictated that they learn quickly.

Pino was deathly afraid of medical duty and was relieved to hear his name called for fire-brigade. The sight, and in some cases the smell, of the wounded upset his stomach to the point that he thought for sure he'd vomit. The smell of burning flesh was not something he was prepared for and even from a distance he felt nauseous. It would be days before his constitution returned to normal, to say nothing about his ability to sleep. His moonlit dreams of tranquil waters and the soft murmur of the sea, with Gia by his side, were replaced by dreams of smoke-filled skies, air-raid sirens and the cries of the wounded, until sleep in general was almost unknown.

Those first few days were complete pandemonium with the new arrivals waking up and assembling only very briefly before breaking off and heading in different directions with their various attachments looking for something to do. This managed chaos continued for several weeks until the base was back to some semblance of its former self. The rag-tag nature of the work was not efficient but it got the job done. Pino was pleased to learn that the soldiers he met down there had a much greater knowledge of what was going on in the war and were more than willing to share.

"Was it just the infantry that was kept in the dark?" he mused. He could have hoped for better news because he soon learned the Greek invasion wasn't going as well as had been expected. He thought of the assurances of the officers back in basic. "Success is virtually assured," he remembered them saying.

"I guess *virtually* was the key word in that statement," he laughed to himself, though he knew it wasn't funny. As he heard more, his heart sank. Apparently, with barely two weeks' worth of preparation under their belts, Italian troops were ordered to cross the Albanian-Greek border. Seven ill-fated divisions of the 9th and 11th Armies were dispatched with no naval or air support at all. To add to the misery, torrential rains fell during the invasion and as the temperature dropped below freezing, the infantry found itself woefully unprepared for what quickly became a winter battle.

There was also a great miscalculation of the Greeks' willingness and determination to fight. The Greeks were more than prepared and with the support of English Royal Air force bombers, they pummeled Italian positions in Greece and Albania. It wasn't long before the Greek military posture changed from defense to offense. As the battered Italian army retreated back into Albania, the Greeks followed, not merely to the border but into Albania! After a month of fighting, a full one-third of Albania was securely under Greek control.

It was a disaster and a humiliating discovery, one that further shook Pino's already shaky confidence in his military commanders. The weeks and eventually months spent in Taranto preparing for the "second wave" of the Greek enterprise proved no great relief either. It became readily apparent that no Plan

B had ever been devised. So sure were they of their success, a defensive posture had never even been discussed.

Pino shared the information with his comrades and saw their faces fall. It was clear that even Bernardi wanted no part of any re-vamped invasion. Pino prayed nightly for a miracle that would spare them from deployment on the Greek front and after only a few short weeks, his prayers were answered.

CHAPTER FIVE

TIME TO SAY GOODBYE

THE WOOL UNIFORMS THEY WERE ISSUED were designed for all seasons and all types of weather – or so they said. Doing his morning exercises in the cold rain, Pino thought about how miserable the wet clothes would feel for the next two days, but they were the only ones he had. He didn't dare say a word about it, even to Amonte, for fear of rekindling his "mama's boy" image, which had to some degree silently gone away. The cold and the constant dampness kept Pino in a perpetual state of sore throat and sinus congestion. He had never before missed his clear mountain air so much. The misery index, as he liked to call it, didn't seem to have the same effect on his comrades and he was jealous. Despite a runny nose and watery eyes that gave the constant impression that he was sick, he clung to a manufactured tough exterior.

One foggy spring morning as the men were doing their daily running, a siren blast was heard. At first, panic set in; the thought of another sneak attack was remote but not unthinkable. As the men frantically headed back to base, Pino pulled out his sister's Saint Christopher medal, which he never took off, and kissed it for luck.

The base was abuzz with electricity but not the kind Pino had expected. No one was running to battle station or for cover, rather they were assembling as if for inspection. As they reached their barracks, scrambling soldiers told them the CO was about to address them, so they quickly fell in behind the rest of them. Reaching the reviewing grounds, they formed ranks and waited in great anticipation for their captain. They didn't have to wait long. Captain Adamo strode confidently before his men, looking almost radiant as he prepared to address them.

"Gentlemen," he barked characteristically, "today, I have the great honor of sharing with all of you your new marching orders, concerning occupied Greece. As I'm sure you've all heard by now, last fall, the Italian army executed a daring invasion of northern Greece." He paused and surveyed their expressions. "Despite a well-planned, well-executed campaign, due to circumstances beyond the control of *Comando Supremo*, the Greek army repelled our advances."

"How reassuring," muttered Pino.

"Did he say 'occupied' Greece?' noted Bernardi.

"Maybe it was a slip."

"Yeah, or wishful thinking." The commander stopped speaking and looked in the direction of Pino and Bernardi.

"Shut up back there!" he yelled, and the stone-faced soldiers did as ordered. The commander resumed, "Despite the valiant efforts of our troops, superior numbers and tactical advantage allowed the Greeks to postpone their *inevitable* downfall. However, last week, our allies to the north, 50,000 Nazi storm troopers finished the job that we began. Two days ago, Athens fell and the occupation was complete. We now have the proud and honorable task of securing the new eastern border of the Axis powers. Tomorrow at 0800 hours, you will board ships and armored transports bound for Piraeus, Greece. Have your gear stowed and checked and ready for inspection at 0700. That is all."

As the men walked back to their barracks, the debate began.

"I'm not so sure about this," Pino whined.

"Are you crazy?!" yelled Amonte. "Occupation is the best imaginable scenario. It's like baby-sitting!"

"Yeah, no shells exploding over your head, no machine guns, no snipers trying to pick you off," Carlucci added. Once again his comrades' arguments seemed to make perfect sense, but something bothered Pino, something that he couldn't put his finger on.

"I've been thinking about why they're sending us to Greece," said Bernardi with an uncharacteristic softness.

"What's the big mystery?" interjected Amonte. "It's like Carlucci said in basic, Hitler thinks we're rotten soldiers and he'll never trust us again to mount any kind of offensive. So, he'll stick us with a job that even us stupid macaroni eaters couldn't screw-up: playing nursemaid to the Greeks!"

"Yeah! It makes perfect sense to me," agreed Carlucci. "He sticks us as far away from the real action as he possibly can."

"Exactly," said Bernardi as though he had figured out a puzzle none of the others were even aware of.

"What are you getting at?" Pino asked, irritated.

"Okay. He just overran Greece a week ago, right? And right away, he's so anxious to hand it over to the very same troops that bungled the invasion the first time? I mean, it's still the front isn't it? It may not be the Russian front, but it's still the frontier of his *empire*, right? And suddenly he completely trusts the Italian army to protect his southeast flank?"

They all sat in silence pondering the words, but still no one quite understood the significance of what he was saying.

"Are we playing nursemaid to the Greeks?" Bernardi continued. "Or are we lambs being led to the slaughter?" That thought had never entered Pino's mind, but now it hit with all the subtlety of a sledgehammer.

"You mean, you think...he feels that we're expendable?" Pino stuttered. "That's the way I see it, choirboy," Bernardi stated. "It's not like Greece has a wealth of natural resources that he desperately needs, or needs to protect."

"Can I just make a point here...*So what?*" answered Amonte. "Are you guys nuts? I'd much rather be guarding something that nobody wants, anyway. Isn't it safer?"

Less than twenty-four hours later, they packed up their gear and boarded a ship bound for Greece. It was part of a great convoy of warships headed east from Taranto across the Ionian Sea. Coming from the mountains, Pino had never been on a ship before and the experience was strangely thrilling for him. For a brief moment, he almost forgot he was headed to war. He was again the wide-eyed boy who cried at La Scala. Unfortunately, his wonderment was short-lived. After only a few hours on board the boat, Pino began to feel a dull pain between his eyes. Then a similar discomfort manifested itself behind his ears at the base of his head. He wrote it off to the dampness, or perhaps he was catching yet another in an endless stream of colds. He went on deck to get some fresh air. Rain was beating down, again, and Pino walked out into it. The ship was tossed gently by the waves and the motion, which at first had a soothing effect on Pino, was now beginning to bother his stomach. He deeply inhaled through his nostrils and exhaled through his mouth. He did this for several minutes. He thought his old breath control exercises might help clear his head, but they had little effect. He stepped back out of the rain into a doorway on deck. The sound of the rain hitting the deck of the ship reminded him of something but he couldn't remember what. "Frying eggs!" he thought. The rain sounded like a griddle with eggs frying. The thought gave him a momentary feeling of warmth all over. Eggs and bacon frying in the kitchen downstairs, a simple pleasure, like so many others, that he never fully appreciated, until now. He closed his eyes and tried to imagine himself back in the warm comfort of home, underneath his covers, listening to breakfast cooking downstairs in the kitchen. He got goose bumps thinking about it.

Suddenly, he didn't feel well. He opened his eyes and tried to focus them. They weren't cooperating. Pino's stomach was in an uproar. He panted and gasped but he was dizzy and nauseous. He ran to the railing and got violently sick overboard. He had never felt so awful in his entire life. At that moment the door swung open and Amonte stepped out onto the deck. At first, he didn't notice that it was Pino only a few feet away leaning over the railing. Amonte lit a cigarette and coughed. Pino turned his head and looked at him.

"Jesus Christ," Amonte called out, "You're green!"

He ran to Pino's side and helped him away from the railing and out of the rain. He helped him back to his hammock and out of his wet clothes.

"Call the medic," Pino implored, but Amonte just laughed.

"What's so funny?" Pino demanded.

"The medic won't come because you're seasick."

"Seasick?" Pino muttered.

"Get some sleep. You'll be fine when the rain stops." Amonte said with a wink, and he walked away.

"Seasick," Pino said again, disappointed. This entire military existence was finally getting to him. He desperately tried not to cry, but he was losing the fight. The next day, the rain had still not ceased. The men were called together for a briefing, but Pino couldn't get out of his bunk. He was in another world, a delirium. He hadn't eaten anything in seventy-two hours and he was becoming severely dehydrated. Finally, the medic came to see him. The medic looked as if he had been in the army since the last war, maybe the last century. He had an impatient air about him and didn't appear to have much sympathy for his patients.

"What's the problem here?" the old doctor asked. Pino gulped and tried to answer, but his mouth was too dry. "Hmmm. I see," the medic replied. He reached into his bag and took out several bottles of pills. He opened each one and took out a multitude of colored pills. "Sit up," he ordered Pino, and Pino struggled to obey. "You've got to get up and about. I want you to sit on deck and look out at the horizon. Take these every four hours till you feel better. And I'm going to give you a vitamin shot so you don't catch your death before we even reach shore."

After the medic left, a dizzy and weak Pino got out of his bunk and lumbered up to the deck. He had chills and a fever and thought seriously about diving overboard to end his misery, but after a few minutes, his stomach started to feel a marked improvement.

"The old medic was a magician!" he thought. For the first time in days, Pino began to believe that he might just survive the voyage, after all. The meeting that Pino had missed was an important one. However, given his condition, it was probably best that he didn't learn what was in store for them next. In the morning, the men assembled in the ship's hold, where they boarded armored amphibious personnel carriers. They were packed in like sardines.

Pino was feeling much better now. His head still ached, probably as a result of the dehydration, but his stomach was back to normal. He stood silently in the personnel carrier. Loud grinding noises could be heard all around. A tarp covered the soldiers so they couldn't see what was going on. Suddenly, they began to move. They could feel the inertia of the vehicles as they slowly rolled forward. Then just as quickly, they splashed into the water. The motion hit Pino like a thunderbolt, but he refused to give in to it. He could hear the rain pounding the tarp above him. The tarp was water-resistant but as soon as puddles began to form on its surface the men quickly learned the difference between water-resistant and water-proof. Whichever this tarp happened to be, it proved insufficient. Soaked and miserable, the men stood quietly. Only Amonte moved about the vehicle. Like the mayor of the boat, he was buzzing around chatting with virtually every soldier on board. He reached Pino and sat down on the floor. Pino started to kneel down to talk to him but just then, a wave struck the craft and tossed it around like a cork. Pino nearly lost control. He pushed his way to the edge of the vehicle and poked his head out from under the tarp. He pulled it back in, soaked, cold and miserable.

He closed his eyes and dreamed of Collagna. No matter the trouble, no matter the strife, no matter the pain, the peace of Collagna and the stillness of the Apennines could never be disturbed in his mind. The mountains were his refuge and when he returned there he knew that the flowers would be blooming, the trees would be blossoming, the birds would be singing and the trout would be swimming. He could smell the chestnuts and the oleander and taste the fresh figs.

"You, OK?" Amonte asked, bring the dream to a crashing halt.

"Huh? Oh. Never felt better," said Pino.

"Well, it's official," Amonte blurted.

"What's official?"

"There's absolutely no one onboard that speaks a word of Greek."

Pino burst out laughing but quickly checked himself.

"Is that what you were doing?" he asked.

"Hey, someone's gotta be able to communicate with the natives."

"I guess," Pino said with a smile.

"Hey, Sassani said that they have a totally different alphabet than us. Is that right?"

"How the hell would I know?" Pino retorted.

"Well, you're an opera singer, right?"

"Yeah, so?"

"So, you probably know more languages than anybody else here," answered Amonte.

"You ever heard of a Greek opera?" Pino asked sarcastically.

"No. But I never heard of a Russian or German opera either till I met you. So, I figured maybe they have opera in Greek, too."

"Well if they do, I've never heard of it."

"Bah! What good are you?" said Amonte.

Pino poked his head from under the tarp only to get soaked by the rain again. He pulled it back in and shook the water off like a dog.

"Antonio, in your travels, did you come across anyone who knows where we're headed?"

"All anyone's saying is Greece," Amonte said with a yawn. "Whether it's the mountains or the islands is anyone's guess. I'm hoping it's the islands."

"Any particular reason?"

"It's warmer. What about you?"

"Anywhere but the islands."

"Why's that?"

"I heard back in Taranto that the British have been attacking the islands. *And* I don't think the islands have any kind of communications, no mail or anything. That kind of worries me."

"You worry too much."

"Yeah, I know. I'm working on it."

"Hey, I never asked you, you married?"

"Engaged," he answered with a bashful smile.

"Uh huh. That explains a lot.

"Like what?

"Like why you'd rather be near a mailbox than the beach!" Amonte chided him.

Pino smiled as he thought about Gia for the first time in days. He was really beginning to rely on Amonte for emotional support; the two had become fast friends. Pino looked at his friend lighting a cigarette and thought that if they both survived the war, they would certainly be friends for life. Amonte took a deep drag from the cigarette and blew the smoke outside of the tarp. Pino reached over and grabbed the cigarette from Amonte and took a drag himself. Amonte just stared at him, perplexed.

"Isn't smoking bad for the voice?" he asked slyly.

"The worst," said Pino, taking another drag.

Amonte smiled. "In that case," he said, "here, keep the pack." The two soldiers shared a laugh and a smoke. They could just as well have been in a cafe in Milan or Florence. The only thing missing was the coffee.

The personnel carriers rolled out of the water and onto a rocky beach. The beach appeared to be immediately next to a fairly large port. "Piraeus," they surmised. The vehicles pulled up to a line of covered military trucks, neatly lined up waiting for them. The men disembarked the carriers and immediately boarded the trucks. Bernardi climbed aboard a truck and sat down with a massive groan, followed by his three friends, who piled in and sat on wooden benches that lined the sides of the truck.

"It'll be nice to finally sleep on something that's not moving," Bernardi said with a yawn.

"I just want to put on some dry clothes," Carlucci added.

Pino looked out of the back of the truck. Wave after wave of soldiers poured out of personnel carriers and boarded trucks. This was the real thing, he thought, and for the first time since he started basic training, he was really, really afraid. He thought about what Bernardi had said about being expendable. It stuck with him, like a gently nagging pain he always knew was there. As he watched, some trucks pulled away and headed north, while others headed south. He was confused. Were they being split up?

"I hate to sound like a broken record, but does anybody have a clue where we are?" he inquired as the truck started to pull away.

"Who cares?" Bernardi growled. "We are where we are. All that matters is that you keep your eyes open and stay alert." Again, his words seemed uncommonly logical to Pino.

"Keep your eyes open and stay alert," Pino repeated to himself almost like a mantra. He didn't believe it. Still, he kept repeating it, or some derivation of it. He concluded it had significantly more impact when someone else said it. Amonte looked at Pino and flashed a nervous smile, which Pino returned. Then he stood up and walked up to the cab of the truck.

"This is ridiculous," he said and banged on the back of the driver's window. The driver pulled open the curtain. "Hey, where are we headed?" Amonte asked.

"Athens," was the reply. A hush fell on the soldiers. Whether it was surprise or fear or delight, none could say. What was certain was the relief that Pino felt. For some strange reason, he always felt safer in a city. Perhaps it was the massive stone buildings that he remembered from Milan, the ones that appeared so indestructible. Maybe it was the thought that they'd never want for food or provisions in the city. He seemed to remember that Athens was on a hill or a mountain. In any case, his brain told him that in a war, high ground was better than low ground. He didn't remember why, but he definitely remembered that the captain had said that: "Due to the strategic advantage of a high-ground position the Greeks repelled the advances of the Italian army."

"Athens?" Bernardi spouted.

"Wow! The big city!" Carlucci beamed.

"I guess that settles that," Amonte said with satisfaction.

"Yep, all the comforts of home," Bernardi added with a half laugh.

"I hear Athens is absolutely beautiful," Carlucci said.

"Oh yeah, the architecture is supposed to be just spectacular," Amonte spouted sarcastically. "Just spectacular."

CHAPTER SIX

ATHENS

THE RIDE FROM THE COAST to the city was far shorter than any of them had expected. Along the way, the soldiers peered out the back of the truck. The view inspired little confidence. In every direction, all that could be seen was devastation and destruction: fallen buildings, rubble, storefronts with smashed windows, women and children in the streets.

"Oh, yeah, great architecture," Bernardi remarked. Pino felt his heart begin to race and his throat go dry.

"Man, those Nazis don't fool around, do they?" he nervously added.

"You know," said Amonte, "I think I can safely say for the first time...I'm kind of glad they're on our side."

As the trucks slowly drove through the outskirts of the city, the men didn't see the Acropolis, or the Parthenon or any of the antique structures for which Athens was famous. All they saw was destruction. Looking at the devastation all around him, Pino began to doubt that the ancient ruins were even still standing, but after a while he noticed the destruction seemed to come to an abrupt halt. In fact, once they entered the city proper, it appeared that no shells had been dropped at all. The truck came to a stop and the driver climbed out and walked around back.

"Welcome to Athens, boys," he said dryly as he opened the gate. The men got out and started hauling their gear. They looked around but didn't see anything that even vaguely resembled a camp. This was the middle of town. There were shops everywhere. Confused but undaunted, their backpacks in place, they started across the street to where all the rest of the men were assembling. Aside from the fact that the place appeared deserted, the part of town they were in looked like it hadn't been affected at all by the war.

"Hey, how come the city didn't get hit with any artillery?" Amonte asked the driver.

"Open city," the driver retorted, "like Rome. No fortifications either, by mutual agreement. We don't shell Athens, they don't shell Rome. Too much historical stuff."

Pino was shocked. In all the madness, someone had the presence of mind to think of preserving historical treasures? This was the first sign of civilized thinking he'd come across in some time, and he was shocked the Nazis would agree to it. If it was true, then he was just delighted to sleep under the peace it provided.

"I'm going to find out what's going on," said Bernardi. He bumped into Pino as he passed, offering no apology, then he was gone, moving up through the mass of assembled soldiers. Amonte and Carlucci smoked cigarettes and giggled nervously, as Pino surveyed their surroundings. The street was not unlike any number of Italian streets that he knew, not quite in the center of the city but certainly not on the outskirts either. He was surprised to see so many apartment houses built so close to one another; they appeared to be on top of each other. They didn't have to wait long for Bernardi's return.

"This is it," he announced.

"This is what?" Amonte inquired.

"This is home," Bernardi declared, pointing to a small building just a few feet away.

"I don't get it," Pino replied.

"I didn't either, but now it makes sense. We're commandeering hotels around the city to use as barracks."

"How does that make sense?" Amonte asked.

"You wouldn't understand," Bernardi quipped impatiently. "But, more importantly, we get to sleep in real beds. Can you understand that much?" A great groan of relief passed among the men. This was certainly a good sign; perhaps a small and insignificant one, but a good one nonetheless. They followed the rest of their company through the door of the modest Hotel Aegean. Once inside, Pino looked around, examining the place, and found nothing particularly special about it. It was clearly a low-end hotel for travelers on a budget, but it might as well have been the Excelsior to Pino. The rooms were tiny and Spartan. What had been single rooms now housed three beds.

With the usual randomness, Amonte and Bernardi were assigned to the same room as Pino. Carlucci was on another floor on the other side of the building. He was annoyed and felt like he was consistently being left out, maybe he was. As Amonte and Pino began to unload their gear, Bernardi dropped his pack on the floor and flopped onto the bed.

"Home sweet home," he muttered.

"Not bad," Pino said with a smile, testing the mattress. "Not bad at all."

"Not bad?" Amonte yelled. "This is goddamn paradise! Think of all the poor suckers out there sleeping in ditches tonight! Admit it, we hit the jackpot, boys."

"Keep your shirt on," Bernardi admonished, "It's still a war, and you can bet that the natives aren't too thrilled about us being here."

Once again, Bernardi surprised Pino with his sober grasp of the situation.

"No, no, no. You're right. You're right," Amonte agreed. "All I'm saying is, we could've done a lot worse." They all silently agreed and Pino was feeling a lot better about his situation than he was only an hour earlier. His body told him to lie down and get some rest but his mind raced.

"So, what do we do now?" he asked. "See anything posted? Any orders? An agenda, or something?"

"Vaggi, why don't you take a walk around and see if you can find out where and when we're supposed to report. And see if you can find some food, too," grumbled Bernardi, regressing to the primordial beast Pino had come to know.

"Anything else?" Pino replied sarcastically.

"That's all. Dismissed."

"Sorry I took so long to write, but for a long time I had no idea where we'd be stationed. And after a seemingly endless trip by bus, train, boat, and finally truck, we arrived in Athens. I guess we got lucky being sent somewhere that's probably not going to see much action. But we've got to be extra careful not to relax too much, because you only have to look around at this place to remember why we're here. The devastation is unbelievable. This beautiful and proud city is practically a wasteland now. But none of the great historical places were touched. Still, the emptiness is creepy. Being on the winning side does have its advantages. Instead of sleeping in tents or barracks, we've actually commandeered an empty hotel, and we're sleeping in real rooms on real beds. Not bad, eh? It doesn't look like there'll be any tourists coming here anytime soon, so the army decided to borrow it for a while.

I'm bunking down with two of the guys from basic, Amonte and Bernardi. Amonte is my closest friend out here. I think I mentioned him in my last letter. He's the son of a butcher down in Todi. And Bernardi, well, let's just say we tolerate each other. He's a big ox from Naples whose only two joys in life are eating and sleeping. All in all, it's not so bad. If it stays quiet, I may even try to study my music a little. I guess that's all for now. I'll write again as soon as we're a little bit more settled. Please tell my family I'll write them all very shortly. And give Maria a big kiss for me. You're in all my thoughts.

Te adoro, Pino"

CHAPTER SEVEN

THE PLEASURES OF OCCUPATION

IN 1941, THE POPULATION OF ATHENS and its surrounding area was nearly nine hundred thousand, yet judging from the silence in the streets after the Nazi occupation, one might easily have thought that the city was deserted. The Nazis imposed stringent regulations on movement. Food rationing was commonplace and a strict curfew was in effect. The German soldiers were not the most tolerant creatures, and stories of atrocities were rampant. Rumors spread of people disappearing in the night never to be heard from again.

When the Italian army was dispatched with the task of occupying the city, the Greek people didn't know exactly what to think. One thing was immediately clear, however, and that was that the Italian soldiers were neither as vicious nor as unsympathetic as the Germans. But it was still occupation, and one of the world's oldest and proudest civilizations could hardly be content in that condition. The Italian soldiers sensed it immediately and never failed to remember it while on patrol.

Patrolling was the general order for the occupation forces. The soldiers spent most of their days patrolling the nearly empty streets, not knowing exactly what they were on the lookout for. In any occupation, there is always a fear of insurrection, but from the outset, that never appeared a likelihood in Athens, where the vast majority of the remaining population was comprised of women, children and old men. The second most common fear was snipers and it was a real fear indeed, so the soldiers on patrol needed to remain alert at all times.

Pino walked with Amonte down a particularly hard-hit street. In spite of the "open city" designation, it seemed the German's just couldn't help themselves. Rubble was everywhere: smashed stone and cement, broken glass and a particularly foul smell about which they did not wish to venture a guess. It wasn't an ancient and mossy smell like in a church or some hallowed place; rather it was like rotting garbage. Pino had had a peculiar notion that all the buildings in Athens were made of marble, yet in the weeks that he had been there, he had yet to see any. The streets were almost identical to those in Italy, only they smelled much worse. There were some scattered fruit vendors, flower stands, sponge vendors, all with relatively few customers. A constant flow of old women and children were hurriedly moving about. It was almost a week before Pino saw his first male of the species in Athens. At first he couldn't figure out why, but he checked his own stupidity and the ugly reality of the situation set in: there probably weren't any left. His wandering thoughts were interrupted by Amonte.

"As I see it," Amonte said, as if he'd just figured out the meaning of life, "we're really just playing police here, right? I mean, this isn't exactly the Russian front." Pino didn't say anything. He'd heard all this before but he was waiting to see where Amonte was going with it this time. "After all, what are we doing here?" Amonte continued. "We break up a fight here and there. We look sternly at the natives to inspire fear and intimidation. We're just like goddamn policemen!"

"All the same," Pino said, "I'm not going to sleep easy till I'm back in Italy."

"Of course you will. It's just a question of getting used to the place. If you'd just relax a little, you might get to like it here. There's really a lot to like about Greece."

Pino stopped dead and looked at Amonte with disbelief.

"Are you out of your mind? Do you even hear what you're saying? I don't want to get used to this place! I want to do my time without getting killed and then get the hell out of here!"

The two men stopped because, as if on cue, two old women appeared, in the midst of a heated argument, yelling loudly at each other. Amonte laughed.

"What did I tell you? Eh?" Then, turning to the ladies, he cleared his throat loudly.

"Ladies! Ladies! That's enough! That's enough, go on home now." The two women gave the soldiers disdainful glances then left in opposite directions. "Yep, police work. I'm telling you, we've got it made here. You ought to let yourself go a little. There's a lot to like about Greece."

They continued to patrol street after street, repeatedly seeing the same scene being played out. It made Pino sad. He wondered if he was too soft. Would it get him in trouble somewhere down the road, or would it get him dead somewhere down the road? He reminded himself that he was an artist and that he possessed the heightened sensibilities of an artist. It was only natural that he should feel things more deeply than most. It was, he told himself, a blessing that would bring great intensity to his life, if he lived long enough to enjoy it.

The routine of daily patrols with no specific objective was beginning to grate on the collective nerves of the men. Weeks and months of mind-numbing routine with no tangible results had produced a tired, weary, and increasingly complacent mob. The sharp, alert soldiers that left Italy some time ago were now a distant memory. The daily calisthenics that were the trademark of basic training were also a distant memory. There was just no denying that this group of soldiers was becoming soft around the middle. Little by little they stopped taking breakfast, lunch and dinner in the mess hall, and started partaking of the wonderful cuisine that surrounded them. For some, the gastronomic style of Greece was a hard sell and a real learning process. For others, it was pure delight.

At first, Pino had some serious doubts, preferring to eat at the base canteen, but soon he found himself in the minority, and occasionally found himself alone! His first venture into the Hellenic culinary arts was at a small *koulouria* stand. *Koulouria* were a kind of pretzel, a bread ring covered with sesame seeds. Pino tried one, then another, and another. Needless to say, it wasn't long before he was hooked and they became a staple of his daily breakfast routine.

Many of the little idiosyncrasies of the Athenian locals were beginning to rub off on the soldiers. Italians and Greeks were such inherently social peoples that it was inevitable for interaction to occur. On sunny afternoons, large groups of soldiers would often join the locals in a game of *koum-kan* or Greek rummy, in Omomia Square. Still others would work the black and gray markets of Athens to secure liquor, cigars or other contraband. Times were hard for the Athenians, so bargains were plentiful.

One brilliantly sunny morning, while on patrol, which consisted of walking in small concentric circles around the "camp," Pino and Amonte came upon a young boy hanging posters. Amonte walked up to take a look at the poster. He tore it off with a laugh.

"Hey! Well how about this! They must have known you were coming! There's going to be an opera tonight!"

"You gotta be kidding," Pino said. "Here?"

"Apparently. I can't read Greek, but that definitely says "opera" and the date is today."

"Who the hell would want to put on an opera here?" Pino demanded.

"Beats me. Maybe the Nazis?"

"Maybe. Look, it's *Fidelio*."

"Is that good?"

"Well, it's just about as German as it gets: Beethoven," Pino said, scanning the poster for clues. "Wait a minute," he said with a start. "This says Athens

Opera. Hmmph, I guess it's not the Nazis after all. Think they'll sing it in Greek?" Pino laughed.

"You know what? Who cares who's putting it on? Who cares what language? We should go. It's just what you need to calm down. Let's ask the captain for liberty. What do you say?"

Pino smiled and shook his head in disbelief.

"Well, maybe you're right. It might be a nice little diversion. Why not?"

Amonte put his arm around Pino.

"Now that's more like it! You'll get the hang of this occupation business yet!"

The two men walked down the street arm in arm, laughing. As soon as they left, the young boy returned and hung another poster where they had taken down the previous one. The poster was hardly the work of art that a *La Scala* opera poster was but it had one feature that no *La Scala* poster could claim. At the bottom of the poster, in small block letters was the word 'Kalogeropoulos'.

The same poster was hanging in a glass box on the outside of the theater. The theater was a large outdoor amphitheater; almost a "theater in the round" style edifice. People were filing in through enormous stone archways.

As Pino arrived, he immediately sensed that the theater was something extraordinary. It stood right in the shadow of the Acropolis, and was clearly built in antiquity.

Finally, Pino was seeing the famous Greek ruins up close, and they did not disappoint. Here, he thought, was the birthplace of philosophy and democracy, and in extraordinarily well-preserved condition. He made a mental note of where the theater was and vowed to return to see it during the daylight hours.

One thing, however, that stood out like a sore thumb was the enormous German flag that was flying from a pole on top of the Acropolis, right in front of the Parthenon. It could not possibly have looked more out of place. It made Pino angry, but he knew better than to say or even think about it.

It was a picture perfect August night, warm and dry. Pino, Amonte and Carlucci stood outside the theater talking and generally enjoying the evening like civilians might. They passed around a bottle of *retzina* that Carlucci had gotten from a street vendor.

"This is really nice," Carlucci said with satisfaction as he took a swig of *retzina*. "Just like the Arena in Verona, eh, Vaggi?"

"Something like that," Pino answered, somewhat preoccupied. "Hey, just how long are we going to wait for him?" Bernardi was late. He had told them that he had some business to attend to before the show and would meet them in front of the theater. Now he was late.

"Relax," Amonte admonished him. "He'll be here any minute. He said he had something important to do first." Then he took a drink of the *retzina* and coughed violently. He looked at the bottle, then at Carlucci. "What *is* this shit?" he asked with a grimace.

"It's *retzina*. Greek wine. It's traditional," Carlucci answered gleefully.

"It's awful! Tastes like wood. Couldn't you find anything else?"

"I asked for a nice *Marchesi di Barolo* '27, but they were all out. They say when you drink this stuff you tell the truth!"

"Then keep it away from me!" said Amonte, "What I wouldn't give for a little of my Papa's Chianti right now." Poking Carlucci playfully, he pointed at Pino, who was pacing back and forth. "Hey, Pino, will you quit pacing already? He'll be here!"

"Yeah, and I'm sure whatever he's doing, it's very important. But this isn't the movies, you know, it's the opera. If you're not in your seat when the doors close, you're screwed! They don't let you in!"

"What do you mean they don't let you in? If you've got a ticket, they have to let you in!" Carlucci protested.

"No, they don't! Not once it starts. Latecomers have to wait outside until the end of the act, and this particular opera only has two acts. They won't interrupt the performance. Those are the rules." Pino kicked the dirt and shook his head impatiently. "And I'm not gonna sit outside because that fat bastard is out getting laid somewhere."

"Is he for real?" Carlucci asked Amonte. "Maybe at La Scala they don't let you in, but not here in this dump. Let's see them try to keep me out."

"Shut up, both of you! Here he comes now," said Amonte. Bernardi approached the soldiers with a swagger. He was smoking a big cigar and carrying a bag.

"It's about time," said Pino. Bernardi walked right by him as if he wasn't even there.

"Shut up, Vaggi. No one's gonna spoil my night," Bernardi bellowed, grabbing the bottle from Carlucci.

"What's this?" he asked contemptuously.

"It's *retzina*. Greek wine."

"It's cow piss," he said as he threw it away. Then, he dramatically reached into the bag and pulled out a large wineskin. "Now, gentlemen," he said, "if you please, try a little real wine!" One after the other, they each took a drink from the skin and moaned with ecstasy. Amonte was the first to venture a guess.

"Chianti? No, Barbera?"

"Mmm...Mother's milk! Now I can die!" groaned Carlucci.

"No, no, no," Bernardi interrupted. "Don't die just yet! First...," he said as he reached into the bag again, "Cubans!" he proclaimed, pulling out a handful of enormous, fat, cigars.

"You're a God!" whispered Carlucci.

"Yeah, yeah, I know. It's a tough job but somebody's got to do it."

They smoked the cigars and drank the wine in perfect bliss for a moment. Their smiling faces spoke of a degree of civilization none of them had known since leaving home. They stared at the starlit night and the madness of the war was light-years away from their thoughts. Pino thought about his father for a moment. He considered just how happy his father always was just to have a cup of coffee, a cigarette and a glass of *grappa* after dinner. For years, Pino had hated the thought that his father was so provincial, that he had lowered his goals and his dreams so much so, that a simple cup of coffee and a little *grappa* seemed like paradise to him. At that moment Pino felt closer to his father than ever before. Maybe the old man knew something Pino didn't, after all. The old expression, that you don't know what you've got till you've lost it, was bouncing around in Pino's head. When Pino hit a perfect high C in an aria, there was nothing to compare with the thrill and the sheer joy of it, yet on this warm August evening, a mouthful of good wine and a fine cigar was the closest thing to paradise that he could think of. He leaned back against the wall and took a long drag on the cigar and coughed violently. He really didn't know how to smoke a cigar, but it didn't matter. It was perfect.

"This is turning into a really special evening. Where the hell did you get all this stuff?" Pino asked wistfully.

"Vaggi, you want to make this evening really special for me?" Bernardi asked.

"Not particularly."

"Don't talk. Just shut up."

"Hey, boys," Amonte interrupted, "I hate to break up the party, but take a look over there. We've got company." Amonte was pointing to a large contingent of German soldiers filing into the theater in their full dress uniforms. "*Der Fürher* likes his opera, I guess."

"There sure are a lot of them. Maybe we shouldn't drink in front of them," Pino said.

"There you go again, Vaggi," Bernardi complained. "If the Germans don't like it, they can kiss my ass." Just as Bernardi said this, a German soldier stopped and looked at the men. He shook his head in disgust and headed into the theater. Incapable of leaving well enough alone, Bernardi felt compelled to answer the German's indignant glance.

"What are you looking at? Huh?" he called out. Amonte and Pino immediately jumped in front of Bernardi and led him away.

"Listen! *Stronzo*. We don't want any trouble with these guys," Amonte admonished him.

"Screw 'em! They want trouble, I'll give them plenty," Bernardi bellowed loudly.

"Just calm down! We're here to have some fun, not get into a brawl."

Bernardi's body relaxed and the others released their grip on him. What they failed to realize was that to a guy like Bernardi, getting into a brawl *was* fun. He lived for just such occasions, and on this night, fate was on his side.

The men entered the theater and gasped. It was truly breathtaking. Pino guessed that it was easily over a thousand years old. It was actually over two thousand years old. Once again a feeling of wonderment filled his body. When they found their seats, Pino was pleased to see that the row in front of them was completely empty. He thought he would take a moment to show off to his buddies his opera knowledge. But the chance was fleeting, for only moments after they sat down, a group of German soldiers took the empty seats right in front of them. Some people believe in fate. Some do not. On this particular night, fate was playing a cruel joke on Pino and his comrades, as the soldier who gave them the dirty look outside just happened to be seated right in front of Bernardi!

Bernardi started to giggle at the bizarre coincidence. Amonte shook his fist at Bernardi with a very stern look. Carlucci put his hands together as if praying and mouthed the words: *"Please, no trouble!"* Bernardi gave them all a look as if to say: *"Who? Me?"* He then smiled and also put his hands together as if praying.

"You make a rotten angel," Pino quipped as the lights went down.

As the glorious *Fidelio* overture began, the majestic strains of Beethoven washed over the crowd and filled Pino with indescribable pleasure. The overture to *Fidelio* was a magnificent creation. Pino had read that Beethoven labored terribly in its composition. In fact, there were several versions of the overture discarded by the master, which were luckily preserved and became standards of the concert repertoire. Pino found himself conducting the score as he listened. Although German music was by no means Pino's preference, he simply could not deny the extraordinary power of the music. He thought about it for a moment and laughed.

What an odd choice of repertoire for a Greek opera company, he thought. After all, *Fidelio* was the story of a man unjustly imprisoned by vicious captors. The man's only hope for escape was his loyal wife, Leonore, who stopped at nothing to free her beloved. She dressed as a man - Fidelio - to deceive the captors and ultimately to free her husband. More significant than the plot was the opera's unquestionable condemnation of oppression and repression in any form. Was this really the kind of thematic material that one would perform in public in a state of hostile occupation?

Suddenly a light went on in Pino's mind. The choice of *Fidelio* was no accident. It had to be by design! The Greeks must have flattered the Germans by suggesting a Beethoven opera in their honor, only the Germans didn't see the underlying message and the irony of such a performance. Very, very clever! It made him a little bit nervous. He felt like he possessed a dangerous secret. He looked at the thousands of people in the audience and wondered how many of them knew. How many suspected? For Pino, there was no suspicion at all. He was absolutely certain he was correct. This knowledge brought about another epiphany for Pino; he was secretly enjoying the fact that, in a small way, the Greeks had gotten the best of the Nazis. This presented a serious and fundamental problem: the Greeks were the enemy, the Germans, the ally. At that moment, Pino was filled with dread about his own conviction. What exactly did the Greeks do to deserve such a fate? And could he ever call the Germans his *paisani*, with a clear conscience? He remembered his father's words from years ago as if he were standing before him speaking them himself; "they are a cold and cruel people, Rosa. Never forget that."

He looked at the German soldiers in the row in front of him. He marveled at the precision of their haircuts. It unnerved him a little. These were truly an exacting, highly disciplined people, capable of unspeakable cruelty. Yet the music that he was listening to was the art of a German, and it spoke of a better, more perfect world. It was glorious in the truest sense of the word. God himself must have moved the composer's hand across the page to create such beauty.

"What a paradox," he muttered, half to himself. Pino's thoughts were disrupted by Bernardi waving the wineskin in front of him. Pino took the sack and drank deeply, then passed it to the others who drank from it noisily. A German soldier sitting in front of Bernardi glanced back over his shoulder to see what the noise was. Seeing them drinking from the wine sack, he sighed heavily in disgust, then turned around again shaking his head.

There was a fundamental difference in the way Germans and Italians perceived opera. In Italy, going to the opera was quite often as much a social occasion as a cultural one, with intermissions regularly outlasting the acts of the opera. By sharp contrast, to the German mind, attending an operatic performance was often akin to attending religious services: music was considered a "holy art" deserving of reverence. A clear illustration of this difference was beginning to transpire.

The German soldier glanced back over his shoulder a second time and shook his head in disgust. Bernardi had had enough and a twisted idea formed in his wine soaked mind. Just as the German soldier turned back to face the stage, Bernardi leaned forward and belched loudly into his ear. Furious, the German soldier jumped up and turned around, but before he could do anything, Bernardi shoved him and the soldier fell backwards into the row of seats in front of him. A huge melee broke out. The audience was screaming in Greek, German and Italian. Fists were flying everywhere. Pino was hiding on the floor. Bernardi was hitting everyone in sight. Several of his blows even landed on Amonte, who was trying to break up the fight. Carlucci was nowhere to be found.

The orchestra continued to play as the fight carried on. Finally, Pino looked up and saw Carlucci sneak out the door. In an instant, Pino's brain decided that it was a wise move and he leaped to his feet and ran to join him. Amonte saw Pino out of the corner of his eye and he, too, made for the door. On the way, he grabbed Bernardi's belt and dragged him kicking and screaming out of the donnybrook.

The commotion inside the theater provided the Italians a perfect opportunity to escape, but as Bernardi was heading out of the theater, he stopped and picked up a garbage can and threw it at the brawling Germans. One soldier saw them and gave chase. Soon, a dozen others joined him.

"Split up! They'll never find us!" Bernardi called out.

"*Stronzo*! They know we're soldiers! They know exactly where to find us!" Amonte cried out. Nonetheless, they did split up and headed off in different directions. Pino stopped after only one block and ducked into a dark doorway to catch his breath. As he stood there, four German soldiers ran right past him, oblivious to his presence. After they were safely out of sight, Pino leaned out of the doorway. He looked in both directions to make sure the coast was clear. Then, he stepped out and started slowly down the street. He took off his army jacket and shirt, folded them and tucked them under his arm. In just an undershirt, he thought he might look a little less conspicuous, but he was perspiring like a beast of burden and hoped to find a water fountain. He decided to head back through the park at the base of the Acropolis. No one would expect him to be headed toward the scene of the crime, and because the night was black as coal and they'd never find him there. He guessed right; they didn't even look. He wandered aimlessly through the woods, following the moonlight, hoping he was heading in the right direction. He kept the Acropolis on his left as he proceeded, and in no time at all he emerged from the woods into a neighborhood of narrow twisting streets. He knew he was lost, but at least he felt he was safe. Despite his sense of security, he walked slowly and cautiously, stopping at each intersection to check for German soldiers. None were around.

Amonte ran west, down a different street, looking over his shoulder as he went. The only person he saw was Carlucci, who seemed to be following him. Amonte cursed him under his breath, "Stop following me, you fucking idiot!" Amonte turned a corner and nearly ran head on into the back of a group of German soldiers, but luckily, they were headed in the same direction he was and didn't see him. Amonte slammed on the brakes and silently retraced his steps, but as he turned the corner Carlucci crashed into him! As they slammed to the ground, Amonte had the presence of mind to immediately cover Carlucci's mouth to smother any scream. The two men lay intertwined on the street for several seconds, holding their collective breath and praying that the Germans didn't hear them. After a few moments of tense silence, they got up, brushed off their uniforms and continued their winding journey home.

Pino was soon walking more confidently through the streets. He still didn't know exactly where he was, but he didn't care. The night was clear and the Germans were far away, or so he thought. After seeing no sign of the Germans anywhere for a few minutes, Pino ceased pausing at intersections to check. His recklessness soon caught up with him. At the very next corner, Pino saw a water fountain. Parched, he headed straight for it, but as he leaned over to drink from it, he noticed a lone German soldier a block away, headed toward him. He froze. He had to think fast. He couldn't run. He didn't want to create the appearance that anything was wrong. He simply finished his drink, yawned over-dramatically and continued down the street. As soon as he passed the corner, he stopped and leaned against the building on the corner. With his heart in his mouth, he crept back to the edge and peeked around the corner. To his horror, the German soldier was running toward him! He panicked. Without looking, he turned to run but crashed into an empty fruit cart, chained to a broken streetlight.

Jesus! I'm dead, he thought. He quickly surveyed the street for somewhere to hide. If he didn't do something fast, he'd be finished. He could hear the

German's footsteps just around the corner. At that instant, he noticed the apron around the fruit cart and darted beneath it. No sooner had he pulled the apron down behind him, than the German's shadow could be seen on the cloth. The shadow paused for the longest second of Pino's life, then continued running down the street. Pino thought his heart would explode. He could hear German voices in the distance. His brain raced as fast as his heart. What could he do? He sat on the ground and tried to compose himself. He decided that the only thing to do was to get comfortable and wait it out. He pulled out his St. Christopher medal, held it tightly and kissed it, then he made the sign of the cross on his forehead with it and kissed it again.

Bernardi lumbered down a narrow street, totally out of breath. He stopped and leaned against a building to rest. He could hear the Germans hot in pursuit, and knew he couldn't stop for long. He started to move again but felt a sharp pain in his abdomen. He doubled over in agony. He rested his hands on his knees and caught his breath.

"Man, do I gotta pee," he thought aloud. He heard a German voice that seemed to be right on top of him. He looked around but saw nothing. He realized that he would never outrun them, so he looked for an alternative. He saw a dark alleyway and ducked into it. The foul smell was overwhelming. There were garbage cans everywhere and he guessed it was rotting food that he smelled. One of these buildings must be a restaurant, he thought. As he reached the far end of the alley, he saw that it was a dead end. He was trapped. He quickly scanned the alley for a place to hide. There was none. He'd never fit in one of the garbage cans. Then, he saw it; a fire escape on the left side of the alley, but it was too high for him to reach. He jumped, but missed the bottom by several feet. He grabbed the biggest garbage can he could find and stood on it. It teetered precariously (the alcohol in his system didn't help) but he managed to get a hand on the bottom rung. He yanked, but it wouldn't come down. He yanked again, but he only succeeded in losing his footing, which left him hanging there. Taking a ferociously deep breath, he lunged upward, dragging his hulking body along. It took all of his strength, but he managed to ascend the ladder, two stories, to the roof.

When he got there, he climbed over the edge and fell onto the roof with a titanic thud. He lay there motionless for a few minutes staring at the star-filled before pulling himself up into a sitting position. He sat with his back against the low wall that circled the perimeter of the building, listening for the Germans, but heard nothing but the sound of his racing heart. He didn't think it would ever recover.

Thank God for basic training, a thought he never expected he'd have. Slowly, he regained his breath and with it, his confidence. He remembered the wineskin. He took it out and raised it to his lips, but much to his chagrin, it was empty. *Va fan cullo!* he cursed, and carelessly tossed the wineskin off the roof. Unfortunately, when the wineskin reached the ground it landed with a loud crash among some glass bottles. "Shit!" he muttered in disgust. He prayed that no one heard the noise, but it was too much to ask. Seconds later, two German soldiers appeared at the head of the alley. Bernardi peeked over the edge at them as they started looking under the junk and the garbage cans.

What idiots, he thought with a slight laugh. *Smells great, huh boys?* Looking down at them, another truly demented idea formed in his inebriated brain. He silently got to his feet and stood near the edge of the building, fighting desperately not to burst out laughing. Then, in a move of unbridled defiance, he unzipped his fly and began to pee off the roof into the alley!

Down below, the German soldiers were continuing their cautious inspection when one of the soldiers felt something gently striking the top of his hat. He looked up and was splashed in the face by the stream. In the darkness, he couldn't quite see where it was coming from. He cupped his hands and caught some of the stream, which he then held up to his nose and sniffed.

"Aaaaugh!" he recoiled in disgust at the smell. Bernardi burst out laughing uncontrollably. He thought he would give himself a hernia. Beneath him, the Germans were screaming, but he had no option except to continue his business until he was tapped out. As one of the Germans tried to reach for the fire escape ladder, Bernardi directed the stream onto him. Finally, Bernardi's bladder gave him the signal that he could move along, and he fixed himself. He leaned over the edge and laughed at the furious German soldiers.

"*Auf wiedersehen, meine Freunden!*" he called out with a mock salute. Then, he gathered himself and took off across the rooftops.

Pino was cold and cramped. He had no watch on, so he had no way of knowing just how long he had been under the fruit cart. He guessed that it had been over an hour, but he couldn't be sure. He was prepared to stay there all night, if necessary. It had been a long while since he had heard any sign of the Germans and he decided to poke his head out and take a look around. He lifted the apron slowly and glanced up and down the street. It was desolate. He began to think that the Germans were all probably in bed by now, sleeping soundly, while he sat wondering whether he'd ever have feeling in his legs again.

With extreme caution, he crawled out from under the fruit cart. He tried to stand but couldn't, so he rubbed his mangled legs which had both fallen asleep. While he limbered up, he looked at the cart that had been his salvation. As he dragged himself off the sidewalk, he took a few coins out of his pocket and left them on the cart, hoping they'd still be there when its rightful owner arrived in the morning.

Walking down unfamiliar streets, whistling softly to himself to curb his nervousness, nothing looked familiar. For the first time in his life, he wished he had his gun with him. Remembering that they'd walked downhill to the theater, he intuitively started back uphill. After about a half-hour of wandering aimlessly, a familiar-looking, broad square appeared. The street at the far end ran north and south and it would eventually lead in the direction of his camp. The street sign revealed it was *Via Patisson,* a street he'd patrolled several times before and he realized he wasn't that far from the base at all. Following the cable car tracks, Pino came upon a large fountain. Although it seemed a relic from a different time, at that moment it was a veritable oasis. He stopped and drank deeply; the water was warm and tasted of metal piping, but nonetheless it was nectar to the parched wanderer. Sated, he sat next to the fountain to relax for a moment and to try to guess the exact route that had brought him there from the theater. Something was different. The night, which had been deadly silent, was silent no longer. In the far-off distance, Pino thought he heard a woman's voice singing.

The opera? he thought to himself. *Must be, but wait, the opera must have ended by now!* He was already well beyond his curfew so he really had no reason to hurry home and decided he'd follow the voice. It seemed as pleasant a compass as one could ask for.

Drawing nearer, the voice grew stronger, along with the sound of a piano accompanying it. He recognized the piece but couldn't identify it. It was certainly Italian and it was absolutely an aria, but the title eluded him. He closed his eyes and began to sway to the music. *It's sure not Fidelio,* he mused. Drifting down the street toward the voice, trying to remember the name of the aria, Pino looked up at the windows of the houses he passed. The street was lined with small shops with apartments above them. Finally, the house from which the music was coming was in sight. It emanated from an apartment down the side street. He followed it. At the back of the building, there was a second floor balcony with French-style doors that opened to a tiny balcony. Pino stopped and again closed his eyes, drinking in the voice. It was extraordinary. It wasn't quite beautiful, but it was powerful and dark and had a tortured quality. It was quite different, quite special, possessing a stunning vibrance and immediacy. He knew right there that he had never before heard its equal. As he listened, he slowly sank to his knees and put his hands together as if praying.

"Incredible. What a sound," he thought aloud. As the voice finished the aria, Pino opened his eyes and put his hands over his heart. *"Brava! Brava, Signorina!"* he uttered quietly. He stared at the open door for several minutes but there was only silence. "Go on. Please sing something else. Please, just one more," he implored internally, but no sooner had he uttered the words, German voices could be heard coming from around the corner. "Damn!" he thought as he looked up at the window one last time. As he got to his feet, he made a mental note of the address. The voice had already made its own mark on him.

CHAPTER EIGHT

THE CONTRACT

T HE GREEK SUN WAS ALWAYS STRONG. It reminded Amonte of visits to his family in Sicily. Todi, his hometown, was a medieval city of towers and walls, all designed to repel advancing armies. Athens was a different story altogether. The city was thousands of years old. The thought made him shake his head with awe. So much of the Western world's history had taken place here and the entire world was directly affected by the writings of the ancient Greeks. He wondered if his time in Athens would one day be written about in history books. He supposed not. After all, occupation was hardly the sort of thing that made the headlines. Battles made headlines, but, in retrospect, he knew he'd gladly trade in the headlines to avoid seeing any real action.

The wheels of the war machine kept turning, and Athens needed to be fortified against attack. Although Athens was declared an "unfortified" city, a demarcation designed to preserve the historic city from bombardment, that didn't stop the Germans from installing massive anti-aircraft gun turrets in the hillsides around the city. Amonte and Pino were part of a special detachment of soldiers building a gun turret on a hillside just north of the Acropolis. The plan was to dig deep irrigation ditches to channel away the runoff of the rains from affecting the foundations of the gun turrets. The ditches were then filled with stones which were covered with sand and then more stones on top of them. These stones were held in place with mortar to form a wall to hide the gun. The guns were enormous. Amonte guessed that its shells would have to be 50 caliber, or 35 at the very least.

"This isn't exactly what I expected when I enlisted," Amonte said, tossing a mammoth stone into a ditch.

"A little sunshine and exercise never hurt anybody," said Pino, uncharacteristically chipper. The warm climate and sunshine agreed with him and for the first time since he'd reported for basic, his head cold had disappeared and he could breathe freely. Amonte stopped digging to wipe the sweat from his eyes and rested for a moment on his shovel.

"Where the hell is Bernardi?" he asked. "He's supposed to be digging this ditch, too!"

"Are you kidding? He's busy bragging to anyone who'll listen about how he pissed on those German soldiers."

Amonte shook his head with a laugh.

"If I were him," he said, "I'd be careful whom I told that to. You can bet those Nazis are none too happy about it. And frankly, they didn't strike me as the forgive-and-forget type."

"I doubt anybody would squeal on him," Pino said.

"No, not on purpose, but this is wartime, buddy, and I wouldn't trust my own *mother* to keep quiet if them Nazis started gettin' pushy. Hey, what happened to you last night? You have any trouble getting back?"

"None at all. In fact, I took a little stroll around the town on my way back," Pino said with a grin. Amonte sensed that there might be a story attached, so he played along.

"Oh, did a little sightseeing, did we?" he inquired.

"Something like that."

"And just what sights did you see?"

"Didn't *see* anything. It's what I *heard*!"

"I don't get it," said Amonte, puzzled.

"Well, while I was walking around, I came to a fountain, not too far from the base. So, I stopped for a drink and sat down to rest for a second, when it happened."

"What? What happened?"

"I heard a voice, but not just any voice. It was like a dream, a vision or something. She sounded like...like I don't know what. There was something beautiful and terrible in her voice."

"She?" said Amonte with a smirk. "Ah! It's a girl we're talking about."

"Not a girl," Pino corrected him, "An angel. A goddess, with a dark, tortured voice, singing in perfect Italian, the most beautiful aria I've ever heard."

"She speaks Italian! Hey, good work, Pino! What's she look like?"

"I have no idea."

"*What?*"

"Before I could see her, the Germans showed up and I had to run."

"Hey! *Amici!*" interrupted Bernardi, from the bottom of the hill. "Take a break for a minute, our first mail's here!"

"Well, all right!" Amonte declared, tossing aside his shovel. The soldiers sat under a tree and drank from their canteens as Bernardi passed out the mail.

"OK, gentlemen, let's see who still loves us," he joked. The remark struck Pino in an odd way. For the first time, he realized that he hadn't received any letters from home at all. It obviously hadn't bothered him too much, because this was the first time the thought occurred to him, but it stirred in him a sudden desire to hear even the slightest news from his little hamlet in the hills.

"Hurry up," Amonte said, "before the Captain sees us sitting around."

"You boys need to relax," said Bernardi, leafing through the letters.

"I don't think we can afford to relax after your little episode last night," Pino retorted.

"Vaggi, don't get me angry or I'll piss on you, too. Take your goddamn mail and shut up." Bernardi threw a thick stack of letters at Pino. He continued throwing letters to the other soldiers and put two in his own pouch. "That's it," he said.

"What do you mean, 'That's it'?" Amonte asked.

"Just what I said. That's all there is," Bernardi answered.

"Great. Some family I've got. I could be dead out here and they don't give two shits. Hey Pino, maybe mine got mixed in with yours." Amonte reached over and started pulling letters out of Pino's pile.

"Help yourself," Pino said sarcastically. Amonte looked through the letters dejectedly, then suddenly he got a curious look on his face.

"Who's this Gia Mastrangelo? She sent you like a dozen letters!"

"She's my *fiancée*," Pino said sheepishly.

"Whoa!" Bernardi roared. "Your *fiancée*? You never said anything about a *fiancée*."

"Well, Bernardi, I never knew you cared," Pino said with a grin.

"You got that right. In fact, I was pretty sure you didn't like women, know what I mean?" Amonte laughed and shook his head, but Pino didn't find it amusing.

Was that it? he thought. *Did Bernardi think he was a fenocchio? A homo?*

"I totally forgot you were engaged," said Amonte. "Hey, maybe you shouldn't be out chasing that girl on the balcony!"

"What? What girl on the balcony?" Bernardi demanded. "What did I miss?" Pino took the opportunity to give Bernardi a taste of his own medicine.

"That's right, Bernardi! Two girlfriends, one here and one back home."

Little things such as tact and discretion were qualities unknown to Bernardi, and for a big lumbering Neapolitan, he gossiped like a fish wife. It was like air and water to him: essential; and no one was spared his scrutiny nor his dissection kit.

Among the pile of letters from Gia, there was one letter that stood out. It was oversized and had a hand-written note on it saying: "Open this one first!"

The handwriting was unmistakably that of his sister Maria, and if she wanted him to open that one first, he would do just that. Inside the envelope was another envelope of ivory color with a gold border and a beautiful red wax seal. The seal had been broken. Obviously somebody else, probably Maria, had already examined its contents. Pino's eyes examined the letter and suddenly his jaw dropped. On the back of the letter was clearly written, in big ornate letters, *TEATRO ALLA SCALA*. His heart stopped. His lungs ceased breathing. His mouth agape, he held the letter in front of him for a long moment then pressed it to his chest. He was in suspended animation. He didn't hope. He didn't pray. He didn't think at all. A year earlier, receiving the letter might have been the defining moment of his life, but here, in Greece, that life, with all its trappings, seemed completely foreign. It was almost as if Giuseppe Vaggi, *the tenor*, had been a character he'd read about in a book. That man bore no resemblance to Pino Vaggi the soldier, the warrior, who proudly dug ditches for his country in faraway lands. Slowly, as if in a trance, Pino opened the letter. Despite his surroundings, he was determined to treat the letter with appropriate respect. He was pleased to see that whoever had opened it was careful to tear it open along a crease to protect its contents. His hands trembled as he withdrew the letter from the envelope. He unfolded it slowly and began to read.

Amonte noticed how silent Pino had become and watched him out of the corner of his eye. Pino's eyes went back and forth, then stopped. Whatever it was, it was important, because as he stared at it, his eyes grew wider than Amonte believed humanly possible. Just then, he let loose a blood-curdling scream.

"Aaaaaaaahhhhhhh!"

The scream scared them half to death. Pino stood up, still screaming, and thrust his arms up in the air.

"Jesus Christ, Pino, what is it?" Amonte cried.

"Vaggi! What the fuck?" Bernardi called out. But Pino was on another plain of existence. He ran around in a circle and started up the hill still screaming. When he reached the top he stopped. He was panting uncontrollably. He looked down at his terrified friends and sang out at the top of his voice.

"*Esultate!*" It was the opening to Verdi's *Otello*, sung by the Moor upon his victorious return to Cyprus.

"This had better be good or I'm gonna fucking kill you!" Bernardi yelled. Pino lowered his fists and again looked at the letter, then crushed it in his hands and fell to his knees crying.

The mess hall was buzzing. The news of Pino's outburst, or as some called it, his breakdown, had traveled throughout the company.

"Let me get this straight," Carlucci stated, "*Teatro alla Scala* in Milan offered you a contract to sing there next season, correct?"

"That's right," said Pino.

"Unbelievable! Just unbelievable!" Carlucci marveled.

"And La Scala is the *crème de la crème* of the Opera world, right?" asked Amonte.

"Uh huh," Pino answered.

"Wow! That's great, Pino." Amonte said, like a proud father.

"I can't wait to see the look on my old man's face," Pino said with a smile.

"You're being awfully quiet," Amonte said to Bernardi.

"I'm just trying to figure how they justify doing operas with a war going on," Bernardi sniped. Pino smiled at Carlucci and Amonte, who returned the smile and gave him a delighted "thumbs up." Their sincere happiness for their friend was apparent, Pino felt and appreciated it. He realized he could never fully explain what it meant, nor would they be able to fully grasp it, so he didn't try. Pino never had a brother of his own, but tonight, despite all their differences, he felt more like a brother to Amonte and Carlucci than a friend. He desperately wanted to share a glass of champagne with them to celebrate but that would have to wait.

After dinner there were puddles of water everywhere outside the mess hall from a brief thunderstorm. The soldiers splashed around in them while contemplating the evening's agenda.

"I say, we play some cards and see if anyone has any cigars left, before turning in." Bernardi threw out the idea rhetorically, expecting full compliance from the group.

"Nah, I'm gonna take a little walk and get some air," Pino replied.

"Suit yourself," Bernardi said, not entirely upset at the thought.

"Don't get caught up and forget curfew, Pino," Amonte reminded him.

"Don't worry, I'll be fine," said Pino, with a smile. *"Buona sera."*

Leaving his friends and heading off into the crisp night air, he walked through the city streets humming to himself. He pulled the La Scala letter out from his pocket and kissed it. He was now a tenor in every sense of the word and no one could ever take that away from him. War or no war, he had achieved his life's goal. But he couldn't share it with those to whom it meant the most and who meant the most to him.

He imagined how happy his sister must have been upon receiving the news, probably as happy as he was! She was the only one that had complete and unwavering faith in him. He pulled out the Saint Christopher medal she'd given him at the train station and kissed it. Each night he placed it at the bottom of his footlocker. It was his most treasured possession. Of course, from now on, it would have to share that place of honor with his La Scala contract. Somehow he didn't think Maria would mind.

Nearly an hour passed before Pino reached the fountain from where he had heard "the voice". He took a drink of water, still warm and metallic, from the fountain. Then, he wet his hair down and combed it back with his hands. He took a deep breath and walked toward the window where he had heard the voice.

The street, which had the appearance of being a busy urban thoroughfare during the day, was desolate at night and Pino was pleased at the privacy it afforded. He turned down the side street which lay in complete darkness except for the glow of the lights in the houses. The window was wide open but there was no light or sound. He stood there for a minute and wondered if it was a fool's errand.

Maybe she didn't sing every night? He dashed that idea immediately. *Of course she did! No one could sing like that without total dedication. She must vocalize every day! Perhaps she'd practiced earlier in the day?* There was only one way for him to be sure. He would wait.

He glanced around the street hoping to find a place to sit down and fortune presented him a lone wooden stool in an alleyway just across the street from her window. Picking up the stool, he looked for a suitable yet unobtrusive spot to sit. Unfortunately, there was none. The only spot available was a tiny alley between two stores, used to store garbage cans. Pino moved the trashcans a little deeper into the alley and placed the stool against a wall just a few feet away from the mouth of the alley. The stench was overwhelming.

In relative obscurity, he sat down and got as comfortable as he could. He stared up at the window, but there was still no sign of life. A deep sigh essayed from the bottom of his lungs as he prepared for what he suspected might be a long wait.

Evening turned to dusk and dusk to night, but the window remained silent. Pino sat and stared indifferently at the peaceful night sky, trying his hand at amateur astronomy, but he could only make out the Big Dipper. In the street before him enormous puddles lay like black glass left behind by the storm. In the puddles he could see twinkling lights. Leaning forward to get a better look, he realized that the lights were actually the reflection of the stars in the inky black sky. He thought to himself that he must look ridiculous sitting there among the trash staring into the gutter. If any of his friends saw him he'd have a lot of explaining to do.

The evening had begun with nervous anticipation but it had worn off quickly, and he now found himself bored. With nothing to do but compare the various smells emanating from the alley, it wasn't long before Pino fell asleep. The stool leaning precariously against the brick wall didn't exactly provide the ideal sleeping quarters but he managed to drift away nonetheless. His slumber was brief, however, as the sound of an old man digging through a nearby trash can broke his repose. He hoped the old man wasn't picking through the trash for food but that was the first thought that came to him.

As Pino yawned and stretched, he felt a sharp pain in his neck. He tried to straighten up but couldn't. The unnatural sleeping position, however brief, had done something terrible to his upper back and neck muscles. The pain was blinding and as he tried to gently roll his neck, shooting pain shot up to his brain and down through his spine.

This is just great, he thought. He tried to compose himself but the pain was enough to bring tears to his eyes. The thought occurred to him that he cried entirely too much for a grown man, let alone a soldier. He should make an effort to better control his emotions. Just as he was about to completely give in to dejection, he glanced up at the window and the light came on. His heart missed a beat. He leaned forward on the stool, the pain a distant memory. For some reason, he fumbled through his pockets in search of his letter from La Scala, took it out and clutched it intensely. He leaned forward, straining to listen, but heard nothing. There was a slight sound, as that of people talking. As it grew louder, he could clearly discern laughter.

"I didn't come here to listen to the daily gossip," he thought to himself, but the conversation continued. It seemed interminable. He stood up and paced around the alley, wondering how long he'd stay there before his patience ran out. He didn't have to wait very long before the decision was made for him. The conversation coming from the window abruptly halted. It didn't fade out. It halted, as though a meeting were being called to order. Something about the sudden silence struck Pino as strangely familiar. He slowly stood up and stepped out of the alley and at that moment, the silence was broken.

It was a piano.

"Yes!" he cried to himself. "At last!"

The piano sounded bright and crisp but badly in need of tuning. That could be deadly for a singer still trying to fully develop a sense of pitch. Still, to Pino, it sounded like an old friend. Someone was playing very basic scales, presumably to warm up. Pino tapped along with the piano on an imaginary keyboard floating in front of him. He had always hated practicing the piano, but now it was the most welcome exercise he could imagine. The nostalgia of it was like an old song that you never cared for years ago, but now didn't seem to bother you quite as much, and you even kind of liked it. Pino hadn't experienced anything like it in quite some time and he savored it like a fine wine.

Then there was silence again. The silence didn't last more than a minute before Pino heard a voice humming. It was humming a single note as if a Hindu chant. Then, it stopped. A distant sound of pages turning. Then, it happened. His hopes were answered. Through the window a gentle, covered voice began to sing, softly at first, then with more vigor, more power, more confidence. It was her. There was no mistaking that sound.

She sang very basic warm-up exercises which Pino knew by heart. He hummed along with her as she vocalized, occasionally stopping to blurt out comments, "Bravo!" or criticisms, "Flat!" Scale after scale, higher and higher into the register she went, and Pino went along with her. The discordant sound of the piano began to annoy Pino a bit, but all things considered, he'd heard worse in fancy drawing rooms *not* during a war.

A peculiar thought came to Pino just then: Athens was one of the world's oldest and greatest cities. Compared to Collagna; well...there really was no comparing it with Collagna. Yet this girl, in the heart of Athens, practiced the *exact same vocalizations* that the maestro had taught Pino years ago in a little hilltop village in the heart of nowhere. Pino was filled with melancholy at the thought. Perhaps his musical education wasn't quite as provincial as he'd assumed. Although he rarely thought about it anymore, the subject had gnawed at him for years. The La Scala contract was, of course, the ultimate validation but this little footnote gave him a completely different sense of self-affirmation. He suddenly felt a little less ashamed of his hometown, his family, his education, everything.

While his thoughts were elsewhere, he hadn't noticed that the music had stopped. He looked up to the window and was greeted by stony silence. Suddenly, Pino realized that he was standing in the middle of the street. He looked around hoping nobody was watching and he quickly slithered back to his stool in the alley. Just as he got himself reacquainted with the sights and smells of the alley, the music began again. It was a soft arpeggio, maybe Verdi, maybe Donizetti. He wasn't sure, so many of these pieces sounded similar at first. Then it began to sound more familiar. He was certain he knew it but again he couldn't place the title. While he puzzled over the title, the voice began to sing: *Casta Diva.*

No, no, no! Pino thought to himself. *Don't sing that yet! You've got to warm up more than that!* He stood up and paced around in a circle shaking his head. *Casta Diva* from Bellini's *Norma* was indeed a virtuoso piece of bel canto, a difficult piece for even the finest sopranos. Pino couldn't believe she would attempt such an aria after warming up for only a few minutes, but when the voice began to sing, Pino stopped pacing. He listened in astonishment, crossing the street toward her in a dream-like trance. It wasn't an especially beautiful voice, nor a particularly powerful voice. He thought the sound was too covered in the low range, larynx depressed, and too open on the top. In fact, there was not one singular quality that he could point to that was particularly special about the voice. Yet only moments later, he was convinced he was listening to the finest singer he had ever heard.

As he crossed the street, a gentle breeze blew and tossed his hair, sending a chill through his already goose-bumped skin. He reached her house and placed his hands on the stones, caressing them as he listened. He moved to the corner of the building and leaned his head against it, closed his eyes and drifted away.

In his mind there was a velvety black night filled with crystalline stars, glittering from horizon to horizon across the firmament. A mist slowly rose diffusing the light of the stars in all directions. Through the mist Pino began to see a large ancient coliseum, something from classical antiquity. Majestic and proud, the coliseum stood starkly on the horizon, glowing from within. Pino floated through the night sky and onto the floor of the coliseum. The entire structure was full; there was not a single empty seat, and every man and every woman held in their hands a small white candle. The effect was mesmerizing. At the far end of the coliseum there was a stage and a performance of *Norma* was taking place. At that moment, Norma was center stage, dressed in a light blue robe, with a long white veil that concealed her face. She was surrounded by several dozen handmaidens, all of whom were in black with white veils. The stage was fog-filled and very dark except for a ghostly blue light from behind, which silhouetted the singers. The veils blew in the breeze giving a spectral quality to the scene. The great druid priestess wept as she sang and as she removed her veil, her wavy curls of thick black hair hung about her face like a shroud. As she finished the aria, she replaced her veil and turned to go, followed by her handmaidens. The music faded, and so did Pino's dream.

When Pino opened his eyes, he found himself staring up at the dark nighttime sky. He discovered that he was perspiring profusely and he took out his handkerchief to wipe his brow. He stepped away from the house and into the street, holding his heart melodramatically.

"*Brava! Brava!*" he gently spoke, but the window stood hard and silent. He looked both up and down the street, and seeing not a soul, he cupped his hands to his mouth and called out again, slightly louder. "*Brava! Brava, Signorina!*" Still nothing. He bit his lip tensely, then called out, louder still. "*Brava! Brava, Signorina!*

Suddenly an arm reached out and slammed the window violently shut. The smile drained from his face. He'd received his answer; not the answer he had hoped for. He wasn't exactly sure what he expected, but not this! *How rude!* Here he was, in violation of his own curfew, risking his neck just to hear her sing and this was how she repaid him. He stared up at the window and as he did, the light went out. There was little more he could do, so he collected himself, heaved a heavy sigh and wandered slowly away down the street.

Unbeknownst to Pino, as he walked away, a tiny hand pulled back a lace curtain in the window and its owner watched and carefully studied the solitary soldier walking slowly down the alley toward Patisson Street.

CHAPTER NINE

PATROLLING THE PERIMETER

THE ACTUAL MILITARY PRESENCE IN GREECE was not that impressive in size. At its most expansive it numbered some four hundred officers and eight thousand soldiers. Although the occupation of Greece was split into four sections, Athens being in the German sector, it seemed that as more Italian divisions landed, an equal number of German divisions departed. The war was not going at all well for Hitler and the Axis powers. The siege in Russia was proving to be the bloodiest conflict in the history of mankind and drained every able bodied soldier Hitler could find. The unwelcome specter of American intervention was hanging thickly in the air around Berlin, as well. Consequently, occupying Greece simply was not a top priority. The "mission" in Greece was somewhat cloudy and lacking definition. The daily activities of the military were very much like Amonte's original assessment: "police work".

However, the deplorable conditions and the troubling number of deaths from starvation had begun to catch the eye of neighboring nations and soon relief in the form of food shipments were making their way to Greece. German command viewed the shipments as simply one more spoil of war and very little of it actually reached the ones most in need.

The daily marches and patrols had become monotonous for Pino and his comrades. They never saw action of any kind. Carlucci even suggested that they might as well be a marching band carrying tubas instead of rifles. It was obvious that the patrols were simply a display of power, designed to demoralize and frighten the locals, but after a while, it seemed that the locals carried on their business oblivious to the presence of the soldiers.

On one especially hot and humid May afternoon, Pino and his company found themselves once again on patrol, but with a much greater sense of purpose. They were a group of about thirty soldiers, in formation but not marching. On this occasion, Captain Adamo had chosen to accompany the men, something he seldom did. Adamo was a lifelong soldier, clearly a warrior in his own mind. He seemed, in Pino's estimation, to be one of those people who could tell you exactly in which regiment his father, grandfather, and great-grandfather had served; and could provide a list of their respective heroic deeds and notable accomplishments.

It all bored Pino. The thought of spending a lifetime in the military was absurd. It took a different kind of person, the "not-too-bright" kind, he thought, and now Pino's life lay in the hands of just such a man.

Adamo was from Naples. Beyond that fact, Pino knew very little about him. Most of the *Napolitani* that Pino had met in his life were cut from the more familiar mold of Bernardi, but the Captain was nothing like Bernardi. He carried himself with a tremendous amount of dignity and grace. Maybe it was the years and years of precise military drilling? Pino couldn't be sure. At any rate, the Captain inspired confidence in his troops, which was just about as much as you could ask, Pino thought.

As was the routine, the men spent either the morning or the afternoon on patrol, generally in much smaller groups than the one they were in currently. Today's patrol was different. Everyone could feel it. There was tension and confusion in the air and the captain was unusually quiet. All of the men were tired of the mindless repetition of their rituals, but none dared speak up. That is to say, until this particular afternoon when a tiny pebble found its way into Bernardi's boot, causing the kind of nagging pain that couldn't be ignored. Finally, unable to bear the pain any longer, Bernardi spoke.

"What's the point of all this?" he asked.

"Captain says we've got orders to patrol this quarter of the city daily. Smaller units will be dispatched hourly," answered Carlucci. Annoyed at the clinical nature of the answer, Bernardi repeated his question.

"I repeat: What...is...the...point...of...this?" he said in a *staccato* voice, which caught the attention of the Captain, who stopped short. The platoon followed suit.

"Halt!" he called out, as though his stopping short didn't already do the trick. He turned around and angrily addressed the men.

"Gentlemen, our orders are to patrol this sector. We do not question orders, we follow them. Insubordination of any kind will not be tolerated."

He walked back through the ranks toward Bernardi, who stood stiff as an oak.

"Is that clear?" he shouted into Bernardi's face.

"Yes, Sir. Very clear, Sir," Bernardi barked back.

"Good," smiled the captain. The soldiers began to move down the street with a renewed sense of seriousness.

"I don't like this at all," said Pino.

"Will you please stop saying that? You're like a broken record," Amonte replied.

"The Captain is really uptight about something."

"That's his job."

"Today he seems edgy. He's never edgy. I think it takes an awful lot to make a guy like him nervous."

"All I know is you're making *me* nervous," Amonte retorted. As they continued their modified march passing street upon street, townspeople came out of their houses and businesses to look on, their faces pained and angry. "Bernardi was right about one thing," Amonte stated matter-of-factly, "We're not gonna win any popularity contests around here."

Sassani ran up alongside Amonte, whispered something in his ear and pointed in the direction of the Acropolis. The two men looked at the great Acropolis and burst out laughing.

Pino turned and looked in curiosity but didn't notice anything funny. It looked exactly the same as it always – wait! He saw it!

The gigantic German flag, the Reichstag, that had been flying from the Parthenon since the Germans arrived was gone!

"That explains everything!" said Amonte.

"What are you talking about?" asked Pino.

Sassani got in step with Pino and told him what he had just learned from the captain's driver. Apparently their patrol was in reality a search for the two hooligans who had stolen the German flag!

"Two men, probably students, climbed up the side of the Acropolis last night and pulled down the big Reichstag that was on the flagpole up there. Right in front of the German's noses! They are furious!"

Pino smiled inwardly and realized that once again he found himself secretly rooting for the Greeks. *Imagine the daily humiliation of seeing the Swastika, the symbol of oppression, flying right in front of their Acropolis, the very birthplace of democracy.* No wonder someone pulled it down. And as far as a search was concerned, *good luck* trying to get anything out of these locals!

The incident was an amusing one for Pino, but it also showed him that the sleepy Greeks still had a few tricks up their sleeves and more than ever that he needed to remain alert.

By the fall of 1941, the lack of fresh food caused both by the cutting off of supply routes and by German plundering had hit Athens hard. Famine was fast approaching and there was little hiding it. The Italian army saw little of this themselves as they had more than adequate provisions. What they did not realize was that a good deal of the food that they were gorging themselves on was in fact relief aid sent by other nations to help feed the starving Greeks.

The locals tried their best to continue with business as usual but there was no hiding the hardships that they all faced. The markets still opened each day but there was precious little inventory to go around. Frequently, Athenians would walk many miles out of the city to the surrounding villages and scour the countryside in search of fresh produce and poultry. Luckily, the water supply remained untouched and each morning lines could be seen forming at the local fountains. More often than not, the lines consisted of patrolling soldiers filling their canteens.

On this sunny September morning, just such a patrol paused to fill its canteens at just such a fountain. Captain Adamo stopped and raised his hand to halt the troops.

"Rest here for ten minutes and fill your canteens, but don't wander far."

Pino and Amonte groaned with pleasure as they took off their packs and got out their canteens. Approaching the fountain, Pino looked around curiously, sure he'd been there before. Suddenly it dawned on him.

"Hey!" he called out. "This is where she lives!"

"Who?"

"The girl! The voice! The singer I told you about!"

"Oh, really?" Amonte asked slyly.

"Yeah, really! Right there, second floor," said Pino pointing down the street to a corner apartment house. No sooner had he spoken, the balcony doors opened.

"Hey look," Amonte pointed, "someone's coming out." Pino rushed down the street toward the house with Amonte close behind. He stopped dead in his tracks and his smile became a grotesque contortion. His gaze was fixed on the balcony doors, which swung wide open to reveal an old Greek lady in a housecoat and a hat. Amonte burst out laughing at the sight.

"Not what you expected, eh, Pino?" A second later, Amonte stopped laughing. "Whoa! Who's that?" he asked, as a beautiful young girl in her early twenties joined the old lady.

"Aha!" cried Pino, "that's got to be my angel. I knew it!" Pino said nervously. "*Signorina*, sing! Sing!" he called out.

The two women looked at each other in confusion, then the older one whispered something in the younger's ear and the younger quickly departed.

"Now, you'll see just what I was talking about!" he said. The door leading into the house opened and the pretty young girl came out and approached them.

"What are you doing down here? Aren't you going to sing?" he asked.

"No signore, I no sing," she answered in broken Italian.

"Sure you can. You must," Pino implored. "I've told all my friends about you."

"No, *Signore*, no."

"Look, Pino, if she doesn't want to sing..." Amonte offered, but Pino would have none of it.

"Nonsense, of course she'll sing. You've got nothing to be afraid of. You sing beautifully. I *know;* I'm a tenor, myself."

The young girl just grew more and more frightened.

"Signore, you don't understand..." she started.

"Please, just one aria. Any aria," Pino begged.

"Aria?"

"Please, you have no idea how much it would mean to all of us. We miss Italy so much, and when you sing, it reminds us of home."

"Italy? I don't understand," said the poor girl, overwhelmed. Losing all patience, Pino grabbed her hands and squeezed them hard.

"Please don't do this! Go upstairs and sing like you did the other night."

But it was hopeless. She just stared at him, confused and frightened. Suddenly the old woman looked down from the balcony and let out an angry yell in Greek. As the girl responded, the old lady did a double take and stared at Pino suspiciously. Sensing he may have offended, he thought it might be wise to try to diffuse the situation.

"Signora, let me explain," he said gingerly.

The old lady cut him off before he could get out another word, yelling in Greek. Just as the situation was becoming comical, Amonte appeared almost magically with a little old Greek man in a suit and tie, sporting a sardonic smile. The old man, whom Pino recognized as Kostas, the fruit vendor, quickly grasped the situation and proceeded to translate for them.

"Gentlemen, my daughter would like to sing a song from your homeland for all of you, but first we kindly ask that you display a small gesture of your appreciation for her art. Your generosity is appreciated."

First, Pino stared at the old man wondering where on earth Amonte had found him, then at the old lady in total amazement. She was half theatrical agent and half carnival barker. Amonte tapped Pino on the shoulder and looked at him suspiciously.

"Does that mean she expects us to *pay* her?" he asked contemptuously.

"I guess so," Pino said. The girl stood before them and in make-shift Italian made the point crystal clear.

"*Signore*, anything at all. Food is very very scarce."

Her words brought a lump to Amonte's throat. Both he and Pino were unaware it had come to this.

"Aren't we giving these poor folks tons of food? What the hell is in all those Red Cross packages anyway?" asked Pino.

"Singing for your supper, huh?" Amonte said holding up a finger. "Hold on a minute."

He opened his pack and took out some rice and dry pasta he'd been carrying and handed them to her.

"How's that?" he said with satisfaction. "They're only weighing me down anyway."

"*Grazie, Signore. Grazie.*" As she thanked him, a piano could be heard from the balcony.

"You better hurry back up there, if you're going to sing," Pino said anxiously.

"I don't sing," she said putting away the food. Pino knitted his brow in confusion.

"Pino, why did I give her food if she's not gonna sing?" Amonte added sarcastically.

"I don't understand," said Pino.

"I tried to say, *Signore*. I don't sing. My sister sings."

"Sister?" was all that Pino could get out when a voice, *her voice*, could be heard from the balcony. He turned up his head to the voice. The melody was *"Vissi D'arte"* from Puccini's *"Tosca"*. Pino closed his eyes in ecstasy and drifted away.

- *Vissi d'arte*
- I have lived for art…
- *Vissi d'amore*
- I have lived for love…

The words penetrated Pino viscerally. While she sang, as if a magic spell had been cast over them, more and more soldiers began walking over to listen. The aria was well known and the effect on the men was immediate. Some smiled, some hummed or quietly sang along, some sat down as if to pray. The tragic words and sublime music produced a catharsis in the lives of the home-sick warriors.

Tosca's final plea at the climax of the aria ripped Pino apart

'Nell' ora del dolore, perchè, perchè Signore?

In my hour of pain, why? Why, dear Lord?

"Perchè me ne rimuneri così?"

- Why have you repaid me like this?

The words tore at the men's hearts and tears flowed. Through it all, the sister passed among the men with a basket in hand collecting coins, food and various small tokens. Amonte emptied his pockets of their contents, placing coins, matches, and cigarettes into the basket as it passed. There was a solemn church-like quality about the entire scene. Pino would have noticed the parallels had he not been enraptured by the voice. Eyes closed, mouth opened, hands folded, on one knee, he was in a state of bliss.

Bernardi wandered over to the crowd of soldiers to see what all the fuss was about. He came up behind Pino with a grimace on his face, looking like he smelled something foul in the air. He looked at everyone listening and shook his head in disgust.

"What *is* this?" he asked.

"Shhh!" said Pino firmly and Bernardi was quiet - but not for long. Once more, he looked at all of his comrades and laughed.

"Sounds like funeral music to me," he cackled.

Two soldiers silenced him, "Shut up! Be quiet!"

But he wasn't done just yet.

"Hey! Don't you know any happy songs?" he yelled up to the balcony.

"Shut up!" yelled a chorus of voices at him. Furiously, Pino stood up and walked toward Bernardi, but before he could reach him, a loud whistle was heard. The Captain was listening to the girl as well and her singing moved him, but there was work to be done. He once again blew his whistle calling the men back to attention. As they started to slowly fall in, Pino ran over to the young girl and put several bills in her basket. She smiled deeply.

"Tell your sister she's a great artist and she should pursue a professional career. She's wonderful. She's extraordinary!" The captain could be heard in the distance calling the men to order. "I've got to go, but I'll be back," he promised as he turned and ran down the street to join the platoon.

On the balcony, first a hand, then a girl's face peeked out around one of the doors. Only one eye and a little of the nose and hair were visible. The hair was dark and straight, the nose rather large with thick, horn-rimmed glasses adorning it. From her door, she watched again as her soldier ran away.

CHAPTER TEN

BRIEF ENCOUNTERS

ETWEEN THE THREE OF THEM, Bernardi, Carlucci and Amonte had written a grand total of one letter home. Amonte felt guilty for having waited so long to write. When he finally did, he made reference to several fictitious earlier letters, hoping his family would just accept that they were late or lost in the mail. Carlucci and Bernardi had no such compulsions. They would write when the mood struck them, and it simply hadn't yet. This selfish attitude didn't go unnoticed by Amonte, who gave serious thought to how these two might conduct themselves if they ever did see any real action. The thought bothered him, and although he didn't want to dwell on it, he couldn't seem to get it out of his head. Who would he rather have watching his back, Pino or Bernardi? Clearly, Bernardi was a better soldier, stronger and more resourceful, but did he trust him? *With his life?* More and more, this kind of thinking pervaded Amonte's restless mind. Bernardi would certainly be a killing machine in the heat of battle, but was he likely to give a shit about anybody else but himself? Would somebody like Pino, who had to think things over ten times before putting on his socks, ever be decisive in a clutch moment?

"Are you in or not?" Bernardi barked, bringing Amonte out of his daydream and back to the present. "Well?" Bernardi persisted.

"I'm in," said Amonte without even looking at his cards.

"Something's going on here," said Bernardi, chomping on an unlit cigar.

"What do you mean?" asked Carlucci.

"You talking about the Captain, again?" Amonte interjected.

"Yep," said Bernardi.

Carlucci looked around like he was the only one not "in-the-know."

"I don't get it," he protested. "Did I miss something?"

"Probably nothing, but we both noticed that the Captain's been jumpy lately," said Amonte.

"*Really jumpy*," added Bernardi.

Carlucci was petrified. How had he not noticed?

"What do you think it is? An attack coming? We're moving closer to the front?" he babbled.

"We are the front, idiot," pointed out Bernardi with his usual sensitivity.

"Yeah, but it's been a real quiet front so far," Amonte stressed. They sat in silence, staring at their cards, not touching their drinks. "Hey, where's Pino?" he asked. "Is he gonna join us?"

"I bet I know where he is," Bernardi said with a smirk.

In truth, their assessment of the Captain's behavior was more accurate than they could have guessed. He had been particularly edgy since receiving his own assessment from his German superiors, which was not glowing.

1) *Inadequate technical knowledge*
2) *Poor understanding of communications equipment*
3) *Map reading and use of the compass*
4) *Lack of knowledge about field fortifications and fields of fire*
5) *Poor physical conditioning*
6) *Overall complacency*

As if that wasn't insult enough, his own military acumen was brutally condemned:

1) *Total administrative ignorance*
2) *Lack of command authority*
3) *Timidity*

He was horrified. For a career soldier such an assessment was anathema, but he knew better than to dispute the findings of his commanders. He needed to mend his impugned reputation in the eyes of his masters through action; that was the only language they spoke or understood. He needed to shape up his soft-bellied group, and fast. He hoped for some large-scale opportunity to present itself that could rehabilitate their image in one grand gesture, namely a military success. A multitude of sins could be forgiven easily with one act of heroism on the battlefield, but Athens was hardly a battlefield. Sitting on the balcony of the Hotel Grand Bretagne, staring out across the *Plaka* at the Acropolis in the distance, he sipped a glass of mineral water and thought about the hundreds of battles that had been fought right there over the centuries. While no one who's ever been in a battle looks forward to another, he knew that short of an armed conflict of some sort, he'd have a tough job changing the preconceptions and misconceptions of his German masters.

Word of the Italian army's heavy losses in Africa did nothing to ease his troubled mind. He had learned that on the Mediterranean, Libya had fallen to the British. Further south, Italian Somaliland and Abyssinia had been lost as well. All in all, the current state of the Italian campaign looked frightfully bleak, and the future held no great promise either.

The Captain made the executive decision that it was too nice an evening to sit and stew, so he closed his eyes and turned his mind to more pleasant thoughts. The nicest surprise he'd gotten lately was the impromptu concert in the street by the little Greek girl. It was remarkable how wonderfully she sang the aria from *Tosca* with such depth of emotion, such pathos for one so young. He surmised that living under occupation might produce such an effect, but the somber dignity with which she sang revealed a poise and maturity that belied her age. Her voice and her song spoke to him of all the virtues that were in his mind uniquely and unmistakably Latin – virtues his German masters would never possess or hope to understand. He wanted to hear her again and made a mental note to increase patrols in that sector of the city.

Across town, Pino was violating his curfew once again, sitting on the little stool in the alleyway, looking up at the French doors that never seemed to want to open. He checked his watch and looked back up at the balcony. Fortune smiled rarely on Pino of late, but on this chilly autumn night, he was given at least a little grin. As the light came on and the doors opened, Pino bristled with excitement. Light shone through the archway and the curtains blew softly in the night air. The moonlight in the alley played tricks with Pino's now piqued imagination and he swore time and time again that he could make out a woman's shadow traced on the long white curtains.

First there was silence, then the low mumble of distant voices, and finally...the piano. The French doors stood half-opened letting the music pour out into the alley below. The familiar ritual of scales began and he hummed along happily. The exercise continued for several minutes, then suddenly stopped. Silence. He looked up to the balcony in curiosity and saw a shadow appear on the curtain. The silhouette pulled back the curtain and peered out the window. The street lamp didn't throw enough light upward for Pino to see her features. The figure looked out for just a moment, then closed the curtain again. Pino stood up from his stool and squinted to see inside the open doors, but it was no use.

He started to pace impatiently when the piano started again. He leapt to attention when he recognized the music: *"Sempre Libera,"* the conclusion of Act One from *La Traviata* by Verdi. Suitably impressed by the selection, he nodded his head in approval, then returned to the stool and listened intently.

She sang the aria in the proper key, which pleased Pino immensely. Her voice was dark and heavy and Pino wondered if she possessed the necessary agility for the piece. She lacked tonal richness in the upper middle register but more than made up for it with burnished chest register, and, as he noted the first time he'd heard her, a positively ghostly high *pianissimo*. But this aria required a completely different set of skills. Thus far she'd navigated its obstacles with exemplary suppleness but Pino wondered if she would attempt the interpolated high E flat at the conclusion of the piece. He would have to wait to find out because she suddenly, without warning, stopped singing. The silence lasted for just a few seconds. Then, the piano began again, but not where it had left off, but a few bars earlier. Pino hummed along until the piano stopped again. He sat in silence for a moment. Then the music began yet again, from the same spot in the piece.

What the heck was she doing? It finally dawned on him, that the place where she kept stopping was the point in the aria where the tenor, Alfredo, joins the soprano, Violetta, in a "call and response" verse. As Pino was having this realization, the music began again and he stood up and stepped out of the alley. This time he anticipated the music stopping, and it did stop, at the exact same spot again.

Suddenly, the curtain was yanked back and the silhouette appeared. Stunned, Pino stood like a deer in the headlights for a moment before jumping back into the shadows, hoping despairingly that he hadn't been seen. The silhouette remained at the window staring into the darkness of the alley. She certainly must have seen him, he thought. He could not have been more terrified if he were facing German soldiers. The moment lingered on interminably for Pino. He felt perspiration forming on his upper lip but dared not move a muscle. Maybe she hadn't seen him? No, she must have seen him. Still, he didn't want to do anything to draw her attention. Maybe, she saw something but didn't realize what it was. All he had to do was remain still. Soon, she would get tired of waiting and he could escape unseen.

"Well?" the silhouette called out the window, dashing any hopes that he hadn't been seen.

Pino stared up at the silhouette, frozen, but didn't say a word.

"Well?" she called out again, louder than before and with a distinct air of impatience. It was decision-making time, so Pino swallowed hard, blessed himself and slowly stepped forward into the light of the street. He felt like a child who'd been caught stealing. He bit his lip, fidgeting like a nervous schoolboy until his accuser spoke, and with one simple question, all terror was washed away.

"Are you really a tenor?" she asked in a shy but authoritative voice. His relief and simultaneous disbelief were immeasurable. His heart filled up so fully and quickly that he could barely speak.

"Yes. Yes, I am," he stated proudly. "In fact, I..."

"You missed your cue," she interrupted, curtly.

He stood dumbfounded and when he regained his composure he said something to the effect of: "Wha...oh...I...uh...didn't realize...uh that..." As he babbled, she disappeared from the window and Pino once again found himself in silence. *Great. Just great.* He kicked the gravel and looked back up to the window. Silence. Disgusted, he started to walk away. Then the piano began again. He turned back to the balcony and cleared his throat. This time, when the tenor entrance arrived, he was ready to sing with gusto. Unfortunately, his voice had other ideas, and to his profound embarrassment, he cracked horribly several times.

As the two artists were becoming one in song, house lights were coming on up and down the street. Pino was in his element for the first time in ages and he sang *fortissimo* and for a moment the war melted away. However, for the residents of Patisson Street, the nocturnal duet was not especially welcome. There was yelling from windows and doorways. Some came out into the street. It was utter mayhem, but Pino was blind and deaf to everything but the sound of the piano and her voice. But just as the madness around him was reaching fever pitch, the music stopped. Pino found himself singing *a capella* to a growing crowd of angry faces. He stopped and looked up to the balcony but the doors were shut and the light was out. It was almost as though it had never happened. The smile drained from Pino's face.

Abandonata!

He looked at the angry mob and forced a nervous smile. Confused howls and threatening gestures got closer and closer and he was glad he understood no Greek. Bowing politely, the smile never leaving his face, he made another of his now familiar mad dashes down the street.

CHAPTER ELEVEN

Back to School

THE NAME ATHENS WAS TAKEN FROM the mythological goddess Athena. According to legend, the goddess Athena presented the city with an olive tree as a token of her promise to protect the city after her battle with the god Poseidon. It would seem that her promise of protection was a somewhat empty one as Athens was often overrun by invaders. Beginning with the Persians in the seventh century B.C., followed by the Romans, the French, the Catalans, the Neapolitans, the Turks and finally the Germans, Athens was no stranger to occupation.

The Acropolis, the ancient hub of the city, was surrounded by treacherous steep cliffs on its sides. Until the advent of flight, the fortress on top was nearly impervious to invasion. However, this marvel of nature and man had an Achilles heel: water, or more specifically, the lack of water. Attacking forces could surround the citadel and simply wait for its provisions to run dry.

Pino knew virtually nothing of the city's history when he arrived. Initially, he had little interest, but that was beginning to change. He had fallen under Athens' spell and, fed by weeks of endless patrolling of the city, his natural curiosity had taken over.

Pino and Amonte especially enjoyed patrolling the *Plaka*, which, of all the neighborhoods they'd patrolled thus far, showed the most activity. As the soldiers walked down the street they passed several cafes, which, while not exactly bristling with business, were determined to remain open. Adorable little awnings unfurled, protecting patrons from the unforgiving effects of the brutal midday sun as they drank their dreadful Greek coffee, which to Pino's palate, had the taste of motor oil and the consistency of tar. The fruit and vegetable vendors were open as well, a sight that pleased Pino considerably and reminded him of home, but closer inspection revealed their inventories were severely depleted and the items they did have appeared to be of questionable quality. He looked around hoping to find Kostas there but didn't see him.

Pino's relationship with Kostas began harmlessly enough on the night of the opera. Pino was the first to arrive at the theater and while waiting he had bought an orange from a fruit vendor. The vendor was a tired-looking old Greek man with no teeth and nearly no hair named Kostas. To Pino's surprise and pleasure, Kostas spoke excellent Italian. The two men struck up a conversation about the ancient ruins and Pino learned more about Greece in ten minutes than he had in all his years at school.

While he was reluctant to become too friendly with any of the locals, Pino did see Kostas numerous times while on patrol and always had a friendly word for him. Kostas would never reveal his age, but he had no problem bragging that he was the youngest of seventeen children. Their topics of discussion could be as mundane as the freshness of the fruit, or as fascinating as the aspects of Athenian architecture. It was from Kostas that Pino learned about *entasis,* the slight bulging of the Parthenon's columns around the middle. The reason for this was that perfectly straight columns gave the appearance of being slightly concave in the middle. The almost imperceptible widening of the columns in the center countered that appearance and added to their strength and stability. Pino could not have been more impressed with this simple man whose knowledge of all things Greek seemed virtually limitless. That vast reserve of knowledge also included certain interesting details concerning the Italian invasion of Greece; details which for some reason Pino's superiors had neglected to mention.

According to Kostas, Italy had invaded Greece from neighboring Albania in October of 1940. Pino had no idea that Italy had even occupied Albania! The Italian offensive had continued until April of 1941, when Germany took the helm of the invasion. During that year, not only had the Greeks repelled the Italian forces but they actually drove the invading army out of Greece and pursued them into Albania! Embarrassed, Pino could clearly see why his commanders wouldn't be anxious to share that tidbit of information with the rank and file. Kostas explained that in March of 1941, Italy made one last ditch effort to attack Greece. The offensive had failed miserably. The Italian army suffered a staggering 12,000 casualties in five days without taking a single Greek position. Apparently, it was at that moment that Hitler had seen enough. In April, the German army swept into Greece like a tornado.

Pino had heard enough. He didn't need to hear the details of the German invasion. He could see its effects all around him. A thought occurred to him: *But this is 1941! What happened here in the last twelve months?* The thought made him curious but he decided fairly quickly that he probably didn't want to know the answer.

"Not to beat a dead horse, but has anybody figured out what we're on the lookout for, yet?" Amonte asked, snapping Pino out of his daydream.

"Forget it," Pino said. "I bet the Germans are giving the Captain heat again and he's making us march round the clock just so we look like we're doing something."

"Maybe," Amonte said with a yawn, before getting to the subject he really wanted to talk about. "So? Did you see her last night?"

"Kind of."

"Kind of? What do you mean, *kind of?*"

"She came to the window but it was really dark, and I didn't get a good look."

"Well, what does she *kind of* look like?"

"Well let's just say, she may have gotten the talent in the family, but her sister definitely got the looks."

"Ah, really? Too bad."

"I don't mean she's ugly or anything, but she's sort of chubby."

"Ooooh, chubby's bad."

"And she's got a real honker, too."

"Ouch! Double trouble!"

"And did I mention she wears glasses?"

"Perfect! Three for three. Gee, Pino she sounds like a real catch."

"Yeah, but God, can she sing! I mean *really* sing. She's better than most of the singers I've heard working in major theaters."

"Well, that's very important, of course," Amonte said, rolling his eyes. As he scanned the street, a scruffy-looking old man in a coat far too heavy to be worn in this weather, winked at him and beckoned for him to come over. It was Kostas!

"Hey, Kostas!" he said pointing at the old man.

"You know Kostas?" Pino said with a start.

"Come on! Everybody knows Kostas!"

Amonte and Pino walked over and chatted amiably with Kostas for a moment when the old man got a devilish look in his eye.

"You like *grappa*, Pino?" he asked with the grin of Lucifer himself.

"Well, I guess," said Pino, thinking of his *grappa*-laced misadventures with his father.

"Lend me a few *lire* and I'll see you back at camp."

"*Lire?* What's wrong with *drachmas?*"

"*Lire* go a lot farther around here," said Kostas.

Pino looked suspiciously at Kostas, then even more so at Amonte.

"How do you two know one another?" Pino inquired.

"Kostas is the guy that translated for us, remember?" Amonte said and Pino's mental fog lifted.

"Of course! How did I forget?"

"And remember Bernardi's cigars and *grappa*?" Amonte asked with a smile.

"You're kidding." said Pino.

"Nope," Amonte replied. "Kostas is our little one-man-contraband center!"

"Gee, Kostas," Pino said with a laugh, reaching into his pocket and finding a few bills. "How come all you and I ever talk about is the latest news and current events?"

"I like to keep a little mystery until I know I can trust you," the old man proudly said.

"Well you never cease to amaze me, my friend," Pino said holding the bills out in front of him.

"Great," said Amonte, grabbing the bills. "See you in an hour."

With that, Amonte put his arm around Kostas and the two men disappeared into the winding streets of the Plaka. Pino shook his head with a smile and wondered if there was anything which Kostas was *not* capable of.

As he walked along surveying the shops, Pino stopped at a small vegetable stand and glanced down at a bunch of sad-looking tomatoes. They reminded him how sorely he missed the red blood-oranges from back home. The tomatoes simply didn't cut it. He picked one up and squeezed it then held it to his nose and smelled it. Not ripe. Disappointed, he glanced up from the cart for an instant and caught a glimpse of a young girl walking toward him from the shadow of an alley. He looked back down at the tomatoes, but suddenly something inexplicable made him look again. The girl was now close enough for him to get a good look. She was heavy set, with brilliant dark hair. She was attractive in a plain sort of way, but she had a rather large nose, crowned with thick glasses. He continued to watch her come out of the shadow and into the street. She didn't notice him at first, but either the heat of his stare or divine providence caused her to turn her gaze in his direction. When their eyes met, she stopped dead and her jaw dropped. It was her! He knew it! He dropped the tomato and ran around the stand toward her.

"Hello! It is you, isn't it?" he said awkwardly.

She didn't quite smile, but she didn't quite frown.

"You're the tenor, right?" she asked, in perfect Italian, eyes nervously looking at the ground.

"That's right, yes. We never finished the aria," he said.

"You have a nice voice."

"Thank you."

"But you need to warm up more before you sing," she instructed. Pino was caught by surprise and was tongue-tied. "But I can't talk right now," she said with urgency. "I...I have to meet my cousins. They are waiting for me."

"Oh," said the dejected tenor. "Well, I'd love to talk to you sometime, and hear you sing."

"Fine, fine, yes, but now I've got to go." she said, rushing past him. Pino laughed and shook his head, when suddenly he realized something and turned back toward her.

"Hey! What's your..." but she was gone. "...name," he finished with a sigh.

Later that same day, Pino was finishing his circuit of the *Plaka* and preparing to head back to base, all the time wondering what goodies Amonte could secure from his "connection". Pino didn't smoke, so the cigars that Bernardi regularly brought back to camp held no interest to him. However, he inexplicably appeared to be developing a soft spot for *grappa, Perhaps it was in his genes?* Of all his childhood memories, Pino's father bringing a bottle of *grappa* to the dinner table and leaving it there until everyone finished their meal, was one of the most indelible.

Dinner was the exclusive responsibility of his mother and one that she handled with great relish, but once dinner was complete, his father was king, swinging into action making espresso for everyone. Pino started drinking *espresso* at the age of eight and was quite addicted by his early teens. Mr. Vaggi made three separate "blends" for the family. First, for Mama Vaggi, he made a light, sweet *espresso* with just a nip of *anisette* in it. Mr. Vaggi personally found the taste of *anisette* repulsive. He also possessed a particular distaste for *anise, galliano, sambuca* and any other variety of sweet liqueurs generally considered "southern Italian." The *grappa* bottle would sit on the table keeping watch, like a cordial sentinel, as the family ate, and would continue the watch as Papa prepared the second blend for Pino and Maria. Their blend was similar to Mama Vaggi's in that it was light and sweet, but the sweetness came from a dash of sugar rather than alcohol - although, Pino soon learned to sneak little sips of *anisette* and hold the liquor in his mouth until his coffee was ready. He would then swish the two together in his mouth and swallow them as one, hoping his parents hadn't noticed. Finally, after the rest of the family was served, Mr. Vaggi got down to the real business. His own blend was a mixture of two different coffees, one Italian, one Turkish or Greek. It was one of the only indulgences he allowed himself. Needless to say, the coffee was as strong as diesel fuel. Once brewed, he would add the secret ingredient to make the mixture complete: one ounce of grappa.

Pino marveled at the joy his father derived from this simple pleasure. At times, it made him happy to see his father in this way, able to enjoy life's most basic pleasures. At other times it bothered him terribly, because it told of just how common his father really was, and how low he had set his sights in life, and just how provincial they as a family really were. Thoughts swirled in Pino's head, frustrating and mocking him. For reasons he could neither identify nor explain, the thought of being "common" was unbearable to him, that was, until he became a soldier. The expression, "try not to distinguish yourself" learned in Basic, came to mind and he always tried to remember it.

Pino couldn't enjoy a glass of *grappa* without thinking of his father, but on that particular day, the thought of *grappa* with his father brought back another memory: his mother's kitchen and the aroma of chestnuts. For a moment, he wasn't sure if the smell was real or imagined. Nevertheless, it intoxicated him. He inhaled deeply through his nose and the smell of roasted chestnuts filled his soul. He held his breath in his lungs as long as he could, savoring the flavor, then he exhaled. The sensation was gone as quickly as it arrived.

The street car bell made him open his eyes. Like everything else, the street cars had been commandeered for army use. Pino now found himself standing in the middle of the street, wondering how long he had been daydreaming. He looked around and no one seemed to be paying attention to him, so perhaps it was just a second or two. In his mind, it was hours, days, maybe even years.

He wasn't sure if he had done it consciously or unconsciously, but Pino's tour had somehow brought him to Patisson Street - *her* street. He couldn't conceal his pleasure and thought he'd wander around for a few minutes, in case she showed up.

First thing: gotta get her name, he told himself. He looked at his little alleyway and concluded that it looked better at night. In the light, it seemed to be no more than a storage area for garbage cans. *Jeeez...no wonder it smelled so bad! What must she think of somebody who hides himself among the garbage?* There would be time to worry about that later, he thought as walked to fill his canteen at the fountain. The water was very cold, for a change, and after his canteen was brimming, he washed his face and hands. The sting of the water brought a fresh alertness.

What exactly am I doing here? he asked himself soberly, *this is foolishness. In fact, it's worse than that. It's the exact kind of distraction that I promised myself I wouldn't allow to happen. Damn it.* He sat down for a moment to compose himself. *If anyone from the base saw me, I'd be a laughing stock. Or maybe worse - there might be some disciplinary action.*

But what about Bernardi? And Amonte? Aren't they violating some kind of regulation every ten minutes? Buying black market liquor, tobacco and who knows what else? What am I doing wrong? I'm just listening to a damn girl sing, that's all, and what's wrong with that?

"Yeah! What the hell is wrong with that?" he barked angrily. Getting to his feet, he kicked the dirt viciously, furious at something, but not exactly sure what. Pino shouldered his rifle, stowed his canteen and marched down the street toward the base, grimacing with a newfound resolve as he walked. He was a soldier. This was a war. Soldiers that lost their focus died. He wasn't going to die. No one was going to distract him again.

As he turned the corner, he collided headlong into his "distraction." It was difficult to say who was more surprised; the girl, who gasped, Pino, whose "resolve" disappeared like water through his hands, or the two rain-coated young men walking on either side of the girl.

"You gave me such a scare," she said putting her hand over her heart.

"Sorry. You startled me, too!" Pino said catching his breath. The two other men smiled nervously and the girl bit her lip. "Hey! These must be your cousins?" Pino offered. The men nodded and continued to silently smile. He guessed that they didn't share her command of Italian.

"Yes, but we really can't talk now," she said anxiously.

"That's all right," Pino said sympathetically. "I just wanted to..."

"Why don't you pass by tonight," she interrupted, "around the same time as usual? When I am practicing, all right?"

Pino could sense that something was strange, forced, about her behavior. He wanted to talk to her, to help her, to calm her, but it wasn't the kind of attention he wanted to deliver in front of an audience. From their movements, he correctly concluded that her cousins didn't understand a word of Italian, but he still preferred to speak with her privately.

"Great," he said. "Then I guess I'll see you tonight. Same time. *Ciao.*"

"*Ciao,*" she responded mechanically as she rushed past him. The other two men nodded their heads again and scurried after her. Pino watched as they made their way down the street.

"That was odd," he said to himself. He skipped along back to base gently whistling "Sempre Libera" to himself. *Tonight, we'll finish that duet. She'll hear my real voice. Better remember to vocalize first. Tonight...*" he paused and thought for a moment, *Tonight, I've got to remember to find out her name!*

Dinner was some sort of barley paste and cold vegetables and Pino ate very little. His thoughts were elsewhere. His comrades in arms were not very talkative and that suited him just fine since he really wanted some time alone to warm up his voice before heading out to his appointed destination.

Just before the end of dinner, Pino excused himself and went to the latrine, which always provided wonderfully warm acoustics. He dared not sing at full voice in there for he'd surely be heard all around the camp, so instead he simply hummed his scales to himself to get loose. It was really a poor substitute but it was better than nothing. He could vocalize more on the way over.

The night was cloudy and gray with a hint of mist in the air. Pino hated this kind of weather, but there was nothing that could dampen his spirits. He felt his pulse quicken as he walked, his stride growing in length and speed as he went. When he reached Patisson Street it was quieter than usual. Everything looked the same but something was different. He found the little stool in its usual place and pulled it out into the light at the edge of the street, as there was no longer any need for subterfuge. He cleared his throat loudly and sat down to await his cue.

The window and the French doors were shut and there was no sign of life within but he wasn't concerned. He passed the time trying to guess which duet she would choose tonight, worrying a bit that she would choose one to which he didn't know the tenor part.

After about an hour, Pino showed the first signs of impatience. It was still too early for him to be angry but a hint of disappointment had already crept inside him. Nothing had stirred in the house across the street all evening. That wasn't normal, but it wasn't enough reason for concern, yet.

Another hour passed and Pino was angry. He'd been rocking back and forth on the stool maniacally for nearly two hours and disappointment was setting in. He stopped rocking and buried his head in his hands. His brain was sending a message that his heart refused to hear. Was he making more of this than there really was? Was this all the dreamy illusion of an inexperienced heart? Feeling foolish, another more painful thought returned to him from earlier in the day. He fought it off for a few minutes but his inner voice was getting louder and making more sense. *What am I doing here?* He had no desire to hear it again, so he stood up and replaced the stool in the alleyway. He debated whether or not he would even look up at the window one last time. He decided not to. He walked briskly and noticed that he had trouble swallowing and his chest felt heavy. It was an unfamiliar feeling and he didn't like it. He tried his best to file it away in his memory for use in some role he might play in the future, but at that moment there was nothing good about it.

She may have had the best reason in the world for not showing up but he didn't care. He was exhausted and longing to sleep. He thought about his bed back home, his flannel sheets and goose down pillows. But he could see her chubby, young face and hear the warm elegantly Penelopese-accented vowels pouring out her nervous and hurried words. This silly little romance – *was it a romance at all?* Was he imagining it all in his own over-fertile imagination? What was a wartime relationship anyway? A fling?

He wanted desperately to go home, to sleep in his own bed...to see Gia. He wanted the peace of mind that Collagna brought, the sound of the bees in the day and the crickets at night, the smell of bread in the morning and of burning wood in the evening. He wanted to feel the permanence of the mountains and the consistency of the seasons. He wanted the security of familiarity and routine of people he knew and trusted.

Back at the hotel, he crept quietly to his room and into bed. He laid back and closed his eyes, grateful for the warmth of the sheets. He wished his racing mind would relax and pass into sleep, but it would not. It whirled round in a sea of noise, music, faces and images. He knew sleep would not be coming. He tossed and turned for an hour or so before giving up.

He tiptoed out of the room and up the stairs to the roof, where a small patio with deck chairs stood empty. He sat in one of the chairs and let go a deep cleansing breath. All of Athens seemed to stretch out before him. He gazed at a panorama of structures he could not identify, were they apartments? Hospitals? Office buildings? He had no clue. Kostas could tell him. After so many months it was remarkable how little he knew about his surroundings. He knew how to get to her house and back. That was about it. At a time when staying alive and returning in one piece to his fiancé should have been his paramount concern, he seriously needed to readdress his priorities.

To the south, in the distance of the misty night, he could just about make out the lights of a ship on the line where the sea met the sky, but he wasn't worried. It could be friendly or it could be an Allied invasion. He just wasn't all that concerned. All he could think about was her.

CHAPTER TWELVE

The Battle of Collagna

THE WHITE TRUFFLES FOUND in the Reggia Emilia were renowned across Europe. During truffle season, every chef worth his toque was breathless with anticipation of the arrival of the first truffles of the season. The process of cultivating the truffles, however, was hardly an exact science. In fact, since the precious fungus was actually found below the soil, a rather primitive method of detection was employed: the pig. No animal in creation could sniff out the delicate aroma of truffles quite like a pig.

Gia Mastrangelo was probably the only living person in Collagna that detested the taste of truffles. It was more than simply their taste. The fact that they were a fungus really bothered her. At this time of year, when the aroma of truffles wafted from virtually every household in town, Gia was at her most miserable. At first she busied herself with her singing lessons, but after her falling out with Alfredo, singing became somewhat less important in her life. She continued to sing in church but without the passion of an artist.

She began spending hours each day watching her mother prepare food. After all, soon she'd be a wife and she needed to learn how to cook and sew and do any number of other domestic chores that heretofore she had largely ignored or taken for granted. She was determined to be the most complete wife imaginable by the time Pino returned. It was a lot of work, between school, lessons and learning home economics, but she knew it was worth it. Day after long day, she went through the same rigorous ritual. She told herself that she was gaining the discipline she'd never had before; it would build character. "A little suffering is good for the soul," she learned in church, and she was certainly suffering. Not merely physical suffering from the long days, but mental suffering from the mind-numbing tedium of her daily routine, and finally, and most importantly, emotional suffering from Pino's absence.

His letters had become less frequent and Gia was trying not to be concerned. At first she was annoyed, but she quickly wrote that off to her own selfishness. This was a time of war, and even if it meant not hearing from Pino for its duration, that would be all right if it meant his safe return. Still, her eagerness to communicate with him, to touch him, filled her days with madness and longing.

In his absence, Pino had taken on a larger role in Gia's life than he had ever occupied when he was with her. She now spent half of her time at Pino's house, not just visiting Maria, but getting to know Mama and Papa Vaggi. It wasn't long before she actually began to feel that they were part of her own family. She had always loved Maria like a sister, but Mr. and Mrs. Vaggi now also occupied a warm and secure place in Gia's heart. Despite all the fear and uncertainty that lay before them, somehow Gia just knew that in the end they would all be happy together.

Mrs. Vaggi enjoyed Gia's company as well and often showed her little cooking tips from her own batch of secret recipes. Gia especially loved the experience of shopping for food for dinner. Learning the process of how to choose the freshest meat, fish and vegetables was a chore, but an immensely satisfying one, and the market quickly became her home away from home. The war caused a great deal of rationing and the variety of choices were severely diminished but Gia viewed it as a challenge, almost a game, trying to compose a meal with whatever happened to be available on that particular day.

One day, she saw lovely veal chops in the window of Vaggi's butcher shop, something she hadn't seen in quite a while. Knowing her future-father-in-law's penchant for veal, she decided to allow herself this one extravagance. She waited until Mr. Vaggi was in the back room then stealthily entered. She whispered to Giancarlo, the young boy whom Mr. Vaggi had taken as an assistant. Giancarlo was a troublemaking fourteen year old who had gotten himself in hot water for public drinking and spouting off about how he would spit in Mussolini's eye if he ever met him. Ordinarily, the boy would have found himself shipped off to a school for wayward children, but owing to the fact that his father was in the army and his mother was trying to raise three children in his absence, Captain Biaggi was pressured into letting him off easy. Mr. Vaggi stepped in to assist in the process, offering to employ the boy part-time to keep him out of trouble. Secretly, Mr. Vaggi admired the boy's moxy and relished the opportunity to confound Biaggi, in even a little way. The idea didn't go over as well with Mrs. Vaggi who thought her husband certifiably insane for adding an employee to the payroll given their economic hardship. But she took a liking to the boy immediately and with Pino away, there had been a fairly significant drop in their grocery costs, so she softened her stance.

"Gianni, I need you to put those veal chops aside for me and don't sell them to anyone. I want to make them for dinner for Signor and Signora Vaggi tonight. I'll be back at lunch time when the shop is closed to pick them up. *Va bene?*" He winked and smiled at her and she knew she could count on him.

Peter Danish

She went about the rest of her morning errands and returned just before noon. She checked and saw no sign of Mr. Vaggi, so she entered. Giancarlo put a finger to his lips to signal her to be quiet and pointed to the back room; clearly, Mr. Vaggi hadn't left yet. She nodded in understanding and came close to the counter where Giancarlo was giving her the all-is-well sign.

"*Tutto bene,*" he said with another wink. Gia bristled with excitement. *What a wonderful surprise this was going to be!* She'd never cooked for the Vaggis before and was anxious that it be a success. The veal chops, she knew, would ensure it! The bells on the door clanged as another customer entered the shop and Giancarlo left Gia to attend to him.

"*Giorno,* Giancarlo" said the customer.

"*Buongiorno,* Signore Biaggi," answered the boy.

Gia froze. She didn't want to talk to the Chief Magistrate after the way she had so roundly insulted his son, and she slowly slid down the counter away from him, turning her back in hope of remaining unseen. It was too much to hope for.

"Gia!" trumpeted Mr. Vaggi, emerging from the back room. "What are you doing here?"

The cat was out of the bag and there was no point in further subterfuge.

"*Ciao,* Signore Vaggi, *come sta?*" she said with a big warm smile.

"What brings you here?"

"I just dropped in to say hello."

"That is so sweet!" he said. But no sooner had the words left his mouth, the smile ran from his face. Chief Magistrate Biaggi had wandered over to join them.

"Nice to see future in-laws getting on so well," he said and they nodded in acknowledgment. "That reminds me of a joke I heard at a party the other night!"

Gia tried not to let her discomfort show, as Mr. Vaggi was trying to understand how anyone could be throwing or attending parties at a time like this.

"Oh, yes! It goes like this: if marriage were outlawed…then only outlaws would have in-laws! Get it?" he said, laughing at his own joke. Gia and Mr. Vaggi smiled and chuckled politely. "Oh well, enough frivolity, back to business!"

"You're here on business?" asked Mr. Vaggi with a modicum of concern.

"Yes, indeed," replied the magistrate, "the business of dinner!"

An audible sigh emitted from Gia's relived lungs, but a different kind of tension was soon to emerge.

"Vaggi, do you have any veal chops? I don't see any in the case." Indeed there were none, because Giancarlo had removed them and placed them in the freezer in the back.

"Certainly," replied Mr. Vaggi, "some beautiful ones." But as he looked for them they were gone. "That's odd." He said scratching his head, looking around to see if they'd somehow moved. Gia looked at Giancarlo who met her glance but was perspiring heavily. If his boss asked, what would he say? If he said he'd sold them, Mr. Vaggi might ask "to who?" or "when?" In either case, he had no answer, and should his boss check the register, the draw would be light. If he got fired, he'd be sent to the juvenile home, and he was not about to let that happen.

"Gianni, what happened to the veal? Did you sell it?" Mr. Vaggi asked.

Gianni looked at Gia and didn't want to disappoint her but he couldn't risk the alternative. What happened next, he could not quite explain. It seemed his brain sent one message to his mouth, but his mouth delivered another.

"*Si, Signore*, I did. Only a few moments ago. Sorry, Signore Biaggi!"

Gia stealthily clenched her fists with glee, as the magistrate made a sour face.

"Well, then," he said with marked disappointment, "I guess it will have to be *cinghiale*. Or, have you sold the last of those also?"

"Coming right up!" said Giancarlo.

It was a small and insignificant victory but it meant the world to Gia. She'd managed to please her new father-in-law and foil the magistrate in the same motion. With this priceless tidbit safely tucked away, she skipped down the lane, gaining speed as she went along, and all she could think about was the look on Mr. Vaggi's face when he learned who it was that had bought the veal chops.

CHAPTER THIRTEEN

Betrayal

THE BODIES BEGAN TO APPEAR in the fall of 1941. The older folks were the first to go. The famine in Greece spread faster and worse than anyone in the occupying forces had expected or believed possible. Any items of value that could be confiscated were confiscated to help pay for the feeding and housing of the occupation troops. Little concern was given to the local folk, whose country was teetering on the verge of complete financial ruin as a result of the occupation costs levied upon it. Such was the way of the Nazi machine. Not only did the Greeks have to suffer the humiliation of occupation and starvation, but they had to pay for the privilege, as well.

Word spread throughout the camp that the *Duce* himself was coming to Athens to visit with the Greek Prime Minister and to review the troops. Pino and his comrades in arms quickly found themselves back in basic training mode. They were drilled and drilled for hours daily in ceaseless marching and formation exercises. For Captain Adamo, the inspection couldn't have come at a worse time, hot on the heels of his harsh review from his superiors. He barely had time to begin preparing a plan of action for the shaping up of his band of infantry.

Vehicles were freshly painted, flags flown all around town, uniforms were pressed, boots shined. Sadly, Pino felt it all had the feeling of a grand charade. It seemed that their actual state of readiness was completely irrelevant. All that mattered was that they cut a fine figure before the *Duce*. For Pino, the one really difficult part of the new order was that, going forward, the curfew was to be strictly enforced. That meant he could no longer see or hear his angel, at least not on a regular basis. He knew the next time he saw her he had to make some significant contact. He thought about what he'd say to her but drew a blank. He did know one thing for sure: even if he had to tie her up, he would absolutely not let her leave without learning her name. After that, he'd get her to commit to a meeting, maybe in the park, perhaps on Sunday after church. Did she attend church? He had liberty only in the afternoons; the evenings belonged to the officers. He was jealous of the freedom they had, the freedom to go to cafes and restaurants in the *Plaka* to eat and drink like little kings, the freedom to listen to music in the clubs at night, the freedom to sit in the dark of an alleyway, under a window and listen to a young girl sing, if they so pleased. It was so unfair.

The actual date of Mussolini's visit was kept secret until the day before he arrived. At that time, the entire Italian occupational force swung into action. The *Duce*'s meeting would be at the Government Center, wherever that was, thought Pino. He would then travel by motorcade through town and inspect the assembled troops along the way. Pino was pleased to learn that his battalion would be assembled on Patisson Street, not far from his angel's house. He was thrilled that the captain seemed preoccupied with that sector of town lately and he hoped to make the most of the situation and speak with her if the opportunity presented itself.

The troops gathered in preparation for their long march up to Omonia Square and then back south along Patisson Street. Pino couldn't help noticing the incredible difference in the uniforms between the troops and the officers. Despite their best efforts, even when pressed, the infantry uniforms looked shabby and disheveled. By contrast, the officers looked like royalty! Never had Pino seen so many shiny jackboots! The distinction was unmistakable.

The march was long and boring and seemed completely unnecessary. Why couldn't they simply march directly to the reviewing points? Along the way, they passed an ocean of sad and hungry faces, but missing were the faces of the beggars, the sick and dying that had increasingly populated the streets for the past several weeks. Pino immediately suspected a round-up of undesirables must have taken place during the night to make the place less "unsightly" for the *Duce*'s inspection.

Just as *her* house came into view, the company halted and assembled along the curb of the street at parade rest. From where he stood, Pino could clearly see the house, but not her window, which was just around the corner, on the side. As more soldiers passed and assembled further down the road, he scanned the crowd hoping she might be among the residents that had come out to witness the display. Not surprisingly, very few Athenians cared enough to watch the spectacle.

First the infantry, then the motorized infantry, then armored unit after armored unit slowly passed. But for the lack of cheering, one might easily have mistaken the procession for a parade passing a reviewing stand. To Pino, it was a mind-numbing show of force that served no purpose at all. *Who are they trying to impress? These people are dying of starvation in the streets! Tanks are the least of their worries!* Throwing his head back in disgust, he noticed a figure on the roof of a building opposite them, then another. It was *her!* She wasn't in her window. She and her sister had gone to the roof to watch the procession.

In the distance, Pino heard music and then cheers. The *Duce* must be close, he thought. He was correct. The *Duce's* motorcade was just a few hundred yards away. As it approached, the soldiers assembled cheered. Pino got caught up in the excitement and felt like cheering himself. He never dreamed he'd be so close to the "great" man and the excitement of the moment was undeniable. The last armored units passed and the *Duce* was in view, sitting in the back seat of a convertible military touring car. He waved regally as he passed. All of the practice, all of the drilling was for naught. Whoever the *Duce* passed waved frantically at him and he returned the affection.

Pino looked up to the roof, anxious to see the reaction of his angel as the *Duce* passed. What he saw astounded him. He could never say with absolute certainty because of the distance, but he could have sworn that as the *Duce's* car passed beneath, he saw his angel spit at him from the roof!

Unbelievable! What defiance! The young girl just spat at the *Duce* of Italy. *What nerve, what unmitigated gall!* If he wasn't already in love with her, he was now. The man solely responsible for her oppression and misery was within her reach and she showed her distain in the only way she could. He thought how proud his father would have been! Clearly there was more to this girl than met the eye.

Mussolini's trip to Greece, while a noble gesture, provided little relief. Upon his return to Rome, the *Duce* sent a letter to Hitler informing him that the Greek situation was much worse than had been expected. The government was on the verge of total collapse. The treasury on the brink of bankruptcy as a result of the heavy occupation costs. And the population was literally starving to death. Mussolini firmly believed that if Greece collapsed, it would have dire consequences on the Axis on many levels. Hitler, however, was indifferent to his plea, stating the Greeks had no one but themselves to blame for their situation, and he would say nothing more.

The night of Mussolini's visit was a merry occasion for the Italians and impromptu parties erupted in the various cafes around Omonia Square. For the occasion, Captain Adamo granted his men liberty to enjoy the celebration, but with the stern admonishment that "the real work begins tomorrow."

Bernardi and Amonte were anxious to get out and take full advantage of the opportunity, as the new restrictions imposed of late had severely curtailed their evening recreation. There was a club frequented by several of the officers that they wanted to check out that supposedly had good food, lively music and women of questionable virtue. Pino had a different destination in mind but he dared not share it, so he reluctantly tagged along.

Noticeably absent on that evening was Carlucci, who lately had been keeping more and more to himself. At first no one had noticed or particularly cared, but this night was a celebration and it was odd for him not to accompany his comrade on such an occasion. Amonte heard a rumor that Carlucci was smitten with a Greek girl he'd met on patrol, but chose not to share the information with his pals. He'd been seen chatting with her more than once and Amonte suspected his pal was just out sowing his oats.

Good for him! Amonte thought, *Maybe tonight I'll sow some of my own.*

Omonia Square was the heart of the city in terms of nightlife, if you could call it that. Of the dozen or so cafes and clubs in the square only a handful remained open and those remained solvent largely due to the patronage of German and Italian officers. The three soldiers decided to first visit the club which they had heard about from the officers. If it was too stuffy or if they felt awkward around the officers, they'd leave and check out one of the other spots on the square. They washed, shaved and combed their hair, trying in vain to look presentable. It was no mean feat.

"Tonight, some chicks are gonna get plucked!" bellowed Bernardi as they stepped out into the cool, crisp night air. "So, Vaggi, tell me, do opera singers pull a lot of chicks?"

"You'd be surprised," Pino said trying to sound confident.

"You bet I would, shocked even!"

"Relax guys," Amonte interjected, "I heard that in town there's plenty of girls just ripe for the picking. One of the officers was telling me at breakfast that the girls were literally throwing themselves at him the other night. He had his pick of a dozen."

"Why pick?" said Bernardi, "Why not take 'em all? For a little bit of rice or sugar you can have your own harem. I'm telling you guys, this place just keeps getting better and better." Bernardi's manner suggested to Pino that he spoke from experience.

The thought of paying for or "buying" a girl repulsed Pino, but it didn't seem to bother Amonte at all.

"Yep, Vaggi, we all have to do our part to support the local economy."

Outside it was a dull grey and muggy evening: this was Athens at its worst. Clouds of mist ascended from the streets like steam in a hot jungle swamp. The walk to Omonia Square was a short one and they could hear the welcome sound of music in the distance.

Turning off the boulevard into the square, Pino saw Kostas on the far side of the square pushing some kind of cart. He hadn't noticed the soldiers and Pino started to wave to him but quickly thought it best to leave him alone to whatever nocturnal intrigue he was up to.

Pino had begun to take a real liking to the little, grizzled old man with the encyclopedia-like memory. He was one of those colorful characters that both blended into the background and stood out at the same time. Pino noticed that Kostas appeared out of breath as he labored with the cart and wanted to help him with his load but decided against it. It wasn't the right night to be seen fraternizing with the locals. He'd see Kostas again soon enough and make it up to him.

The Olympia Café was jumping to the sound of German drinking songs when Pino and his comrades arrived. A cursory glance of the crowd revealed a largely Italian clientele, with the exception of one table of German officers neatly situated right in front of the café's small stage. The orchestra, if you could call it that, was comprised of a dozen elderly Greek musicians, all of whom gave the appearance that they'd rather be anywhere but where they were. Given the economic conditions they surely couldn't complain; at least they were working. In all likelihood their wages for the evening might very well be paid out in food, but that was more than acceptable.

Bernardi led the way inside and quickly found a table close to the stage, across from where the Germans were seated.

"Red wine's OK for everybody?" he asked, and they nodded. "Waiter! Red wine, Italian!" Rubbing his hands together he announced, "Boys, tonight we are *all* getting laid, even Vaggi."

The comment didn't bother Pino nearly as much as the oom-pa-pa music, which after only minutes, began to grate on him. The noise and the smoke annoyed him and brought back an unpleasant memory of *Café Fritz*. He looked around and noticed that no one else seemed the least bit bothered so he decided to suck it up and try to enjoy himself. Bernardi was talking but Pino wasn't listening. He sipped his wine and wondered how long they'd remain in this place before striking out to another more inviting one. The hordes of loose women that they'd heard about were nowhere to be found and their absence, Pino was sure, dictated that departure for another destination was imminent.

The evening took a turn for worse as Captain Adamo suddenly appeared and sat at a table of Italian officers immediately next to Pino and his friends. The captain nodded to his troops and they returned the formality, but his appearance changed the entire dynamic of the evening. They exchanged unhappy glances. Unspoken was the agreement that they obviously couldn't leave the moment their Captain arrived. It would be unseemly and they were already the unfortunate holders of a spot not very high on his esteem scale. So, they settled back in, at least for the moment, to watch the entertainment in the company of their CO.

"That changes things somewhat," said Pino.

A pretty young woman, perhaps eighteen years of age, walked passed and without a word, Amonte was off in pursuit.

"Not for him!" said Bernardi with a belly laugh.

Amonte's departure left Pino alone with Bernardi, a position he didn't relish. Bernardi produced and lit a cigar, further annoying Pino. The smoke rings he blew wafted around the table making ghostly images in the air. It came as no surprise to Pino that Bernardi would be so adroit at something like blowing smoke rings. It seemed to fit his personality to a tee. He was also the best card player and dice thrower in the group; skills which Pino imagined were far more highly prized in Napoli than in Collagna. All of these charming little traits combined with a sparkling personality made Bernardi arguably the least appealing person Pino had ever met. He watched the hulking mass of Neapolitan fury sitting next to him and wondered what dinner must be like in the Bernardi household. He imagined a band of loud, foul-mouthed baboons yelling at each other at the top of their lungs while they fought over the last meatball.

A smattering of applause and a few cat-calls from the audience greeted the next singer to take the stage. Pino was indifferent to it all, preferring to continue constructing imaginary pictures of the barbarous Bernardi family at Christmastime or at Easter dinner. The tinkle of the piano caught his attention. A familiar melody was forming in the orchestra, an Italian melody.

"Finally," he thought, "enough of this beer-drinking noise." He knew the song well, *"Il Bacio,"* by Arditi. A melancholy smile broke across his face as he drifted with the melodic line. His peaceful trance was smashed when his eyes happened upon the face of the singer. His angel! *She's going to sing popular songs?* he thought. *Can she?* He was in another world for just a moment before Bernardi's hand waved in front of his face.

"Earth to Vaggi. Earth to Vaggi. Are you there?" he said with a sardonic laugh, when the singer's identity finally registered to him. "Hey! Wait a minute! That's her isn't it?"

Pino was red with embarrassment and he didn't even know why.

"Well, alright now. This is going to be fun!" said Bernardi, chomping on his cigar.

She sang the song with delicacy and poise and the crowd went wild. Even though it was no more than a trifle. Pino was impressed. She immediately launched into another song, this time in Greek. It was some kind of plaintive folksong, and Pino hated it. He didn't want her talents wasted on such pedantic rubbish. She was an artist of the first rate and this was all beneath her. Still, he could not help but be moved by her performance. She sang with deep sorrow in her eyes and deeper sorrow in her voice, the kind of sorrow that bespeaks a lifetime of unhappiness. Not merely the somberness of war and the bitterness of occupation, but the kind of misery that only an artist can sense, feel, interpret and share. Her eyes met his for just a moment when suddenly a hand touched him on the shoulder. He turned to see a young girl wearing too much makeup smiling at him and speaking in broken Italian.

"Would you like to buy me a drink?"

"Not now!" he said. He tried to signal to her that he was listening to the song but it was no use.

"C'mon, Honey! Sit right down here and join us," Bernardi spouted. "What's your name?"

"Stella," she replied.

Pino smiled politely and resumed watching the performance but Bernardi wouldn't let up.

"Forgive my friend, sweetie, he has no manners," said Bernardi. Then, he added in a whisper. "Besides, confidentially: I think he prefers men. You know how it is." He slapped Pino in the back of the head and roared at him: "Hey, Vaggi! Pay attention! We've got a guest. Hey Stella, you got any girlfriends looking to meet some handsome Italian soldiers?"

Pino turned around and was shocked to see his angel singing directly to Captain Adamo, who was wrapped in attentive splendor. She looked as if there wasn't another person in the world and he was eating it up. Pino couldn't conceal his outrage, which Bernardi found impossible to resist.

"Yeah, tough luck there, Vaggi. You know the old saying: Why take a soldier when you can have an officer?"

The song ended and the audience erupted again. The appeal of the folksong to a crowd of homesick soldiers was undeniable. Even if they didn't understand the words, the message rang clear. She stood there drinking in the adulation. She was in her element after all.

Pino stood and began to approach the stage when he noticed Captain Adamo doing the same. The Captain kissed her hand, then led her back to his table where she joined the group of officers in their merrymaking. The sight ignited in Pino a fury he'd never known himself capable of. His temples throbbed and he felt dizzy. He slammed back his drink in one gulp and stormed out, with Bernardi's voice trailing behind him: *"Kali nichta* Vaggi!*"*

Soft wood, Pino, like pine. That's what you're made of. His father's words echoed in his ears as he ran home. *You bend but you don't break,* the voice reminded him.

"Yes," Pino added, "but don't forget about the marks, the dents!"

As he walked, he saw dozens of his fellow soldiers in the streets. Most were chatting up the local girls. He detested them all. He detested this country and this war, but most of all he detested *her.* As he turned the corner leaving Omonia Square to head down the hill toward the Acropolis and his base, he saw a welcome sight: Kostas. The old man was pushing a cart filled with cardboard boxes up the street.

"Kostas! Come here!" Pino called.

"Are you alright, my friend?" the old man said.

"No. Got any *grappa?*"

Kostas drew back in shock and scanned the street to see if anyone heard Pino's outburst. He put a finger to his lips and waved for Pino to follow him out of the light and into an alley.

"You should know better than to say such things in public," scolded Kostas. "I could get in big trouble if the Germans knew about my little business."

Pino realized Kostas was right. One stupid little slip of the tongue could land his friend in jail or worse.

"Sorry, Kostas, I'm having a bad day."

The old man's ancient eyes glistened in the moonlight and looked right through Pino. His penetrating stare caused Pino to turn away, but Kostas squeezed his arms reassuringly.

"Is it a woman?" he asked.

Pino blinked in amazement. The old man had powers of perception like no one he'd ever encountered.

"No. Well, yes. Kostas, how the hell did you…"

The old man waved for him to be silent again.

"Pino, my friend, wise men speak because they have something to say; fools because they have to say something." Pino digested the pearls of wisdom.

"Plato said that, not me! But we are both Greek!" said Kostas with a hearty laugh. "Plato also said that love is a mental illness!"

"He did not say that!" said Pino, already feeling better.

"He did indeed, my friend. Look it up!" There was no need to look it up. If Kostas said it was so, it was so. "Now to business. This woman, she is Greek?"

"Yes."

"Oh that's bad. Very bad. Greek women are the worst kind of women. I am afraid *grappa* won't help you, my friend." Pino couldn't stop smiling at the performance. "I am afraid you need something that does not come in a bottle." He reached into his pockets and dug around for a minute. "Ah, here we are." He pulled out a string of brightly colored ceramic beads and handed them to Pino.

"What are these?"

"*Komboloia.* Worry Beads. When you are in times of deep distress, which will be often if you are in love with a Greek woman, you hold them in your hands and rub them. They will give you relief from your stress."

Pino held the beads like they were a string of diamonds, like the rosary beads his mother gave him as a child for his first holy communion.

"Now you say, 'Thank you, Kostas!'"

Pino burst out laughing and hugged the old man.

"God bless you, Kostas! When this shitty war is over, I promise to come back and visit you!"

"Ya, ya, don't worry about Kostas. Just you stop worrying about Greek girls! Concentrate on being soldier first, getting home safe. Greek girls aren't going anywhere."

"I will," he promised. "*Kali Nichta*, Kostas."

Kostas pulled Pino close and kissed the top of his head, then shoved him away and started up the street toward the square, whistling as he walked.

CHAPTER FOURTEEN

THE MEETING

OVER THREE HUNDRED THOUSAND PEOPLE died of starvation in Greece during the occupation. Food shipments from America were re-routed to feed the Italian troops in Africa and Germans on the Russian front, and the International Red Cross was powerless to stop it. There was virtually no bread, oil, rice or sugar in the entire country. In what he considered a humanitarian gesture, Hitler loaned ten thousand tons of wheat to the starving nation. Unfortunately, the nation required ten to fifteen thousand tons *monthly* to survive! Vegetables, legumes and garlic were all that the helpless population could count upon for sustenance. Long treks out of the city and into the surrounding countryside in search of food became the norm and often the roads were littered with the bodies of the poor souls that didn't make it.

The sight of decomposing bodies greeted patrols more and more often and eventually trucks were dispatched to remove them. What was worse, Pino wondered, to be shot and killed in battle, or to die a slow death from starvation? The sight of an old man dead on the side of the road upset Pino almost to the point of tears. The secret, they said, was never to look at the faces of the corpses. The man could have been sixty or he could have been ninety, there was no way of telling. Pino said a quick prayer for the old man. Then, another for himself, that he never get assigned the task of collecting the remains of these poor wretches.

Another familiar sight was the daily exodus of Athenians out of town to the fields searching for food. Pino followed their path and watched with little emotion as he delivered a dispatch to a checkpoint on the northern outskirts of the city. With all day to do it, he was in no particular rush. The checkpoint was patrolled by both German and Italian troops and he had no desire to linger, so, his dispatch delivered, he turned and headed for base.

He hadn't gone ten yards before he stopped dead in his tracks. In front of him stood a group of about twenty Italian soldiers crowded around something. His curiosity got the better of him and he endeavored to investigate. Unbelievably, there *she* was, his former angel, taking all sorts of gifts from the soldiers and stuffing them into a large sack. There was olive oil, dry pasta, wheat, barley, rice, soap and even wine! What was the meaning of this?

"Please sing for us again sometime soon, Maria!" one of the soldiers called out.

Maria! That's her name! It was too bad that he hated her now that he finally knew her name.

"I promise," she replied, "but now I need to get back. My mother will be worried." She lifted the heavy bag over her shoulder with a grunt and Pino jumped into action.

"*Signorina*, I'm going in your direction. Let me carry that for you!" he offered, trumping the rest of the soldiers who stood around muttering and wondering why none of them had offered first.

"*Grazie. Molto Grazie*" she answered, and they were off.

For the first hundred yards they walked in stony silence, nervous or otherwise. Pino was torn between emotions. He felt tremendous affection for the girl, there was little point in denying it. But how much of that was really his awe for her incredible artistry? He certainly did not find her attractive in the same way he did Gia. His feelings for Maria were altogether different but equally passionate. He couldn't explain it.

After recent events, he also worried that she might be just another opportunistic girl looking out for the best thing to come her way. Like Bernardi said: why choose a soldier when you can have an officer? He desperately wanted to talk to her about music and singing. He knew it was just a matter of breaching the subject correctly. Perhaps, some small disclosure on his part might open the doors.

"I saw you at the club the other night," he said.

"Yes, I saw you too."

"You sounded lovely."

"Hmmm. You don't lie very well. I was ghastly."

"No! You were not. You had them eating out of your hand!"

"I could have sung *O Sole Mio* and gotten the same response. They wouldn't know the difference."

"I would have known. Besides, what's wrong with O Sole Mio?" Pino asked with a flirtatious grin. They continued in silence for many blocks, passing the theater of Herodias Atticus and reaching the Plaka.

"So, tell me, *tenore*," she asked, "where do you sing?"

A knowing smile crossed his face as he considered his answer.

"Well, it's hard to say. Before I was drafted, I was studying at the National Conservatory in Milan."

"Really?" she asked, impressed. "What's it like?"

"Well, like any other conservatory, I guess. But most of my training came from my music teacher back home in the mountains."

"Oh, so you are not from the city, then?"

"Not at all!" laughed Pino.

"I was born in New York."

"Really?" he said, completely surprised. "New York City and now Athens, you must be very…very sophisticated."

Now it was her turn to laugh.

"Oh *yes!* I am quite the modern sophisticated woman!" she said with a chuckle. "Aside from my music lessons, I'm afraid I have very little knowledge about…well, about anything, really!"

"Me neither!" said Pino with a smile. "I really have no other interest than music. My father thinks I'm a disgrace to the family."

"My mother thinks the same about me!" she said. "But my teacher believes in me. And I believe in myself."

"It seems we have a lot in common," said Pino.

Maria just smiled a shy little grin.

"So tell me, do you sing professionally or are you still studying?"

"Well, the truth is, I was actually just about to make my debut at La Scala when the war broke out."

She laughed out loud, incredulously. Then, noticing his serious look, she stopped cold and studied his face, like a tiger, probing, seeking.

"La Scala, you say?"

"La Scala. They offered me *La Bohème* for next season. Well, actually this season, but unfortunately, as you can see, I'm here in Athens."

She scowled and threw him a fierce glance.

"Are you serious?" she said.

He was reminded that there was much more to this girl than met the eye. She looked hard at him, scanning his eyes for something, perhaps a trace of fear, but there was none. He simply smiled a cocky smile and nodded as he resumed walking. He felt like Nemorino walking away from Adina in *Elisir d'Amore*, and he began to whistle softly. For the first time since he'd met her, he felt he held the upper hand. She trailed close behind, lost in thought. He'd struck some kind of nerve. Her harshness was gone.

"I'll sing there, one day," she said in a faint voice, which Pino was not certain was meant to be heard.

"I'm sure you will," he said. "I'd say you are already better than any soprano I've heard in Milan."

Her eyes exploded with excitement, as if it were the greatest compliment she'd ever received.

"Do you mean it?" she asked.

"Of course, I mean it. You have a remarkable gift! But be careful not to squander it." Pino decided to roll the dice a bit. "I'd love to sing with you sometime, if you don't mind." She looked at the ground and smiled a Inervous smile. She was the shy little girl again, but underneath a bubbling energy was trying to burst free.

"Me too," she said. "I would like that very much."

"Great!" he said with relief, "When would be a good time?"

"Can you go for a walk with me on Sunday, say after lunch?"

He wasn't sure, but he agreed anyway. He'd sneak out if necessary. As they reached the corner of her house, she stopped and took the sack from Pino. They shook hands like old friends and said goodbye. She entered the building carrying the spoils of war and he skipped down the street with a song in his heart.

That Sunday, as planned, they met on a bench in front of Herodias Atticus. At first, there was awkward silence, but Maria was far too curious to remain quiet for long. She pummeled Pino with questions about his training, his instructors, his favorite operas, his biggest obstacles, his greatest fears. Once they started talking about music and singing there was no distance between them, no nationalities, no war. They chatted like life-long friends because they spoke the same language: music. It was the happiest Pino had been since he'd left Collagna. Finally, he'd met someone who completely understood him.

Their Sunday meetings became a regular event for several weeks, with Maria packing her music and Pino packing provisions for a small picnic. They always went to the same spot in the park in front of Herodias Atticus, outside the Acropolis. They walked rather than take the street car and would never be seen walking too close or holding hands or doing anything that might be considered unseemly. They sang songs and shared anecdotes about the opera and their studies.

After they had already met several times, Pino decided that he would show her his La Scala letter. When he did, she stared at it in reverence as if it were a holy relic. But always resolute in her conviction that she'd soon join him in their ranks.

Maria confided in Pino that she was a member of the Athens opera and he was impressed. She was embarrassed to tell him. After all, he'd already been contracted by La Scala! But the fact of the matter was that Maria actually had more stage experience than Pino by that time as a result of her contract with the Athens Opera and he was very much in awe of her.

She constantly told him that he had the most beautiful voice she'd ever heard and he repeatedly told her she was the most gifted singer he'd ever heard.

Often, he'd ask her to sing an aria for him but usually she refused, preferring to sing duets. He treasured hearing her singing solo because each opportunity to listen was like a lesson for him. She sang in a style so honest and completely foreign to him that he was riveted by each word. She was so completely at one with the text that it was almost as if she were writing it herself, there on the spot, as she sang.

Despite her protests, he implored her to sing anything: "something easy...something simple."

She admonished him in words that were permanently seared into his heart.

"No aria is *simple*. No aria is easy. You of all people should know that. Infinite possibilities swirl in my head with every note and every word. It takes ages for me to consider every aspect of an aria; to think, study, practice and aspire to master it. I'm not so conceited to say that any aria is easy."

Frozen, goose bumps ran up Pino's spine. He didn't believe in ghosts, but he looked into her eyes convinced that she was somehow channeling Maestro Ivaldi. She spoke in words almost identical to his. It gave him pause, but it also drew him to her in a way he could not explain.

They often sang together in the park, duets from *Tosca, Bohème, Norma, Lucia* and especially *Traviata*. That was the first duet they'd ever sung, back on that autumn night on her balcony and it remained very special.

Their relationship was deepening and despite the horror surrounding them, they managed to find a little corner of the world to sneak away to and remember how beautiful life could be. Unfortunately, the war was never far off and its grim reminders always managed to find a way into their lives.

Pino told Maria that all he knew about the events of the last year had come from old Kostas. She laughed and told him that the old man had sugar-coated everything. Her eyes grew noticeably darker whenever she discussed the Nazis, and he learned not to ask for too much information at a time. Apparently, in the days prior to the Italian arrival in Athens, things were much bleaker and she wasn't sure they'd survive. He found it odd that she spoke as if the war were over and survival no longer in question.

"When the Nazis completed their conquest," she said, "we had to sit through day after day of the most humiliating parades in the streets. They came down from Syntagma Square, along Panepistimiou Street, then right past our house on Patisson."

Pino smiled inwardly as he remembered watching her spit on the *Duce's* car as it passed.

"Tanks and guns and motorcycles and armored cars of all kinds in the most ostentatious display imaginable. It was terrible. The Germans are cold, cruel people. I hate them!" The venom in her voice and the fire in her eyes unnerved him. She looked like a wild animal ready to devour its prey. He was convinced that this inferno that raged inside of her was unmistakably the source of her brilliant singing. Nothing learned in a conservatory could possibly compare with the raw sensuality, the power and passion of her profoundly human emotions. Her singing was ripped right from her soul and no amount of embellishment could mask the brilliance of the storyteller. The unbridled emotion revealed an honesty that Pino *knew* was exactly what Maestro Ivaldi spoke of and said all singers should aspire to. To her it came as naturally as breathing.

Pino also knew that the apparent ease with which she employed her gifts was the result of years and years of sacrifice and slavish devotion to the art. He'd lived it himself.

One afternoon Pino decided to breech the subject.

"Do you ever wonder if all the sacrifice is worth it?" he asked.

The smile drained from her face and her eyes narrowed.

"How can you even ask that? To even be given the *opportunity* to sacrifice for art is a gift from God. It's an honor. A privilege."

It was the second time she'd spoken words that had also flowed from the maestro's lips. He simply couldn't believe his ears. The words were like music to him. In no time at all, he came to trust her implicitly.

Pino enjoyed their little sightseeing tours almost as much as singing with her. Together they visited the Acropolis and all its temples as well as the ancient theater of Herodias Atticus. The two would often sit on the millennia-old marble and have picnics, pretending to watch great performance of ages past.

On the occasion of Pino's twenty-first birthday, Maria baked him a lemon cake and hoped desperately that he was partial to lemons. It was not her first choice. She had hoped to make an almond torte which she was certain no Italian could resist, but couldn't find any almonds. The lemon cake required merely flour, baking soda, salt, sugar, eggs and of course lemons. The baking was easy. Concealing it from her mother proved dicier. First, she needed to call her voice teacher, Elvira Hidalgo and tell the diva that she was not feeling well and would need to miss her lesson. If her mother ever learned the reason, there would be hell to pay. Her hands shook as she put the cake in a paper bag and wiped the powdered sugar from the counter to conceal the evidence.

Pino waited in the usual place and as usual Maria was late. He was no longer troubled by her lateness. He'd come to expect it. He sat back and listened to the wind blow through the pine trees all around him and wondered how many of the world's greatest minds had sat in this very spot through the ages thinking deep thoughts, pondering the meaning of life. For the better part of the last year, the meaning of life had been simple: stay alive. In the last few weeks all that had changed. Maria burst into his life like a supernova, and in her wake she re-ignited the creative passion for art and the interpretive passion for singing that he'd allowed to pass into his subconscious for so long.

He heard a voice humming in the distance. *Lucia di Lammermoor*, the duet from the end of Act One. How appropriate, he thought!

"Ah, verranno a te sull'aura I miei sospiri ardente, udrai nel mar che mormora l'eco dei miei lamenti."

- Ah, on the breeze will come to you my ardent sighs, you will hear in the murmuring sea the echo of my laments.

Pino's heart filled as he prepared to sing the next verse, but just as Maria appeared from among the bushes, his heart sank. She was dressed in a manner he'd never seen before with an ill-fitting floral print blouse and a doughty-looking black skirt around her ample midsection. Well-worn, low heeled black sandals rounded out the ensemble. In short, it was not exactly a sight that engendered much passion in him. Unfortunately, Maria saw it in his eyes instantly.

She didn't say much. In fact she said nothing at all. The one element that punctuated most of their early conversation had been silence. While that seemed to suit them well before, this time Pino sensed that beneath her silence a cauldron was bubbling, just waiting to spout. He never knew just what to say to unlock those unspoken words. He imagined how much easier this would be if the two of them were sitting on a couch in her living room, without her silly outfit and her omnipresent mother around.

"I made you a cake," she said.

"Oh! Wow, thank you," he mumbled.

"Buon Compleanno."

"Thanks."

She leaned forward and gave him a peck on the cheek and allowed it to linger. He wished he had the courage to tell her how he felt, but instead simply bumbled his way through a series of awkward motions suggesting interest and intent, hoping that the message would be understood and well-received. Why this silly outfit? Why couldn't she dress like she usually did? For some reason, he wondered what Amonte would have done. He always seemed so smooth. First of all Amonte wouldn't be here. He'd made it clear he found Maria pitifully unattractive, but if he were here...

Just then Maria lunged forward and kissed him. His heart thumped in his breast and he thought it might explode, but touching her lips caused his mind to go blank. He felt nothing, only the tenderness of the kiss. And it all seemed so right and so natural, not melodramatic like in the movies. He heaved a mammoth sigh of relief through the kiss and she giggled.

"Deep sighs? Should I be worried?" she asked.

"Not at all."

They sat in silence holding hands and eating the cake, a peaceful silence that brought comfort and warmth in its wake. A gulf had been bridged. After a few minutes they got up and walked, holding hands. At least until they exited the park, where they became two ordinary pedestrians in the *Plaka*. They walked all the way up to Omonia Square and down the alley next to Maria's building.

"I have to go," she said. "Mother will worry."

"When do I get to meet her?" Pino asked.

"It's probably best you don't. She's old fashioned. She wouldn't understand."

"I see," he said with obvious disappointment. "You haven't told her about me have you?" She looked away. "Why not?"

"I have to go. My mother..."

"Okay, okay," Pino sighed, frustrated. "Wait. Take these." He pulled a package out from his pack. "It's salted, so it'll keep well."

"Thank you," said Maria with a hint of embarrassment.

"Doesn't your mother wonder where the food is coming from?" he said sarcastically.

"What are you suggesting?" she asked indignantly.

"I'm not suggesting anything. But, doesn't she even want to know who's sending all the food?"

"She doesn't care," she said as she took the package and hid it under her dress.

"Why are you hiding it? You're only across the street. No one will see."

"Old habits," she said nervously.

"You're not going to share it are you?" Pino asked.

Maria began to walk across the street without looking back.

"Would you think less of me? Does it pain you to think of me as one so selfish?"

"It only pains me to think of you perishing here, and the world not getting the chance to hear you."

She stopped then ran into his arms and started to cry.

"I can't imagine God giving you this gift then taking away any chance for you to share it," said Pino. "That's a thought I can't bear."

He wiped away her tears and she looked deeply into his eyes.

"Pino, what would happen if your captain found out you were giving us food?"

"Don't worry about that."

"I'm serious. Please tell me."

"Well, strictly speaking, you are the enemy, so...I'd probably be in big trouble."

She held him tighter.

"I really do need to go now."

They kissed goodbye tenderly.

"Happy Birthday, Pino."

"*Il mio Tesoro,*" Pino said softly.

She crossed the street and disappeared into the house.

CHAPTER FIFTEEN

Ecco il Mondo

A T THE HOTEL BRETAGNE, Captain Adamo sat at his desk reading the latest orders from HQ and sinking deeper into despair. He was allowing his personal feelings to creep deeper and deeper into his work and he knew that to be gravely dangerous. This time it could not be helped.

What does any of this nonsense have to do with the war? he mused with disgust as he put down the communiqué instructing him to ascertain the names and addresses of all the Jews in his sector. For all their ruthless efficiency, the Nazi's senseless obsession with the Jews was something he simply couldn't fathom. It was a distraction and detracted from the overall efficiency of their operation. Adamo had seen with his own eyes the heated demonstrations this policy provoked in Italy and knew his soldiers would have trouble following such orders. The timing was awful. Just as he was prepared to whip his troops back into shape, this order could eat at their sense of scruples and fairness and ultimately impact their morale in the worst way. He was tempted to throw the order into the fireplace and pretend he'd never seen it. That was what he should have done, but he knew he couldn't. Not now. Not after the scathing report he'd just received about his troops and his own command. He was in a jam.

He'd heard a story in the officers' club about a Nazi officer stationed on one of the Greek islands who was given the order to round up the Jews in the community. The officer demanded of the governor a list of all Jews on the island. The governor insisted there was no way of telling the Jews from the general population. Undeterred, the German visited the Bishop of the Greek Orthodox Church on the island to illicit his support. Apparently, the Bishop had studied in Munich and had even known Hitler many years ago, thus the officer felt confident in securing his assistance. The Bishop told the officer to return the next day and he'd have a list of all the Jews for him. Upon his return the Bishop produced an envelope containing the list. When the German opened it he saw the list contained only two names — *the Governor and the Bishop!*

Such pride and moral courage made Adamo sympathetic to the Greeks, but he was a soldier and could ill-afford to let sympathies get in the way of his judgment. Hopefully, the war would end soon and with it, Italy's alliance with Germany. Until then he had a job to do.

In the distance, he heard revelry beginning. His problems weren't going anywhere, so he decided to go and join his men in some much-needed debauchery. He needed to relax for a while and not think so much.

He got up to put on his coat and hat, but as he did a corporal burst in with an urgent dispatch. At first, Adamo read the letter with his usual disdain, but suddenly his demeanor brightened and he crushed the dispatch in his fist.

"This might be just the opportunity I've waited for," he thought with a hopeful nod. He rushed out of his office.

Captain Adamo entered the mess hall to find Pino, Amonte, Bernardi and Carlucci playing cards. His entrance brought the men to attention.

"Vaggi, Amonte, come with me," he said and turned to leave, not waiting for the men to acknowledge.

The men looked at each other as if to say: *What did we do?* They didn't dawdle. They were up and out the door in an instant.

"Sure! Right after he wins three straight pots! I bet the captain's in on it," said Bernardi.

Outside the mess hall, the captain and two other soldiers dressed in full combat gear were awaiting Pino and Amonte. The sight of them turned Pino's stomach into knots. No matter what the reason, this couldn't be good news.

"We've got a little job to do tonight," the captain said calmly. "You've got ten minutes to get your gear and meet me in my quarters. Go!"

Pino and Amonte ran like rabbits back to their barracks to grab their gear and suit up. Ten minutes wasn't much time. Was it another exercise?

"Any idea what this is all about?" Amonte asked.

"No clue," Pino replied on the verge of panic.

The two men were now bunking down in different rooms, because there were so many empty ones available. It annoyed Pino, because he wasn't sure exactly what he should take with him and he had hoped to watch Amonte. He grabbed his backpack, shouldered his rifle and put a box of cartridges into his breast pocket. His pistol came next, followed by his long blade for hand-to-hand combat, a weapon for which he had had absolutely no training whatsoever. He prayed he would never need to use it. His helmet completed his preparations and as soon as it was strapped across his chin, he was as ready as he'd ever be.

In the street below, Amonte waited for him. Then, they took flight toward the captain's quarters. When they arrived, the other two soldiers stood at the door. As Pino and Amonte entered, they were nearly knocked over by the captain coming out.

"OK Let's move!" he barked.

Pino looked at Amonte in terror. *Move? Move where?* Amonte was just as confused as Pino. The next thing they knew, they were running through the streets at a heated pace. They turned a corner, then another, and another. They proceeded at such a clip, making so many turns that Pino became disoriented. He thought he knew these streets well enough by now not to get lost, but he was wrong. Amonte was softly talking to one of the other soldiers when the captain put his finger to his lips to signal "quiet."

They came to a corner and the captain raised his hand to halt them. He pointed to Pino and Amonte and motioned for the two of them to take the other side of the street. They crossed over and waited for his next order. The captain pulled out a pair of odd-looking binoculars and looked through them down the street. Pino took the opportunity to get out a question.

"What in God's name are we doing?" he asked.

"Sassani just told me they got a tip that two escaped English pilots are going to be smuggled out of the country through Athens."

"You're kidding."

"Wish I was."

"Are they armed?" Pino asked. Amonte shrugged. "Great," Pino muttered in horror.

The captain waved to them and took his rifle from his shoulder. Pino and Amonte did the same.

"Oh, Jesus," Pino said, a little louder than he expected.

"Shut up and calm down," Amonte ordered.

The captain motioned for them to move forward. They slowly proceeded down the street in the dark. The captain waved for them to stop and they froze. They were at the mouth of a small street or a large alleyway. It was about ten yards wide and was lined with trashcans and wooden crates that Pino imagined were fruit or vegetable boxes. The captain and the other soldiers crossed the street and stopped at the other side of the alley entrance. The captain again peered through his binoculars down the alley.

"Thirty meters down on the right is the side door to the house we're hitting," he said.

Hitting? Thought Pino.

"Cocia, stay here. Sassani, you proceed to the end of the alley and cover the front entrance, but stay out of sight. Nobody goes in or out, got it?" Both men nodded silently. At least now Pino knew the names of his comrades. "Cocia, once Sassani gives the 'all clear,' you join Vaggi and Amonte with me," the captain continued. "We knock. Say we need to conduct a routine inspection of the premises. Nothing special, just routine. Cocia, you're the mouthpiece. Got it?" Pino and Amonte nodded, not exactly sure what they were agreeing with. "As soon as we're inside, we secure the site. Vaggi, you check upstairs. Amonte, you the basement. I've got the ground floor. Cocia, you keep the old lady busy while we're looking." Pino guessed that by "mouthpiece" the captain meant Cocia spoke Greek. Just then the captain's voice darkened. "We got word that two English fighter pilots are being stashed away here on their way out of the country. We may already be too late."

"Do we know if they're armed, Captain?" asked Amonte.

"Can't be sure. Assume the worst. We do know that both men were wounded in their escape. So they shouldn't be too much trouble. OK, let's move."

Pino wiped the sweat off his brow and blessed himself. He reached into his shirt, pulled out his St. Christopher medal and kissed it. This time he wasn't thanking the saint, he was praying to him. He put the medal back and followed the captain down the alley. Thirty yards later, they stopped at a side door. The three men remained there until Sassani reached the end of the alley and assumed his position.

"All clear!" he called out, and Cocia ran down to join them.

"Ready?" asked the captain.

Pino and Amonte nodded nervously. The captain knocked on the door so loudly that the noise caused Pino and Amonte both to jump. Inside the house, voices could be heard, but they were not audible enough to make out what was being said. They waited a few seconds. Then, the captain knocked again. The voices stopped. Footsteps could be heard coming downstairs, growing louder as they got closer.

"Cocia, get ready. Boys, check your weapons," the captain whispered.

Pino and Amonte had their rifles cocked and ready, their perspiring fingers on the triggers. The sound of footsteps stopped right behind the door that was in front of them. The captain motioned Pino and Amonte to the other side of the doorway and they quickly moved. The sound of locks being undone startled them. Finally the door handle started to turn. The tension was palpable as the door slowly opened.

"*Buona Sera, Signore.* How can I help you?" said a young girl in perfect Italian.

Pino didn't realize it, but his jaw hung wide open in shock. It was Maria.

"*Signorina?*" said Captain Adamo, with a distinct note of surprise in his voice. He quickly regained his composure. "We are conducting a routine inspection of certain homes throughout the city. It's just routine. Is your mother home?"

"Yes, she's upstairs," she answered, looking only at the captain. "I was just practicing my piano and mother was listening."

"That's fine," the captain replied with a smile. "You just continue your practicing. We don't want to inconvenience you at all. We'll be done before you know it."

She hesitated for just an instant but Pino caught it.

"Of course," she said. "Come right in."

The men entered, Pino bringing up the rear. He avoided making eye contact with her as he passed.

"Is there a cellar?" asked the captain in an offhand manner.

"No, sir. Our apartment is just what you see and two bedrooms around back."

The captain nodded approval and slowly scanned back and forth.

"You'd better get back to practicing. I don't want you getting in trouble with your mother."

"Thank you," she said without a hint of nervousness. She turned and went back up the stairs. The captain watched her disappear, then he pulled his men close.

"OK, let's be quick and thorough. Use your pistols. If you see anything, yell. If they're armed, don't hesitate to shoot. Amonte, you're here, Vaggi, Cocia, you're with me. Go!"

It was all happening too fast. They separated. Amonte entered a large sparsely decorated living room, and began to look around. The living room had a look like no one had set foot in it for years. Aside from a clock and the drapes, the walls were barren. There was no one there.

Pino and the captain moved into a narrow hallway. There were two bedrooms, a bathroom and a hall closet. The captain entered the first bedroom on the right where he was greeted by the old lady.

"Buona Sera Signora," said the captain, respectfully.

"Sera," she replied, grimly.

"I'm so sorry to disturb your daughter's lesson, but we'll only be a moment," he assured her, but she waved her hand in dismissal, she didn't understand a word. Cocia jumped into action and translated.

"Would you care to sit down?" she offered.

"Well...alright," he agreed and reluctantly sat on the couch next to the old lady. Pino moved slowly through the hallway, checking the closets. Everything seemed perfectly normal. Next, he came upon the bathroom. It, too, was empty; nothing out of the ordinary. The shower curtain was pulled closed and Pino knew he had to check it. His heart began racing. He quietly took his pistol out of its holster and aimed it at the center of the curtain. He eased into the bathroom sideways with his back against the wall and reached out toward the curtain with his left hand, the gun in his right. He took a deep breath and ripped the curtain back. Nothing.

Amonte left the living room and entered the dining room. He got down on one knee and looked under the table. The room was empty. There were no closets of any kind, just a hutch with china and a small chest in the corner.

The captain was still sitting on the couch with the old lady. Impatiently, he tried to make small talk.

"So, tell me *Signora*," he asked, "Is it just you and your daughter living here?"

"No, no. I have two daughters. My oldest is out getting some vegetables for dinner tonight."

"I see," said the captain with a nod.

The old lady knitted her brows and leaned forward, straining to hear something. Her face contorted angrily.

"Maria!" she barked, "I don't hear you!" From the other room, the girl's voice answered.

"Sorry, Mama," she said, and immediately a piano was heard.

"Ah! You must forgive my youngest daughter, she is a good-for-nothing," the old lady said, "Lazy and stubborn."

"But she's young, yet." the captain politely protested, trying his best to sound interested. "Give her time. She may surprise you."

Pino stood still in the hall, his emotions in a whirl. *How was this possible? Could Maria possibly be complicit in such a thing? This was espionage. She could be shot for this. I could be shot for this!*

Well, Maria, he thought to himself, *you never cease to amaze me.* This time, however, it was he who held the upper hand, not to mention weapons. He entered the room where Maria was practicing. From the doorway, he slowly scanned its contents. There were two single beds against one wall, French doors leading out to the balcony on another wall. An upright piano stood against the third wall, with Maria seated before it. There was a large ornamental mirror on the wall above the piano. The fourth wall was barren except for double doors leading to a large closet. Pino strolled slowly and nervously around the room as Maria practiced. It was oppressively hot in the room and he was perspiring profusely. He didn't want to wipe his forehead in front of her, but the mirror kept him plainly in her sight no matter where he stood in the room. He tried not to look at her but it was impossible. He glanced out of the corner of his eye at her back as she played. He then looked up at the mirror and caught her sneaking a glance at him, but she quickly looked away. The tension was too much for him. He needed to breathe.

Stopping at the French doors, he looked out. He could see the little stool in the alley where he had spent so many evenings. He opened the doors and moved out onto the balcony. Once out of her sight, he wiped his face with his coat sleeve. The night air wasn't much relief. It was rather hot and humid, but the balcony provided a welcome break from the tension of her bedroom. He looked again at the little stool across the street and thought to himself that from this vantage point it really wasn't very well concealed at all. In fact, had she been looking that way, she would most certainly have seen him. He suddenly had one more reason for concern. *How many times had she seen him? Did she know that he was out there all along?*

The piano playing stopped and Pino's thoughts returned to the reason he was there. Reentering the room, he saw that Maria was leafing through some music. He was curious to see what it was, but he didn't want to appear interested. He coldly resumed his patrol around the room. There was little left to explore, other than her closet. She began to play again and Pino knew the piece well, but could not name it. Chopin? Liszt? It was all he could do not to hum along. The music was a pleasant diversion, easing the tension somewhat as he strolled across the floor toward the closet doors. As Pino got nearer to the closet, he noticed Maria's playing became stiffer and awkward. To the untrained ear, the difference might have been imperceptible, but to Pino, it was night and day. It set off an alarm in his head. *The closet.* He pulled out his pistol. The sound of the piano and the sound of the captain in the next room faded from Pino's consciousness. His tunnel vision focused on the doorknob of the closet. Maria continued to play, watching him in the mirror.

Suddenly, he heard a rustling sound from within the closet. He froze. His mouth was dry and his temples pounded as he grasped the doorknob and raised his pistol. He yanked open the door.

A birdcage? There was a canary fluttering about in a cage hanging from a hook in the closet. Pino laughed to himself and let out a huge sigh of relief. It was a large closet, almost deep enough to walk into. The contents were merely some clothes on hangers and two shelves with boxes.

"Captain!" Amonte called out. "Could you come here a minute? I think you need to see this."

Pino looked at Maria, who stopped playing and was nervously looking down at some music on her lap.

Why was she so nervous? He could hear the captain and Amonte's voices, too low to be understood. The captain cleared his throat loudly.

"*Signora*, you said you live here alone with your daughters?" he stated in an accusing tone.

"And I do!" she replied tersely.

"Then perhaps you can explain these, they are clearly men's clothes."

As the captain questioned the lady, Pino turned away from Maria and returned his pistol to its holster. He was just about to close the closet when his eye stopped dead on something. The top shelf was piled high with cardboard boxes, canned soup and beans, flour, and some folded clothes, but there was something else.

"They belong to my husband," the old lady protested, downstairs. "He's living in America."

"America?" said the captain.

"Yes, the United States. We used to live there. My daughters were born there, but we missed the old country and..."

"You and your daughters returned to Greece, in the middle of a war, alone?"

"My husband planned to join us shortly, but then the war prevented him."

"I see," the captain replied, suspiciously.

Pino's eyes were riveted to the ceiling of the closet. His heart stopped beating as he stared at a drawstring that connected to a small door. An attic. Once again, Pino's hand instinctively reached for his pistol. The salty taste of sweat filled his mouth as he raised the pistol slowly and stepped into the closet. The cord hung down above his head like a noose. He held his breath and reached up for it with the caution one would approach a snake. As his fingers grabbed the knotted end of the string, he took a hard swallow and...

Dang!!! Maria slammed a loud chord on the piano, nearly causing Pino to jump out of his skin. His heart raced like a humming bird and he looked at her in disbelief, trying to catch his breath. As she played, Pino looked at her in the mirror. Her face was ashen and tears filled her eyes. Pino was terrified, his worst fears confirmed. They were in the attic. In the mirror, Maria was slowly, almost imperceptibly shaking her head "no". Pino looked back at the door, then at Maria. Tears were beginning to stream down her face. Pino wiped the sweat from his palm on his jacket, then slowly raised his pistol. As he did, he looked back at Maria in the mirror. She had closed her eyes and folded her hands as if praying. The sight tore at Pino's heart. Then, without opening her eyes, she whispered the word "please". His brain was racing out of control. He was bathed in sweat, and his grip on the pistol was slipping. It was now or never. He looked back at the door.

"*Vaggi!*" yelled the captain, startling Pino once more.

"Y-yes, Captain?" he replied.

"Is everything in order in there?"

Pino looked at Maria in the mirror. She was pale and there were shadows under her eyes but she didn't say anything.

"*Vaggi?*"

"Yes, Captain. Everything's fine."

Maria let out a sigh of exhaustion and relief and put both hands on her heart.

Pino rushed out of the closet and closed the doors behind him. As he did, the captain entered, followed by Maria's mother.

"All finished up here, Vaggi?"

"Yes, Sir. All finished here. Everything's in order."

"All right then," the captain said turning to Maria. "You're not practicing! Now get back to work, so your mother doesn't get angry."

"*Si, Signore,*" Maria said with a smile and immediately began to play again.

"There you go. *Signora*, I'm very sorry to have disturbed you and your family. I hope we haven't inconvenienced you too greatly."

"Not at all *Signore* Captain. Not at all."

Looking at Maria, the captain beamed like a proud father.

"That's Mozart, isn't it, my dear?"

"Yes it is." she answered, still playing.

"'*Rondo alla Turka*' correct?" he continued, to Pino's astonishment.

"Yes."

"You play it very beautifully. But I have a request. Do you think you could look through your music books and find something in Italian to play for myself and my men? I seem to recall hearing you sing something in Italian at the café the other night, isn't that right?"

As the captain spoke, the door to the closet swung open a few inches. Maria saw it and tried to remain calm.

"Well..." she stammered

"Of course you can!" her mother interjected. "*Signore*, my Maria is also an accomplished singer. She is a member of the Athens Opera!"

"Really?" the captain said exuberantly, as if he had no recollection whatsoever of the reason they were there. "That's wonderful!"

"Hey! What a coincidence," said Amonte, entering the room, "Vaggi here is a ten..." but he was cut short by a vicious elbow to the ribs from Pino before he could finish the sentence.

"You must share an aria with us. Any one at all," the captain insisted.

Maria turned around to the piano, but she was actually looking at Pino in the mirror. She made a small jerking motion with her head. Pino knit his brow in confusion. She looked through her music then made the jerking motion again. This time, Pino glanced in the direction she was gesturing, and gasped at the open closet door. He looked at the captain who was now seated on the edge of the bed facing Maria. Thinking fast, Pino walked toward the captain, blocking his view of the door.

"Captain," he said, "I'm sure the *Signorina* would need time to properly warm up her voice in order to sing something as demanding as an opera aria. You are from Napoli are you not, Captain?"

"I am indeed." the captain answered proudly.

"Well, then perhaps she could sing a Neapolitan tune in the captain's honor?"

The two men looked at Maria. She paused, then nodded her head in agreement.

"The captain must forgive my bad pronunciation. I am not very familiar with the Neapolitan dialect."

"Ha! My dear, the majority of Italy cannot master the Neapolitan dialect, and they've had a lot more exposure to it than you!" he quipped, positively enchanted with her.

Maria cleared her throat and began to sing "*Santa Lucia Lontano*". The captain groaned with ecstasy as she began the song. It was an ideal choice, a song about immigrants who had left Italy behind but longed to return. He closed his eyes and drifted away, quietly singing along. The instant he closed his eyes, Pino slid in front of the open closet door and quietly shut it. Maria finished the song and the captain applauded loudly, tears welling up in his eyes.

"*Brava! Brava, Signorina!* You have a passion in your voice that belies the number of your years."

"*Grazie, Signore,*" she said bashfully.

The captain stood up and walked over to Maria. He bent down on one knee and kissed her hand.

"My sincerest hope is to one day hear you sing at the San Carlo Felice in Napoli. You possess an extraordinary gift and it is your duty to share it with the world."

"And it is *your* duty Capitano to stop all this fighting!" the old lady admonished him.

"Mama!" Maria yelled, embarrassed.

"Be quiet, Maria!" her mother scolded.

"That's all right my dear. Your mother is right, and hearing you sing reminds us just how much we long to go home. We won't bother you further. *Buona notte.*"

"Thank you, *Capitano. Buona notte,*" said the old lady.

"Let's go, boys," the captain ordered. The men nodded respectfully to the women and left the room. Once they were gone, Maria and her mother exchanged sighs.

As they left the house, the captain signaled to Sassani, who scurried to join them. At the end of the alley, they turned onto Patisson Street and headed south back to base.

Amonte had seen something in Pino's eyes in that room, but said nothing. Pino knew that Amonte's sense of loyalty would not allow him to speak, but he never knew just how much his comrade suspected. Both were keenly aware of something hanging heavily in the air but neither would dare risk opening that Pandora's Box. For the duration of their march back to base, they didn't so much as glance at one another.

As they walked, unbeknownst to them, a pair of eyes watched from the window. As the soldiers turned the corner, Maria was sure she saw one of the men look back over his shoulder. She held back the curtain and moved closer to the windowpane. She bit her nails as she watched them disappear. Then, she raised her hand and gently blew a kiss to her soldier.

CHAPTER SIXTEEN

Maintaining Focus

THERE HAS ALWAYS BEEN DEBATE as to which country grows the world's finest olives. Some say Italy, some say Greece, still others say Spain. While largely a matter of personal taste, there can be no denying that the olives grown in and around Athens are among the world's best. There were no olive trees in the mountains of Reggio Emilio, so it was no surprise that Pino was indifferent toward them. He wasn't even certain whether they were a fruit or a vegetable. That indifference was not shared by the Italian population as a whole, whose passion for olives and olive oil made the country the world's largest producer of both.

Marco Bernardi was passionate about olives. Not in the sense that he could identify different types (other than to say that one was black and one was green), but rather in terms of their consumption. He fell quickly and madly in love with the olives he found in Greece, and regularly carried a jar of them in the pocket of his uniform, and often another jar in his pack. They were the ideal breakfast, snack, or even dinner, if you happened to have enough of them!

If you were resourceful, they could also be a source of entertainment. One afternoon, sitting inside a gun turret, which they were supposed to be building, Bernardi explained to Carlucci exactly how this was possible. Leaning back against the sandbags, smoking a cigarette, Bernardi produced three large green olives from his breast pocket.

"Now, pay attention," he instructed. "The object is to toss the olive from the right hand into the air just above the left hand. Then you toss the one from the left hand above the right hand, *capische?*"

Carlucci looked at Bernardi as if he were insane, but nodded anyway.

"Got it."

Bernardi began to move his hands in small circles, pretending to juggle.

"Pretty soon you develop a rhythm and they all fall into place. See?" he continued.

"What do I look like? An idiot?" Carlucci responded.

"No comment. Go on then. Try it." Bernardi challenged him.

"Look, I haven't seen you actually *do* it yet either. You just talk and talk and wave your hands in the air."

"Hey! I'm trying to teach you."

Bernardi kept doing his mock-juggling act and Carlucci just shook his head.

"Where did Pino go?" Carlucci asked, bored with the demonstration.

"He's either working on his sun tan or communing with nature. Check it out," said Bernardi, pointing to a rocky ledge above their position. Carlucci looked up and saw Pino sitting cross-legged on the ledge with his hands folded as if he were praying.

"I hear they had a close one the other night," said Bernardi.

"What's that supposed to mean?" asked Carlucci.

"You know those English pilots that were supposed to be hiding out somewhere in town?"

"Yeah. I heard something about them. So?"

"Well, the captain got a tip that they were holed-up in some house in town. So he grabs Vaggi and Amonte and goes to check it out." Bernardi started to laugh a deep belly laugh.

"I don't get it," Carlucci said. "That's funny?"

"Wait!" Bernardi said, composing himself. "So they go to this house and it turns out to be the home of Pino's little girlfriend, the song bird!"

"You're kidding!" said Carlucci.

"Honest to God! Amonte said Vaggi nearly swallowed his tongue when she answered the door!"

"Jesus! What happened? Were the Brits there?"

"Nah, of course not, and even if they had been, they were long gone by then. But, Amonte said you had to see Vaggi to believe him. Tears in his eyes, like he had been *betrayed* by his beloved!"

"Ah, poor Pino," Carlucci said sympathetically.

"Yep. So I think that's what he's doing up there on that cliff."

"Looking for spiritual guidance?" Carlucci asked.

"Hell no." Bernardi chirped. "I think he's gonna jump. End it all. Poetic, right? Perfect death for an opera singer."

Pino sat there, deep in thought or deep in despair. Deep in something.

Captain Adamo was admittedly no great fan of the Nazis, but, as a career soldier, he couldn't help but be impressed with the success of the German army's campaigns. The planning and execution were brilliant. As a man, he couldn't help but be disgusted by their brutality and their Philistine attitude toward unnecessary cultural devastation. The destruction of works of art and houses of worship repelled Adamo. He was not a particularly religious person and it could not be said that he possessed a taste for art, but there was something he found fundamentally repugnant in the baseness of such acts. From the start, it was clear to Adamo that the German army had no real intention of turning over the occupation of Greece to the Italian army. The day he received orders to feed misinformation about the failed Italian invasion to his men, he sensed trouble brewing. In his mind, it indicated a clear mistrust of Italian military acumen. Nothing that transpired since then suggested to him that his initial assessment was mistaken. There was no clear objective, no real mission, no sense of purpose. What was worse was that he knew his men were beginning to sense it, too. All of this made the routine "spot checks" by German command all the more insufferable.

Without a specific objective, Adamo had the ignoble task of manufacturing goals for his company. Adding insult to injury, he would then have to defend and justify these synthetic operations to his German superiors. Establishing gun turrets at strategic defensive points around the city was a no-brainer on several levels. It made perfect military sense. It didn't require any extraordinary skills on the part of his men. And, most importantly, it was time consuming, both in planning and execution.

The greatest danger facing his company, Adamo knew, was complacency. Long-term projects created an air of purpose among the men, something to strive toward. It wasn't the kind of action that would erase all of their doubts but it did provide something concrete he could point to as an accomplishment. It was clear that soon he would need to come up with another such project and the thought worried him. For days he had racked his brains for ideas but none were forthcoming.

"How much farther is it?" asked Major Meier.

Adamo's other thoughts would have to wait.

"Just another hundred meters or so. You can almost see it from here." Adamo said, as he walked up the hill toward the gun turret with his German counterpart. "You'll see Herr Major. We've installed turrets with fifty caliber machine guns nests at eighteen strategic points on the hillsides surrounding the city." The German officer nodded his approval. "The turrets are manned twenty four hours a day and the watches are shifted at four-hour intervals to keep the men fresh and alert."

"Very impressive," Meier replied, much to Adamo's surprise. This might just work after all! They continued to trudge uphill through short shrubs and myriad patches of strong smelling flowers, beneath a scorching Athenian sun. This exercise was designed merely to get the Major off Adamo's back for a while whilst he developed a more comprehensive strategic plan, but if the Major was actually impressed by this! Damn! That would be a great boon for the Captain indeed.

It was too much to hope for. Something was wrong. They stopped about a hundred feet before the turret. The captain knit his brow in confusion. *Where the hell were the men?* The turret was clearly unmanned and the captain was beginning to hyperventilate. He looked left, then right and saw nothing.

"No, no, no," he muttered to himself.

"Are you all right?" the German officer asked. "Is something wrong?"

The *coup de grace* came when he spotted Pino, sitting like Buddha up on the cliff. He snorted like a bull and furiously started to run up the hill, leaving the confused German in his dust.

"So help me, Vaggi, when I..." Before he could finish the sentence, and just when he thought he couldn't possibly get any angrier, he reached the side of the turret and witnessed a sight that nearly caused his brain to explode. Behind the sandbags, Bernardi and Carlucci were smoking cigarettes and juggling olives. They saw him and stopped dead, jaws dropped in shock. The captain just stood there, stunned, his jaw in exactly the same position as theirs.

By the time Major Meier had made it up the hill, the cigarettes were extinguished and the olives disposed of or swallowed. The German officer had no idea what had transpired, but it didn't matter, the damage was done. Captain Adamo stood there, frozen, looking as though something had snapped inside his head. Bernardi and Carlucci had never seen him look like that before. In reality, they'd never seen *anyone* look like that before. Captain Adamo closed his eyes and silently walked away, down the hill, with Major Meier following, more confused than ever.

No one was exactly sure just what happened to the captain that afternoon. For whatever reason, he never discussed it with anyone. However, one thing was absolutely certain: from that point onward, Pino, Bernardi and Carlucci's relationship with their captain had reached a new low, a low that they didn't even think was possible.

CHAPTER SEVENTEEN

The Descent

THE MANIFESTATION OF THE CAPTAIN'S ANGER toward Pino, Bernardi, and Carlucci first appeared in the form of a week's duty scrubbing the toilets with toothbrushes. The work was humbling, but Pino tried to take it in stride, finding a silver lining in the bathroom's acoustical qualities for vocalization.

"You know, there really is something about the sound of a bathroom," said Pino matter-of-factly. Bernardi, failing to appreciate the acoustical qualities, took a handful of water out of the toilet and threw it in Pino's face. Cleaning a few toilets was hardly the worst assignment a soldier could draw, but it was meant to deliver a message. If at first they were concerned that the captain was angry with them, the feeling had soon passed. Now, it seemed like they no longer existed at all to him. His complete indifference was disquieting. The assignment, while obviously a punishment, and a humiliating one at that, could actually be viewed as a positive sign: at least the captain was still aware of their existence.

The relationship between the soldiers, while never exactly rock-solid, was also beginning to show stress fractures. The "we few, we happy few, we band of brothers" mentality had almost completely disappeared, replaced by a more first person singular mentality. The card games that had once filled the evenings with diversion became tedious. It was difficult to find enough men willing, let alone interested in playing. The men weren't sure if the captain was even aware of this breakdown in morale. If he was, he did an exceptional job of concealing it, or perhaps, he simply no longer cared. It was difficult to say, judging from his actions, and even more difficult judging from the lack thereof.

The entire time they were confined to latrine duty, they saw neither hide nor hair of the captain and they viewed it as a lucky break — out of sight, out of mind. Despite the gravity of their situation and the potential ramifications of another slip-up, Pino resolved to sneak out after curfew to see Maria again. He wanted to confront her about the English pilots. He had to learn the truth of the matter. Was she an unwilling participant or had she been complicit in the deception. He wanted her to fully grasp the potentially disastrous consequences of her actions. He wanted her to know precisely what he had been willing to risk for her. The danger she had put him in. But most of all, he needed to hear her sing again. The sound of her voice had become his opium and her singing, the syringe that delivered it. In quiet moments when there were no toilets to scrub and nothing to divert his attention, he pondered over it and found himself sighing like a love-sick school boy.

It was critical that he keep his comrades unaware of his plans because they would undoubtedly attempt to stop him. He'd have to be more careful than before and leave later. It was more dangerous than in the past but his need was greater.

Exiting the hotel was easy. Returning unnoticed in the wee hours of the morning would be the tricky part. The short walk from base to Maria's house was always pleasant when in a state of eagerness and anticipation, but tonight was different. Pino was too impatient to walk and he hopped aboard a street car headed north on Patisson. Since the curfew had gone into effect, the cars stopped running at 9pm, so he could take it out but not back. It was just as well. He could be stealthier among the shadows of the streets and alleys, which by now he had come to know as well as the back streets of Collagna. He no longer passed the front of the building on Patisson. He used the entrance to the alley from around back that he discovered from Captain Adamo. His fateful visit to her room proved all too well that he had no hope of remaining unseen on his previous perch. So, upon reaching his familiar spot among the trashcans, he immediately rearranged the "layout" of the alleyway to provide better cover.

He wasn't sure if he wanted to be seen or unseen just yet. He'd keep his options open. He knew he'd have to confront her eventually but standing amid the wafting stench of garbage, he realized his resolve wasn't as solid as he'd thought. With a thud, he dropped himself onto the stool to begin his vigil, but only seconds later the lights came on and the doors opened. It was much sooner than he had expected or hoped and he was not prepared to face her yet.

A figure stepped out onto the balcony and could be seen in silhouette. The cloudy night hid the face, but not the glow of a cigarette. Pino instantly knew it could not be Maria. Instinctively, he knew she didn't smoke. As the clouds parted momentarily the figure came into view and Pino's heart stopped. Captain Adamo was standing on the balcony with one hand on the rail and the other tossing a cigarette carelessly into the night air.

Pino's head spun in disbelief. What the hell was *he* doing here? Pino stood up and in the process knocked the lid off of a can, making a loud racket. Ordinarily he would have panicked at the sound, but he didn't move a muscle. He was too shocked at the scene unfolding before his eyes. At hearing the sound of laughter coming from inside the house, the captain stretched his arms, then turned and re-entered. It was too much for Pino's brain to process. In a split second of uncontrolled fury he grabbed the first object he could find, an empty soda pop bottle, and violently flung it at the window. It hit the stone balcony and smashed to pieces in a crash loud enough to wake the entire building.

The noise broke Pino's trance and in a moment of clarity, he ran for his life back down the alley as lights came on all around. He knew that he'd never clear the alley in time, so he darted into a darkened doorway and prayed. He was on the side of the alley opposite the balcony and as he leaned slightly out of the darkness, Pino could clearly see Captain Adamo, Maria and her mother on the balcony looking wildly in all directions. He slid back into the darkness and waited. Perspiration droplets formed from his nose and chin, but he didn't bother to wipe them. His only movement was to gently pull out his sister's St. Christopher medal and kiss it. It had gotten him through tight squeezes in the past and right now he needed all the help he could get. He gambled that the captain wouldn't leave the women alone to investigate and he was proven right. After the longest five minutes of his life, Pino emerged from the shadows and tiptoed the rest of the way out of the alley and all the way back to base.

Pino had known disappointment in his life: his father, his career, but never in matters of the heart. He recalled the maestro's words: "in matters of the heart, fate's blows while often unspeakably cruel and capricious, were very rarely fatal." He tried to cling to these words as he repeatedly told himself he was not in love with Maria. It was not real and he was not pining for her. It *was* the dreamy illusion of an inexperienced heart. Nevertheless, he cursed her and he cursed Captain Adamo. He cried, *"Maladicione!"* like *Rigoletto* before him, but he knew it would be equally fruitless. *Why didn't curses ever work out in real life like they did in the opera?*

When he returned to the hotel, he made no effort to remain clandestine, walking into the lobby like a busy impatient tourist. Inexplicably, the sentries, the guards and the MPs didn't so much as bat an eyelash! He hadn't even realize it until he'd ascended the stairs and dropped with a crash onto his bunk. *I guess if you look like you belong — you belong,* he thought with a cryptic laugh.

Rolling over onto his back, he stared at the ceiling. The venetian blinds let in thin slivers of pale moonlight, which gave him the distinct impression of prison bars. In another life, he'd laid on his back in his soft bed in Collagna and thought of his fair little hamlet as a prison. Back then, he thought, he was just young and stupid. Now he was....still young and stupid, probably stupider. He didn't know what he was. He was no longer an opera singer, certainly not compared to her! Some little Greek girl only maybe seventeen years old made him seem like a rank amateur. He was a total wash out as a soldier. He couldn't get out of his own way in this army; and if they saw any real action he knew he'd be done for. Was he still engaged? In his heart he knew he'd been unfaithful, at least in spirit, if not the flesh. He couldn't focus on anything anymore. His world was a mess. At times like this in the past, he'd always found himself retreating, fighting off the urge to cry, but not anymore. The hurt and the anguish passed through him as if he were made of gas, touching everything and touching nothing, leaving a trace, a residue, but otherwise no sign of contact. He was no longer the soft wood his father once called him. There would be no dents, no marks from this point onward.

CHAPTER EIGHTEEN

SILENT NIGHT...CHRISTMAS IN COLLAGNA

THE ONLY THING IN THE WORLD more beautiful than Collagna in the springtime, thought Gia, was Collagna at Christmastime. The breathtaking vistas of the snowcapped mountains surrounding the picturesque little village were truly something out of a fairytale. She told herself repeatedly how lucky she was but she wasn't convincing, anymore.

At night, Christmas carols echoed though the lonely stone streets of Collagna and partly drowned out the loud drunken babble of the old men in the pubs. But the sound of the carols only made Gia more miserable. She hadn't heard from Pino in over six months and she was despondent. Autumn had been hard but winter and especially Christmas would be simply unbearable. It made no sense. According to the radio, there was no fighting going on in Greece at all, and Athens had been declared an "open city" free from attack. So why had Pino's letters stopped? She had read all his previous letters over and over and could practically recite them from memory. But her memories were fast becoming like the newsreels they had watched in the cinema, grey and out of focus, of the past, not the present. For the last eighteen months, her life and his had become mutually exclusive, untouched and unknown to each other.

She was ashamed of her feelings, her selfishness and her yearnings, but they couldn't be stopped any more than time itself. She also hated herself for the persistent nightmares she'd been having about Pino's adulterous behavior in Greece. She tried desperately not to think about it. She trusted him implicitly and had complete faith in his sense of honor and decorum, yet she still felt wretched and paralyzed by the distance and growing silence between them.

Their life together was beginning to feel more and more like a dream that would never come true. She hated the Duce for this. His damned war was causing her dream to fade and life to pass her by alone in Collagna. His muddle-headed radio messages gave no peace to her inner turmoil either.

The last straw for Gia was seeing *Signora* Biaggi in church wearing a new fur coat with a silver fox collar. It nearly caused her fury to boil over publicly. More and more often it seemed all the occupants of the village were groveling at the feet of the chief magistrate and it sickened her. She blamed them and their fellow Fascisti for all the shortages in the stores and the escalating prices, as well.

When she overheard Mrs. Biaggi say: "Damn this war! The stores are all out of my favorite silk stockings," it took all of Gia's fortitude not to strike the woman.

The only solace was her newfound domesticity. Nightly, after dining and doing the dishes with her family at her own house, Gia would hurry over to the Vaggis for coffee and pastries in front of the fire and the chance to listen to the radio for news.

It was there, listening to the radio that she had a brilliant idea. She suggested that they all gather and spend Christmas dinner together like one big family. The idea was warmly received in both homes, bringing a spark of happiness to what surely would have been a painful holiday for all of them. Still, deep down, she realized that despite all of her intentions, the absence of a letter from Pino had cast a pall over the entire season and no amount of lamb and eggnog was going to erase it.

CHAPTER NINETEEN

THE BOILING POINT

ANY LINGERING DISAPPOINTMENT PINO had felt early in his military tenure at being summarily dismissed from the elite Alpine Division was quickly erased when he learned that the Alpine Units were being dispatched to the Caucasus Mountains to assist Germany in its ill-advised Russian campaign. He'd unwittingly managed to dodge yet another bullet, but recent developments had wrapped him in a blanket of fatalism from which he could not shake free. He felt himself drifting more and more and caring less and less.

The frequency of daily patrols persisted and even increased. The pressure of German influence was felt across the board. The patrols, sometimes expanded to groups as large as ten or twenty, more frequently in groups as small as two, appeared to occur more randomly. If there was any rhyme or reason to it, it was lost on the men.

The first day after completing latrine duty, Pino was back among the ranks of the patrols. The afternoon was a real scorcher and ten overheated Italian soldiers were miserable in their march. It was another day of Athens at its worst, grey, muggy and humid. Despite the captain's best efforts, marching was not really an accurate description for their movement. They walked together loosely in pairs.

They passed the usual array of street venders, who by now had become used to the sight of them, and no longer displayed any outward hostility. Pino was paired with Amonte, who, being sick on the day of the German inspection, had managed to avoid the latrine duty. Even so, he had no illusions about the captain's regard for him. Like it or not, he was lumped in with Pino, Bernardi and Carlucci, guilty by association.

"So, d'ya hear where the captain's been spending his nights lately?" Amonte asked with a know-it-all grin. Pino uncharacteristically ignored the remark, keeping conspicuously silent. "Yeah, while you guys were busy cleaning up the shitter, I saw him pick up your little girlfriend in his car and bring her back to the hotel where all the officers are staying. I think she sang for them, some kinda private concert."

As they turned down a street dotted with fruit and vegetable vendors, Amonte reached out and grabbed an apple from a stand. The owner, who looked to be around ninety, started screaming bloody murder. Amonte quickly put a finger to his mouth to quiet him down, but there was no stopping him. Not wanting to attract any attention, Amonte angrily dug into his pocket and produced a coin which he promptly tossed to the old man. He caught it and spat on it. Then he spat at Amonte, but he didn't throw the coin back. It quickly went into his breast pocket for safekeeping. Amonte rushed back up through the ranks until he was back alongside Pino. He could see that Pino was in a gloomy mood and thought he might have a little fun at Pino's expense, and he knew just what nerve to touch.

"I understand that yesterday, she and her mother went up north to Salonika to do a concert and the captain went along as chaperone. That was real thoughtful of him, don't you think?"

This latest tidbit was news to Pino, and he nearly allowed it to penetrate his armor. He made a mental note to ask Kostas about it the next time he saw him; he'd surely know – *he knew everything*. Pino realized that he hadn't seen Kostas in a while. The old man moved in mysterious ways, he thought. Amonte's taunts, however, were beginning to grate on him. Pino was disappointed that his best friend should be so inconsiderate about a subject he knew to be an open wound, but the digs kept coming. .

"Hey, lover boy, what gives?" Amonte teased him. Pino ignored the comment entirely. "You getting jealous?" Pino shot him a cold stare but remained silent. Their path would eventually lead them past Maria's house and Amonte knew it so he bided his time whistling a tune. As they marched south along Patisson Street, Pino glanced to his left at her window, not sure what he wanted or expected to see. Sure enough, Maria and her sister were on the balcony looking down at the parading soldiers. Pino half wondered if the sisters would spit on them as they passed. Noting the pathetic look on Pino's face, the devil in Amonte took over.

"So, tell me," he asked with a devious grin, "have you heard from Gia lately?"

That did it. Pino whirled around and decked Amonte with one punch, a devastating right cross. As Amonte crumbled to the ground, half in pain, half in shock, Pino pounced on him and chaos ensued. Before Pino could land another punch, Bernardi, who had witnessed the entire attack, caught his arm and bent it back. Another soldier leaped onto Bernardi's back and the two of them crashed to the ground on top of Pino and Amonte.

As Pino tried to crawl out from under the pile, another soldier grabbed him by the back of his collar and tried to drag him away, but there was too much weight on top of him. In the midst of the ruckus, Captain Adamo was screaming at the top of his lungs for them to break it up. The soldier who had Pino by the collar grabbed with two hands and yanked as hard as he could, but this time, his second hand unwittingly caught hold of the chain that held Pino's dog tags. As he pulled, the chain dug into Pino's neck, cutting off his breath. Pino tried to get a free hand under the chain but he was quickly beginning to feel faint. The ground was spinning and his eyes failed to focus as he struggled to remain conscious. He tried to scream but he had no breath. Then, just as he was about to black out, the chain snapped. Trying desperately to catch his breath, Pino suddenly felt a great weight lifted from on top of him, and then everything got quiet.

The next image that his clearing vision focused upon was Captain Adamo standing above him with his hands on his hips. Pino thought he was going to be sick. He took a deep breath through his nostrils and held it, fighting off the urge. He was about to attempt to stand when two soldiers grabbed him under the arms and lifted him up. He shook like a wet dog, trying to clear his head.

"You two are this close," said the captain holding his index fingers about an inch apart. "You understand me?"

"Yes, Sir," said Amonte, whom Pino just realized was standing next to him. Pino nodded affirmatively to the captain, not exactly sure what he was agreeing to. The captain stepped closer and stared at Pino.

"I didn't hear you," he said quietly.

"Yes, Sir," Pino quickly retorted. "Captain! It was completely my fault. Amonte didn't do anything. I just lost it for a minute. It won't happen again." He turned to Amonte and put out his hand. "I'm sorry. *Mea culpa*, OK?"

"No problem," said Amonte, feeling a pang of guilt about the entire incident.

"Wrong," said the captain, interrupting their reconciliation. "Big problem. I want to see both of you tonight in my quarters at 1800 hours sharp. Is that clear?" Before they could even nod, he added a final blow, "And bring that baboon Bernardi and his little sidekick Carlucci, too." He then turned to the rest of the men and with one look, they fell back into rank.

Without a word, the captain turned and began marching with the men following close behind. As they moved down the street, the dust from the brawl began to settle in their wake. In the middle of the street, amid the dust and the dirt, a number of small objects glimmered brightly in the morning sun. There were three objects to be exact. They appeared to be metallic in nature, two of which were of a silvery color and one of gold. Several hours would pass before Pino would even realize his loss. For there in the gutter lay his dog tags, alongside of which laid his most treasured possession, his sister's St. Christopher medal. Sadly, the street was far too busy for them to remain there very long and a second later, they were gone.

The melee resulted in Pino and Amonte receiving the most unpleasant assignments of their careers thus far: sanitation detail. After spending countless nights among the trash cans beneath Maria's window, the assignment held no special terror for Pino, until he fully understood the definition of sanitation detail during a military occupation. For three days they would be collecting the company's trash and driving it to the dump down near Piraeus, where, Pino guessed, it would be loaded on barges and dumped at sea.

The next morning they had their eyes opened. The collection of dead and decomposing corpses was at the top of the list of responsibilities for the sanitation detail. Bodies needed to be found, collected and disposed of quickly to prevent the spread of pestilence. As the number of bodies was growing daily, the problem would not be getting better any time soon, thus, immediate and decisive action was critical.

The image of the old Greek man's dead body that Pino had come upon when delivering dispatches weeks ago was freshly raised in his mind. It wasn't an image he'd forget any time soon. His only defense was the pair of gloves he was given. They were not rubber or specially insulated gloves but rather the kind a gardener might wear. He remembered what the other soldiers had said about never looking at the faces, and he also remembered he'd failed to do so last time. If he was going to survive this week of "Stiff Patrol," as the detail was nicknamed, he'd have no choice.

Climbing into the back of the open truck, Pino and Amonte began their distasteful assignment. The first few hours were uneventful and Pino began to delude himself that he might actually get through this without getting his hands dirty. But the midday sun revealed that his pipedream was over. On the north side of the Acropolis, near the theater of Herodias Atticus, they were greeted by the unmistakable stench of rotting flesh. Pino thought he would wretch from the smell. To his surprise, the odor didn't seem to bother Amonte.

"Forget it, Pino. Might as well get used to it. It ain't going away," he said hopping off the back of the truck. Pino desperately tried to breathe through his mouth only and for a moment it seemed to be working. Unfortunately, the smell was the only trail they had to follow. Amonte headed into the park and stopped before going very far.

"Ok, here's our boy," he said with a sigh of resignation. "C'mon, let's get it over with."

Pino knew he was right, but still his hands shook as he approached the body lying peacefully beneath a tree. It appeared to be curled up and resting from a long journey, with its head buried in its folded arms. If not for the morbid stench, it would have appeared perfectly normal, just a tired old man stopping under a tree to get out of the sun for a moment's repose.

"Grab his legs," Amonte instructed, as he himself took hold of the body's arms. As Amonte lifted the arms, Pino collapsed to the ground. Before him, he saw the pained expression frozen in the face of the body and it broke his heart. It was Kostas. The eyes were squinted as if crying tears that no longer flowed and the corners of the mouth were turned down as if bemoaning his loss of dignity. Pino began to cry uncontrollably. Kostas was more than merely an acquaintance. Pino had grown extremely fond of the old man, his wealth of knowledge, his wit, his wisdom and his courage. Pino crawled next to Kostas lifeless body and held him. Amonte dropped to his knees and looked on helplessly.

Two sad and exhausted soldiers concluded their three days of sanitation detail in silence before returning to regular duty. Although it was a welcome return, their first march together proved a continuation of the same pattern. Pino was hoping, that without having to say it, Amonte would not share news of his breakdown with anyone, especially not Bernardi.

Before long, their usual patrol brought them down Patisson Street. In the most thoughtful voice he could muster, Amonte asked the question that he knew was eating Pino up.

"So, if she's here, you gonna talk to her?"

"What? Oh. I don't know."

"Well, you better decide fast. There she is," Amonte said, pointing to Maria's balcony.

Pino was in no mood to deal with her at that moment but he sensed he might have to. On the balcony, Maria was looking their way, vocalizing in full voice. She wore a white sundress. To the best of his recollection, Pino had never seen her dressed quite so brightly. In fact, everything about her manner seemed brighter and more joyful than before. As the soldiers approached, she stopped singing and yelled to the captain.

"Buongiorno, Captain Adamo!*"* she called out.

The sight of Maria brought about a complete change in the captain's demeanor. His usual irritable disposition melted into enchantment.

"Buongiorno, Signorina!" he called back to her.

"Would *Signore Capitano* like to hear a song from bella Napoli?"

"Ah, *Signorina,* it would warm the captain's heart!"

Maria cleared her throat and began to sing a popular Neapolitan song, *"Mattinata."* As the soldiers passed by, several of them joined in the song. Some tossed coins up onto the balcony. Some tossed bread. Maria laughed and tried to catch the coins as she sang. Soon the entire platoon was singing. It was amazing. Pino recalled another time such a transformation occurred where only moments earlier, the entire squadron was at one-another's throats, fighting like dogs in the street, and moments later they were singing together like brothers. He marveled again at the power of music. All of his comrades were singing a song from their home, led by a young girl who was for all intents the enemy. All of them, that is, with the exception of Pino.

The entire time Maria was singing, she scanned the crowd to try to find Pino. Her extreme near-sightedness didn't make it easy. Finally, she saw him and leaned over the balcony to get his attention. She waved, but Pino would not look at her. She was confused, but she continued to sing. Pino got closer and closer until he was just underneath the balcony. Again, Maria leaned over and flashed a big smile as he passed, but he completely ignored her. She stopped singing, but her song continued among the soldiers. The look of confusion on her face dissolved into one of trouble. As it became clear that his snub was no accident, the troubled look became one of hurt, and she ran back into the house.

The fountain at the end of the block had become one of the soldiers' usual rest spots. They stopped, and one by one, re-filled their canteens. Pino didn't bother to refill his canteen. He walked over and sat against a wall alone with his thoughts. The strong midday sun that baked his face proved too much for his closed eyelids so he pulled his hat down over them. Anyone passing by might have mistaken him for a vagrant sleeping in the street or another of the dead waiting to be collected and disposed of.

Pino's heart was sick. He felt tired and old, his lack of experience in worldly matters, matters of conscience, matters of the heart, only confused the issue further. He wasn't even sure he was angry anymore. His racing thoughts permitted him no rest and closing his eyes only made matters worse. With his eyelids down, countless images flashed before his mind's eye in rapid-fire succession.

A gentle breeze blew across his face and cooled his sun-drenched skin, but even these near idyllic conditions couldn't help him find peace of mind. It was always windy on Patisson Street and the breeze stirred up little, dirty dust clouds. In the clouds, Pino saw the powdery images of faces: angels, demons - he couldn't tell which. The arid outline of Kostas' face, contorted by rigor mortis or by the shame of his condition, formed in the dust of Pino's mind and he reached out toward it before it disappeared. Kostas had always possessed an understated dignity that even war and occupation couldn't take away. It was this quality that made his humiliating death all the more tragic.

Kostas' death made Maria's betrayal seem trivial and Pino's self-loathing for feeling such heartache was brimming over. He recalled how in the past his personal woes were quickly put into perspective by the larger events around him, but none of that provided him with any solace now. He tried to clear his mind altogether, to concentrate on his breathing, like he had been taught to do by the maestro. He focused on the sound of his breath passing through his nostrils, penetrating his sinuses and filling his lungs, then the sound of its release. The exercise worked better than he could have imagined and he soon felt the tension in his neck and shoulders begin to release its stranglehold.

He decided to treat himself to a drink of water from his canteen, but the water was warm and distasteful. When was the last time he changed it? He drank no more but lifted his hat and poured the rest of the water over his head. He languished as it cooled him and rolled down his cheeks and the back of his neck.

Suddenly, a burst of applause could be heard among the men. The sound brought Pino back to reality rather abruptly. He lifted up the brim of his hat to see what the commotion was about. He wasn't pleased by what he saw. Maria was standing among the men carrying a pail to fill at the fountain, and the soldiers were all lavishing praise upon her. Pino felt his nostrils flare and he pulled the hat back down over his eyes. He didn't see the captain push his way through the men towards Maria.

"*Signorina,*" the captain said, visibly gushing, "You do us too much honor. When all this is over, I think your voice will be one of our fondest memories of Greece."

"*Molto grazie, Signore Capitano,*" she replied in beautiful Italian, to the delight of the men. Then the captain kissed her hand, and the men all hooted and hollered. Pino feigned indifference to the entire performance and attempted to return to his meditation. He needed time to sort out his feelings and right now he knew he was far too volatile to address them. Unfortunately, the decision was taken out of his hands a few moments later.

A shadow crossed his face, blocking the sunlight and he felt a gentle kick against his boot. At first he ignored it, pretending not to notice, but then came the voice which he couldn't ignore.

"Hey! Caruso!" chirped the voice, with just a hint of mockery. Pino didn't look up, but from under his hat he could see two feet in old beat-up sandals, and a large bucket of water. He allowed her to stand there for several moments without acknowledging her as the tension mounted.

"Mi scusi!" she continued. "Hey, *Gigli?*" she said, this time with a more playful vulnerability in her voice. Pino didn't know what to do. His heart pounded like a bass drum in his chest. The sound and tone of her voice nearly melted away his anger, but not quite. She had consorted with the enemy, and he, for all intents and purposes, had helped her. His complicity, even if it couldn't be proven, might be considered treason, and could conceivably place him before a firing squad. How did he allow himself to get mixed up in this? Why the hell didn't he just turn in those damn English pilots? It was his duty. What was she to him, anyway? She didn't care for him. She was just playing with him. He wished he'd never met her and that she would just go away, but the two feet standing before him weren't going anywhere.

"Hey Caruso, I wanted to ask you something," she continued in an almost flirtatious voice. "How many tenors does it take to screw in a light bulb?" she asked with a chuckle.

The humor was lost on Pino who, finally acknowledging her presence, looked up angrily. Maria was standing in front of him holding her pail in front of her with both hands. She could have been a painting, he thought, trying to maintain his sense of composure. She smiled at him, a warm, melancholy, almost-but-not-quite-loving smile. Then, she went just a little bit too far.

"What's the matter?" she asked with a laugh. "Did you lose your voice again?"

Incensed, Pino leaped to his feet and grabbed her viciously by the wrists. Her face registered agonizing pain but she didn't say a word. She cringed but continued to look right at him. He stood looking eye to eye with her for a long moment. Despite the pain, her expression grew more confident, even defiant. Then she flashed a disarming half-smile. Pino's eyes began to well up with tears and his blood boiled. He bent her arm backward and raised his hand to strike her.

"Vaggi!" the captain called out angrily, apparently witness to the entire event.

Pino released her wrists and let her fall to the ground. He stepped away from her. Maria swallowed hard and flared her nostrils. For a second, she looked as if she would pounce upon him, but instead she quickly glanced about to see if any of the other soldiers were watching. She lifted her bucket, and started walking home, slowly at first, then picking up speed.

"*Signorina*, wait!" the captain called out after her. She looked back over her shoulder at Pino who stood defiantly, with his back to her. She was breathing hard and her eyes were red with tears. She didn't want to be seen this way and she ran, wiping a tear away from her eye with one hand while carrying the bucket with the other. As fate would have it, she stumbled and fell. She hit the ground with a cry and a loud crash as the bucket went flying, spilling the water all over.

The noise startled the soldiers, several of whom came running over to see if she was all right, but her eyes were fixed on one soldier who made no attempt to help her. Seeing him so cold and unsympathetic, she started sobbing uncontrollably. As she raised herself from the street it was clear she was injured more in spirit than in the flesh. She regained her lost composure and grimaced; her beautiful dress was filthy and torn. She straightened it out nonetheless and ambled quickly back to her house, leaving the bucket in the middle of the street.

Pino stood rigid and impassive. He couldn't bring himself to look back. Suddenly, through the crowd, he saw the captain rushing toward him with blood in his eyes.

That evening Pino, Amonte, Bernardi and Carlucci were summoned to appear at Captain Adamo's quarters in the Hotel Bretagne. The other soldiers hadn't seen Carlucci for days and had begun to wonder what happened to him. Some joked that he was on a secret mission for the captain. Others guessed his Greek girlfriend was occupying all of his time.

The Hotel Bretagne was palatial in every sense of the word. Despite its opulence, Captain Adamo's quarters could appropriately be described as spartan. He was a warrior who had little use for decorative trappings. He sat at a simple wooden table that served as his desk, smoking a cigar and reading some papers. A large map was spread out before him on the table. A knock was heard at the door followed by a voice from outside.

"Captain, your guests have arrived," the voice announced.

"Show them in," he replied.

Amonte, Bernardi, Carlucci and Pino walked in and stood before the captain's desk. He let them stand there for several minutes without bothering to acknowledge them and they glanced nervously at one another as he smoked.

"I've spent the last hour reviewing your files," he said softly. "I've found nothing in them that would have suggested that you men were going to be trouble-makers."

Pino wasn't sure what to make of the observation, but he certainly didn't like being branded a 'trouble-maker.'

"By nature, I'm not a very patient man," the captain continued. "That's not your fault, but I'm afraid it is your problem. I will not expend any more energy on you. I don't believe that spending time in the brig is the answer to anything..." He paused to let the thought sink in to each of the soldiers' heads. "So, I've assigned all of you to two weeks of hard labor. Specifically, you will be on minesweeping detail. During that time, in the evenings, you will be confined to quarters."

Their faces crumbled. Pino hadn't even realized there was a mine sweeping detail. He thought nothing could be as bad as sanitation, but again he was proved wrong.

"Any more trouble from any of you, and I mean *anything*...and you'll be riding this war out in military prison. Have I made myself clear?"

"Yes, Sir," they answered in stunned unison.

"Dismissed."

CHAPTER TWENTY

PRESENCE OF MINES

CARLUCCI HELD THE MINESWEEPING DEVICE like a broom. It looked like a long stick with a round plate at the end. Its wires ran from the plate to a backpack that he wore. He was instructed to slowly wave it left and right, about a foot above the ground as he walked through the streets.

"What are you doing?" Bernardi asked.

"Practicing," Carlucci retorted.

Bernardi shook his head in disbelief and raised his hand to shade his eyes as he scanned the street.

"I can't believe I'm guilty by association with all of you. I know what Amonte and Vaggi did, but I had no idea you were such a little rascal."

It was true, all of Bernardi's shenanigans since they'd gotten to Greece, had somehow managed to go completely undetected and, consequently, unpunished. Pino, it seemed, was always the lightning rod that trouble found on a regular basis. None of them could have guessed that Carlucci was actually the one on the verge of finding himself before a firing squad. His offense was a crime of the heart. As many had suspected, Carlucci had found himself a cute, little Greek girlfriend. What no one could have suspected was that she was Jewish and he had been stealing army rations to feed her and her family.

The Italian command was completely oblivious to Carlucci's nocturnal endeavors and in truth probably would have found them harmless even if they had known. The German Command however did not. Their patrols spotted an Italian soldier making repeated visits after curfew to a house occupied by a Jewish family and got suspicious. Carlucci was never arrested or even detained, but Captain Adamo was alerted to the situation and told how "unseemly" it was for his soldiers to be providing "stolen" rations to the enemy.

Initially, the captain almost hoped the Germans would call it a war crime and have him shot, such was his anger. Eventually, he decided mine-sweeping would be a comparable punishment.

"What time did Amonte say they'd meet us here?" Bernardi asked.

"Pino said they were stopping by his buddy's fruit stand on the way to get some figs for breakfast." Carlucci answered.

"Figs? I hope he gets some olives too."

"Ha! Don't bet on it."

Pino and Amonte were sharing a cup of Greek coffee, for which Pino was slowly developing a taste, in the café where they used to meet and talk with Kostas. Kostas had informed them, as was his habit, that Greek coffee was in fact of Turkish origin. But, he had strongly advised them not to say it too loudly in Athens. Those early morning meetings with Kostas had become part of Pino's regular social schedule and even Amonte had started looking forward to coffee and *baklava* with the old man. Each encounter had been a civics lesson in culture and history. They even managed to pick up a few words in Greek. Pino recalled that their last discussion, several months ago, was culinary. As Amonte savored his *baklava*, Kostas explained that Greece's cuisine had over the years been greatly influenced by the Turks. After so many years of Turkish occupation, the gastronomic traditions of the two countries had melded (though very few Greeks would ever admit to it!) In fact, Greek coffee, *baklava, halvah,* even *moussaka,* all had their roots in Turkish kitchens.

Pino glanced at his watch and tapped Amonte on the shoulder.

"We better move it. We can't be late," Pino said. Amonte, mouth filled with pastry, gave Pino a thumbs-up. Pino reached into his pocket for money and felt the beads that Kostas had given him. With a heavy heart, he pulled them out and stroked them, remembering the evening that Kostas had given them to him. In his mind's eye he replayed the exchange and the pearls of wisdom his friend shared with him.

"Plato said that love is a mental illness! This woman, she is Greek? Oh that's bad. Very bad. Greek women are the worst kind of women. These are Komboloia. Worry Beads. When you are in times of deep distress, which will be often if you are in love with a Greek woman, you hold them in your hands and rub them and they give you relief."

Pino held the beads like they were diamonds and he remembered Kostas' final admonition: *"Don't worry about Kostas, just you stop worrying about Greek girls! Concentrate on being soldier first, getting home safe."*

Pino fingered the beads as he finished his coffee. Since the day he'd lost his sister's St. Christopher medal, the Kamboloia beads that Kostas gave him had taken up a special place in his heart and more and more he found himself turning to them for comfort. If he made it home to Collagna, he promised himself, he'd give the beads to his sister as a special gift and let her know just how precious she was to him.

"I don't think there are any mines on this road," Bernardi declared. "I don't think there ever were any mines. I think this is the captain's sick idea of a joke."

He followed behind Carlucci with a shovel on his shoulder. On this particular day the men were assigned to clear the dirt roads climbing Mount Lycabettus.

"You can't be too careful with landmines," Carlucci replied.

"All I'm saying is, who would put them here? Think about it," Bernardi reasoned. "Certainly not the Germans. They'd put them around their perimeter. Since they took Crete, the mainland is nowhere near their perimeter. The Brits are going to have to take back the islands before they hit the mainland, right? I heard yesterday that Canada and New Zealand declared war on us this week. D'you believe that? Canada! What the hell did we ever do to Canada? Anyway, my point is: we've been up and down these same roads for days and haven't seen a single mine and I for one don't believe we ever will."

"I don't care. One more day of this and it's back to regular duty," said Carlucci.

"Amen to that," exclaimed Bernardi. "Thank God, tonight's the last night I have to spend confined to quarters with Vaggi's singing! Two goddamn weeks! I'm starting to hear his singing in my sleep."

That night, Pino couldn't sleep at all. Each time he closed his eyes his mind was bombarded by millions of rapid-fire images. He tossed and turned for several hours before he gave up and sat up in bed. He looked around the room in total darkness. His vision had adjusted enough for him to see his comrades sound asleep. He quietly slid out of his bunk and opened his footlocker. In the past, he would have done a little reading. That usually made him drowsy. He missed his music books. They were his friends, his constant companions, and he treasured them. His *Ricordi Anthology of Tenor arias* had been the dearest and he'd thrown it away. His next favorite was the copy of *Lucia di Lammermoor* that the maestro had given him as a present, years before. He remembered how the maestro loved to tell the story of how a mutual friend, *"Lucia,"* had introduced him and his wife. The thought emboldened Pino. He got dressed and tiptoed lightly toward the door carrying his boots. A moment later he was gone.

Pino walked the narrow streets as quietly as he could. He realized that breaking curfew in the past might have resulted in nothing more than a slap on the wrist but now it would surely have dire consequences if he got caught. Still, something inside his head told him he must and minutes later he found himself standing in the shadows across the street from Maria's house. He had no plan.

He wasn't even certain why he'd come. The house was completely dark. He sat down on the pavement and stared up at Maria's window. There were no signs of life. He checked his watch. It was very late, they were surely asleep. He looked both ways down the silent empty street, as he had done so many times before, then he stood up. He wiped the dirt off of his knees and backside. He decided that what he really needed was a good stiff drink, so he headed south toward the *Plaka*, where he knew he could find an open *taverna*.

The streets of the *Plaka* were particularly difficult to navigate, twisting and turning, displaying no rhyme or reason to their layout. The streets were, strictly speaking, little more than alleyways, and half of them, dead ends. Prior to the war it was a thriving community, but now it had been reduced to shell of its former glory, populated by a handful of old men playing *koum-kan* or backgammon.

Pino lumbered into the first *taverna* he came upon and sat at the bar. He didn't want a table, thinking that might draw too much attention. He ordered an ouzo and nursed it gently. The sweet viscous liquid reminded him of the sambuca his mother was so fond of. He really wanted a glass of *chianti*, but that was a pipedream and he simply couldn't stand Greek wine, red or white. So, ouzo it was. The sweetness of the liquor, which usually repulsed him, was a friend this evening, like a forbidden pleasure. Pino luxuriated in each swallow. He remembered that Kostas had once told him that every civilized country on earth had its own kind of ouzo, or more specifically a liqueur derived from Anise. The Turks had *raki*, Greeks had *ouzo*, Italians had *sambucca*, and Colombians had *aguardiente*.

"Colombia?" Pino thought, wondering how Kostas could possibly have any knowledge of South America. But Kostas seemed to know a little about everything. Pino wished that Kostas were there with him in the *taverna*. He imagined that the old man would be the perfect drinking partner, with stories, anecdotes and little facts abounding.

In the corner, an old man with greasy black hair and an incredible moustache was playing a *bouzouki,* a handcrafted, eight-stringed, kind of lute, or long-necked mandolin. Its steel strings produced an unmistakable sound. Pino had heard a great deal of bouzouki music since his arrival in Greece, mostly accompanying dances. The instrument was almost always played in a bright major key. After another *ouzo*, Pino thought the best way to describe the *bouzouki* was as a "happy" instrument. He couldn't imagine sad songs being played on it. But tonight was different. Maybe it was his sour mood, or maybe the liquor, but somehow, the *bouzouki* sounded sad, mournful. It was a sound, the likes of which Pino had never heard before.

The old musician began to sing along to the melody in a dirge-like drone and Pino listened, mesmerized. He didn't understand a word, yet he was profoundly moved. The song was full of pain and longing, but ripe with life. The singer never got emotional or melodramatic. He let the melody and the words speak for themselves.

When the song was finished, there was surprisingly no applause from the few people in the bar. Pino fully expected them to roar out approval, but none came. He was puzzled. The old musician put down his instrument and strode over to the far end of the bar. He made a gesture that the bartender was apparently familiar with because he immediately brought the old man a drink. Pino watched intently as the old man lit a cigarette and deeply inhaled. He really wanted to talk to him about the music but he was afraid that the old man might think it unwise to speak to a soldier. Still, he had to try. He slid down along the bar and smiled at the old man, who much to Pino's surprise smiled back a beaming grin of broken, yellow teeth.

"Good evening," Pino said pleasantly. The surprises just kept coming when the old man replied in stilted but certainly understandable Italian.

"You are Italian soldier, no?" he said with big, eager eyes. Pino didn't know what to say. The old man seemed happy, almost thrilled to speak to him. Suddenly, Pino wondered if it was wise to be speaking to the man.

"Yes, I am," Pino replied hesitantly. "You speak Italian?"

"*Si, certo!*" the old man boasted.

"That's wonderful!" Pino replied and motioned to the bartender for another ouzo. "That song you were playing just now, did you write that yourself?"

"No, of course not," the old man said bashfully. "It was *rebetika.*"

"Is that the composer or the name of the song?" Pino asked.

The old man laughed and took another long drag from his cigarette.

"Neither!" he said with a smile. "*Rebetika* is a style of song. It is song of the Greek immigrants from Turkey."

Pino shook his head in ignorance. The old man didn't seem surprised that the young soldier knew little of Greek history. It seemed that to the rest of the world Greek history ended two thousand years ago.

"After war with Turkey, many, many refugees come to live here in Piraeus, the port of Athens. They bring with them these songs of better times, happier times. Songs of longing for home and old way of life."

The old man's words tore at Pino's heart. He never longed so much for his little village.

"What do the words to that last song mean?" Pino asked.

"It go like this:

I sing from an alien land where it's cold and I grow old.
I can't take it anymore, Mother; my body is wearing out.
This alien life is full of bitterness, of misery.
It takes us far from home and wastes us, body and soul.
I'm leaving, Mother. I can't take it anymore; I'm coming back
To you, Mother, away from the misery of this foreign land.
But I met a woman, Mother, here in this alien land.
I'm bringing her back; and all three of us will try to live together.

Pino was speechless. The icy cold feeling gripping his heart had almost completely thawed. It was as though this stranger was looking into the darkest regions of his soul and reading his deepest thoughts and feelings. He knew if he didn't change the subject, he'd weep uncontrollably. He cursed his own frailty. Everything made him cry. He wanted to go home. The old man saw the change in Pino and he reached out and patted his hand gently. This simplest of gestures made Pino feel better.

"Where did you learn to speak Italian?" Pino inquired.

"From the music."

Pino didn't understand.

"The music?" he asked.

"*Si*, I learn from listening to the opera." As the words left the man's lips, Pino's jaw dropped, in stupefied silence. "What? You don't like the opera?" the old man said, trying to read Pino's expression.

"Oh my God! That's incredible." Pino muttered, his open mouth becoming a broad smile. "You have no idea!" Now it was the old man's turn to be confused. "What is your name?" Pino asked, smiling radiantly.

"*Sono Spiro.*" the old man said proudly.

"*Piacere, Spiro*" Pino replied, putting out a hand for Spiro to shake. "*Sono Pino.*"

"You like the opera then or no?" Spiro asked gingerly, "Because I know many songs from Napoli also. *'Torna Sorriento', 'Cor'e Ingrato', 'O Sole Mio'.*"

Pino thought he was going to faint. A wonderful warm chill passed throughout his body. The hair on his neck stood with a delight he hadn't known since the first night he heard Maria. He wanted to hug the old man.

"Spiro, you won't believe this but I am an opera singer! Or at least I was one before the war!"

"No!" Spiro said with slight incredulity.

"Yes! A very good one, too." Pino bragged.

Spiro squinted at him with a hint of disbelief. He put down his drink and walked over to his *bouzouki*. He picked it up and tuned it as he walked back to the bar.

"OK my friend, we see just how good you are," Spiro said with a challenge.

Pino thought he'd burst, but he quickly came back to earth when faced with the difficulty of finding an opera aria that could be accompanied on *bouzouki*. The two musicians racked their brains for nearly ten minutes trying to think of a piece that they both knew when finally they had it! *"Questa o quella"* from *Rigoletto*. The accompaniment was little more than a trifle, but it was perfect!

Spiro and Pino strode over to the tiny bandstand, which was actually a one-step riser in the corner. Spiro spoke a few words to the patrons that Pino didn't understand, excepting his name, and then the old man began to clap his hands to set the tempo. With no rehearsal at all, they began. They began and time stood still. Pino was on the stage at La Scala at last. No singing in his entire life had pleased him as much. He threw himself into the aria with reckless abandon. Spiro was loving it, too. He sang along as he played, mispronouncing words all the way through. Pino ended the aria with a tremendous cadenza, in the middle of which Spiro winked at him and said "show-off!" The aria ended and the entire bar, all six patrons, applauded. Pino gave Spiro a bear hug and kissed him.

"What should we do next?" Pino exclaimed with unabashed enthusiasm.

Before the night was over, they would perform *"Questa o quella"* three more times, to the delight of the increasingly inebriated crowd. They also played several of the more well-known Neapolitan tunes, including *"O sole mio"* a half-dozen times!

As Pino got drunk on *ouzo* and drunker on the music, he began to wax philosophic.

"Spiro, my friend, this has been the best night of my entire life," Pino said nodding his head like a drunken donkey.

"It was magical, my friend, but you must get back to your base soon, no?" Spiro said in a fatherly fashion. "I don't want the Italian army looking for me tomorrow."

Pino laughed and nearly fell off his chair. He was very drunk. Spiro was right. He'd better get back before anyone noticed he was gone. He looked Spiro in the eye and took both of his hands in his own.

"We must do this again, my friend," Pino implored.

Spiro kissed Pino's hands and squeezed them tightly.

"Anytime, Maestro," he said softly.

"Maestro?" Pino thought with a grin. Unknowingly, Spiro had just paid him the greatest compliment he had ever received. Pino stood up and bowed to the men at the table, then without another word he headed for the door.

"*Kalinichta*, Pino!" Spiro said as the door closed behind him.

Pino deeply inhaled the night air and started the long walk back to the base. On the way, he studied the stars that filled the deep blue night and he remembered the words that Amonte had said to him so long ago.

"Maybe Amonte was right," he said aloud. "If you give it a chance, there really is a lot to like about Greece."

On the way home, Pino walked down Patisson Street and past Maria's house. He stopped for a second and looked up at her window. He was no longer filled with the heated emotions he had felt earlier. He wanted to tell her about his evening, about the pleasure he felt, the *kefir* as the Greeks called it, the unbridled joy. Defying every rational bone in his body, he walked down the alleyway to the side door, the one that they had used to enter and search the apartment. When he reached it, he stopped and stared at it. He reached out his hand and extended his index finger. With that finger, he gently caressed the doorknob. Then, he sat down on the step and rested his chin on his fists. A cat ran through the alley and startled him, slightly sobering him. He stood up and looked at the door handle once more. Then, he scanned up the door to the brass knocker. There was a small label with a name written on it. He hadn't noticed it before.

KALOGEROPOULOS. He said the name out loud several times, "Maria Kalogeropoulos," although after the first time he knew he would never forget it. But, just to be absolutely certain, he reached out and tore the label off the knocker and stuffed it into his pocket. On the walk home, Pino touched the inside of his pocket several times along the way to make sure the paper was still there. It was. In a pleasant way, it made him feel like he was carrying a small part of her with him.

CHAPTER TWENTY-ONE

So Close Yet So Far

THE NEXT DAY WAS TO BE their last of minesweeping detail and a brilliant sunny sky welcomed them. Amonte and Pino got up early and, as was their habit, headed to the café for coffee. Bernardi and Carlucci took in as much sleep as they possibly could before beginning the day's labor. The assignment had turned out to be something of a bust. In thirteen days they had yet to come across a single mine, a fact viewed differently by each of them. Carlucci was still terrified about the whole thing and prayed to God each time he put on the sweeping equipment, certain that only divine intervention had allowed them to survive the past two weeks. Bernardi, on the other hand, was convinced that the entire exercise had been a farce, and took a *laissez-faire* attitude toward it.

The final morning, they were on the northernmost outskirts of town, where the apartment buildings and paved roads turned into rural country houses and gravel cart paths. There were one or two paved roads, but today their assignment was to clear the cart paths.

As Carlucci held the sweeping device in his hands, headphones on, he looked perpetually worried. Bernardi stood behind him, leaning on a shovel, and yawning. He stretched his arms and scratched his head. He looked around and saw Pino and Amonte across the field on another dirt road doing virtually the same thing, Amonte holding the sweeping device, Pino the shovel.

"Hey!" he yelled with a laugh, "Did you catch anything?"

"Not a nibble!" Pino responded.

"You see? I told you!" Bernardi said to Carlucci who was oblivious. He shook his head in disgust and looked at Carlucci who was still very serious and hard at work. "Did you hear me?" Bernardi bellowed, but Carlucci continued with his head down. "Have you heard anything I've said? Hey, I'm talking to you!" Carlucci didn't appear to hear a word and kept right on sweeping. "I'm surrounded by idiots." Bernardi said with a sigh.

He leaned forward and yanked the headphones off Carlucci who whirled around in surprise. "I've got a better way of doing it," he said with a wicked smile. Then, picking up a large stone from the side of the road, he stepped around Carlucci and tossed it in front of them. The stone hit the ground with a mighty "thud" and Carlucci winced. Bernardi walked up to the stone, picked it up and tossed it again. Again it slammed into the ground.

"Are you out of your goddamn mind? Cut it out!" Carlucci screamed.

But there was no stopping him.

"Just proving a point," said Bernardi, picking up the stone again.

"Hey! *Stronzo*! You're gonna get us all killed!"

Bernardi paid no attention and continued tossing his stone, whistling pleasantly as he did so.

"The locals use these roads every day and nobody has been blown up by any mines," Bernardi reasoned. "And you know why? Cause there aren't any!"

Carlucci winced and covered his head each time Bernardi tossed the big stone. Until, finally, he snapped. He rushed Bernardi like a bull and tackled him from behind. They hit the ground with a crash. Carlucci had lost his wits completely, screaming madly and punching Bernardi like a crazed animal. At first, Bernardi was so shocked that he couldn't even defend himself. Only after a few blows struck him squarely on the chin did he mount his own offensive.

By chance, Pino happened to glance over in their direction and saw the soldiers rolling around in the dirt like two little boys. His eyes nearly popped out of his head.

"Unbelievable!" he said, shaking his head in disbelief. "Hey!" he called out, "Listen! Quit it will ya! The captain sees you and you're dead meat! You hear me!"

Pino's yells caused Amonte to stop sweeping and remove his headphones.

"Bernardi! Carlucci! Knock it off!" Pino screamed.

"Hey Pino, the captain sees this and we're all dead meat."

"Holy shit!" Pino exclaimed, realizing Amonte was right.

Pino took off his helmet and slammed it to ground.

"Screw that!" he said as he took off, running across the field toward them, still carrying his shovel.

Bernardi and Carlucci were rolling around on the ground fighting like children.

"Hey! Cut it out! Goddamn it!" Pino screamed, coming closer. But they paid no attention. Pino ran like a gazelle, a gazelle carrying a shovel. He was only a few dozen yards away from them. As he ran, he tried to wipe the sweat from his brow with his forearm, and accidentally whacked himself in the face with the shovel.

"Goddamn it!" he cursed and threw away the shovel. Just as the shovel hit the ground, there was a massive explosion! The fury of it blew Pino through the air, sending him crashing to the earth flat on his back ten yards away.

"What the fuck?" screamed Bernardi. All he could see was a huge cloud of dirt and debris. Carlucci's face froze with a look of dread. The next thing they could see was Amonte rushing into the field through the smoke, screaming like a maniac.

"Pino! Jesus Christ!" he cried.

He reached Pino lying in the field covered with blood, his uniform tattered, and dirt falling all around him like black snow. He fell to the ground and cradled Pino's bloody head in his hands.

"Get a medic! Get a fucking medic! Hurry!" he screamed to the stunned Bernardi and Carlucci. Carlucci took off like a bullet, but Bernardi was frozen, his eyes fixed on the terrible sight of Amonte crying, wiping the dirt from Pino's bloody face.

PART THREE:
NEW YORK 1964

CHAPTER ONE

THE CRUCIBLE OF GOD

THE AREA BETWEEN BROADWAY and the Bowery, south of Prince Street to Canal Street in New York City is known as Little Italy. With more Italian inhabitants than Florence, Little Italy is at any given time the sixth or seventh largest "Italian city" in the world.

In the late nineteenth century, the Italian feudal system created such economic hardship for the vast majority of Southern Italians, that immigrants left their poverty-stricken homeland in droves. They set out across the Atlantic with virtually nothing but the clothes on their backs and a strong willingness to work.

Since the day the first immigrants settled in the neighborhood, music played an integral role in the community, and that role saw no sign of fading. It was said that after performing to the cultural elite at the Metropolitan Opera, the great Enrico Caruso would regularly drop by the neighborhood for a late-night poker game and some Neapolitan espresso.

In the years shortly after World War II, Little Italy underwent another population explosion, with Italian expatriates by the thousands arriving in search of a new life and opportunity. They brought with them a cultural renaissance in the neighborhood. At night, the sounds of Neapolitan love songs filled the air, wafting from one sidewalk cafe or another.

In 1964, as the entire country was in the grip of civil unrest, with the civil rights movement at its height and terrible rioting taking place as far away as Los Angeles and as nearby as Newark, somehow, New York was spared from any real violence. In Little Italy, the civil unrest was virtually unknown. In fact, the overwhelming social issue of the day was the ever-encroaching expansion of Chinatown, which lay just south of Little Italy. News and events from the old country were at least as important, if not more important, to the largely immigrant community than what was going on in their adoptive country.

One source of local pride within the community emanated from inside St. Dominic's church. It was the sound of the church choir. Despite the noise of the traffic and the general hustle and bustle of pedestrians, and tourists, the sound of the choir could always be heard, clarion clear, throughout the neighborhood. In the multitude of cafes that lined the streets and sidewalks of the neighborhood, customers would routinely delight in the sound of St. Dom's choir.

St. Dom's was a smallish church, squeezed between two four-story, walk-up apartment houses. Consequently, it too was long and narrow. The church had a tiny vestibule that was three steps up from the sidewalk. Inside, the church was extremely dark, due to the lack of any real sunlight and the dark-stained oak pews and woodwork. Yet in spite of the darkness, the church was anything but dreary. An abundance of candles constantly flickered near the altar and in the sacristy, creating a wonderful warm glow inside the church. Thanks to the neighborhood's generosity, there was never a dearth of flowers.

At the far end of the church, there was a choir loft that ran the entire width of the building. Its centerpiece was a mammoth pipe organ of brass and mahogany, which seemed a bit too large for the space it occupied. The organ was not the church's original instrument. It was a gift from some local businessmen when the old organ died.

Some years before, during a Sunday morning Mass, Father O'Brien had alerted the congregation to the fact that there would be no musical accompaniment during the Mass because the organ had been "acting up," again. Frustrated, music-loving members of the parish spoke to one of the area's leading "benefactors" and explained that the church was in dire need of a new organ. The meeting was legendary in certain circles. One of the local business owners explained that having no music in church was eating away at the spiritual conscience of the parish and, by extension, the neighborhood. Another petitioner said that his two daughters were in the church choir and no longer had an organ to accompany them. But the final straw was when a certain delicatessen owner stood before the "benefactor" and explained in clear, concise terms:

"A church with no organ is like a hotdog with no mustard. Like pasta with no cheese. Like a woman with no tits." Two weeks later, engineers from an Italian organ maker were measuring the choir loft for its new organ.

There were great divides in the Catholic Church in New York at the time and almost open hostility between the Irish Catholics and Italian Catholics. The problems stemmed from neighborhoods where Italian immigrants were replacing the German and Irish in greater numbers. Priests rarely had the language skills to deal with newcomers to their congregations and these newcomers usually had no command of their adoptive country's English, either. The church hierarchy pointed to the fact that ninety percent of the Irish Catholic population attended Mass every Sunday, compared to twenty-five to thirty percent of the Italian Catholic population. Add to that the fact that most Italians spoke of one day returning to the "old country" and one can see why the church had difficulty in gauging the commitment of these new comers to their parishes.

This was not really a problem at St. Dom's, whose congregation was probably ninety-five percent Italian. Father O'Brien, the church's Irish-American pastor, had received his training in Rome and worked extensively with Bishop Scalabrini and Mother Cabrini for years in their immigrant social programs, providing language classes, nurseries, orphanages, and other critical services to the immigrant community. For an Irish-American, he was uniquely qualified to shepherd a flock in the heart of Little Italy.

The choirmaster took his seat at the organ facing his choir. Much like the organ that accompanied it, the choir was rather large for such a small church; there were no fewer than fifty members, about thirty women and twenty men. Their sound was dense and lush like velvet. Clear to even the casual listener was the fact that this was not a typical church choir. The quality of the voices, the individual technique and the wonderful blending of colors suggested a professional ensemble of the first order. Yet, these men, women and children were, in fact, rank amateurs, none of whom had any serious musical training. What they shared was a rare passion for and commitment to the music they sang. They also shared a chorus master named Giuseppe Vaggi.

That afternoon, the choir was working on the *"Quando corpus morietur"* section from Dvorak's *Stabat Mater*. It was not by any means a favorite of the choir. In fact, they had never performed it at all. But, it was a special request from Father O'Brien. The old priest so rarely made any requests of the choir that when he came before them the week prior, asking for the obscure Czech piece, they had no other option but to agree. Apparently, the Sunday Mass was being said in some late parishioner's honor and the departed's family expressly wished for the piece to be sung at the Mass. Pino was totally unfamiliar with the piece and had a devil of a time finding a vocal score for it.

The Dvorak *Stabat Mater* was not terribly complex, but it was certainly not the sort of piece a local church choir could be expected to handle. Then again, theirs was no ordinary church choir! Pino relished the challenge like a football coach looking forward to a big game against a superior opponent. He drilled and drilled his troops, using just the right combination of honey and vinegar to maximize their potential. The piece called for four soloists and large choir. Pino always felt that the size of the choir was relative; if their hearts were in it, they could sound like a hundred voices.

The *Stabat Mater* was a Latin poem written around 1300 by a Franciscan monk named Jacopone da Todi. Pino had sung the Rossini version numerous times in his youth. But, Dvorak held a very special place in Pino's heart. Although he knew relatively little of the Czech composer's work, it was Dvorak that first brought Pino and Gia together, so many years ago in Maestro Ivaldi's studio. The sound of Gia singing the lovely "Hymn to the Moon" remained one of Pino's most treasured memories. There was even a brief period when Pino had tried to learn the words - a very brief period. The lyrical beauty of the aria and the lush, textured score of the opera from which it was taken, *Rusalka*, had always reminded Pino of Puccini. For some reason, to Pino, everything in creation could be explained in terms of its Italian parallel. He used this very example when breaking the news to the choir that they had a little over two weeks to learn the exotic Eastern-European piece. But, as expected, the men, women, and children of the choir attacked the piece with their usual professionalism and the unique zeal that made them special.

This would be their final rehearsal before the performance and Pino was pleased at their progress. There were still a few rough edges, some of them his own organ-playing limitations, but overall, he was satisfied. He just wanted to run through the finale one more time, but fate was determined to prevent him. Just as he raised his hand to give the downbeat to start, a loud, piercing, ringing noise could be heard. Several of the younger choir members smiled or giggled, the older ones wore sad or sympathetic faces. Their choirmaster was gently rapping his fist against his left ear. He continued this peculiar performance until the ringing stopped. He then loudly cleared his throat and raised his hand again as though nothing had happened. But modern technology wasn't through with him just yet, for once again, just as he gave the downbeat to begin, the ringing returned. He began violently whacking himself on the side of the head, but the ringing continued. The choir watched the bizarre scene in silence (they'd seen this play before) until the ringing turned into a buzzing. The temptation to laugh was incredible, especially for the younger members. Finally, one of the younger boys did. It wasn't much of a laugh, but it was enough.

Pino stopped trying to make the noise go away and stared at the child. The boy, who was no more than twelve, fidgeted, nervous and embarrassed. At that moment, Pino removed the hearing aids from his ears.

"Very nice," Pino said softly. "Very nice. That's it for today, gang. See you all on Sunday. Try to get here at least a half hour before Mass, Okay?"

They nodded affirmatively and began to dissemble. As they filtered out, Pino buried his face in his hands and let out a deep cleansing sigh. He was tired in body and soul, and he longed for a hot bath and a *grappa*, not necessarily in that order. A young girl stood before him waiting for him to come up for air. As he looked up and saw her, the smile returned to his face. This was why he did it all.

"Maestro Vaggi?" the child asked. Pino rested his chin on his fists and smiled back at her warmly.

"What is it, Sweetie?"

"Father O'Brien says your wife called and she wants you to come *straight home* after choir practice." As she uttered the words, "straight home" she gave him a very serious look that made him laugh out loud.

"Thank you, Sweetheart." She ran off and Pino closed his music and turned off the organ.

Pino walked down Mott Street with his music books under his arm, humming the Dvorak to himself. He stopped at a storefront and glanced in the window. The coast was clear. He entered. On the front window, bright red letters read: VAGGI FINE PASTRIES.

Pino went behind the counter and put his music books on a shelf. Then he rubbed his hands together greedily as if he had just found gold. A smiling female customer carrying a white box tied with red string came toward him, but she simply waved as she passed by. Pino nodded politely with a smile, pleased that she chose not to engage in a conversation.

"See ya, Joe," she said letting the door slam shut behind her.

"Yeah, yeah. *Ciao*, Irene," he said absently before turning his attention to the cookie case. After carefully examining its contents, Pino changed his mind and moved down the counter to the pastries. He reached under the counter and pulled out a fine looking mini-*cannolo*. He admired it for a second before taking a small nibble. Perfect.

"Hi, Pop!" called out a voice from behind, startling him.

He turned around, hiding the *connolo* behind him, and saw his daughter Maria.

"Hi, Honey," he said, crumbs falling from his lips.

From behind the far counter, Maria skipped to the door and locked it.

"Perfect timing, Pop!" she said. "You can help close up."

Maria was Pino's pride and joy, and then some. Fifteen years old, going on thirty, a straight A student, and even more beautiful than her mother. She had the same deep wide-set eyes that first attracted him to Gia and his own chubby cheeks that gave her face a distinctly cherubic quality.

"Maria?" called out a woman's voice from the back room. The voice was heavily accented, Italian of course, and as big as a house. It could usually be heard up and down the block, when the windows were open.

"Yeah, Mom?" Maria answered.

"When your father gets here, tell him to take out the trash before he comes up." Maria giggled and stuck out her tongue at her father. "And don't let him have any sweets. Dinner's almost ready," her mother continued.

"You got it, Mom," Maria answered.

"And you, too! Hurry up and clean up down there," her mother concluded.

Maria looked at her father disapprovingly. Pino returned the look, and then he looked at the pastry.

"You heard the boss. Drop it!" Maria ordered.

Pino bit his lip. It was bargaining time.

"Tell you what," he said with sheepish grin. "Why don't you run upstairs? I'll clean up for you down here."

"*And?*" she added.

"And what?" he asked.

"And take out the garbage!" she answered shaking her head.

He made a mock fist as if to slug her. She smiled and ran up the stairs. Pino resumed eating his pastry, grabbing a broom to sweep the floor. His shop was immaculate. He insisted upon it. Every morning at 4:00 am, the first thing he did, even before he started baking, was to dust the shop and mop the floors. It was the first thing he did in the morning and the last thing he did in the evening; it was a matter of discipline. He started to sweep, then paused to straighten out a picture on the wall. Not quite right. He tried again but he couldn't get it straight. He stepped back and looked again and again and again, each time adjusting it slightly, until finally he was satisfied.

It was a picture of Maria Callas on stage in a production of *Tosca*. Pino didn't know exactly where the photo had been taken but he was pretty sure it was not Italy. *Perhaps England?* It was a very old black and white shot that had begun to yellow around the edges, and he was determined to one day learn its origin. It hung on the wall next to another picture of Callas as *Violetta* in the La Scala production of *La Traviata*. Next to that one was Callas as *Lucia*, from the

Met, next to that *Medea*, from Dallas, next to that *Leonora*, from Covent Garden, next to that *Norma*, from Paris, and so on, and so on. One photo of Maria Callas after another filled the entire back wall of the pastry shop. There were also artist renditions, album and magazine covers, all framed and hanging in tribute. Pino gazed at them in silent adoration for a moment. By any standards, it was an impressive shrine, one that he'd painstakingly assembled over many years. In the neighborhood, it was legendary.

CHAPTER TWO

La Famiglia

THE KITCHEN OF PINO'S HOUSE was in modest 1960's style with green linoleum floors, baseboard heating, built-in, wall-unit cabinets from Sears-Roebuck, a large stove with six gas burners on top and a massive refrigerator. In the center of the room stood a round kitchen table with four chairs. The table was set for dinner.

An attractive, slightly heavyset woman with immaculate blonde hair was at the helm of the dinner preparations. She was at least thirty years of age, but few would have guessed that she was past forty. She wore an apron, on which was embroidered: *Never trust a skinny cook!*

Pino snuck into the kitchen and observed the table setting.

"Gia, perche mangiamo qui?" he asked, a little annoyed. Gia whirled round in surprise.

"When did you get in?" she asked, "I didn't hear you."

"I get lighter on my feet as I get older," Pino replied, grabbing a spoon to sample the brewing sauce. "But why are we eating in the kitchen and not the dining room?"

"Who cares? It's just us tonight," she said, dismissing the question.

"I guess," he muttered, not entirely satisfied, as he sipped the sauce from the spoon.

"Before you sit down, go take out the trash, before it starts to stink," she ordered.

"Already done," he said smartly.

"Oh? Well, then go help Maria clean up the shop."

"Also done," he said with a yawn.

Gia was losing patience.

"Then get the hell out of here for five minutes and let me cook!"

"All right, all right!" he replied laughing.

He got up to leave, but stopped to give her a kiss on the top of the head.

"Out!" she screamed.

As Pino left the kitchen and headed down the hall to the dining room, he picked up the mail from the table and went through it.

"By the way, your mother called," Gia called out from the kitchen.

"What did she want?"

"Same as always. She wants to come stay for a few days."

"When?"

"Who knows? Antonio called too. He and Millie invited us to dinner next Saturday night."

"Millie? *Milagros*, if you please!" he said to himself.

"I told them that's fine. Is that alright?"

"Sure. Sure," he blurted out. "Hey, Honey, did you remember to stop by the drugstore to pick up my batteries?"

"On your dresser."

"Grazie, amore."

"OK, call Maria, dinner's ready."

Generally speaking, Teatro alla Scala did not make a habit of hiring deaf tenors, (although some critics have accused them of hiring more than one "tone-deaf" tenor) and they were not going to make an exception for Giuseppe Vaggi.

After the landmine incident, Pino spent over two months in a military hospital somewhere, he never actually found out where, having his burns and internal injuries tended to. At first, it didn't look like he would survive, but after several surgeries and blood transfusions, the details of which he also never learned, his strength slowly came back. Limited access to antibiotics made recovery from the various surgeries take a bit longer than the doctors would have liked, but during a war they didn't have the luxury to be choosy. It was almost six months before Pino had the strength and the inclination to send a letter home.

Sadly, during the time between his last letter and this one, Pino's father died. It seemed that he sensed it coming but didn't say anything to anyone. He was suffering from cancer of the liver but made no effort to seek treatment. He had been working longer and longer hours to make ends meet, as the war had fairly well ruined most of the businesses in Italy, but he never complained. As he felt his strength diminish and his weariness grow, he wished his son had been there for him. Pino had never been particularly helpful around the shop, probably by design, but that didn't matter to his father. Papa Vaggi's only regret was all the time he had wasted being angry with his son. He felt like a tired old cliché. He'd always told himself that it was for Pino's own good that he was so firm, but now, he was having doubts. It was a painful realization that he might never see his son again, but he took solace in the fact that they had had a reconciliation of sorts before Pino departed. It was all he had.

To make amends, Papa Vaggi had vowed that he would treat Gia like his own daughter. He showered her with gifts (that he couldn't afford) and with fatherly love, the love that he could never quite express to his son. His daughter Maria was thrilled that Gia was practically part of the family, as she already thought of her as a sister.

Gia's parents had never been overly fond of Pino, and his prospects as a husband and provider. But Gia regularly quoted biblical passages of how a girl must leave her father and mother and stand with her husband. Her parents never fully understood that and unfortunately a rift began to form, one that would last a lifetime. Soon, Gia would come to call Mr. and Mrs. Vaggi, "Mom and Dad," the grass always looking greener.

Whenever a letter from Pino arrived, whomever it was addressed to, the family, including Gia, would gather together in the dining room and read it together. If there was a passage too personal for sharing, it was conveniently omitted. The practice went on regularly for months. They had thought themselves lucky to have a son (and a fiancée) who cared enough to write so frequently.

As time passed, however, the letters came less and less frequently, before eventually stopping altogether. It had been easy to understand; everyone assumed it was because the mail was unable to get through, or that Pino was simply too busy to write. But after several months without a word, a distinct gloom had begun to fill the house. Papa Vaggi had taken it the hardest, often going for entire days without speaking. Maria and Gia consoled and cheered each other up, never allowing a negative word to pass from their lips. Mrs. Vaggi was a rock. Somehow, she had summoned up inner strength that even she had no idea she possessed. Always doing the daily chores, always having the meals prepared on time, always with a smile - not a sad smile, but a hopeful smile.

One evening, after a painfully quite dinner, Pino's father had gone to bed early, complaining about being tired. After a few minutes, he called out from the bedroom asking for a *grappa*. Gia leaped up to fetch one for him. She picked out Papa Vaggi's favorite bottle and poured the clear liquor into an espresso cup. She got a *biscotti* from the table and placed them both on a plate and brought them to him. He was sitting up in bed with a lamp burning at his bedside. Gia came in and placed the plate next to the lamp.

"I brought you a *biscotti*, too. In case you got a little hungry," she said sweetly. He smiled at her but said nothing. "Anything else?" she asked pleasantly. He looked up at the ceiling as though trying to think of something, and scratched his chin. Then his face contorted slightly and he had the look of someone who wanted to ask for something, but wasn't sure if he should.

"You know," he started, then stopped.

"Yes?"

"There is one thing."

She looked at him quizzically.

"Uh huh?" She said.

"You know," he continued, "in all the time we've known you, even before you and Pino, well you know." She smiled, a little confused. "Well," he finally said, "I've never heard you sing." Gia laughed and smiled, embarrassed. "I'd really like to sometime," he said, "If you don't mind."

"Don't be silly!" Gia gushed, "I'd love to. In fact, I'd be honored."

They sat in awkward silence for a moment before Gia leaned over and kissed him on the cheek. Papa Vaggi blushed.

"It doesn't have to be soon, you know, whenever you can," he added unnecessarily.

"Anytime you like," she said. "But, now I think you should get some rest."

He nodded and drank his *grappa*. Gia winked and shut the door as she left.

Papa Vaggi took a bite of the *biscotti* and pulled up the covers to his chin, he didn't want to get any crumbs in the bed. Pino found himself a real gem, he thought. Gia would make him a good wife and a good mother, most importantly, she would make him happy. And with that pleasant thought floating in his mind, he rolled over and fell into a deep and very content sleep.

Papa Vaggi finally heard Gia sing, but he was listening from far, far away on that September morning as she sang a beautiful *Ave Maria* in his memory.

Pino had learned of his father's death upon his return to Collagna. It was a crushing blow. He decided shortly thereafter that there was nothing left for them in Collagna. Even before his convalescence had ended, it was abundantly clear to him that he would never have a career as an opera singer. He spent many a night lying in the hospital bed staring at the ceiling wondering what he would do with the rest of his life. The thought of returning home and working in his father's butcher shop was too painful to bear. Now, fate had stepped in and thrown him yet another curve. The only thing Pino had left to be grateful for was that Gia had waited for him, and her love was unwavering. She had decided long ago that she would be there for him through thick and thin, no matter what road lay before them.

At the kitchen table during dinner, Pino, Gia and Maria quietly devoured a feast that might have been mistaken for Christmas dinner in any other household, both in terms of quantity and quality of the food. The first course consisted of lightly breaded baby scallops in lemon wine sauce. Fresh green salad from the garden followed. Next, was a delightful dish of chestnut pasta (Pino's favorite) wrapped around a stuffing of ground beef, fontina cheese and pine nuts. As if that weren't enough, the main course was big fatty, delicious veal chops. Surveying the bacchanal, Pino wondered how he managed to stay so fit and trim. The truth was, he hadn't. He had developed into a hefty, forty-inch waisted, Italian baker. He wasn't altogether unhappy with his appearance, and he certainly felt healthy enough. As long as Gia didn't have any problem with him, he was content the way he was.

"How was practice?" Gia asked, with a mouth full of food.

"Aside from my damn hearing aids going on the blink right in the middle of the finale," Pino answered, a bit embarrassed, "I think it went very well."

"When are you guys performing that thing?" Maria inquired.

"*That thing?*" Pino said with obvious disgust. "Is she really my daughter? Where did you find her?"

"Who knows, Pop," Maria said playfully, "Maybe it was the milkman or the post man, or one of Mom's *secret admirers.*"

Pino laughed at the comment.

"Go on, Mom. Tell Pop about your secret admirer!" Maria said defiantly.

"Excuse me?" Pino said, displaying a newfound interest.

"Yeah, you better watch out, Pop! This *really* handsome guy has come in the shop every afternoon this week," said his daughter. "I think he's got a crush on Mom."

"Maria!" her mother yelled. "Don't be ridiculous! I'm sure it's nothing like that."

Pino stared at his daughter, who smirked a *wisenheimer* smile. Then, he looked at Gia, who stared down into her food. She was blushing. He wasn't quite sure he liked what he saw, but he would make light of it.

"Oh, well that's OK. I forgot to tell you that I've got a date tomorrow with Gina Lollabrigida. If that's alright with you?" Pino joked.

"Ha! Be my guest!" Gia laughed.

"Don't laugh, Pop. This guy has come in three days straight, and he's always dressed to kill!" Maria continued. "Why would somebody dress that way in the middle of the afternoon unless he was trying to impress someone?"

"I assume you mean, other than for my pastries, right?" Pino said.

"In all honesty, Pino," Gia said, "I think he comes in more to look at your pictures than for the pastries."

"What?" Pino half uttered.

"It's true!" Gia said. "He orders a coffee, a *svaliatelle* or a *canolo,* then he sits at a table and looks at your Callas pictures."

"C'mon Mom. Give it up. I saw the way he looks at you!" Maria said with a big smile.

"Maria! Really!" Gia said, blushing.

The effect of Maria's comment didn't go unnoticed by her father.

"Okay, Maria, that's enough." Pino said authoritatively. "Your mother is a very beautiful woman. It's only natural that men are going to look her way and occasionally smile or wink. It's nothing to get upset about." He took Gia's hand in his own and gently patted it. "That's what marriage is all about, trust. You'll understand that when you're a little older."

"Pop, I understand perfectly. But *you* don't understand, this guy is *hot!*" Maria blurted out.

"Maria!" said her mother, shocked, "Where did you learn to talk that way?"

"Hey," Pino interrupted with a laugh, "you were the one who insisted she go to Catholic school!"

As father and daughter shared a laugh and mother stewed with embarrassment, Pino gave Maria a loving wink and they all settled down to eat, but it wasn't all that long before Pino broke the silence.

"Of course, I guess it wouldn't hurt to meet this *Don Giovanni* in the flesh," he said.

"Don't be silly," Gia said. "You'll be asleep by noon. You're like a clock."

"Hey!" he yelled, "If you were up at 4:00 am to bake the goddamn bread every day you'd be sleeping by noon, too!"

"I know. I'm not saying I wouldn't! That's why I think it's foolish for you to try to stay up until 3:00, just to see this guy." Gia said defensively.

"Aha!" said Maria, "See! She even knows exactly what time he arrives!"

"You are gonna get it, but good!" Gia said firmly.

"Relax, both of you!" Pino interrupted. He paused for a moment to allow things to cool off, then continued. "I suppose I could finish up early tomorrow and take my nap a little earlier too. That way I could be awake in time for our guest."

"Honestly Pino...never mind. Fine. Do whatever you want." Gia said.

"OK, that settles that," Pino declared. "Now, what's for dessert?"

CHAPTER THREE

THE BRAVE NEW WORLD

IN 1949, NEW YORK CITY was hot. The baby boom was in full swing, the economy was exploding and immigrants were arriving by the boatload in hope of a better future than the one they had left behind.

Pino and Gia were married by the captain of the ship that carried them from Genoa to New York. There was no fanfare and only Pino's mother and sister as witnesses, but a finer, more noble wedding there never was.

Their trip was hardly a first class passage. The cramped quarters and foul stench of steerage reminded Pino of his disastrous voyage to Greece. However, he refused to allow himself to be seasick. He had to be strong for the women, or so he told himself. The truth was that the three women were of far stronger stock than he imagined. He guessed that they'd been hardened by the war and by his father's passing; they were oak solid.

Arriving in New York with no friends or family to rely upon, with the war still fresh in the minds of so many, made the early years of *la famiglia* Vaggi's American experience quite an adventure. They had some money to tide them over, but had hoped to use that money as a nest egg for a home. Mrs. Vaggi had sold the butcher shop the year before and used the proceeds to book the passage to America. Unfortunately, the Italian lire continued to fall and a good portion of the money gained through the sale of the butcher shop had been used just to sustain them immediately following the war.

After several nights in an immigrant shelter, the family got a tip on an inexpensive apartment in a part of town known as the Bronx. At first it seemed like an eternity away from the city, but soon Pino discovered the glory of the IRT subway system. For a mere five cents, he could travel from his new home on Belmont Avenue all the way through Manhattan and into Brooklyn to look for some of his *paisani* whom he learned had settled there.

Antonio Amonte had moved to the New World six months before the Vaggis. He had the advantage of family in America who set him up with a place to live and a job in the family bakery. On one of his excursions, Pino encountered someone in a bar who knew someone who knew Amonte. The two war buddies had a tearful reunion over strong coffee and light pastries at

Ferrara's Café in Little Italy. They filled one another in on the developments in their lives since they had last seen each other.

Pino learned a great deal about the events immediately following his injury, many of them, upon reflection, he'd wished he'd never found out. Amonte told the tale as if he were reading it from a book with an actor's sense of drama. Apparently, he'd told the story numerous times to friends and family after the war and had it down by memory. He related it to Pino, who listened calmly and detached, as if it had happened to someone else completely.

After the mine detonated, Carlucci had taken off in search of a medic, but there was none to be found for miles. Amonte had wrapped Pino's head in his own shirt to try and stop the bleeding, but it was no use, and they were almost certain that he would die from his wounds. In a panic, Bernardi had grabbed Pino as gingerly as he could and displaying superhuman strength carried him over half a mile back into town. At the hospital, no one spoke Italian and the staff were slow to help the Italian soldier. That lasted until Bernardi took out his rifle and placed the barrel against the throat of the doctor in residence. He then fired a blast into the ceiling of the emergency room, to make them aware of his seriousness. The effect was immediate. Nurses came out of the woodwork to attend to Pino. A difficult night of surgery had followed and Pino's fate still was uncertain in the morning. Bernardi and Amonte had remained at the hospital the entire time. Carlucci was dispatched to inform the captain of the incident.

Pino was astounded to learn that Bernardi was almost single-handedly responsible for his survival, but Amonte assured him it was true. It was almost too difficult to believe. He resolved to find Bernardi and thank him properly, but the task would not be easy. After the Allies liberated Athens, Bernardi had disappeared. No one was sure if he went AWOL or if he was killed. Years later, Amonte tried to contact his family in Naples when he returned to Italy, but he soon realized the futility of his errand, as there were over three thousand "Bernardis" listed in the Naples phone directory.

It remained a nagging piece of unfinished business in Pino's mind for many years. He decided the only decent thing to do would be to include Bernardi in his nightly prayers thereafter, which he did. But he never heard from or of Bernardi again.

Carlucci's fate also remained somewhat of a mystery, but not a particularly pleasant one. Soon after the landmine incident, he was arrested by the Germans for "trafficking stolen goods" to the enemy. In essence, he had merely provided food for a starving family. His motivation was irrelevant to the Germans and he was arrested and moved out of Athens pending trial. When the roundup of

Athenian Jews began, a mass exodus took place and thousands escaped to the hills north of Athens seeking refuge, before eventually traveling to the northernmost mountain ranges to find permanent hiding places. Fortunately, Carlucci's girlfriend and her family were among the lucky ones that escaped. He was not so lucky. Although none of his friends ever learned the exact truth regarding his fate, the punishment for such offenses was quite severe and in all likelihood he was either interred in a death camp or shot before a firing squad. Sadly, his girlfriend and her family would never hear from him again and never know the extent of his sacrifice for them.

Pino learned the pastry business working at Amonte's side in Brooklyn. It was a hard business with insane hours, but it could be very lucrative if you had an affinity for it, and Pino did. Gia taught music and voice students to help augment the family income and the students' presence was like therapy for Pino. He still couldn't hear very well but just being around the piano had a positive effect on him. The concussion from the blast had ruptured both of his eardrums but the damage to the right ear was significantly worse than the left. Initially, he was considered stone deaf, however, in time the hearing in his left ear began, ever so slightly, to return. His joy was immeasurable. Although he was still very hard of hearing, he could finally hear music again. It was the greatest gift God had ever bestowed upon him, and even though his right ear never really improved, he was content.

A few years later, divine providence and the miracles of modern science changed Pino's life forever. Amonte told Pino that in his doctor's office, he had seen a brochure for a new electronic hearing aid made in Germany. Pino noted the irony: the Germans took away his hearing and now they might be the ones to restore it! It promised miraculous and immediate results, but in fact, it provided neither. What it did provide, however, was hope. At such a critical juncture in his life, he often wondered why God saw fit to bless him so, and he renewed his daily devotions that he hadn't practiced since childhood. He also remembered Maestro Ivaldi telling him that Beethoven was completely deaf by the time he composed his miraculous Ninth Symphony. That piece of music, widely regarded as the greatest ever composed, took up residence in Pino's heart and mind like no other. He developed an affinity for it that he could never put into words. It boggled Pino's mind, that after having been dealt so cruel a hand by fate (*imagine the cruelty – a composer losing his hearing at the very zenith of his creative powers!*) that despite all this, the master could create a piece of music so wonderful, and of all things, bursting with rapturous joy! If it were indeed the work of a mere mortal, then he was certainly one upon whose brow the Almighty had laid a finger.

Pino reflected on the only other Beethoven performance he could remember, the *Fidelio*, in Athens during the war. He particularly remembered the glorious overture, which caused him to reconsider his feelings toward German music in general. Twice in his lifetime Beethoven had brought about cathartic moments, and for this, Pino included the master in his daily devotions.

Eventually, he did find a hearing aid that helped him. Even his problematic right ear showed the signs of improvement. For the first time in years, he began to open up his old scores and sing along as he read. The hearing aid produced a new confidence in him that pervaded everything he did. It provided him the confidence to open his own business, the confidence to teach students, the confidence to accept the choirmaster position, and the confidence to be a father.

Maria's arrival was gloriously unexpected. Though Pino and Gia hadn't exactly been trying for a child, they certainly weren't doing anything to prevent one. Maria was the first Vaggi born an American citizen and named after Pino's sister. The elder Maria was, of course, thrilled and then doubly honored when Gia and Pino asked her to be the child's godmother. It was an exceptionally happy time in all of their lives. They were adjusting well to their new homeland and it appeared to take to them as well. They were happy, healthy, employed, and now, a family. Norman Rockwell could have painted their portrait for the cover of the Saturday Evening Post.

Pino worked in the shop every day and in church teaching the choir on weekends. He even doubled as church organist on odd occasions when the regular guy couldn't make it. He wasn't really a trained organist but he retained his basic piano skills from childhood and that made him more of an organist than anyone else in the parish.

On weekends he would allow himself one guilty pleasure, hunting through the record stores for new recordings. His collection had become so vast that Gia was running out of places to put them. Every trip to the record store included a perusal of the Callas LPs. He owned all of them and waited with baited breath for new releases.

One of the simple joys of record buying was that it was something he could do with Maria. Pino worshipped his daughter as much as any father ever had, yet he had virtually nothing in common with her. She was a sports-loving tomboy and a dyed-in-the-wool New York Yankees fan. Pino really had no affinity for sports at all. He occasionally watched a soccer match from Italy, when a big game was on and when the reception was good on VHF but that was it. His talent for baking was never passed down to his daughter. Maria didn't like to cook and ate a steady diet of hot dogs and pizza. But the one thing that perplexed Pino most was that despite having two talented musicians for parents, Maria's taste in music was dreadful, at least as far as he was concerned. She loved the Beatles (what 16-year-old girl didn't?) and the Rolling Stones and the Beach Boys, and a host of other "non-talents" as Pino referred to them. For some years, Pino and Gia had tried to get Maria to sit still long enough to listen to some "real music," Verdi, Puccini, even Mozart, but it was no use. She simply didn't care to listen to any music she couldn't dance to. Her indifference to the classics bothered Pino more than Gia, who only laughed at the way Pino wrestled with this particular demon.

Eventually, Pino arrived at the sad conclusion that Maria would never derive the same joy from music that he did. He desperately wanted Maria to feel the intensity and the passion that music had brought to his life, but the dream was fading fast. He regularly took her to concerts and encouraged her to join the choir, but she never displayed even a modest interest. And, she was at an age where she didn't mind letting him know just how much his efforts annoyed her.

One way in which she exacted her revenge was by forcing the entire family to assemble before the television set one Sunday night to watch the Ed Sullivan Show. The Vaggis weren't big television watchers as a rule, but Pino did respect the fact that the Sullivan Show often featured singers from the Met. In the past, he'd seen Robert Merrill, Joan Southerland and Birgit Nilsson perform, so on this particular evening he indulged his daughter and tuned in.

He had no idea what he was in for. Along with seventy-three million other viewers, the Vaggis witnessed the dawn of Beatlemania. Four long-haired young men in matching suits sang and gyrated while the audience, composed mostly of young girls, went absolutely insane. Pino had never seen anything like it and hoped never to again.

"This is music?" he complained to Maria, "You can't even hear them, let alone understand the words."

It was wasted breath on Maria who bopped around the room like a lunatic dancing to her mop-topped idols. Pino would never understand this kind of music and wasn't likely to try. It was like the maestro used to say, his tastes "were of the last century, not this one."

Another phenomenon that he could never quite grasp was the unique relationship between his two Marias: his sister Maria and his daughter Maria. His daughter always possessed a very special affection for his sister. She was, of course, the child's godmother and that created a particular kind of bond between them, but there was something more. From the time she was very young, little Maria adored her aunt, or, one might even say, worshiped her. In the early days, Gia was more than a little jealous of her sister-in-law. Pino found the whole situation very amusing, much to Gia's consternation. The child was always asking "where's *Zia* Maria?", "When is *Zia* Maria coming over?" and Aunt Maria tried her best to accommodate her niece, not realizing for an instant that she was starting to drive Gia crazy with her constant presence.

This lead to, "Can I sleep over *Zia* Maria's house tonight?" and worse, "*Zia* Maria would let me do it!" The irony of the situation was, of course, that the two women had been best friends, practically sisters, since childhood, a point which Pino felt compelled to point out to both of them, regularly.

On Christmas Eve of little Maria's tenth year, the situation had come to a head. Pino and Gia knew that Maria wanted a gold necklace for Christmas, one like her friend Claudia from school wore, so Pino called Claudia's parents and politely inquired of them where they'd purchased the necklace, but to his profound disappointment, they explained that they'd bought the necklace in Florence while on vacation. Claudia's mother said that she was pretty sure she still had the receipt and that she'd look for it. Pino thanked her, but explained that little Maria really had her heart set on having the necklace *now*, and they shared a laugh that only parents could comprehend let alone appreciate.

The way Gia saw it; she and Pino had two options: get Maria another necklace or order it from the jeweler in Florence, wait for it to arrive and give it to her later, maybe for her birthday. Pino predicted that Maria would forget all about the necklace in a few days and he voted for the third and unspoken option: get her something else entirely and don't sweat the necklace. Gia wasn't quite as convinced, but eventually she came around. They decided that a nice sweater would do the trick, but just to play it safe, they also purchased a pair of tiny diamond stud earrings. Pino was absolutely certain that little Maria would be thrilled and the necklace would instantly be forgotten.

The tradition of opening presents on Christmas Eve was one that the Vaggi family had always held firm. Christmas Eve dinner was usually prepared by Pino's mother and it generally consisted of several cold antipasti, followed by fish or lobster. The desserts were nothing short of spectacular from Pino's pastries to Maria's homemade candies. After dinner, dessert and drinks came the opening of presents.

Unfortunately, on this particular Christmas Eve, only one present had the chance to be opened. As the family moved en masse to the living room, to begin the ritual, Pino's sister insisted that little Maria open her gift first, and what seemed at first like a harmless request precipitated the single greatest crisis in Pino and Gia's marriage. Somehow, the entire scene took place in slow motion before Pino's eyes yet he was powerless to stop it. As little Maria sat under the tree and searched for the gift from her aunt. Pino sat next to Gia on the couch and held her hand warmly.

"I found it!" Maria called out with glee.

As she started pulling the ribbon off of the box, Pino felt a sudden chill through his body. At once, he had a premonition that terrified him and he wanted to scream, but the air never even left his lungs before his worst nightmare unfolded before his eyes. Maria opened the box and slowly removed a beautiful gold necklace, the gold necklace that she wanted so desperately. As she screamed with joy, Pino grimaced in agony, knowing only too well what was coming next. Gia looked at little Maria in shock as the young girl leaped into the waiting arms of her aunt. Next, Gia turned to Pino, who was staring at the floor. As little Maria cried out, "I love it. I love it!" Gia's nostrils flared and her jaw trembled with anger. In his entire life, Pino had never seen her looking this way and it worried him, but before he could say a word, she stormed out of the room.

It seemed like years, but it was actually only weeks, before Gia and Maria made amends, ultimately realizing that they couldn't live without each other. Tearful apologies flowed like rain and soon no one would have guessed there was ever a problem - except little Maria. The young girl was terribly confused about the entire matter and no one seemed to have a reasonable explanation. The episode would color her Christmas memories for years to come.

Pino was in the middle of a huge yawn. He rubbed his eyes, half-asleep, and checked his watch.

"Are you done yet?" called Gia, from the front of the shop.

Pino looked down at a large tray of small square pastries, half of which had icing, half of which were awaiting his handiwork.

"Why can't Maria do this stuff?" he complained.

"She doesn't get home from school till three," Gia said.

Pino glanced at his watch, which showed 2:30pm. He yawned again, blinked away as much sleep as he could manage, then continued icing the pastries.

Thirty minutes later Pino was fast asleep on a stool, his head resting on his folded arms on the table. From the front, a bell rang, waking Pino, who blurted out semi-consciously: "I wasn't sleeping!" He shook the sleep away once again and gathered his wits slowly.

Someone was talking in the front -- *to him?* He was about to call out to Gia when he heard a male voice. Freshly alert, his curiosity piqued, he listened intently to the voices coming from the front.

He strolled over to the curtain that separated the backroom from the front to investigate further, but he could only hear the voices faintly and it frustrated him. He slowly pulled back the curtain about an inch from the doorframe and peeked out. He could see Gia behind the counter but not who she was talking to. He scanned the shop and through the counter he could see someone but couldn't make out any features. He closed the curtains hoping he hadn't been seen. He thought for a minute. *Did he look foolish?* He really didn't care. He pulled back the curtain again and looked for the stranger. This time there was no missing him. Maria was right. He was a very handsome, distinguished-looking man in his mid-to-late thirties. It struck Pino that he bore a striking resemblance to Omar Shariff. Tall, slender, and impeccably dressed, in a tan blazer, black slacks, white collared shirt with a gold silk ascot, the stranger cut quite a figure.

Pino stepped back for a second and let the curtain close. He looked down at his own bulging belly encased in a white tee shirt and seersucker pants. For the first time in as long as he could remember, Pino felt seriously out of shape. He had flour dust on his hands and face. His hair was matted with sweat. This was not the way he wanted to look when he faced his "rival," so he ran to the sink and washed his hands and face. There was no mirror in the back room to check his appearance and there was no time to go upstairs into the house. He threw a handful of water onto his head and ran his fingers through his thinning hair to comb it down as best he could. He then tore off his Stanley Kowalski tee shirt and pulled out a fresh white baker's shirt from the closet. He rarely wore the shirts, thinking them silly-looking, but at that moment, he was glad he'd kept them handy.

He walked back to the doorway and pulled back the curtain again. The stranger was smiling and laughing as he talked with Gia, who was visibly blushing. Pino stepped back from the door, ran his hands through his hair one last time, and took a deep breath. He tucked in his shirt, sucked in his gut and strode to the door. He yanked back the curtain with authority and stepped into his shop, but Gia was alone. The stranger, coffee and canolo in hand, was walking along the perimeter of the shop, examining the Callas photos. He seemed to be intently studying one particular photo when he stopped and turned to Gia.

"*Signora*, this *canolo* is simply divine, *molto delicato*," he said. "My compliments."

"All the credit goes to my husband. He's the baker," Gia responded, unaware of Pino's presence.

"Your husband is not a baker," he continued, "but an artist. Only an artist could create something as delicate as this."

Pino smiled suspiciously, not convinced of the stranger's intentions. Unseen by Gia, he again sucked in his stomach and stuck out his chest as he moved behind the counter. He grabbed an espresso cup, and filled it nonchalantly. Gia saw him and started to speak, but Pino gently quieted her with a wave of his hand. He proceeded around the counter toward his guest. He stopped and looked at the Callas picture farthest away from the stranger. Then, slowly and methodically, he moved along the wall in the stranger's direction, all the while watching him out of the corner of his eye. After a few minutes, the two men found themselves studying the same picture. They both observed in silence for a moment. Then without even looking at one another, first contact was made.

"This one is really quite amazing," the stranger remarked, firing off the opening salvo.

"Hmm? Oh, yeah." Pino responded awkwardly, caught off-guard.

"Do you know what opera it's from?" the stranger asked.

"Do I know? Ha!" said Pino, mockingly, "Is that a rhetorical question?"

The stranger turned to Pino, confused.

"*Do* you know?" he inquired, again.

"Of course," said Pino with an air of superiority.

"Which?" demanded the stranger.

"*Fedora*, La Scala '57." Pino replied mechanically as though reading it out of some encyclopedia, "That's Corelli with her. It's the only time she sang the role. Lousy role for her."

"I completely agree," responded the stranger. "I still can't believe she ever agreed to do it."

"Have you seen this one?" Pino offered, pointing to the photo above and to the left of the one they were looking at.

"The Rome walkout? Many times," retorted the stranger unimpressed.

"Oh? How about this one?" Pino continued, pointing to a particularly ugly photo of Callas looking like a tiger about to devour its young.

"Dallas, November 17th, 1955. The process server," said the stranger, casually.

Pino, impressed, rushed down the wall and pointed to another.

"How 'bout this one! It's pretty obscure." He said with glee.

"Hmmm. Well the opera is obviously *Norma*, but..."

"Nope," said Pino, gloating.

"Not *Norma?*"

Pino closed his eyes and shook his head.

"Wait. Don't tell me. Ah, I have it! Lady Macbeth!"

Pino smiled a victorious smile and whispered in his rival's ear.

"How about...*Medea?*"

"Ah! Of course! Dallas also?" the stranger cried out. Pino nodded, secure in his supremacy. "My friend," said the stranger, "you know this wall like a good librarian knows her books. I see I'm not the only one who enjoys coming here, to this ... this shrine!"

"Well, actually, I never leave," Pino said.

"What? Oh! You must be Maestro Vaggi! The great pastry artist!"

Pino smiled, embarrassed and nodded.

"I should have guessed it! Someone who creates such culinary delights would appreciate the genius of Callas!" the stranger said.

"Oh, you'd have to look far and wide to find a bigger Callas fan than Joe Vaggi." Pino said proudly.

"Permit me to introduce myself," the stranger said with tremendous grace, "I am Christian Biscini. At your service."

The two shook hands like old friends.

"Biscini?" Pino said with a start. "Then I guess *'parla l'Italiano'* no?"

"*Certo!*" replied Biscini.

"Well, in that case, I'm really *Giuseppe* Vaggi, and my friends call me Pino."

"*Piacere, Pino!*" Biscini laughed.

"*Piacere, Christiano.* I didn't recognize your accent or I would have guessed sooner." Pino said.

"Forget it!" said Biscini with the wave of a hand. "That's because I'm Greek. Don't ask! It's a very long story, I'll tell you some other time."

Pino looked at Biscini with new eyes and he decided that he liked what he saw. Christian really was coming to the shop just to see what new Callas pictures Pino would hang. This was certainly not your average run-of-the-mill opera buff. This was a man with a passion, a devotion, maybe even greater than Pino, if that was possible. One thing was for certain: he wasn't after Gia! The thought made Pino snicker to himself. He couldn't wait until dinner to tell Maria that she was wrong. The little wiseass!

"I'm sorry, did you say something?" Biscini asked.

"No." apologized Pino, "I was just thinking, wow, you must really love Callas to be so knowledgeable."

Biscini squinted as if in deep thought and choosing his words with the utmost care.

"For me," he said, "she is not merely the greatest singer of her generation, but the greatest artist of this century. There is no other."

"What about Tebaldi?" Gia blurted out from the backroom.

"Tebaldi?" cried out Pino and Biscini in perfect unison.

"Yeah, Tebaldi," Gia repeated, sarcastically. "You've heard of her, right?"

"Come on!" Pino said with disgust. "There's no comparison!"

"None whatsoever!" agreed Biscini.

"Tebaldi could never sing bel canto like Callas!" Pino continued like a man on a mission, "Donizetti, Bellini, Spontini. How many of these does Tebaldi sing?" Without missing a beat, Biscini continued the barrage.

"And onstage, Callas is sublime. She is a finer actress than Bette Davis. Tebaldi on stage is like looking at wood!"

"I don't know," Gia persisted. "Last year Pino and I heard Tebaldi sing *Tosca* at the Met and I cried."

Biscini wrung his hands in front of him, and his face turned very serious.

"*Signora*. If Tebaldi's *Tosca* made you cry, then perhaps you should never see Callas. For if Tebaldi moved you to tears, Callas would certainly kill you altogether! You will just have to wait until your husband gets home to tell you the details of the performance."

Pino laughed out loud and Gia was more than a little embarrassed, but it was obvious from the start that Biscini was not the type of person you could stay mad at for very long.

"Don't you worry, Honey," Pino said in an attempt to cheer her up. "It'll be a long time before Callas ever sings at the Met again."

"Yes, Pino's right," Biscini chimed in. "It will be months."

It took a second for the remark to register, then Pino looked blankly at Biscini.

"What?"

"It is still many months away," Biscini said matter-of-factly.

"What is?" Pino asked stupidly.

"Callas' return. Haven't you heard?"

Pino's eyes nearly burst out of his head. He froze solid in a stupor. His mouth hung open like a dead fish in a shop window. *What did he say?* All of a sudden the haze burned away and Pino returned to planet earth. He grabbed Biscini by the arms.

"Are you serious?"

"Of course. She will sing *Tosca* and *Traviata* at the Met next season."

Pino released Biscini from his grip and blessed himself.

"Oh, my God!" he screamed. "Gia! Finally!"

He rushed into Gia's arms and hugged her until she cried out. Biscini watched the scene in great confusion, as Pino and Gia danced around in each other's arms, when it dawned on him.

"Oh, I see! You've never seen Callas perform live! Is that it?"

"What?" Pino yelled defiantly. "*Me? Never seen Callas?*"

"Pino!" Gia said firmly, trying to calm him, but it was as if there had been an explosion inside of him.

"You think *I've* never seen Callas!" he went on. "Brother have I got a story for you!"

Pino drew up a chair and triumphantly sat down. He folded his hands on his belly and rocked back and forth on the chair.

"Where should I begin?" he mused to himself with a self-satisfied smile that both perplexed and intrigued Biscini. "Wait a minute!" Pino said, leaping up from the chair. "Christian, why don't you have dinner with us tonight?"

An unlucky grin appeared on Biscini's face.

"Ah, I'm afraid I've got plans this evening," he said. But Pino would not be stopped so easily.

"Christian, trust me. Break them! Dine with us and I'll tell you a story about Callas that I guarantee will leave you in tears. One that will simply amaze you! Trust me!"

"OK, Pino, don't you think you're laying it on pretty heavy?" Gia interrupted.

Pino didn't even hear her. His smile and enthusiasm were infectious. Biscini looked at the two of them, smiled and shook his head with a laugh. He really had no choice.

"Shall I bring red or white wine?" he asked with a smile.

CHAPTER FOUR

A Queen Without a Kingdom

IN THE EARLY 1960S, MARIA CALLAS was probably the most photographed woman in the world. Her face was on the cover of every major magazine world-wide and she was arguably more noteworthy for her chic, jet-setting lifestyle and penchant for high-fashion than for her art.

She was eventually replaced as the world's most photographed and talked about woman by the widow of a certain assassinated American President. Ironically, years later they would compete again in a different venue.

The Callas legend was at its zenith at a time when her career was in chaos. She found herself in the unique situation of being the highest-paid, most sought after singer in the world, who was banished from the opera world's greatest stages. She had become a queen without a kingdom. La Scala, Covent Garden and The Metropolitan Opera had all banned her as a result of her *diva assoluta* antics. Consequently, the number of her performances dwindled and every contract she signed to perform became headline news. Her popularity with fans was mania bordering on insanity, no opera singer before had ever generated the kind of passion among the public. Her romance with Greek shipping magnate Aristotle Onassis insured her of headlines of one sort and her professional behavior *(or unprofessional behavior)* insured her of headlines of another sort. On all fronts, she courted controversy and the press couldn't get enough. Even serious periodicals like Time Magazine did cover stories about her legendary prima donna antics, stories that bordered on tabloid journalism, but that sold millions of magazines. Her return to the Metropolitan Opera after an absence of over five years was certainly the kind of material that the public and the press simply couldn't resist.

The table was set for a king. There were ornate silver candlesticks, which were wedding gifts, unused until that evening. The Vaggi's finest stemware, one of the few indulgences Gia allowed herself adorned the table as well. And food, and food, and food! It was like Thanksgiving and Christmas dinner combined.

The first course was a wonderful multigrain soup that Gia had learned from Pino's mom. It was not really typical of their hometown, but not exactly foreign to it, either. Next, there was wonderful *cannelloni*, made with three meats, fontina cheese and pine nuts. It was one of Gia's specialties and had fast become one of Pino's favorite dishes. The main course was a huge red snapper that Pino was lucky enough to find after closing up the shop. Generally, all the best fish in the market were snapped up by the restaurants early in the day, but Pino had a good friend at the Fulton Fish Market.

At the conclusion of the dinner, only the skeletal remains of the once beautiful red snapper lay in the center of the table. It had proved no match for the appetites seated around it. Pino was seated at the head of the table, passing a selection of pastries to Biscini on his right. Gia was busy clearing empty dishes from the table, while Maria was casually sneaking more sips of wine than her father usually permitted.

"My friend with whom I was supposed to have dined tonight is a remarkable cook," Biscini stated, "and one generally does not break dinner plans with her, but tonight I'm glad I made an exception."

"Ah, so it was a lady friend you were supposed to dine with, eh?" Pino said with a smile and a wink at his daughter.

"Pino, my friend, I don't know what I found more extraordinary; this meal or your story. This was truly an evening I won't ever forget."

"Me, too," Pino said through a slightly inebriated grin.

"Singing duets against the backdrop of a world war," Biscini said grandly, "How romantic, no, more than romantic. It's almost epic!" He paused to compose himself, then went on. "How did she sound back then?"

Pino thought about the question for a few seconds and then labored over his choice of words for the answer.

"Uneven," he finally said. "She needed a lot more coaching. But, the range and the articulation and the passion! Oh, it was like a revelation! It was immediately clear that this was a once-in-a-lifetime talent."

Biscini took a bite of a mini-canoli and groaned with pleasure.

"You know," said Pino, "at the time, I was actually a bit more polished a singer than she was but she had extraordinary fire in her voice and..."

"Did you ever consider a career as a singer?" Biscini inquired innocently enough between bites.

"Consider it?" Pino raged.

"Now you've done it!" Maria said, despairingly.

"I was offered a contract by *La Scala!*" Pino declared.

"Really?" Biscini said, partly surprised, partly incredulous.

Pino turned to Maria. "Honey, go get my..." but before he could finish the sentence, she was off.

"I'm way ahead of you, Pop," she said leaving the table.

"Not to change the subject, Christian," Pino interjected, "but on a serious note, do you think it'll be hard to get tickets to see Callas?"

"The hardest! And the most expensive, I'd say! They'll probably be cueing up for days to get them."

Suddenly, Pino felt depressed. The thought that Callas would be returning had braced him so, that he had never even considered how difficult it might be to get tickets. What if he couldn't get tickets? That would be the ultimate disaster. There was a sick feeling overtaking Pino's stomach, and it wasn't the fish.

"Will you be going?" Gia asked pleasantly.

"I hope so. If I'm in the country," he replied.

"Do you travel a lot?"

"Not too much, but I don't get to New York as often as I used to."

"Oh?" said Pino, his surprise evident. "For some reason I thought you lived in New York."

"Heavens no!" said Biscini with a laugh, "I live in Milan. But I try to make it over here at least once a year. And once or twice a year, I visit my family in Greece."

"Christiano. You must try to be here to see Callas!" Pino implored him, "I'd love to go with you, and of course with Gia and Maria."

At that moment, Maria returned carrying a picture frame.

"That's Okay, Pop, don't worry about me," she said.

"Shut up, you!" he told his daughter. "It would really mean a lot to us."

"What's this?" Biscini asked, putting on his glasses to examine the object in the picture frame. Pino began to read the parchment in the frame, but he really didn't need to see it, for he had committed its contents to memory long ago.

"April 6th, in the year of Our Lord 1941. *Teatro Alla Scala* offers Giuseppe Vaggi the role of Rodolfo in four performances of Giacomo Puccini's *La Bohème!*"

"No kidding!" said Biscini, patting Pino on the back. "That's wonderful! How were your reviews?"

"Ha!" said Pino with a scowl. "Never made it."

"I don't understand," said Biscini.

"I was busy in Greece fighting the war," Pino replied.

"No! That's awful! And you never tried to pick it up after the war?"

"Well," Pino said reflectively, "I was laid up in the hospital for several months after the war and…" He pulled out his hearing aids and put them on the table. "Well, my hearing was pretty well shot, so…"

In shattering silence, Biscini looked at Pino and saw a deeply pained artist, an artist who had never had the opportunity to express himself. So much was immediately clear to him. He took a candy truffle and looked at it for a long moment.

"Do you sing at all anymore?" he asked.

"In church a little, and when I'm alone, sometimes when out with friends," admitted Pino.

"I'd really love to hear you sometime," Biscini said with a smile.

"Nothing would make me happier," Pino said, his eyes tearing up.

Biscini took a bite of truffle and again groaned with ecstasy.

"Gia, these truffles are divine," raved Biscini. "Don't tell me you made these, too!"

"No, I'm afraid not. Pino's sister Maria owns a little shop in the village; I'll take you there sometime."

"I see talent runs deep in this family," Biscini said wiping the corners of his mouth with his napkin. He then took another truffle, held it up and stared at it.

"You know," he said, "these are actually Maria's favorite."

Pino wore one of his patented confused expressions.

"Maria…*my sister?*" he asked.

"No, no, no.," Biscini laughed. "Callas, of course."

"Really? I'd never heard that," Pino said as he stood up to pour himself another espresso.

"Oh, yes. In fact, heaven forbid I visit Greece and don't bring her back some. Ah, I never hear the end of it."

Gia and Maria laughed. Pino did not. Something clicked inside his head and he put down his espresso, mid-sip. He looked at Biscini.

"How's that?" he asked in an exaggerated tone.

"How's what?" answered Biscini blankly.

Pino walked back to the table and sat down.

"You said, 'heaven forbid you forget to bring her back some truffles.' Is that correct?"

"That's right." Biscini continued, "Since she moved to Paris and hooked up with that blowhard Onassis, she rarely visits the old country these days. I've become her pipeline for all sorts of little *contrabando*, you know."

The table got very silent. All eyes fixed on Biscini.

"I'm sorry," Pino stammered. "Did you say…you mean…you *know* her?"

"Well, of course I know her. She's one of my very closest friends."

Silence. Stunned silence. Shock was written on the faces of Gia and Maria. Pino, on the other hand, looked angry. He stood up.

"Christian," he said gravely, "I have invited you into our house. You have broken bread with us. Please don't trifle with me, with *me* about something like this."

Now it was Biscini's turn to look shocked.

"I'm not trifling with you. Are you serious? Pino, please sit down and relax. We're having a lovely evening here."

Pino sat down, but his face was still grim.

"Everything I've told you is the absolute truth. I spoke to Maria only this afternoon. And I hope that I will have the opportunity to introduce you to her as well. So that you can tell her that magnificent story! I know she'll just love it!"

Pino was not satisfied. He stood up again and walked into the hallway. Biscini looked at Gia, who turned away in embarrassment.

"What are you doing, Pop?" Maria asked, breaking the tense silence.

Pino returned to the dining room with the telephone in his hand. He placed the phone down on the table and looked at Biscini.

"Call her," he said.

"What?" asked Biscini.

"If she's one of your closest friends, call her," Pino repeated.

"Pino!" Gia yelled, "Christian is our guest! How dare you…."

"If you don't call her, I don't believe a word of it." Pino said with venom.

"Pino! Christian, never doubted your story," Gia pointed out. "Now you're embarrassing our guest."

"That's all right, Gia." said Biscini, with a devilish smile. "It's perfectly understandable, your natural incredulity and that artistic temperament!"

With that, he picked up the receiver and dialed. He didn't need to consult an address book or anything. The entire time, he smiled and never took his eyes off of Pino. Once he had dialed the number, he waited a moment, then he handed the receiver to Pino.

"You talk to her," he said.

Pino stared at the receiver in Biscini's hand and started to perspire.

"It's ringing," Biscini said. "Come on, don't make her wait."

Pino took the phone and held it up to his ear, then suddenly slammed it down on the base.

"Was it her, Pop?" Maria wailed.

"I don't know. I got nervous and hung up before anyone answered."

"Ah, boo!" hissed Maria.

Pino looked sheepishly at Biscini, who just smiled like an old friend.

"Christian," Pino started, "I'm really so sorry. It just…"

"Say no more my friend," Biscini interrupted, "consider it forgotten. Don't worry, someday, hopefully soon, you'll get to tell your story to Maria yourself."

"Tell her?" said Pino enraptured.

"Of course!" said Biscini. "You must!"

Tears in his eyes, Pino hugged Biscini, and Gia joined the hug. Maria rolled her eyes and took the opportunity to grab another *cannolo*.

The date of March 19th was circled in red on the big calendar hanging on the wall behind the counter of Pino's shop. There was nothing more to signify how important the date would be in his life. He tried not to think about it too much, but somehow everything he saw and did in some way reminded him of it. It was Gia's impression that Pino looked and acted years younger after hearing the news of Callas' return.

The Callas performance meant a great number of things to Pino, but strangely enough, the one thing he considered of paramount importance was the chance for his daughter to see and hear her. Pino decided he would make one last ditch effort to bring little Maria into the fold at the Callas performance at the Met. Pino was convinced that seeing Callas live in the flesh would affect Maria in a way that she'd never known before. He was counting on it. Pino wanted both his sister and daughter to share the Callas experience with him and with each other. Although neither one seemed to share his enthusiasm about the occasion, he harped on them to trust him.

In fact, he became a one-man public relations machine in the weeks prior to the performance. Any poor soul who happened to make the mistake of looking at or commenting on one of the Callas pictures in his shop was subjected to a comprehensive lecture. Maria and Gia stood behind the counter just shaking their heads. Pino had become a man possessed. Before March, Gia mused, everyone in Little Italy would know about Pino's wartime exploits, whether they wanted to or not.

CHAPTER FIVE

TONY AND MILLIE

THE AMONTES WERE THE VAGGI'S closest friends and at least once a week they would dine together at one another's home. In addition, once each month they would go out to eat in a restaurant. The responsibility for choosing the restaurant would change each month. It was the one real indulgence that both families allowed themselves. The choices could be as modest as a new Chinese food place only a few blocks away in Chinatown or as extravagant as one of New York's temples of *haute cuisine*. Sometimes, they made road trips to New Jersey or Westchester, in which case the dinner would typically be reserved for a Saturday night.

Pino's favorite restaurant in New York was Asti's on 15th street. The venerable old family favorite served hearty, pricey, Neapolitan food and the best espresso in Manhattan. But the real reason Pino loved Asti's was that the waiters all sang. Whether it was a Neapolitan tune or a Verdi aria, there was always music at Asti's. Every inch of the restaurant's walls was covered with autographed photos of virtually every opera singer ever to grace the stage of the Met.

In the center of the dining room stood a beautiful Steinway concert grand piano, manned by an accompanist who was nothing short of a musical chameleon. He knew every popular aria and Neapolitan song from memory. He could easily transpose between keys and he even threw in a few Broadway show tunes (for the Philistines in the audience).

Patrons were welcome to approach the accompanist and suggest a tune. If he knew it or had the sheet music to it, the patron was welcome to sing. The stage was small but throughout the years some of opera's biggest names had stood upon it. There was even an unconfirmed rumor that Maria Callas herself sang there under an assumed name when she moved to New York shortly after the war.

It was also the first public stage that Pino had stood upon in decades. As was often the case at Asti's, the first time he got up to sing was on a dare. He was out with the boys and the wine had been flowing freely when the conversation turned to opera, specifically, to tenors. The debate was Franco Corelli versus Giuseppe di Stefano. Pino claimed to have no opinion on the matter, as he didn't particularly care for either of them, thinking both rather vulgar and lacking refinement.

"But di Stefano has a more beautiful sound!"

"But Corelli has more *squillo*!"

"But di Stefano can sing the *bel canto*!"

"But Corelli has more power!"

As the battle raged on, Amonte sat silently, seemingly lost in thought. He was conducting his own internal debate. He stared across the table at Pino sipping his coffee, looking bored, and decided it was time. It was time to push the chick out of the nest.

"I think," said Amonte, interrupting the debate, "in his prime, Pino was a better singer than either Corelli or di Stefano!"

The boys were astonished by his comment. Pino just smiled, embarrassed by the compliment.

"Go on, Pino!" Amonte encouraged. "We're all friends here. Get up there and sing something!"

Pino was horrified at the idea, and wanted to kill Amonte for suggesting it. But as he looked at their smiling faces, he realized that his inebriated friends would badger him to death if he didn't. He looked sternly at Amonte, who just smiled.

"Okay, maybe just one," Pino said, to the delight of his comrades. He stood up and slowly strolled over to the piano and huddled with the accompanist for what seemed like an eternity before finally coming to an agreement. The piece they settled on came as a complete surprise to his friends and within seconds, the entire restaurant was spellbound.

The opening arpeggios brought a solemn silence from the crowd, and Pino sang Schubert's lovely *Ave Maria* with a tonal beauty so lyrical, so tender that even the restaurant staff stopped to listen. He sang softly and passionately, in a manner that spoke of a bygone era, a true *tenore di grazie*. When he was done, there was hardly a dry eye in the house.

Applause exploded throughout the dining room and the kitchen. Patrons banged silverware against glasses and called out: *Biss! Biss!* And *Encore!* Pino politely bowed and returned to his table. He was trembling as his friends all hugged and congratulated him. Amonte just sat back in his chair and smiled, mission accomplished. Pino leaned over the table, took his face in his hands and kissed him on the cheek. His renaissance had begun.

From that day forward, Pino loved to sing at Asti's and the staff loved him too. He loved the adulation and the applause, but most of all he loved the fact that they called him Maestro. Gia would occasionally join Pino in a duet, but generally she preferred to be a spectator. On a typical evening, Pino would sing no less than two or three numbers to his devoted following. As a rule, he would always open with a Neapolitan song. It was usually not long in length, wide in range or taxing on his voice. He never did encores. However, after dinner, he'd always take a leisurely stroll over to the bar to look at the *grappas*, ostensibly to accept the compliments of the staff. They'd cheer him and beg him to do another song, but he would always refuse. It was the same ritual every night. He'd then return to the table, announcing the *grappas* for the evening and detailing all of the superlatives that the staff had hurled at him. Gia would egg him on insisting he do one more number, for his public. He'd reluctantly agree and everyone in the restaurant would cheer. He'd chat with the accompanist and work out the program. Invariably, he would perform an opera aria, almost always in Italian. Occasionally, some French snuck its way into the repertoire in the form of the *"Flower Song"* from *Carmen*, or *"Pourqoi Me Revellier"* from *Werther*.

One particular evening, Pino had worked up a very special number in honor of Antonio Amonte's wife Millie, whose birthday they were celebrating. Mille, or Milagros as she preferred to be called, was of Mexican descent and extremely proud of her heritage. She and Antonio had met on Ellis Island on the day that both of them arrived in America. They didn't see one another again until they both found themselves waiting tables in the same Bayside restaurant. At first, Antonio looked down his nose at the *Mexicana*, but when he learned that she spoke fluent English, French and a little Italian, in addition to her native Spanish, he was impressed.

Millie was quite stunning to look at with straight black hair flowing down to her waist, and perfect mocha-brown skin that was the envy of all her friends because she never needed any make-up at all. Their courtship had been a whirlwind. After only six months of dating, Antonio did what so many native New Yorkers never did; he visited the top of the Empire State Building. He brought Millie there with the specific intent of proposing to her, but when he got to the top, he almost forgot why he was there. The view was beyond extraordinary! It was literally breathtaking and he ran around like a little boy on the observation deck.

It was late afternoon on a crisp autumn day and to the south there was in incredible watercolor sunset of purple and orange. Antonio and Millie stood there, arm in arm, her head comfortably resting on his shoulder, peacefully staring at the natural wonder before them. Suddenly, Antonio remembered he had come here with a purpose and without looking at her, Antonio whispered in Millie's ear.

"How'd you like to come here every night about this time?" he asked. She just groaned with content satisfaction. Then he lowered the boom.

"I think, maybe, if we're planning to come here every night, people might start talking." She didn't stir. "I mean, who knows what they might say."

She turned to him with a slightly confused look.

"What I mean is, I think it would be a good idea if we got married."

Millie was shocked. Her little body was trembling visibly, then came the tears. She leapt into Antonio's arms crying like a baby. He took the reaction as a "yes".

Back on the bandstand, Pino was having a last minute conversation with the accompanist, going over some tricky rhythmic changes in the piece. It was an aria of sorts, from a Mexican zarzuela. Zarzuela was the Mexican equivalent of Italian opera, with a touch of operetta and a hint of American musical thrown in for good measure.

The piece was called *"No Puede Ser,"* and Pino had learned it specifically for the occasion. The endeavor was supposed to be a complete surprise to Millie, but it was taking too long to get off the ground and she sensed something was afoot.

"Please, tell me he's not going to embarrass me and sing 'Happy Birthday.'"

"Ha!" Gia laughed. "As if he could ever do something that conventional."

Without any further ado, Pino began the aria.

"No puede ser, esa mujer es buena,
No puede ser, una mujer malvada."

The piece was intensely dramatic and intensely Latin and Millie was totally unfamiliar with it. She loved it anyway. When Pino finished, the entire restaurant exploded into applause. Millie took a flower from the bouquet on the table and ran up to the rostrum and threw it to Pino. He caught it and playfully put it between his teeth. Leaving the stage, he gratefully accepted a kiss on the cheek from Millie who took him by the arm back to their table.

The relationship of the two couples was something wonderful. They never seemed to tire of each other's company, although, after a few drinks when the Italian began to flow freely and rapidly, Millie would sometimes tune out; it was too much work to keep up.

Ironically, it was Millie who had convinced them all that they needed to learn English and learn it quickly if they really wanted to fit it in their new surroundings. The neighborhoods where they lived were comfortable environments as almost everyone was an immigrant and Italian was, by far, the language of choice. Pino viewed the situation slightly differently. He didn't want to merely fit in. So, for him the decision was an easy one.

English was an ugly and difficult language to Pino, with more irregularities than all the romance languages combined. Even so, in less than a year, he had better than a working knowledge of it. It reminded him of German and he had studied more than his share of German during his days at the old conservatory. The language did not come as quickly to Gia or Antonio. To Millie, the linguist, the language came almost overnight. It took some time and work, and often an awkward situation or two, but eventually they all spoke very well, and they never forgot whom they had to thank.

Pino was in the throes of a heated conversation, drifting back and forth between English and Italian, as was his habit when emotional.

"Not only does he know her," he exclaimed, "when he's in Paris, he stays at her house!"

"Amazing!" said Amonte, shaking his head. "What are the odds, after all this time, that you'd get the chance to meet her again?"

"Antonio, please correct me if I'm wrong," Pino said in something of a boast. "Did I not say it from the very first time I heard her sing that she would be one of the greats?"

"You certainly did," Antonio said yawning, as though they'd been through this many times before.

"But Pino," Millie interjected, "Let me ask you this: How can you be so sure that this young girl whom you knew for only a few months, almost thirty years ago, is Maria Callas?"

"Believe me, *I* know," he responded gravely.

"Don't bother, Honey," Amonte said, in a definitive manner. "If he says it's her, then it's her."

"Do I detect a note of incredulity?" Pino asked.

"Absolutely not! But, let's face it, Pino. It's been a really long time. I saw her almost as many times as you did back then and I wouldn't know her today if she came up and bit me."

The women laughed at Antonio's joke but Pino did not.

"Precisely my point. You saw her. I *heard* her!" Tapping his index finger to his right ear, he said, "I remember."

Millie thought she'd try a little "girl-talk".

"So Gia," she asked, "are you a little jealous?"

"Of what?" Gia responded, dumbfounded.

"Of what? Oh, come on! Obviously, Pino had a big crush on her at one time, and now she's the biggest opera star in the world. I certainly would be."

"That's silly!" Gia said, with a dismissive hand wave. "Pino was simply awestruck by her talent. Who wouldn't be?"

"Yeah, that must have been it," Amonte said with a devilish grin, "because, let me tell ya, she sure was nothing to look at! A real homely-looking thing!"

"Really?" Gia asked, surprised.

"Absolutely! Fat, big nose, big thick glasses. What a mess."

"Now, wait a minute," Pino interrupted. "I think you're being a little hard on her. She was just a teenager after all."

"She was really that homely?" Millie asked, looking for a serious answer.

"Let me put it to you this way," Amonte explained. "She must have been for me not to give her a second look!" They all shared a laugh and the mood lightened. "Anyway," Antonio continued, "has this Biscini guy gotten the tickets yet?"

"Not yet, but he says pretty soon."

"Well you can count us in for two," Antonio said.

"Great!" Gia said, grabbing Millie's hand.

"You know, it's funny," Pino mused. "Suddenly, I've got friends and relatives coming out of the walls expecting tickets."

"Well, if this guy is really as close to her as he says he is, it should be no problem, right?" Amonte said.

"Of course not. It's just that, I'm sure he doesn't like to ask her for too much. You know."

A silence came over the table. Pino stared at his wineglass, swishing the contents around. In the distance, waiters were singing "Happy Birthday" and bringing out a cake to a patron. Millie turned around, horrified that she might be the intended recipient, but was relieved when the entourage stopped at another table to embarrass someone else. She decided she'd had enough of the silence.

"Pino, is that a polite way of saying there might not be enough tickets to go around?"

"No, no, no!" Pino protested. "I was just thinking, so many people are asking me for tickets, I mean, my cousins, Gia's cousins, Father O'Brien! And of course I want to take my closest friends," he said tapping Antonio on the arm, "and my sister, and Maria."

"I thought Maria hates the opera." Millie interjected.

"She'll thank me one day," Pino insisted.

"Don't bet on it!" Gia laughed.

"*Bravo*, Pino!" Antonio said raising his glass. "Here's to blind faith!"

"*Salute!*" they responded and drank up.

Just then, an Asti's ritual began. The lights went out and the entire dining room was illuminated only by candles. The pianist began to play the intro to the *Anvil chorus* from *Il Trovatore* and the entire staff tapped wine bottles with the silverware in perfect time to the music. First-timers to the restaurant were in awe of the spectacle, as several of the waiters put their chairs together and imitated the action of a Venetian gondola. The spaces between the tables served as the canals of Venice and the waiters were the *gondoliere*, singing as they passed by. It was a truly original experience. To some, it was a bit too "*touristico*," to others it was pure magic, but it was virtually impossible to remain unmoved by the scene.

The *Anvil Chorus* was a universally-loved crowd-pleaser, one that even the "bridge and tunnel" crowd could appreciate. The real tug on the heartstrings would follow. As the applause for the piece died down, the pianist quietly played the beginning of another piece, at first very softly, then gradually growing in volume until finally he crashed down a mammoth minor chord that brought the entire restaurant to attention. Then another. Then another. Then a soft *arpeggio* that resembled a butterfly drifting down from the sky to land on the piano next to him. A gentle waltz tempo slowly emerged from the cacophony and then a melody, sublime in its simplicity. To newcomers, what happened next was startling in its beauty. To regulars, it was a catharsis bordering on a religious experience. The entire staff and the vast majority of the patrons began to sing in harmony a chorus that they had known since childhood, but only recently had gained new relevance and deep emotional significance in their displaced lives.

"*Va' pensiero, sull'ali dorate; va ti posa sui clivi, sui colli,*"

Fly, thought, on wings of gold; go settle on the slopes, on the hills.

"*Ove olezzano tepide e molli, L'aure dolci del suolo natal!*"

Where, soft and mild, the sweet airs of our native land smell fragrant!

It was the chorus from Verdi's *Nabucco*, the song of the Hebrew slaves. The piece was by now a universal favorite and the unofficial national anthem of post-war Italy. It echoed the thoughts and dreams of immigrants everywhere. The tearful crowd sang with building passion.

"Del Giordano le rive saluta, Di Sion le torri atterrate...

Greet the banks of the river Jordan and Zion's toppled towers.

"Oh, mio patria, si bella e perduta! Oh, membranza si cara e fatal!

Oh, my country, so lovely and lost! Oh, remembrance so dear and despairing!

"Arpa d'or dei fatidici vati, Perche muta dal salice pendi?

Golden Harp of the prophets, why dost thou hang mute upon the willows?

"Le memorie nel petto raccendi, ci favella del tempo che fu!"

Rekindle our bosom's memories, and speak of times gone by!

"O simile di Solima ai fati traggi un suono di crudo lamento, o l'ispiri il Signore un concento che ne infonda al patire virtu!"

Mindful of the fate of Jerusalem, either give forth an air of sad lamentation, or let the Lord imbue us with the fortitude to bear our sufferings!

The power and the passion of the piece was unspeakable, and the entire restaurant sat in silent contemplation at its conclusion. Even a regular like Pino couldn't help but be moved. The piece held different meaning to each soul but it touched on a universal truth and a sense, not of sadness, but of melancholy; a melancholy that bound almost everyone who had left something of themselves behind in search of a better future.

Pino thought about Collagna, and he remembered singing this piece with his father some thirty years earlier at DeLuca's bar on the day they learned that the war in Ethiopia was over. It was the first time he'd ever gotten drunk and the only time he'd ever sung with his father. He looked around the table at his teary-eyed friends and smiled, but in his head he keep repeating to himself, like a mantra: "Just wait. Just wait. You'll see."

CHAPTER SIX

CAREFUL WHAT YOU WISH FOR

PINO FOUND HIMSELF SPENDING more and more time at the church. He had access to the organ any time he wished and frequently spent hours each day working on his playing and his conducting, or just sitting in the church alone with his thoughts. He remembered Maestro Ivaldi once telling him that there was no quieter place on earth than a church after Mass was over. Occasionally, a parishioner would enter, sit down and pray for a while. Sometimes they'd light a candle in memory of some deceased loved one, but for the most part Pino was alone with God. Although not a deeply religious person, he had recently developed what he liked to call an understanding with his maker.

Not surprisingly, Pino had a great deal of anger when he first lost his hearing. He had spent more than a few dark nights questioning and cursing God. He asked all the same questions that everyone else whom life had dealt a bad hand asked. *Why?* It took him a very long time to come to terms with a passive deity. He realized that he was lucky to be alive and that was something. And he did remember that there were those far less fortunate than him. He was grateful for Gia's love and for the blessing of fatherhood, and a healthy child. But somehow, it wasn't enough.

Why? There was that word again. Why did God give him this extraordinary talent, this ability to move people, to bring joy to their lives through his art, and then take it away so unmercifully? Many times he thought of Iago's soliloquy from *Otello*, "*Credo in un Dio Crudel*" (I believe in a cruel God!) and he tried his best not to harden his heart, but it wasn't easy.

The children from the choir were filing into the choir loft. He had to compose himself. He owed the children a tremendous debt of gratitude, one that he knew he couldn't repay in a lifetime. He knew in his heart that they were the reason he continued to love music. Not all of them, but the one or two in whose faces he saw real unabashed joy when they sang. It was unmistakable, and it filled his heart so that he could hardly speak. They were the moments that he thanked God for when he sat in the silence of the empty church. These were the moments that he lived for.

As the choir assembled and made their greetings and small talk amongst themselves, Pino paged through his sheet music trying to remember what piece they were working on. His head had been too full of Callas lately to remember.

"Okay. Why don't we start with a few warm-ups," he instructed, then proceeded to play a simple exercise on the organ, which they repeated. Before they had even gotten warmed up, an old priest clad all in black walked in. He strode over to the organ and stood behind Pino. He leaned forward and quietly whispered something in his ear, then walked away. Pino stopped playing.

"Hold on a minute, gang," he said, turning to the departing priest. "Father?" The priest stopped just before reaching the stairs and turned around with a quizzical look on his face. "I'm sorry, Father" Pino explained, "That's my bad ear. I didn't hear a word you said."

Some of the younger choir members giggled, only to be reprimanded by the older members.

"Oh, I'm sorry," the priest said. "You had a message. A mister Bee-ski-nee or something called."

Pino smiled.

"Did he leave a message?"

"Oh yes," the priest said, now straining to remember. "Oh, dear, what was it...oh yes. Very strange. He said: 'March 19th, 8pm, don't be late.' Do you understand it?"

Pino was silent for a moment. Then he laughed out loud as tears began to come to his eyes.

"Yes. It means, God is good after all!"

After choir rehearsal, Pino met Gia at the subway station and the two of them took the 1 Train to 66th street. They exited directly in front of the plaza for the brand new Lincoln Center for the Performing Arts which was to be completed the following year. A few weeks earlier they had watched on television as Mayor John Lindsay opened the New York State Theater; which would serve as the new home of the New York City Ballet. This evening, Pino was bringing Gia to the opening of the beautiful new fountain in the center of the plaza at Lincoln Center. Despite television crews everywhere that made it nearly impossible for the public to see, nothing could dampen their mood. Some politician led the crowd in a New-Year's-Eve-like countdown and when they reached zero, the fountain sprang to life! The crowd went wild, confetti and streamers flew and Pino kissed Gia.

After the crowd thinned out, they strolled around the plaza to take a look at Pino's real interest: the new Metropolitan Opera House! The theater was set to open in 1966 and would boast state of the art everything and with three elevators and a revolving stage it could house up to six different productions at once! Finally, he thought, modern technology being used for something important!

Dinner at *Casa Vaggi* was almost always the high point of the day for all parties lucky enough to be in attendance, yet after returning from the fountain, Pino, Gia and Maria sat around the dining room table with somber faces. Pino had hardly touched his dinner of *papardelle* with braised veal in a Barolo sauce; not a good sign at all. Gia knew that he would be difficult to talk to this evening so she waited for him to make the first attempt at conversation. It didn't come soon. The note he held in his hand from Biscini had cast a shadow over the evening.

"Only four tickets," Pino muttered. "I can't believe it."

Maria smiled when she realized it was Mr. Biscini's message about the opera tickets that was eating her Pop. Before she could make any clever remark, her mother, reading her mind, kicked her under the table.

"Pino," Gia pleaded, "look, it's not the end of the world. You're going!"

Pino let out a sigh that seemed to carry the weight of the world in it.

"But this is an event I wanted to share with *all* my family and friends," he said without looking up from the table.

"And you will! But they're just going to have to get their own tickets," she explained.

"Hey, Pop," Maria chimed in, "let me help. Why don't you give my ticket to one of your friends or Nauna?"

"Nice try, but Nauna doesn't want to go. You're going and that's that."

"I can't believe Nauna doesn't want to go to the opera! What kind of Italian is she? "

"It's a sore subject, Honey," Gia explained. "She's still angry at your father for not taking her to see Renata Tebaldi last year."

Pino let out another mammoth sigh, but this time Gia had had enough.

"Okay, the three of us and your sister, isn't that enough?"

"Yeah, I guess."

"I really don't believe you! You should be ecstatic. Look, it could be worse. Christian could be asking us to pay for the tickets!"

That set off a spark that changed Pino's complexion from pallid green to intense pink.

"Gia," he said slowly and deliberately, "please don't insult me in my own house."

Gia was trying and failing and it showed. It took a while, but Pino began to get a glimpse of the bigger picture.

"Maybe you're right," he said. "I guess I'm just nervous." It was as close as he would come to apologizing. "I think I'm gonna go lie down."

"That's sounds like a good idea," Gia said. "Maria and I will clean up in here, you go relax."

Pino got up and walked into the den. It was a big, dark room with a high ceiling and wood paneling that made it appear even darker. The room had a small fireplace that had probably been used fewer than five times in all the years that they'd lived there. There was a new plush, shag carpet that Pino loved to walk on barefoot, but not tonight. Tonight, he simply turned on his hi-fi and started to go through his record collection. He went back and forth through it several times unable to decide what he felt like listening to. He pulled out a Mantovani album and tried to remember when he had bought it. It didn't matter, he wasn't in the mood for it anyway. Next, his attention focused on a Mario Lanza record of Neapolitan songs. He pulled it out and read the notes on the cover. He'd probably done this a thousand times before. It wasn't what he wanted either.

He was getting ready to give up when he came upon a copy of *Lucia Di Lammermoor*. It was in the wrong place. All his opera recordings were in alphabetical order in the wall unit. He wasn't sure how this one managed to get out of place but it proved a welcome mistake. Pino owned three recordings of *Lucia*, all of them Callas performances. There was the 1953 version, conducted by Serafin, which featured her frequent partners Giuseppe di Stefano and Tito Gobbi. Next came the 1955 recording under the baton of Herbert Van Karajan, which again paired her with di Stefano. But the one he held in his hands was his favorite. The critics did not consider it her finest work, but it held special meaning to Pino. The recording was from 1959 and was the only stereo version of Callas' *Lucia*. But the real reason for Pino's particular passion toward this recording was the tenor, Ferrucio Tagliavini. Pino identified with Tagliavini because the legendary tenor was from Pino's "neighborhood." While not exactly from Collagna, Tagliavini was from Emilia-Romagna, and that made him special in Pino's mind; it made him *famiglia*. Pino had discovered Tagliavini at a critical point in his life. After the war, Pino had lost all feeling for Beniamino Gigli because of his political leanings and Pino was on the lookout for a new favorite, a new talent to idolize. Tagliavini possessed a pure, luxuriant, vocal tone that

Pino loved and had always tried to emulate. Not a large or particularly powerful voice, but one of extraordinary beauty. And he was a local boy! He fit the bill perfectly.

Pino placed the record on the turntable and dropped the needle. As the overture began to play, Pino took off his shoes and sat back in his reclining chair. He closed his eyes and let the music wash over him. Just as he was beginning to drift away to sixteenth century Scotland, someone tapped him on the shoulder and returned him to New York.

"I thought you might like a night cap," said Gia, holding a glass of *grappa* in her hand. Pino took the drink and Gia sat on the arm of the chair next to him.

"I don't deserve you," he said, taking a sip of the *grappa*.

"I know," Gia said with a wink. "What are you listening to?" she asked as she crawled onto the chair snuggly next to him.

"*Lucia*, Act One."

He took another sip of the *grappa* and Gia snuggled her nose up against the nape of his neck. The *grappa* and the warmth of Gia's body made him tingle all over.

"Do you want me to get you a blanket?" she asked him.

"No. I'm perfect, just like this," he answered completely oblivious to the reasons he was so angry only a few minutes earlier. "We should do this more often," he said in a flirtatious manner. Gia just smiled and threw an arm across his chest.

A thought came to Pino. It was something that he had wondered about often but never really discussed. He was always too wrapped up in his own world, his own problems, but at that moment of near perfect bliss, he could only think of Gia.

"Honey, why did you give up singing?" he asked tenderly. She didn't answer. "Seriously, how come?" he persisted.

"Because I knew there could only be one in the family, you."

"Yeah, but after the war, I had no chance. Why didn't you continue?"

"It never made me as happy as it made you. And when you returned, all I wanted to do was take care of you. I had no time to worry about singing."

She was so selfless that Pino nearly cried. He often forgot just how selfish he was capable of being. Gia was an extraordinary woman, far better than he deserved. He said that often, but only occasionally did he realize it was true. He rolled over and kissed her. As he did, she started singing softly along with the record.

"*Io di te memoria viva sempre, o cara, sempre.*"

I shall always cherish my vivid memories of you, my dearest, always.

Pino kissed her again.

"This is where Edgardo tells Lucia that he has to leave her. And she responds that 'even though we may be apart, you can always hear my loving sighs echoing in the wind.' You know, it's funny, but that part always reminds me a little bit of her."

"Who?" Gia asked.

"Callas."

Gia leaned very close to him and whispered in his ear.

"Naaaaah, you never had a crush on her!" she laughed. Then she smiled and poked him on the nose with her finger. "I'm going to sleep," she said, and kissed him. "Don't stay up too late."

"Don't worry, I won't. *Buona notte.*" Pino said.

He took another sip of the *grappa* and snuggled deeper into the chair, his eyes closed. He wished he'd said yes to that blanket.

Within moments, he was deep in sleep.

In his dream, a dark midnight blue mist filled his unconscious eyes, a thick velvety mist, moist and damp, like the moors in some Scottish romance novel. He tried to wipe it away with his hand but it was no use, it went on and on, and the more he cleared the more appeared. He moved forward, the soft moss beneath his feet gave a little with each step. Through the mist he could make out the silhouette of trees. They were all around him, tall and foreboding; pine trees reaching up toward the sky obscuring even the moonlight.

He continued on through the darkness not knowing what he was searching for, but certain he'd know when he saw it. Oddly, he wasn't the least bit frightened. He told himself that this forest was no different than the forests back in Collagna, and he was never frightened there. The air was cold but his body was warm and his heart beat rapidly in anticipation, though he knew not of what. The darkness that surrounded was thick as black ink and he couldn't see his footfall in front of him, but suddenly he noticed the ground beneath his feet change. It was less soft, more firm and trodden upon. He sensed he had come to some kind of path, and if he squinted hard, he thought he could see a faint light coming through the trees ahead. He made for the light as quickly as he could, and as he drew nearer, it grew brighter and more distinct. Soon he could see the path before him as it wound through the woods. It was indeed a footpath, narrow but well-traveled.

In the distance, he thought he could hear voices, so he stopped to listen. They were faint but audible, although he couldn't make out what they were saying. As he came closer, the voices got louder and he could definitely tell that there were two women speaking.

They were just around the bend now, in a small clearing in the woods. He moved slowly and quietly so as not to disturb or frighten them. When he reached the clearing, he felt a chill throughout his body. Not a chill of fear, but a chill of recognition. Before him in the clearing stood two women in antique English formal dresses, probably two hundred years old, he guessed. They were standing next to a huge gothic-style fountain, which was cracked and practically in ruins. The entire scene was bathed in a bluish-grey moonlight that created a surrealistic, ghostly glow. The women themselves might have been phantoms given their dress and the eerie surroundings. They stood on the opposite side of the fountain and had not seen him yet. He took care not to be noticed. Stealthily he moved out of the woods toward them, keeping the fountain between the women and himself. He had yet to get a look at their faces but he sensed that one woman was probably the servant of the other, by her manner of speaking and the attending nature of her movement. He reached the edge of the fountain and got down upon one knee to listen.

"Why do you look about so fearfully?" asked the servant girl.

"That fountain, ah! I never see it without shivering. You know the tale: a Ravenswood, mad with jealously, stabbed his sweetheart here and the poor girl fell into the water, which became her tomb. I have seen her ghost!"

His heart was racing. The tale was horrifying, yet familiar to him. But, why? *Ravenswood?* The women continued speaking but his mind was swimming. This story...this fountain...what was it? He leaned forward to gaze into the fountain, expecting it to be long dry, but it was not! There was water at the bottom. He leaned further and saw the moonlight reflecting in the pool and then...his jaw dropped. He saw his own reflection in the water. But it wasn't *his* reflection! It was his former self. In the reflection, he saw the strong, virile young man he had been before the war. The face had no lines, the hair, thick and black. The clothes ...*what?*

He sat back, away from the fountain and for the first time took notice of his own dress. It was a nobleman's hunting outfit from the sixteenth century with high black leather boots, wool knit pants, a gentleman's waistcoat. His astonishment was not yet complete, for as he uttered his first syllable of surprise, the women turned around, alerted to his presence. Seeing him, the young girl instantly excused herself and hurried away into the woods, leaving him alone with her lady. The lady seemed distant, cold, as though she regretted this meeting, or it was somehow painful.

Once again, an overwhelming sense of familiarity struck him, like all of this had happened before. Then the other shoe dropped. The lady turned toward him and for the first time he saw her face, *it was Callas!* His heart stopped. She was so young and beautiful. She couldn't have been more than twenty. She turned away from him and slowly walked toward the fountain.

"Is my suffering not enough? Do you want me to die of fright?" she cried out in recitative. He was dumbfounded and fumbled for words, when something dawned on him. He recognized what she had just said. He'd heard it before.

"Banish all other feelings save love from your heart; a nobler, holier vow than any other is pure love, only love."

"Lucia!" he said in a moment of epiphany, more ringing to him than had he seen the burning bush himself. "Lucia!" he repeated, "Ravenswood!"

Callas turned to him and he heard music inside his head.

"Do as I say," she sang.

"What?" he replied.

"Give way to love," she continued, as music swelled up all around them, overwhelming them. He knew the next line was Edgardo's, but he couldn't remember it. He hummed along with the familiar melody until Lucia's return.

"E tua son io."

And I am yours!

Then like a man possessed, he hurled himself at her and took her in his arms. She quaked and trembled with passion. Their lips almost touching, they began a ravishing duet.

"Ah, soltanto il nostro foco spegnera di morte il gel."

Ah, only icy death can quench our passion.

"Ai miei voti amore invoco, ai miei voti invoco il cielo"

I call upon love, I call upon Heaven to witness my vows.

Then he pushed her away.

"Separaci omai conviene."

We must part now.

"Oh, parola a me funesta! Il mio cor con te ne viene."

Oh, how I dread those words! My heart goes with you, Edgardo.

And my heart stays here with you Lucia!

"Ah, talor del tuo pensiero venga un foglio messaggero, e la vita fuggitva di speranze nutrio."

Ah, sometimes if you think of me, and send a letter, fresh hopes will fortify my fleeting life.

"Io di te memoria viva sempre, o cara, serbero."

I shall always cherish vivid memories of you dearest.

Then Lucia, with newfound strength began her breathtaking aria. As she did, she strode about the fountain, with Edgardo following close behind.

"Ah, verranno a te sull'aure I miei sospiri ardente, udrai nel mar che mormora l'eco dei miei lamenti."

Ah, on the breeze will come to you my ardent sighs, you will hear in the murmuring sea the echo of my laments.

"Pensando ch'io di gemiti mi pasco e di dolor, spargi un'amara lagrima su questo pegno allor."

When you think of me living on tears and grief, then shed a bitter tear on this ring.

Edgardo repeated the strains of her beautiful lament and took her hand as she continued.

"Il tuo scritto sempre viva la memoria in me terra."

Your letters will always keep your memory alive in me.

"Caro!" he cried, *"Io parto!"*

I must go!

"Addio!" she cried, rushing back into his arms.

"Rammentati, ne stringe il ciel!" He implored her.

Remember, Heaven itself has joined us.

"Edgardo!"

"Addio!" They cried out together, in shatteringly beautiful high notes, lost in a longing and forlorn embrace. He fell to his knees and buried his head beneath her bosom crying. Then, tears in her eyes, Maria lifted his chin and wiped away his tears. She smiled a sad smile and ran off into the distance leaving Pino alone.

Suddenly, deafening applause could be heard, seemingly from out of nowhere. Pino looked around to see footlights and a proscenium and an orchestra pit. Beyond the orchestra, a house full of adoring fans, on their feet. Pino smiled as the curtain fell, and the entire scene faded to black.

CHAPTER SEVEN

Quando Le Seré Al Placido

P INO RARELY WATCHED TELEVISION at night. The news usually
made him think too much and his mind, racing with images, wouldn't let
him sleep. For a baker who needed to wake up at 4:00am daily this could
prove deadly. But when he caught the tail end of a story about Maria Callas on
the evening news, he desperately wanted to know what it was about. His first
thought was one of horror; she was canceling! He couldn't bring himself to
accept that possibility. He called Biscini but he got no answer. His fever
growing, he called Amonte to see if he'd seen the story on the news, but neither
Antonio nor Millie were home. With a heavy sigh, Pino decided to stay up late
to watch for the story on the late news. After dinner he took a quick nap, but
just to be sure he'd be awake, he set his alarm clock.

He couldn't sleep. All kinds of worst case scenarios flew before his eyes as
he lay in his recliner with a half empty bottle of grappa on the table next to him.
Maria and Gia said goodnight and he politely but distantly nodded. He was on
his own now.

The 11:00pm news on WCBS opened with a tease of the story: "fans line
up for tickets to see opera star Maria Callas." Pino didn't quite get it. *Where were
they lining up?* This performance had been sold out for months. Was she
appearing somewhere else? A press conference? The story was the last one of
the evening and the twenty five minute wait nearly put Pino in his grave. At last,
the reporter explained that standing-room tickets for Maria Callas' appearances
at the Met next week were going on sale Sunday morning. *But this was Thursday
night!* Unbelievably, fans were queuing up with blankets and thermos bottles on
Thursday night to insure getting tickets on Sunday morning! Pino was
dumbstruck. He'd always thought of himself as Callas' biggest fan but he
realized he wasn't even close. These people worshipped her! They were going to
sleep on the street for three nights just to buy standing room to hear her! The
thought brought a tear to his eye. There really were people here in this country
that appreciated her after all. In an age ruled by Maria's Beatles and Rolling
Stones, there were still some left that cared enough to sacrifice for art.

Amonte was right. This really was the hottest ticket in town. Pino suddenly realized just how lucky he was to have even four tickets, and how lucky he was to have met Christian Biscini. It had been a while since Pino had felt so lucky.

March 19th
6:30 PM

In the large ornate mirror that Pino's mother had bought them for their first wedding anniversary, Pino was trying his best to tie his bow tie. He'd already showered twice and shaved more carefully than he knew himself capable. However, there didn't appear to be an anti-perspirant on earth strong enough for him this evening. He wanted to get a haircut but simply didn't have the time, so he'd just have to apply a bit more styling cream than usual to keep everything in place. *Where the hell was Antonio? He should have been here a half-hour ago.*

"I'll kill him if he's late," Pino swore.

He stopped fumbling with the tie for a moment and cracked his knuckles. He took in a deep breath and held it, then slowly let it out.

Suddenly, he was startled by a tapping at his window. He was on the second floor. Who could be tapping? He pulled back the curtain to see two pigeons sitting on the ledge. They appeared to be deep in conversation so Pino didn't want to disturb them, and he slowly replaced the curtain. They lightened his mood and he returned to his bow tie. He had one that he could simply put around his neck and hook together, but it never looked as elegant as a real bow tie, and tonight he would accept nothing short of perfection.

Gia walked in dressed in a black strapless gown with a fur wrap. It made her look like a movie star, Pino thought. She watched him struggle with the tie for a few seconds before commandeering the situation.

"Here, let me," she said. In a flash she'd made a perfectly balanced knot. Pino examined it in the mirror for a second, pronounced it perfect, then kissed her hands.

"Is Maria almost ready?" he asked, pensively.

"She was ready a little early and decided to run to the florist to pick up the roses for you."

"She is a good kid, you know that," he said proudly. "Mark my words, one day she'll thank me for tonight."

Gia just laughed and shook her head. "Keep telling yourself that!" Clearly, she had other thoughts on the subject, but it was no use, her husband was a man with a mission.

"Oh, before I forget," she said, "Christian called. He said if we could come by a few minutes early, he'd love to have a glass of champagne with you."

Pino nodded his head, pleased. "Now that sounds like a great idea. Let me tell you something, that guy has class!"

"He certainly does," agreed Gia, helping Pino with his jacket, then brushing away any lint from the sleeves. "Don't forget to thank him for getting those extra tickets for Antonio and Millie."

"Already did, but you can rest assured, I will again! I owe him plenty!" said Pino with a laugh.

They looked together at one another in the mirror for one last inspection.

"We sure make a handsome couple," Pino said with a wink. He tried to give her a kiss but she pulled away.

"Later! You'll mess up my lipstick!" she protested.

From downstairs they could hear a door slam shut.

"I'm back!" said Maria. "You guys ready yet?"

With a tremendous sigh, Pino nodded.

"*Andiamo?*" he asked, offering an arm for his wife to take.

"*Sì,*" she proudly replied, taking it.

"P.S.," Maria called out, "I got you a bag of roasted chestnuts too, Pop."

Pino beamed.

"That's my girl!"

CHAPTER EIGHT

IT ALL BEGAN TONIGHT...

TWO CABS PULLED UP TO THE CURB on the corner of Broadway and Fortieth Street. Like a movie star at a premiere, Pino disembarked the taxi followed by his entourage, and what an entourage! One cab carried Pino, Gia, Maria and Mama Vaggi. The other carried Antonio and Millie, and Pino's sister, Maria. Pino didn't say a word for the duration of the ride, he just went over again and again in his head what he'd say when he finally saw her.

In front of them stood the vast, magisterial facade of the venerable old Metropolitan Opera House. The theater that had been the sight of some of opera history's greatest successes: Caruso, Gigli, Tetrazzini, Pons, would tonight make history once again. Pino hoped that some history might be made backstage, as well, after the performance. He had weeks to decide just what he wanted to say when he finally saw her again, but he still wasn't sure. He had rehearsed several brief speeches in front of the mirror but they all seemed phony and stiff. So at the last second, he decided to wing it. He'd allow the moment to speak for itself. He also wondered just what she'd say to him when he told her who he was! The anticipation was making him glow.

The sidewalk in front of the theater was mobbed with hundreds, maybe even thousands of people, far more people than the house could hold. The calls for tickets were everywhere, obscene amounts of money were being offered, left and right.

"Anyone selling tickets? Anyone selling tickets?" cried out a young man directly into Amonte's face. But there appeared to be nobody selling. They pushed their way through the stagnant crowd toward the doors.

"Man, what a spectacle!" Antonio said with a laugh. "Did you ever see anything like it?"

"There's never been anything like it," Pino said.

As they stumbled into the lobby, exhausted from fighting the crowd, they quickly moved to the far right side to catch their collective breath. They hadn't been there more than a minute when a figure in a spectacular tuxedo with a white silk scarf came running toward them, waving both hands in the air: Biscini.

"Maestro Vaggi!" he called out as he leapt into Pino's arms. The two men hugged like small children, their joy unspeakable. As they separated, Biscini addressed the crowd.

"*Ciao tutti*! Are we all ready?" he said with an enormous smile. Then looking at Pino's mother, he put a hand on his heart.

"*Aspetta! Un atimo, per favore. Ma, qui e questa bella donna?*" He walked over to Pino's mother and kissed her hand. "*Piacere signora. Enchante. Encantada. Sono Christiano Biscini.*"

Pino's mother rolled her eyes.

"Pino, does he always lay it on this heavy?" she said, getting a laugh from the crowd and a big hug from Biscini.

"How about some champagne?" Pino suggested, gesturing toward the bar.

"Ah! I almost forgot!" Biscini said putting a hand to his forehead. "A little change in plans."

Pino couldn't conceal his disappointment.

"No champagne?" he said sheepishly.

"There's no time for that," Biscini said with a wave of his hand, "Maria wants to meet you right away."

They all gasped, and Pino turned white as a ghost.

"What? Now? But...I haven't thought about what I'm going to say to her."

"Nonsense!" Gia insisted. "What are you worried about?"

"Yeah, you've had thirty years to prepare." Amonte joked.

"Come on, she's waiting," Biscini said with urgency. Pino licked his lips and wiped his brow. He was stalling and he didn't even know why. It was all happening too fast for him.

"Can I bring the family?" he asked.

"Of course. Bring everyone, but let's hurry!"

The backstage area at the Met before a performance resembled a kind of wonderfully bizarre circus. There were overweight stagehands in tee shirts smoking cigarettes, singers in 19th century costumes warming up in the hallway or the bathrooms, nervous-looking wardrobe personnel running to and fro with costumes draped over their shoulders and needle and thread in hand. The oddest feature about the scene was that there appeared to be two separate and distinct armies at work. One was moving at a frenetic, almost manic pace, urgency written on their faces. The other group seemed to be doing nothing at all. The vast majority of this group appeared to be on one big coffee break. Pino was surprised to see so many people standing around, apparently with nothing to do, so close to curtain. It provided a nice distraction from the showdown toward which he was headed.

The whole group walked down a long narrow hallway past a group of tuxedo-clad musicians carrying their instruments in the general direction of the stage. Pino was starting to get the warm thrill of nerves and anticipation that he used to feel many years ago before a performance. It was a feeling he hadn't known for some time and he welcomed it with a pleasant sense of nostalgia. Biscini was practically running at this point, anxious to get to their appointed destination as quickly as possible. Pino wondered: why the big rush? But when they reached the dressing room area it became immediately clear. If the backstage area had been a circus, then the dressing area was the A train at rush hour. Costumed singers warming up, prop handlers, and assorted legitimate employees were fighting to pass through the sea of well-wishers and members of the press that filled the hallway outside Callas' dressing room.

"This isn't going to be easy," Amonte said, staring in disbelief at the mob before them.

"Relax," Biscini assured them. "This is nothing. Just stick close to me."

"Sounds like a hell of a party," commented Mama Vaggi.

"Oh, it's just her handlers, the press, various maggots and parasites. They all come out of the woodwork whenever Maria performs."

Biscini looked at Pino and took his hand.

"Ready?" he asked.

Pino nodded, clutching his roses.

Biscini pushed through the crowd like freight train. His general disregard for the well-being of the hangers-on allowed him to pass through the crowd with relative ease. Mama Vaggi was particularly impressed. When they reached the door to the dressing room, Callas was nowhere in sight. The crowd was simply too dense. But Biscini wouldn't be denied, and suddenly inexplicably, he started to sing.

"Ma-ri-a! I've just met a girl named Maria! And suddenly that name will never be the same for me!"

The crowd went silent and parted for Biscini like the Red Sea before Moses. At the far end of the room, the reason for all the adulation sat placidly at a vanity table. Much like a queen surrounded by her loyal subjects, she sat in a long silk dressing gown, chatting amiably with the adoring hordes around her. She was already in full makeup, looking very much the vivacious Roman Diva she would momentarily become onstage. This was not the teenage girl Pino had known. He didn't see the shy, self-conscious young girl he'd sung with, flirted with, and maybe was in love with. He saw a mature woman, a worldly woman. Moreover, he saw a diva, a legend. Watching her, he realized that all the qualities she once had lacked: confidence, grace, beauty, intelligence, and wit, she now possessed in abundance. These qualities combined to create unspeakable charisma.

He suddenly felt very insignificant in her presence. He hoped to find in her eyes a hint of memory, of *simpatico*. He wished he could speak to her alone, not in front of all these jackals. At this point, he wasn't even certain that he would get a chance to speak to her at all. There were so many people and only so much of her to go around.

At the sound of Biscini's voice, a noticeable change came over her, on her face and in her eyes. Gone was the suave, confident sophistication that adorned her features only seconds before. In their place was a glow, an exuberance, an almost girlish look of excitement. One word from Biscini had brought about this incredible transformation. Pino was absolutely stunned, and for just a moment, he saw the Maria he once knew. She may have gained all the celebrity that her position bestowed upon her, yet for that one moment, the insecure little girl in the shabby dress and cheap sandals managed to bubble to the surface, if only for a second. But something was missing. The sincerity and honesty that once shaped everything about her, now seemed gone.

"Christian!" she cried out. He dashed up to her and kneeled on one knee in elaborate fashion. Then he took and kissed her hand. "You are really too much!" she said, grinning from ear to ear.

"Maria, darling," he said without the slightest hesitation, "I have brought someone with me tonight, whom I'd like you to meet."

Callas suddenly displayed just a hint of uneasiness. She appeared excited, even nervous and the entire crowd appeared to be on pins and needles, anxious to hear more. Biscini stood up and beckoned for Pino to come forward.

"May I present, my good friend, Maestro Giuseppe Vaggi."

Pino rushed forward with the roses. Callas extended a hand and he took it in a warm embrace.

"*Piacere, Signora. Molto piacere.* These are for you," he said in the most dignified tone he could gather up.

"Oh, they're lovely!" she answered in a slightly affected voice, taking the roses and placing them on the vanity. "You do me too much honor. But, I do thank you."

"And this is, of course, *La famiglia Vaggi,*" said Biscini, with a wave of his hand.

They smiled, waved, nodded, and bowed heads nervously.

"My, my," said Callas, "but you certainly travel with quite an entourage."

The crowd laughed and Callas acknowledged their laughter.

"Well, tonight is a very special occasion," Pino said, removing his handkerchief and dabbing his temples.

"Yes, it is indeed!" she agreed.

"*Signora*, there's so much I want to tell you. So much to discuss!"

But Callas raised a hand, like *Turandot*, cutting him off.

"*Signore* Vaggi," she said with an impetuous grin, "before you begin, I have a confession to make." She paused and took Biscini's hand. "When Christian called me and said there was someone whom I simply had to meet, I was obviously very curious. But I'd never seen him so excited! He was acting like a young child who knew a secret."

Biscini blushed and bashfully looked away.

"Well," she continued, "it took a lot of prying on my part, but finally I convinced him to share his little secret with me."

Pino held his breath.

"So you know?" he asked softly.

"Know what? What is it?" shouted a rude member of the press in the crowd. Callas threw a sidelong glance of disapproval that dizzied him and sent an icy chill through the crowd. The reporter looked away, in mortal shame. Pino was slightly unnerved by the power that Callas seemed to exert. She took a second to compose herself, then continued.

"My friends, the story that *Signore* Vaggi related to my friend Christian is one of the most wonderful and terrible stories I've ever heard. It concerns a time in my life that I very rarely discuss. Indeed, it moved me greatly."

The quiet in the room was monumental. The entire world was silent. Her ability to tell a story was unparalleled and her audience spellbound.

"It seems that during the war years while I was living in Athens, *Signore* Vaggi was a soldier in the Italian army stationed there. Well, I don't think I need to tell you that this was one of the blackest periods in my life. We were starving and frightened. My sister and I often had to walk many miles only to wait on long lines for food rations. My memories of that time are very spotty. In fact, I have, either consciously or unconsciously, chosen to black a great many of them out from my memory altogether."

She paused again, this time to take a drink of water.

"I was a member of the National Opera by the time I was sixteen, and had sung many roles to generally favorable notices." Her face darkened and her voice lowered. "Then the Germans came. The opera was shut down. I was forbidden to sing in public. They even put a curfew into effect and I was forbidden to so much as vocalize after sundown. With Nazi soldiers marching down my street night after night, we lived in constant terror. There were stories of people disappearing in the middle of the night never to be heard from again. It was, as I said...the blackest period of my life."

She appeared overcome with emotion and Biscini rushed to her side and took her hand.

"Maria, darling, you've got a performance to do, if you'd rather not talk about it..."

"No!" she said defiantly. "I must!"

The crowd gasped and Pino was as spellbound as the rest of them, listening to the story as though it was the first time he'd heard it, not as though he'd actually lived it. One thing was certain to him: in Callas' story, there was no mistaking who the star was going to be.

"My friends, it was at this blackest of times that our fates changed dramatically! Perhaps it was divine Providence or simply a stroke of luck, but the Nazis eventually handed over the occupation of Athens to the Italian army, and while all the restrictions remained in effect, it was clear from the start that the penalties for breaking them would not be as severely...as brutally, enforced."

Mama Vaggi was completely lost and looked around shaking her head in confusion, but Callas pressed on with her story, fire in her eyes.

"I was never one to shrink from adversity. Rather, I have always tried to use it to my advantage. I was certain I could use the Italian's passion for music to help our situation. So, my sister and I would regularly perform impromptu recitals on the street corner, much to the delight of the homesick Italian soldiers. We were rewarded with pasta, dried fruit, and the occasional bottle of wine, which at that time, I might add, was quite a luxury, indeed."

They all smiled and some applauded her ingenuity.

"But, I digress! Around that time, that I gathered up the nerve to resume my nightly vocal exercises, in strict defiance of the curfew, mind you. However, unbeknownst to me, one Italian soldier..." She smiled and gestured at Pino, who blushed. "...had the audacity, the temerity to defy his own curfew in order to sit in the dark of an alleyway next to our house...just to hear me sing!"

The crowd cheered and applauded Pino, and he nodded modest acknowledgment.

"And now," she said grandly," thanks to my dear friend Christian, we have, at long last, been introduced."

The entire crowd burst into applause and cheers. Biscini bowed and Pino smiled, but as the crowd saluted him, his smile slowly began to fade into a look of mild confusion.

Introduced? he thought. He looked at Biscini who was attending Callas. He waited for her to continue with the story, but shortly, it became evident that she had said all she was going to say. Pino didn't understand.

"But wait," he said, interrupting the revelry, "tell them the rest!"

Callas just looked at him with a smile.

"Finish the story!" he implored her.

"But that is the end," she said. "We've finally met. Here. Tonight."

Pino was baffled and it showed.

"But we've already met!" he insisted.

"We have?" Callas said, innocently as a schoolgirl.

"Of course we have," Pino went on. "You know very well."

Callas shook her head in confusion, but still smiling warmly, except for her eyes. Her eyes were out of sync. They were not the eyes of the grand diva at all. They were cold, penetrating eyes that looked right through Pino to a distant past and place which no one else could share.

"I'm afraid I don't understand?"

"Oh, come on!" Pino said with marked incredulity. "We met several times. We went for walks. We sat in the park and talked! And, what about your two *'cousins'* remember?"

"But I met so *many* soldiers and it was all *so* long ago," Callas said apologetically.

Pino was shocked.

"I don't believe this!" he said, his voice on the very of a yell. "You must remember singing on your balcony, right?"

"Of course I do!"

"Then you *must* remember! We sang together!"

But her face was a blank smile. Pino was panic stricken. He looked at his family, who were clearly embarrassed by the situation. He began to pace, unwilling to admit defeat.

"*Signore*, please, you must understand," Callas said in a voice that would have melted even the coldest heart. "It was a very trying time for us, and there's so much that I simply can't recall."

Pino stood frozen. Her words cut him like a razor, the wound at first invisible, then just a red line, then gushing blood. Suddenly, a memory emblazoned itself across his racing mind. He looked like he had just found the final piece of an elaborate jigsaw puzzle. Like Calaf solving Turandot's riddles he confidently walked toward Callas.

"Wait." He said slowly and methodically. "The last time I saw you, you were singing for the soldiers, for the captain. You remember the captain, I bet," he said sardonically. "You carried a pail to fill at the fountain. Remember? But, as you ran off you stumbled and dropped…the pail."

As his voice trailed off mid-sentence, he thought he detected a slight yawn emerging from Callas. Something clicked inside his head. He closed his eyes and nodded as if suddenly it was all perfectly clear to him. Somewhere in the back of his mind there was a scream creeping forward from the depths, trying to get out. It took all the *sangfroid* he could muster to contain it.

"I really am very, very sorry, but I simply don't remember," Callas said, putting the final nail in the coffin of Pino's dream. As he stood in silence, he thought: *A performance. Always a performance, and this one is now over. The conquest, complete.*

She took his hand in her own and caressed it. But it was an empty, emotionless caress, much like the way she might have petted the head of a dog. *There, there, Pino. Good boy. Now go lie in the corner and don't bother me any further.*

To this we've come? he thought.

"Well, that's all right," he said, defeated. "It wasn't important anyway."

Gia took his arm.

"Madam Callas," she said, "we don't want to take up any more of your time. Thank you very much. It was a great honor to meet you."

"My dear, the honor was all mine. And please, all of you must come backstage to greet me after the opera as my guests." Callas said turning to one of her handlers, "Albert, darling, please put them all on the guest list, would you?" The lackey nodded and dashed off to do her bidding. "But now, I really must get ready, so all of you must fly away." Callas commanded. "I'll see you afterwards."

The first performance of the evening had concluded and the crowd slowly filed out of the dressing room. Callas turned back to the vanity and touched up her makeup. As she did, she watched Pino in her mirror, out of the corner of her eye. Before he reached the door he stopped. Callas was slightly alarmed, but didn't allow it to show. For some reason, Pino was holding his ear, and then he seemed to be fiddling with something in his hands. Whatever it was, she couldn't tell, but he appeared to tap it several times, then place it in his ear. The last thing she saw was Gia draping an arm over Pino's shoulder as the two disappeared into the bustling crowd.

CHAPTER NINE

TOSCA

THE ROLE OF TOSCA is one of the repertory's most coveted, not merely because it offered the soprano one of the most beautiful and celebrated arias in all of opera: *Vissi D'arte,* but also because of the intensely personal drama at the center of the role. Maria Callas' undisputed mastery of the role both vocally and dramatically was the stuff of legend. Seeing her in the role had been Pino's most cherished dream since he'd heard her sing the aria years ago in Athens, but now, as he entered the auditorium of the famous opera house, the performance held little appeal to him.

The embarrassing display backstage was already a distant memory to his family, replaced by wonder and awe as an usher took their tickets and led them to their seats *in the very front row.*

"Jesus Christ!" Amonte said, too loudly for his wife's taste and she let him know with an elbow to the ribs.

"Oh, my God, Pop! These are the most incredible seats in the world!" Maria said, unable to restrain herself. They sat down and drank in the glory of the evening all around them, gazing upward at the magnificent proscenium and the famous Golden Horseshoe of the Met balcony.

Unfortunately, Pino would not allow himself to relax. He sat silently, stewing in his own world. Gia, seated next to him, smiled and held his hand, sensing his inner turmoil while he just stared into space.

"Honey," she whispered, "don't spoil the evening. Let's forget about it and enjoy the opera."

Pino patted her knee, and gave her a sympathetic smile. He really didn't want to ruin the night for everyone else and debated for a moment the idea of getting up and leaving them there, but he knew they'd be concerned and wouldn't enjoy themselves. He couldn't even put into words how he felt. Every cell in his body hurt.

The lights went down and the conductor appeared at the podium. The audience provided appropriate applause but Pino didn't even look to see who the conductor was. He had known who was conducting the performance for several weeks but at that moment it escaped him. At that moment, everything escaped him. As the applause died down the overture began. The simple, beautiful minor chord strings gave Pino a chill. It was going to be a long night.

The glitz and glamour of the event were gone and with them, Pino's hope for a happier more dignified future. Tears welled into his eyes and one strayed down his cheek as he struggled to check them. They mustn't fall, he thought, for that would signal the very deepest depth of humiliation.

When Callas first called out: *"Mario! Mario!"* from off stage the entire theater held its breath. As she hit the stage, the entire theater exploded into the most incredible ovation Pino had ever heard. It was almost frightening. The ground actually shook. Over two minutes went by before the crowd would allow the performance to continue.

Callas looked radiant. To her credit, she remained perfectly in character throughout the entire extended ovation. But to Pino, it was obvious that she was devouring every second of it. He thought he even detected a hint of a smile emerging from her lips. He could observe more closely than most since he was probably the only person in the entire house who was not clapping. He sat in stoic silence.

The score was second nature to Pino, and he could virtually recite the libretto word for word, but the presence of Callas added a dimension that he had never imagined possible. She was more than charismatic. She was magnetic. Pino had to fight himself to keep from staring in astonishment at how her every movement was embued with the perfect combination of passion and grace, and how each gesture seemed to make an incredibly deep emotional statement and connection with the audience. This was more than art; this was genius.

Halfway through the first act, Pino felt the first tinges of uneasiness in his stomach. He opened his bow tie to breathe with less restriction, not caring if anyone saw him. No one did. Looking around at the mesmerized faces in the audience, he felt as though he could have been on fire and no one would have stirred in the slightest.

When the time finally came for her aria, Pino was past all concern. He was in Athens. He was surrounded by Amonte, Bernardi and Carlucci. Maria was serenading them from her balcony. Meanwhile, at the Met, four thousand men, women and children held their collective breath.

The moment of silence just before she began *Vissi d'arte* was remarkable. It seemed almost as if everything that had gone on before in her entire life had coalesced into one sustained, shattering moment of silence.

As she sang, her voice was replete with sobs, wrought with emotion. She looked as though the aria was literally tearing her apart. Yet the control was sublime and the intelligence of the interpretation was indescribable.

Pino, eyes closed, five thousand miles and twenty five years away in the gauzy haze of a newsreel, toured the devastated city. He passed the beggars in the street, then Nazis marching in formation, hungry children crying, old men playing backgammon in the square, Spiro playing his beloved *bouzouki*. Kostas tending his fruit cart. The ghostly images started overlapping one another, faster and faster they appeared and disappeared. Finally, in his mind's eye, he saw Maria. She was in the street crying. Next to her was an empty pail. Her beautiful white sundress was torn and covered with mud.

Pino opened his eyes to stop his mind from racing, but Callas stood right before him. Her eyes were full of sadness and she looked like she might burst into tears at any moment. Callas kneeled at the edge of the stage looking in Pino's direction. There was no mistaking it: Callas stole a glance at Pino. As she did, her expression distorted into sadness. She was looking directly at Pino and he was crying. Bitter tears were streaming uncontrollably down his face. In an instant, Callas regained her composure and continued.

The audience went absolutely insane at the conclusion of the aria and Pino clutched Gia's hand in a death grip. She hugged him around the neck and kissed him on the cheek.

At the end of the performance another legend was born. Callas had returned and conquered. The stage lights came up for the curtain calls and, as was customary, Callas was the last to appear. When she did, the applause was deafening. Bouquets of flowers rained down from the rafters like manna from heaven. She strode back and forth across the stage like a queen, acknowledging the applause, the outpouring of love, the adoration.

Pino's family was literally jumping up and down, waving, trying to get her attention, but to no avail. With a final wave and blow of kisses she disappeared behind the curtain.

At the opera's conclusion there was pure bedlam. Callas received fourteen curtain calls and would have received fourteen more if she were willing to continue coming out. Her devoted legions would have stayed all night pouring out their love for her. Pino never quite understood this kind of hero-worship. It was one thing to show appreciation and respect for an artist and the performance, but this kind of ostentatious display was complete nonsense to him.

The Vaggi clan left the auditorium in a state of ecstasy, sensing that they'd witnessed a small piece of history. Once again, they had to work their way through a crowd as a good portion of the audience refused to leave, wanting the moment to last forever.

In the lobby, Amonte put his arm around Pino's shoulder and kissed him on the cheek. Pino blushed but didn't say anything. His face still wore a sour smile. Without missing a beat, Mama Vaggi provided the perfect antidote for Pino's gloom.

"I'm sorry. She's pretty good, but she's still no Tebaldi."

Even Pino had to laugh at that piece of wisdom. It was much needed levity. Maria, Pino's sister, held Maria, Pino's daughter, smiling at her brother with a joy that she hadn't seen in her for some time.

"Hey, Pop," Maria said, beaming, "you were right. I'm glad I came."

Pino smiled and messed up her hair. He winked at his sister and lovingly punched her in the arm.

"I guess we should be headed backstage now," Amonte said.

"Yeah, let's hurry before it's too crowded," Millie added.

"C'mon, Pino," said Mama Vaggi, "you lead the way."

"Nah, you guys go ahead. I'll catch up with you in a minute."

"What are you talking about?" his mother asked impatiently.

"Go on. I'll be along in a minute."

"Are you sure, Honey?" said Gia.

"Yeah. Don't worry." he said with a wink to reassure her.

"Okay," Gia said, facing the troops. "Alright everybody, *andiamo!*"

Alone in the lobby, Pino slowly strolled over to the poster announcing the evening's performance. He stared at it absently, perusing the list of performers' names. The poster was adorned by a large SOLD OUT sticker across the middle of it, partially obscuring some of the names. He read down the list until his gaze finally stopped at Callas' name.

He fumbled in his pocket for a minute before managing to find what he was looking for. It was a crumpled up piece of paper. He held it in his hand for a second, as if undecided whether or not he would unravel it. Finally, he did. The paper was old, tattered and yellowing at the edges but the writing on it remained intact. It was only one word and the letters were in Greek: KALOGEROPOULOS. It was the nametag from Maria's door on Patisson Street in Athens. He'd carried it with him since the drunken night he spent singing with Spiro some twenty five years earlier.

Suddenly, someone tapped him on the shoulder. He turned around to see Biscini standing before him, arms wide open as if expecting an embrace, or to ask 'why'?

"Are you all right, Pino?" he asked.

"Sure," said Pino.

"Maria's asking for you."

"Yeah, right," he said with a laugh. He looked back at the poster and took a hard swallow. After a moment, he looked at Biscini.

"Why'd she do it, Christian?"

"Oh, please! She's a *diva*. Who knows? *La donna è mobile* right? Tomorrow she'll probably remember everything."

Pino let out a long sigh, and looked back at the paper in his hand.

"No. I hurt her way back then, and now she's paying me back," he said.

Biscini didn't know what to say. He noticed the paper in Pino's hand.

"What's that?"

Pino looked at the label one last time, then he crumpled it up and tossed it on the floor.

"Nothing," he said.

He started to walk away, but Biscini grabbed him by the arm.

"Pino, my friend. I have never asked you for anything, have I?"

Pino stared at Biscini without emotion.

"Do this one thing, for me."

After a moment, Pino bent down and retrieved the paper. He uncrumpled it, put it in the breast pocket of his tux, and rubbed his hands together.

"Let's go."

The backstage area was precisely the madhouse Pino had expected it would be. He and Biscini joined the long, snaking, receiving line, unable to see where it ended. He came back not for her but for Christian. He was no longer lacking in energy or indignation. If he didn't come, there would be talk, further cementing her victory. He knew this gesture wasn't particularly brave or noble, merely convention, expectation. It made him sick. He would endure this miserable sham for Christian, then be done with her, forever.

As they got closer, Pino heard every conceivable kind of superlative about the performance. Ironically, the very scene that Pino found so thrilling only a few hours earlier, now seemed extremely distasteful. He was tired and wanted to go to bed. 4:00AM would come soon and he had work to do. Besides, there was nothing here for him. After the embarrassing scene in her dressing room before the opera, he never wanted to see her again. He didn't belong in her world and never would. This was a gaudy and synthetic dream and if this was what she'd done with her gifts…

Turning a corner, they could now see Callas. She was dressed in a spectacular gold and red silk dressing gown. She could be heard playing the part of the gracious hostess, a part she played to the hilt. Her honesty, it seemed, was now reserved exclusively for the stage. *How did that charming ugly duckling ever become this, this priestess of affectation?* She was alternately gleeful and solemn at the right moment, but the solemnity seemed forced and unreal; merely another character she was playing.

Biscini squeezed Pino's hand and winked at him. He desperately wanted his friend to end this occasion on a high note and he knew that it was a gamble, but it was a gamble that he had to take.

They were fast approaching her and Biscini was next in line. Pino took a deep breath and looked around defiantly. The label in his pocket gave him courage. He wasn't sure what he would say to her. Maybe he would say nothing at all. He'd simply hand her the label, watch her reaction and know in his heart that he'd won.

"Christian!" Callas cried out, kissing Biscini on both cheeks. "Where have you been? I expected you'd be the first in line," she said, mockingly scolding him.

"My darling, I needed to compose myself. The depth of emotion was simply too great!" he responded with a bow.

Pino listened to the small talk impatiently. He didn't like it when Christian put on bogus airs. Looking determined but anxious, he wiped the perspiration from his brow.

"You are an angel, Christian! Please call me tomorrow. Let's have lunch while I'm in town."

"On that you can depend," he said as he kissed her hand, then gracefully moved along.

As Callas turned her head toward Pino, there was a ringing in his ears, but it wasn't his hearing aids. The entire scene seemed to be unfolding before him in slow motion. Their eyes made contact, but not a word was spoken. It was as if they were in suspended animation. Pino blinked and, breaking the stare, glanced around nervously. Callas showed no sign of nervousness. She glowed like a bride on her wedding day. She smiled at Pino in a way that he hadn't seen in decades. It was a warm smile, a melancholy smile, an almost-but-not-quite loving smile. He fixed on her gaze and looked deeply into her eyes. They were dark but twinkled like stars and he saw nothing but joy in them, joy tinged with an ever so slight hint of melancholy. In them, he read a message of forgiveness.

Releasing his breath, he felt his shoulders drop and all tension disappeared. He remembered the label in his pocket and he started to speak, but Callas gently raised a finger to her lips. She took his hands into her own and squeezed them gently. Without saying a word, she slowly reached her hands behind her neck and appeared to undo something. Then, she reached underneath the neckline of her dressing gown and removed something. Pino couldn't see what it was, but she placed the object into his hands and closed them up around it. She held his hands in hers and squeezed them warmly once more before letting them go. She stared into his eyes. Pino was confused and slowly opened up his hands. As he did, all the confusion was resolved. The ringing in his ears ceased and the background noise of the room returned him from his suspended animation.

In his hand was the St. Christopher medal that he had lost in the war, the St. Christopher medal that his sister had given him on the train platform as he departed, the St. Christopher medal that had watched over him and delivered him safely through so many troubles.

Overcome with emotion, his eyes welled up with tears. He looked up to see Callas, but she had already moved on to the next well-wisher. He smiled with the joy of a child, and clutching the medal, he walked on. Stopping only a few steps away, he kissed the medal like he'd always done and put it away in his pocket. He'd never part with it again. Then, looking back at her in all her glamour and glory, he gently blew her a kiss. Callas was deep in conversation with another guest and didn't react, but, as Pino walked away, out of the receiving area and out of her world, she watched him. She watched him out of the corner of her eye, and she smiled, the same warm, melancholy, almost-but-not-quite-loving smile.

THE END

CPSIA information can be obtained at www.ICGtesting.com
Printed in the USA
LVOW05s2025220514

386948LV00003B/150/P